Understanding Commodity Cultures

Understanding Commodity Cultures

Explorations in Economic Anthropology with Case Studies from Mexico

Scott Cook

ROWMAN & LITTLEFIELD PUBLISHERS, INC.
Lanham • Boulder • New York • Toronto • Oxford

ROWMAN & LITTLEFIELD PUBLISHERS, INC.

Published in the United States of America
by Rowman & Littlefield Publishers, Inc.
A wholly owned subsidiary of The Rowman & Littlefield Publishing Group, Inc.
4501 Forbes Boulevard, Suite 200, Lanham, Maryland 20706
www.rowmanlittlefield.com

PO Box 317
Oxford
OX2 9RU, UK

British Library Cataloguing in Publication Information Available

Library of Congress Cataloging-in-Publication Data

Cook, Scott, 1937–
Understanding commodity cultures : explorations in economic anthropology with case studies from Mexico / Scott Cook.
p. cm.
Includes bibliographical references.
ISBN 0-7425-3490-1 (hardcover : alk. paper)
1. Economic anthropology—Mexico. 2. Indians of Mexico—Economic conditions. 3. Economic development—Mexico. 4. Free trade—Mexico. 5. Capitalism—Mexico. 6. Mexico—Economic conditions. 7. Mexico—Economic policy—1994– I. Title.
GN564.M6C66 2004
306.3'0972—dc22 2003027874

Printed in the United States of America

™ The paper used in this publication meets the minimum requirements of American National Standard for Information Sciences—Permanence of Paper for Printed Library Materials, ANSI/NISO Z39.48-1992.

At the basis of Marx's conception of the world lies the notion of an appropriation of nature by human beings in order to satisfy their wants and needs. This appropriation is a material process embodied in the acts of production and consumption. Under conditions of commodity production, the acts of production and consumption are separated by exchange. But the appropriation of nature always remains fundamental. From this it follows that we can never ignore what Marx calls "the material side" of commodities. To do so would be to remove the satisfaction of human wants and needs from any relation to nature.

—David Harvey (1982:5)

The boundary between nature and culture, the distinction between the material and the mental, tend . . . to dissolve once we approach that part of nature which is directly subordinated to humanity—that is, produced or reproduced by it. . . . Although external to us this nature is not external to culture, society or history. It is that part of nature which is transformed by human action and thought. It is a reality which is simultaneously material and mental.

—Maurice Godelier (1986:4–5)

Contents

Acknowledgments

Given the reflective current in this book, it is appropriate for me to acknowledge some old intellectual debts. First and foremost, I thank Hugo Nutini for first introducing me to social anthropology (structural-functionalism) and to Mesoamerican studies when he was an instructor and I was a fellow in the Pan American Union (PAU) Graduate Training Program in the Social Sciences at the University of Puerto Rico from 1961 to 1963; then for recommending me for a Mellon Predoctoral Fellowship that enabled me to enter the doctoral program at the University of Pittsburgh, where he served as my adviser and scholarly role model during my graduate student years; and, finally, for his role in facilitating my doctoral dissertation fieldwork in Mexico. Although our paths have crossed only sporadically since then, my career got a significant boost thanks to Nutini, and I continue to admire the energy and rigor of his scholarly output.

I am also indebted to Donald Hogg—my thesis adviser and teacher in the PAU program at the University of Puerto Rico—who introduced me to cultural anthropology and to fieldwork, always emphasizing the importance of careful observation (which he had learned under the tutelage of John Gillin at North Carolina and Sidney Mintz at Yale). In that program, I was introduced to sociological theory by Howard Stanton, to the historical sociology of pluriethnic societies and alterity by Harry Hoetink, and to cultural geography by Jim Blaut. It was also in Puerto Rico where Hazel Dubois Stanton planted the idea of economic anthropology in my head and where I ended a brief stint in Oscar Lewis's incipient *La Vida* project in order to begin doctoral studies at Pittsburgh (rather than continuing with Lewis's project and later initiating doctoral studies at Illinois).

Aside from Hugo Nutini, I also owe a debt of gratitude to other teachers at the University of Pittsburgh: Leonard Kasdan for guidance and encouragement with my early work on Polanyi, Arthur Tuden for provoking my interest in comparative political economy, Harold Gould for broadening my understanding of peasantries in complex societies, and George Peter Murdock for allowing me to do a paper on Max Weber in his seminar on the history of anthropological thought (as a trade-off for doing another on Julius Lippert).

Only in the process of writing this book did I have occasion to review my correspondence with Ralph Beals, spanning a period from 1965 to 1975, much of which dealt with substantive issues in economic anthropological discourse. I had forgotten how much time and thought Beals invested in this correspondence with someone who was, until 1968, still a graduate student. The correspondence period included one year (1967–1968) when I served as a research associate in Beals's Oaxaca Markets project, funded by the National Science Foundation (NSF). He was in residence in Oaxaca for several months during that year, and I had the opportunity to talk with him about many of the issues we had corresponded about. Even though I had finished my dissertation early in my tenure with Beals's project, I nevertheless learned a great deal about fieldwork protocol and discipline and about anthropology and Mexican studies from my association with him on that project. Much of what I learned was useful during my own later experience as a principal investigator on an NSF-funded project in Oaxaca.

In addition to those acknowledged here and all those colleagues, officials, and informants whom I have thanked in my previous publications in Mexican studies and economic anthropology, I wish to thank the Visiting Scholar Program at the Long Institute of Latin American Studies and the Office of Graduate Studies at the University of Texas, Austin, for appointing me as a visiting scholar during 2002–2004. Without my ability to acquire faculty privileges at the university's outstanding libraries, especially the amazing Benson Latin American Collection, this project would have been much more difficult, especially since my personal library was scaled down in anticipation of my 2001 retirement and permanent relocation from Connecticut to Texas. In the case of the one serial listing in the bibliography that was not available in the Benson Collection, I am indebted to Darlene Hull of the excellent Latin American Collection at the Babbidge Library at the University of Connecticut for finding and providing me with a copy of same from that library.

I wish to express my appreciation to Daniel Little, Bob Carmack, Paul Durrenberger, Keith Hart, Michael Kearney, Fred Krissman, and Joe Spielberg Benítez for taking the time to read and comment on portions or all of the manuscript in previous versions. Their help was invaluable, and I hope the final version does some justice to their contributions.

I owe a special debt of gratitude to Jaime Rodríguez, editor of *Mexican Studies/Estudios Mexicanos*, for his invitation to undertake a review article on the anthropology of Mexico. This book was an outgrowth of that review project. Also, I am grateful to Jim McDonald, chair of the Department of Anthropology at the University of Texas, San Antonio, for allowing me to meet with his graduate seminar on methods during the spring of 2003 and to teach a graduate seminar on economic anthropology in the spring of 2004. Many refinements in this book were made as a result of feedback from the UTSA experience.

Finally, I express my gratitude to my wife, Hilda, who tolerantly adapted to the constraints of yet another project, and to my grandchildren, Alexandra and Andrew, who compel me to ponder the future.

Introduction

Looking forward from the first decade of the twenty-first century, the production of knowledge about the economic life of Mexicans and Mexico from an anthropological perspective will have to be more attentive to the analysis of commodity value than it was during the twentieth century. This premise derives from a realistic recognition of the broad-based, multifaceted transformation of Mexican economy, society, and culture during the twentieth century—a process epitomized by Mexico's emergence as the third party, together with the United States and Canada, in a project to develop a North American common market. The entire neoliberal project, of which the North American Free Trade Agreement (NAFTA) is a part, seeks to expand integration across international boundaries together with strategic participation in competitive world markets guided by the logic of comparative advantage.[1]

Although Mexico's turn away from a model of independent national development to one of national development through a framework of asymmetrical interdependency is controversial, it was a carefully considered response to a widespread recognition that the postrevolutionary nationalist (and protectionist) approach had reached the outer limits of its capacity to meet the material needs, expectations, and aspirations of the rapidly growing Mexican population. Increasing millions of that population, from all parts of Mexico and representing all sectors and levels of its class structure, had in fact anticipated this policy turn during the late decades of the twentieth century and made it a fait accompli by migrating to the United States in the quest for dollars through labor market participation, traveling there to make consumer purchases for consumption in Mexico, or deploying capital in American and other foreign markets. The common denominator of this activity was deliberative choice by Mexicans regarding the acquisition, use, and/or accumulation of commodity value calculated in money terms. Since the early 1980s, this market-responsive behavior has been generated by conditions of subsistence and/or accumulation crisis in Mexico.[2]

Anthropology, as a field of knowledge, is uniquely organized to enable its practitioners to integrate archaeological evidence pointing to the Stone Age origins of a culture of commodity value in pre-Hispanic Mexico, with historical evidence of its growth and diversification through the colonial and postcolonial periods, and with ethnographic evidence from the lived experience of Mexicans in the computer age global economy. Such an integrative approach provides a unique perspective in demonstrating how lived experience is informed by and shapes the diversifying funds of knowledge that enable Mexicans under economic stress to make culturally informed choices in their material interest. The focus on deliberative decision making, understood as involving utilitarian means–end reasoning necessarily influenced by social and moral considerations, promotes a balanced approach to the economy/culture relationship and to the role of agency in processes of economic crisis or transition. There is ample precedent for imbalance on both issues in the literature lamenting the destructive consequences of capitalist development in the lives of Europeans and peoples of other continents.[3]

Even an antipathy toward the asymmetrical, unequal relations of exchange, value distribution, and power associated with capitalism or a posture that connects the relative loss of control that individuals have over their survival to a "reduction in the influence of moral considerations in economic behaviour—a decline in the 'moral economy'" (Sayer 1997:19)—becomes more informed and not necessarily weakened through an understanding of commodity economics. Concerns like cultural survival, subsistence/livelihood security, use value, ecological degradation, human rights, or the sociocultural connectedness of the economy are not incompatible with a commodity-focused analytical approach to economic anthropology. The point is to not ideologically reject commodity economics but rather to adhere to the heuristic dictum that "values which can be measured in terms of money" are not the "only ones that ought to count" (Robinson 1962:148).

Understandably, a concern with moral decline or with inequalities spawned in market economies may translate into antipathy toward the hegemonic consumerist culture of actual capitalism that callously misdirects social production away from the provisioning of vital social needs. The rise of the new international division of labor has given new impetus to this antipathy over issues like deindustrialization, capital flight, outsourcing, export processing zones, and so on (Fröbel et al. 1978). One downside of such antipathy, however, is its affinity with the unreasonable thesis that economic thought created to understand the development and functioning of capitalism is inapplicable to economic processes outside Western capitalist history. According to this thesis, advocated by Karl Polanyi and the substantivist school of economic anthropology, classical/neoclassical economics, and (by implication) Marxist economics, necessarily distorts knowledge production about those areas of the world, like Mesoamerica, which have deep non-Western, precapitalist histories.

In Mesoamerican and Mexican studies, this thesis has been expressed through antagonism to the concept of "penny capitalism" (Tax 1963) as descriptive of the economic life of indigenous peasant artisans (Palerm 1954; Wolf 1959a:224) and in a corresponding assertion of the civilizational discontinuity between Spain (and the rest of Europe) and pre-Hispanic Mesoamerica as summed up in the term "*México profundo*" (Bonfil Batalla 1996). Bonfil injects the rural Mexican economy with a logic of self-sufficiency according to which all work is undertaken to produce for subsistence security, not for the realization or accumulation of exchange value, and culturally harmonizes that economy through endowing its subjects with a shared autonomous worldview (1990:56–57). This argument applies to agriculture as well as to craft production (1990:63, 1996:32–33). His view evokes the vision of an egalitarian economy in which there is a "unity of human beings and the natural world" (no labor alienation, and land is an inalienable resource) and in which "categories of Western origin" do not exist (1990:55–63, 64; 1996:27, 28–33).

Views like Bonfil's are neither baseless nor frivolous. For the most part, however, they are products of categorical binary reasoning that thrives on dichotomies and resists the notion of the interaction of opposites, in his case carried to the extreme of denying the historical process of cultural mestizoization or syncretism (1996:17). Reality is categorized into mutually exclusive boxes, viewed as antagonistic rather than mutually constitutive: use value versus exchange value, subsistence versus accumulation, Indian versus non-Indian, production versus consumption, formal versus substantive, material versus immaterial, ideal versus real, economic versus cultural, economy versus society, and so on. Not surprisingly, this type of reasoning yields opposed schools of thought or approaches to knowledge production that, in sociocultural anthropology during the late decades of the twentieth century, came to be identified by labels like "political economy" versus "symbolic anthropology" and in economic anthropology by labels like "formalists" and "substantivists."

Roseberry (1989:esp. chap. 2) argued convincingly against rigid oppositional thinking. He rightly rejected Sahlins's (1976:55) notion of a "founding contradiction" between the mental (constraints of the mind) and the material (practical activity) in favor of "an emphasis upon meaningful action . . . that . . . is shaped by the meanings people take to their action even as meanings are shaped by people's activities" (1989:33). In this book, I have applied Roseberry's emphasis to the study of the economic anthropology of Mexico.

The obvious place to start any economic study is with production of use values, or "the material side" of commodities (Harvey 1982:5; cf. Marx 1967, 1:36). This starting point ensures that the satisfaction of human wants and needs remains connected to the transformation of nature by labor. It also requires that a comprehensive understanding of these processes and the relations between them entails a consideration of both qualitative and quantitative aspects (Harvey 1982; cf. Marx 1967, 1). The contribution of economic anthropology to such an understanding resides in its capacity to privilege the qualitative or cultural aspect, including agency, in the labor process of value production in a way that simultaneously recognizes the fundamentally material and therefore quantifiable nature of that process.

Consequently, economic anthropology is uniquely positioned to integrate two separate analytical tendencies represented in the juxtaposed statements by Harvey and Godelier in the epigraph: one that specifies commodity value but does not explicitly mention human agency and culture and another that implies commodity value and stresses the interconnectivity of agency/culture with nature. Harvey makes a strong case for recognizing the importance of use value in Marx's many-windowed exploration of commodity value in the capitalist mode of production. For Marx, he argues, "use value is modified by, at the same time as it modifies, capitalist relations of production" (1982:7–8).

Harvey's case, like Marx's exploration in three volumes of *Capital*, becomes intelligible only by considering concrete examples like the production and use of machines (1982:7, 98–155) and pursuing complex connections between use and exchange value and money to show how the process of capital accumulation affects the "standard of living" of labor (1982:8, 39–56). The challenge to economic anthropology in seeking to understand processes of livelihood and accumulation in societies like Mexico, with its uneven development, persisting cultures of precapitalist origin, yet pervasive involvement in continental and global capitalist markets, is to deal with an unusually diverse array of capital/labor relations as well as with significant sectors of the rural population with combined, if alternating, involvement in capitalist, petty commodity, and subsistence circuits of value production and consumption (cf. Cook and Binford 1990:12–15, 27–32).

The labor theory of value, combined with a focus on class differentiation, has proven to be analytically fruitful in the study of how rural Mexicans in household/family enterprises go about meeting the material requirements of everyday life—food, shelter, clothing, tools, health care, old-age security, and so on—in culturally mediated ways and also how they may or may not accumulate capital in these and other small-scale enterprises. Alejandro Marroquín (1957a, 1957b, 1978) was the first anthropologist to apply his general knowledge of this theory to the study of the indigenous Mexican economy. For him, long before the Spanish Conquest, the premonetary economy evolved to a level of organization requiring the operation of an objective standard for valorizing circulating objects; such a standard developed around the appreciation of physical effort and the intensity of actually felt material and cultural needs by subjects who demanded valued objects. Thus, labor came to regulate the commodity valuation process (1978:33–34). Marroquín's recognition of both material and cultural sources of the need for things would seem to make him receptive to the proposition that the study of socioeconomic phenomena as aggregate consequences of "individuals acting out of a prudent regard for self- or family-welfare" (Little 1991:150) or out of a profit or capital accumulation motive must be attuned to a broad array of cultural meanings and values and not exclusively to labor cost.[4]

Conventional economics, which has served as the theoretical source for formalist economic anthropology, emphasizes the analysis of commodities conceptualized as combining esteem value (utility) and exchange value and has been more focused than traditional Marxist economics on analyzing both sides of the commodity value equation. For conventional economists (and formalists in economic anthropology), commodities are products or goods that are exchangeable and exchanged (that is, bartered or bought and sold) (Fraser 1947:124–25); they are the natural subject matter of market economics. The shortcoming of this approach lies in its penchant for sweeping the antagonistic social relations between capital and labor under the rug of dehumanized algebraic x and y variables (cf. Robinson 1962:61).[5]

The substantivist current in twentieth-century economic anthropology, grounded in the work of Karl Polanyi with an infusion of Mauss (1954), has been sympathetic to the Marxist position that in precapitalist economies, human-made artifacts circulated among and between makers and nonmakers exclusively under regimes of use rather than of gain. According to this approach, artifacts, products, or goods embody use value but not exchange value, which is considered to be exclusively market related. Consequently, for substantivists, use value–laden products are not commodities because of the absence of markets and a specialized division of labor. To the extent that trade and utilitarian exchange are acknowledged to occur in noncommodity regimes, exchange value is interpreted by substantivists as a creature of noneconomic (for example, kinship, political, and religious) forces, and use value is privileged as the economic prime mover (Sahlins 1972:esp. chaps. 4–6). Not surprisingly, substantivism has proved congenial to the study of symbolic structures of demand/consumption (Sahlins 1976) as well as to the study of the global crisis in subsistence provisioning among subaltern populations (Nash 1994, 2001).

Because of the thoughtful critiques of traditional Marxist economics by scholars like Baudrillard, Bourdieu, Chevalier, and Appadurai, there is strong support for assuming that any "useful" artifact also embodies potentially realizable exchange value. Such an assumption weakens the substantivist rationale for pursuing the study of noncommodity economics as advocated by Sahlins (1972) and places a high analytical burden on claims for the exceptional significance of noncommodity activities in any economy of record. This renewed theoretical focus on exchange value, ironically associated with a consumptionist problematic, reinforces the effect of a growing body of evidence from ethnography and archaeology pointing to commodity production and circulation across the entire spectrum of precapitalist economies (Earle 2002). All this bodes well for progress in a new economic anthropology that adapts Marx's analysis of commodity value under capitalism to a wider spectrum of economies through an innovative rethinking of consumption and exchange (Appadurai 1986; Miller 1991).

My consideration of issues raised in preceding paragraphs in the process of writing this book has caused me to be both reflective and reflexive (Rubinstein 1991:27 n. 2). I have reflected on my entry and early participation in the subfield nearly four decades ago so as to form a clearer image of that period from the perspective of the present and have also critically reexamined my subsequent participation as an ethnographer and author. To engage in such a process is a daunting undertaking in today's postmodern world, where the spirit of multivocality and deconstructionism reigns, where systematic thought is scorned as blind allegiance to metanarrative discourse, and where one scholar's "science" is another's "ideology." Indeed, academic discourse about human affairs seems to pride itself today in ridiculing the effort to distinguish scientific from ideological discourse as well as scientific from popular knowledge and seems to delight in collapsing the distinction between subject/object and subjectivism/objectivism.[6]

Under such unsettling conditions, philosophy can help us find our bearings. Daniel Little, in three important books (1986, 1989, and 1991), has provided philosophical legitimacy to positions on several issues that have been of central concern during my career: 1) Marx and Marxism pass muster as legitimate contributors to empirical social science, 2) the modus operandi and findings of empirical social science weigh heavily in favor of formalism as opposed to substantivism in the formalist–substantivist controversy of the 1960s and 1970s, and 3) a modified empiricism, revolving around the interplay between theory and fact but stripped of a rigid rule about observational confirmation or refutation of knowledge claims, is rewarding (Little 1989:24).

Reading Little has convinced me that I was not alone among participants in the formalist-versus-substantivist debate who could have benefited from a more profound understanding of "falsificationism" (Marshall 1998:220–21) and of the methodological implications for economic anthropology of the naturalism-versus-antinaturalism discourse in the philosophy of social science. I am no longer convinced that theories in economic anthropology are falsifiable, either empirically or logically. There is a persisting lack of agreement among economic anthropologists over the content of the corpus of "known facts" about extinct and extant economies. The circle closes if we agree with Karl Popper's Kantian (and profoundly antiempiricist] proposition "that all descriptions of experiences involve selection and interpretation in terms of some prior conceptual framework, or theory" (Marshall 1998:221).

This epistemological vicious circle means that all existing and future theories in economic anthropology are and will be unfalsified and unfalsifiable. Falsification of theories cannot be achieved if the facts they purport to explain are disputed. Under these conditions, the quantity and quality of empirical content, together with logical precision and clarity, must play the key role in evaluating theories for which conclusive proof or disproof is lacking. It is comforting to argue that in the quest to understand complex processes involving multiple causes, a posture of theoretical pluralism is more realistic than one of theoretical purism (Little 1989:25). But the bottom line may be that social scientists "are not strictly enough compelled to reduce metaphysical concepts to falsifiable terms and cannot compel each other to agree what has been falsified" (Robinson 1962:25). Recognition of this fact led Joan Robinson to characterize her own discipline of economics as limping "along with one foot in untested hypotheses and the other in untestable slogans" (1962:25). The same could have been said of economic anthropology then and can be said of it today.

Since philosophers of social science like Little cannot weigh into every controversy as neutral arbitrators like he has done regarding peasant moral economy or the formalist–substantivist debate, effective polemic has an important role to play in social science discourse. Indeed, controversial discussion involving "aggressive attack on or refutation of the opinions or principles of another" (*Webster's Third New International Dictionary, Unabridged*, 1753) is unavoidable in social science discourse and can be especially productive "when it not only shakes the confidence of those it addresses in the correctness of their views, but also demonstrates the superiority of the countersolutions it proposes" (Schaff 1963:21). To be productive or "effective," polemic must fulfill at least three basic conditions (Schaff 1963:20–21): 1) it must be based on proper knowledge and citation of the opponent's views, which must be opposed with pertinent counterarguments; 2) it must single out in the views criticized the problems that account for their attraction and that remain even when it is agreed that the solutions offered for them are false; and 3) it must put forward alternative, positive solutions of those problems. My contention is that during the course of the formalist–substantivist controversy, the critiques of substantivism by formalists more consistently met these three conditions than did critiques of formalism by substantivists. A measure of this positive impact of formalist critiques was George Dalton's liberalization of Polanyi's restriction of formal theory to the analysis of market economies (Dalton 1969; cf. Dalton 1961). In short, effective, empirically informed polemic may stimulate progress in social scientific discourse.

Recently, I was struck by the use of the term "penny-capitalist" in a book by Colin Clarke (2000:79, 249) about Oaxaca primarily because he used it with direct reference to my own work in which I had not used it. This caught my attention because I had long considered Tax's oxymoronic concept to belong to past discourse that had been superseded by the work of subsequent generations of scholars. While not as exhaustive as Tax's, later research was more informed theoretically, more sophisticated in survey methods and data set analysis, and more strategic regarding in-depth interviewing and case studies, thereby facilitating greater refinement of our understanding of economic complexity. In any case, Clarke's use of the term stimulated me to reexamine the topic of penny capitalism by reading books like John Benson's *The Penny Capitalists* (1983) and rereading Tax's *Penny Capitalism*. This inevitably led me to a broader inquiry that would try to reconcile the continuing attraction of concepts like penny capitalism in a world ever more subjected to continental and global market projects of "dollar" capitalism.

Another term that requires clarification is "division of labor" with or without the accompanying phrase "and specialization." In preparing a preliminary index for this book, I was surprised to find thirty-six references to these terms, and this has led me to reflect on their usage and meaning. In economic anthropology, the rationale for the combined usage ("division of labor and specialization") was provided by Herskovits (1960:124–25), who felt that conventional economics downplayed specialization in its Smithian concern with divided labor involved in the production of single commodities (or commodity categories). Economic anthropology, by contrast, should, according to Herskovits, understand "division of labor" in terms of the "splitting up of the total amount of effort needed to keep the economy of a given society operating . . ." (1960:124–25) and regard each of the "sub-groups [based on family, kinship, age, gender, residence, or other identity] whose members perform a particular aspect of . . . [that] work as specialized" so that "the kind of labor each performs in achieving this" is its "specialization" (1960:125). Herskovits downplayed the extent to which economic anthropology would encounter divisions of labor and "specialized direction of effort" in the production of "parts of commodities" (1960:126) simply because his focus was on precapitalist economies rather than on those experiencing capitalist development or penetration. My work among the peasant artisans and petty industrialists of Oaxaca and in the U.S.–Mexico border brick industry has shown that economic anthropology must now address not only the social division of labor but the division of labor in production as well (Mohun 1991:154).[7]

As a key concept, "commodity culture(s)" serves as a thread loosely integrating the separate chapters of this book. I have conceptualized it as a way to operationally immobilize two contradictory tendencies: on the one hand, the tendency to understand the economy as a separate reality from its sociocultural matrix, thus distorting its influence, and, on the other, the tendency to submerge the economy in its sociocultural matrix, thereby diffusing its influence. The concept begins with the assumption that the economic field is a relatively (and variably) autonomous space within an encompassing matrix with which it selectively interpenetrates or "interfuses" (Hornborg 2001:39). Thus, the concept's complexity reflects its relational nature. That is, the knowledge that informs the actions of economic subjects together with the actions themselves, and their results, are all understood "as relations, containing in themselves, as integral elements of what they are, those parts with which we tend to see them externally tied" (Ollman 1971:15; cf. 3–11).[8]

Accordingly, artifacts of human labor are made and circulate only within a sociocultural process organized relationally; individual agent activity is enculturated and socially engaged. This process implies subjective consciousness of a difference between self, thing, and other (that is, labor alienation) that, in turn, provides a basis for reckoning exchange value. Accordingly, others consume what producers make, but producers are culturally empowered to recognize that use values for others are potentially exchange values for their own immediate social unit (that is, contain the possibility of reciprocation in one form or another). From hypothetical beginnings, then, commodity culture(s) develop in complex and diverse ways, interpenetrating divisions of labor and specialization as well as many noneconomic institutional structures in particular social formations. Each commodity made, exchanged, and consumed implies an associated cultural matrix facilitating its making, exchanging, and consumption. The cultural matrix embraces both subjects and their agency as well as objects and their movements on the way to destruction through consumption or material dissipation. The concept implies tension between social structures and individual agency and recognizes the possibility that social structures can subordinate social action but also that social actors can, within limits, maneuver through and around so-called determining' structures.[9]

The multiple value content of commodities is a product of the sociocultural matrix within which they are made, exchanged, and used. Together with the knowledge, deliberations, attitudes, tastes, and meaningful actions involved in their making, exchanging, and use through destructive consumption, the multiple value content of commodities constitutes their culture. Inevitably, given the multiplicity of valuable objects created by humanity to achieve diverse material ends, the realm of commodity culture is diversified in complex ways in nearly every economy of record—but most formidably so in the economies of capitalism. Nevertheless, under the rubric of commodity culture—in precapitalist, noncapitalist, and capitalist economies alike—there are as many discrete subcultures as there are commodities. Therefore, except in the most abstract sense, commodity culture must be understood in plural terms. This is why I have chosen to use the rather awkward term "commodity culture(s)" at appropriate points throughout this book. In the Mesoamerican context, we can speak of commodity subcultures for specific agricultural crops like maize, beans, or maguey; for pottery; for metates; for basketry; and so on. I first used the concept with regard to artisanal brick production (Cook 1998:288 n 2). Specific commodity subcultures are further divided by production and consumption dimensions. These subcultures are specific, instrumental inflections of more generalized forms.[10]

I will use the term "Mesoamerica" to refer to Mexico plus the western Guatemalan highlands, which are closely linked ethnoculturally and historically to the Chiapas highlands. My assumption is that the indigenous peoples of this area since the time of the Spanish Conquest have shared a common economic core culture or, more specifically, what I call "commodity culture(s)" that has pre-Hispanic roots in the presence of markets and merchants—traits that, among others, were identified by Kirchhoff (1968:25) as being distinctively Mesoamerican. This is essentially my justification for considering Tax's concept of penny capitalism to be as relevant for Mexican studies as it is for Guatemalan studies, although ultimately its significance crosscuts area studies boundaries.

A further contradiction regarding the concept of Mesoamerica, for those of us whose anthropological practice is premised on the reality of the nation-state, is that it is subversive of politically defined territorial boundaries (Monaghan 2000:3). The concept envisions a culture area whose territorial boundaries are culturally defined by an immediate pre-Conquest time line and span Mexico south of the Pánuco-Lerma drainage, Guatemala, El Salvador, British Honduras, and western Honduras to an approximate boundary formed by the Ulua River and Lake Yojoa (Sanders and Price 1968:6; cf. Kirchhoff 1968). In short, Mexico and Guatemala, which became sovereign nation-states during the first half of the nineteenth century, are Mesoamerican territories but by no means cover the entire territory of Mesoamerica.

I will refer to Mesoamerica, Mexico, and Guatemala in a way that seeks to avoid conflating the postindependence nation-state with the more encompassing culture area. When the "Mesoamerica/Mexico" usage occurs, a statement is being made that applies to both the pre-Hispanic culture area and the postindependence nation-state. The reader is asked to bear the burden of keeping in mind that even though the contemporary cultures of the nation-states of Mexico and Guatemala embody, in differing degrees, pre-Hispanic Mesoamerican traits, the term "Mesoamerica" is best restricted to a pre-Hispanic culture area or non-Western cultural configuration. From my perspective, the use of a term like "Mesoamerica today" with reference to contemporary Mexico and Guatemala must be understood figuratively and *cum grano salis*. Culture of Mesoamerican origin that survives in these two countries today (with the possible and partial exception of language in some instances) does so as ruins or as substantially changed in either form, content, meaning, and/or function vis-à-vis the baseline of the Spanish Conquest and colonization.

Finally, a comment to the reader on the plan of the book is in order. It is conceived as a collection of essays, in greater or lesser degree integrated by a focus on commodity value and its sociocultural underpinnings. To some extent, each chapter can be read on its own; each is, more or less, self-contained.

The most obvious connective strand between chapters is ethnographic case material from Mesoamerica/Mexico. Hence, both the opening and the closing chapters mainly address such case materials—chapters 1, 2, 3, 6, 7, and 8 focus on the Mesoamerican/Mexican heartland, whereas chapters 9 and 10 focus on the Mexico–U.S. border and NAFTAmerica. Only two chapters, 4 and 5, do not share this ethnographic connection, so readers specifically interested in Mesoamerican/Mexican studies may wish to skip them. However, these two chapters represent an effort to address major themes in the foundations and development of comparative economic anthropology in a way that connects with my review of that subfield in Mesoamerican/Mexican studies. One of the main goals of the study is to stimulate consideration of the connection between these two domains of discourse.[11]

Chapters 4 and 5 also set the groundwork for a new theoretical approach in economic anthropology. This approach hinges on the key concept of commodity culture(s) and its connections to labor alienation, commodity value, and prudent rationality. In this introduction and in the afterword, I attempt to provide the reader with a general orientation, in the first instance about the book's themes and intentions and in the second about its conclusions and implications. To the extent that it is not an easy read, the reader can justifiably blame the author, who, of course, will defend himself by blaming the subject matter.

I will be the first to admit that this book could have been written differently. Two of my prepublication reviewers were in general agreement that an alternative would have been to systematically organize the study to address the inadequacies of knowledge production vis-à-vis changing realities in the perceived order of things. More specifically, it was suggested that rather than critiquing knowledge production piecemeal, author by author or work by work, as I chose to do, it would have been preferable to focus more broadly on approaches or paradigms. Among these latter would be those that embrace economic dualism, natural economism, or a romantic view of indigenous life or those that privilege ethnic identity, cultural survival, or community reproduction over class relations or capital accumulation. The purpose of such a plan would be to explore how these approaches/paradigms are impacted by the structure of research funding that itself inevitably reflects U.S. foreign policy. Indeed, one reader suggested that there may be a link between changing epistemologies and changing U.S. policies with respect to Mexico, the linkage being made through the area studies research apparatus on given academic projects. I agree. Such an undertaking, of course, would also entail producing in some detail a history of the transformation of the Mesoamerican/Mexican economy from pre-Columbian times to the era of globalization with an emphasis on commodity production and markets. This would be the "changing reality" confronted by anthropological representations.

The model of this type of study in anthropological discourse is Antonio Lauria-Perricelli's (1989) dissertation on the Steward group's project in Puerto Rico. Lauria-Perricelli laboriously and convincingly documents the complex ways in which "specific conjunctures of socio-political interests bear on the consumption and repercussion of anthropological images and discourses, as such on the objects, concepts, methods, and products of such research" (1989:3). Replicating Lauria's study in twentieth-century Mesoamerican/Mexican anthropology would be, needless to say, a daunting undertaking, given the multiplicity of major projects in the region over the years that were funded by various agencies and branches of the capitalist state apparatuses of the United States and Mexico. There are other factors aside from "conjunctures of socio-political interests" that influence citational culture, interpretation, explanation, and other aspects of knowledge production, some of which were examined in the pioneering book *Anthropological Perspectives on Rural Mexico* by Cynthia Hewitt. Perhaps the next generation of scholars will extend our understanding of the role of these factors in shaping the anthropology of Mexico.[12]

NOTES

1. NAFTA undoubtedly belongs to the policy cluster that Stiglitz lumps together as "Washington Consensus policies" (2002:74). He characterizes these as "based on a simplistic model of the market economy, the competitive equilibrium model, in which Adam Smith's invisible hand works, and works perfectly. Because in this model there is no need for government—that is, free, unfettered, 'liberal' markets work perfectly—the Washington Consensus policies are sometimes referred to as 'neo-liberal,' based on 'market fundamentalism,' a resuscitation of the laissez-faire policies that were popular in some circles in the nineteenth century" (2002:74). Of course, as Stiglitz also makes clear, the United States as the hegemonic partner in such bilateral or multilateral arrangements with Third World countries invariably manages to practice protectionism for its powerful business sectors while demanding its elimination in Third World business sectors (2002:59–67).

2. With regard to characterizing that segment of the Mexican population of most concern to a study like this one, the controversial matter of ethnic identity must be addressed first. Without exploring the complexities of the matter here (see Cook and Joo 1995), my assumption is that most Mexicans today are ethnically classifiable as either mestizo (mixed indigenous and European) or *indígena* (indigenous or Indian), and these labels will be used to identify the subjects of the studies reviewed in this book. Indigenous subjects will also be identified by the non-Spanish language they speak (although many of them also speak Spanish), such as Zapotec, Mixtec, or Nahua.

For analytical purposes in economic anthropology, once the issue of ethnic identity is resolved, the most crucial identifier is the agents/subjects' (including their household/family) position in the process of commodity production, acquisition, exchange, and accumulation—a position that requires objective determination through the analysis of many variables (see Cook and Binford 1990:43–47, 116–23). My assumption is that, for one empirically verifiable reason or another, the conditions surrounding and influencing these subjects are of crisis—regarding either subsistence/acquisition or exchange/accumulation or these two sets of variables in some combination. We have enough evidence to realize that absolutely destitute subjects are much less likely to have the wherewithal to participate in migration targeting distant labor markets, so that desperate material need is not a sufficient explanation for such migration. In fact, a significant proportion of migrants have the wherewithal to fund such migration and motives, which often reflect strategies for enhancing acquisition/accumulation of commodity value in already viable, if squeezed, family enterprises. The only caveat here is the role of credit/debt relations in migration, whether originating in the sending community or at the receiving end of the labor market (or some point in the network linking potential employers to potential employees) (Krissman 2002a; Peck 2000); an unknown proportion of the Mexican migratory labor force is caught up in these credit/debt relations. In other words, the population of Mexicans participating in migratory labor throughout NAFTAmerica is heterogeneous in credit/debt, class, ethnic, residential, gender, and age terms. Their common denominator is typically a combination of simple reproduction and simple accumulation squeeze (cf. Bernstein 1979:427; Cook and Binford 1990:97), not simply a generalized state of subaltern poverty. Having said this, and at the risk of self-contradiction, there is a bias in anthropological discourse—derived from its subject matter—toward a focus on subjects of indigenous, rural, small-community origin. The scope of the approach I am proposing, however, does embrace a population of other social origins as well (for example, small-town mestizos, periurban *colonia* dwellers, and so on). Of course, given the transformation of Mexico from a basically rural, agrarian to a predominantly urban, industrial economy since 1950, the majority of "urban" Mexicans today are not many generations removed from either "peasant" or small-community origins.

Another assumption that I make regarding Mexicans engaged in petty commodity or petty capitalist production is that they are "subalterns" in the Gramscian sense of being subordinate in the national hierarchy of class and political power where "hegemony" in the state apparatus is in the hands of a ruling class (Gramsci in Hoare and Smith 1971:160). This implies a surrender of independence and autonomy through movements, alliances, and coalitions where the interests of many class fractions are "sacrificed to the intellectual hegemony of the ruling class" (160). In the twentieth-century Mexican corporatist state, representatives of different class fractions participate in the "political class" that exercises/fashions capitalist hegemony in a complex contest between police-military force and popular consent.

3. The term "Stone Age economics" is the catchy title of a book on substantivist economics by Marshall Sahlins (1972). It is clear from his introduction to that book that, aside from its catchiness, Sahlins intended it to convey in three words what the book expounds: economics as a "culturalist study that as a matter of principal does honor to different societies for what they are" or an approach in which economy implies neither

the exercise of rationality nor prudence nor the "need-serving activities of individuals, but the material life process of society" (Sahlins 1972:xii). In other words, "Stone Age economics" is Sahlins's euphemistic catchphrase for a version of substantivist economics that I called "structural substantivism" (Cook 1974b). Sahlins's Baudrillard-influenced sequel to *Stone Age Economics* titled *Culture and Practical Reason* (1976) pronounces his final break with the realm of exchange value–oriented instrumental culture and his embrace of cognitive, expressive culture as prime mover in human affairs. There is little room in this approach for human agency and, therefore, no way for it to promote understanding of cross-societal cultural process dialectically, much less of hegemony in class societies (Roseberry 1989:26–27; Wessman 1981:69–72). Echoes of Karl Polanyi's (1957) *The Great Transformation*, perhaps the single most important contribution to the "literature of lament" in terms of its influence on economic anthropology, abound in the work of Sahlins and other proponents of the substantivist approach.

4. There are those who might object to Little's term "prudent rationality" on the grounds of redundancy. The dictionary meaning of "rationality" is the "quality or state of being rational," and "rational usually implies a latent or active power to make logical inferences and draw conclusions that enable one to understand the world about him and relate such knowledge to the attainment of ends" (*Webster's Third New International Dictionary, Unabridged,* 1993:1885). "Prudent" is more specific in meaning, connoting "wisdom shown in the exercise of reason, forethought, and self-control" or "shrewdness in the management of practical affairs" (1828). Therefore, Little's term implies the informed (by practical knowledge) exercise of means–end rationality and is not redundant. For purposes of economic anthropological discourse, I prefer the term "reasonable" (and "reasonableness") to "rational" (and "rationality") simply because it "usually carries a much weaker implication of the power to reason in general or of guidance by conclusions drawn by reasoning power, rather applying to actions or decisions or choices that are practical, sensible, just, or fair" (1885). It seems to convey in one word the same meaning as the compound term "prudent rationality." "Prudent reasonableness" is a redundant expression. I will use the term "prudent rationality" interchangeably with "deliberative or reasonable decision making" in this book. Prudent rationality is always appropriate to the circumstances in which a given agent is located.

5. Herskovits (1960), for example, used the terms "good(s)" and "commodity(-ies)"—and, less often, "product(s)"—interchangeably throughout his work, which is most disconcerting in his discussion of value and equivalence, where in one key paragraph he refers to commodities initially but concludes by referring to goods (1960:210–11). Consequently, it is not surprising that his discussion of these and related issues is confusing (1960:chap. 17).

It may come as a surprise to some readers that Marx himself identified use value with utility. However, this reflects his schooling in the classical economic tradition. Even if Marx had lived and worked during the period of neoclassicism, he probably would have accepted marginal utility (and productivity) analysis as useful for understanding the surface or objective appearances of the demand (and supply) side of market behavior. He would, of course, have rejected the entire neoclassical project's "unconscious preoccupation . . . to raise profits to the same level of moral respectability as wages" and have insisted on the classicalist recognition of "exploitation as the source of national wealth" (Robinson 1962:59)—a recognition that he single-handedly developed into a systematic approach to capitalist political economy. He would have emphasized that the unequal system of value distribution in actual capitalism exposes the sham of laissez-faire freedom of choice among a level playing field of consumers, each acquiring utility according to his or her needs, wants, or desires. Robinson (1962:48) was right to emphasize the circular reasoning haunting marginal utility analysis: that commodities are preferred because they have utility and have utility because they are preferred. Fraser (1947:76–77) pointed out that the meaning of "utility" in economics discourse differs from popular usage where it implies "wanted as a means to some further end" or "desirable in the sense of satisfying a genuine or worthy desire or need." By contrast, in economics discourse, "utility" implies only that people are prepared to acquire and consume things (Fraser 1947:77), and "the reasons why a thing is wanted have nothing to do with whether or not it possesses 'utility'" (78). Economists traditionally have focused on marginal utility or the difference between the total utility of the amount already possessed by a commodity and of an amount greater than that by one unit (80). They quantify this in price terms, that is, in terms of what the unit is worth in money or some other commodity. According to Robinson, "Price is the measure of marginal utility" (1962:48). This leads to still another important meaning of utility in economics discourse—a commodity's power of inducing acquisition through barter or purchase (cf. Fraser 1947:90). But economists have largely abandoned the attempt to measure utility directly in favor of a method of ranking the utilities of various commodities against each other known as indifference analysis (Schneider 1974:54–60).

6. According to Rubinstein (1991:27 n. 2), "Reflection describes those instances when we look back on our experiences in order to form an image of our earlier work. It is a process which involves the construction and management of self-images. Reflexivity, in contrast, requires the active analysis and application of our experience to improve our data collection and interpretation. Reflexivity necessarily involves the critical examination and use of earlier experience to influence future action, and is thus an epistemologically revitalizing activity."

Durrenberger and Tannenbaum (2002) propose four different meanings of theory in reaction to the role it plays in postmodern discourse and as an introduction to their review of Chayanov's theory in economic anthropology. I agree with their preference for what they call the operational or scientific meaning in which there "is a strong interplay between abstractions and concrete experience, each defining the other in a continual process of self-correction, critical appraisal, and revolution" (2002:139).

The subject(-ive)/object(-ive) relationship continues to bedevil social theory and epistemology. A brief scan of this book's index entries for these terms shows the range of usage herein. Objective economic understanding is often associated with quantifiability and empirical verifiability as, for example, with class indicators or economic action and its results. Somewhat more problematic are objectivity claims made for objects such as economic structures, conditions, or things that are logically conceptualized. The implication of such claims is that the objectivity of such objects derives either from their demonstrable materiality (which is sensually perceptible) or from their amenability to empirical scientific method/procedures (for example, in the case of specific economic structures, conditions, commodities, or other objects). The trick is to submit subjectivity to procedures that promote objective determination in the subject/object relationship.

7. As is so often the case in the study of commodity economics, the theoretical foundation for understanding the role of division of labor and specialization, after the pioneering contribution of Adam Smith (1937), derives primarily from the work of Karl Marx (1967, 1:35–83) Max Weber (1978:114–36), and Emile Durkheim (1964). My approach to commodity culture rejects Marx's insistence that in precapitalist economies there is a "social division of labor, without production of commodities" (1967, 1:42). What is lacking in such economies, at least from the Neolithic, is not the connection between social division of labor and commodity production nor even a division of labor between workers (that is, a "technical division of labor"; Weber 1978, 1:114) but a division of labor between capital and workers (Mohun 1991:154).

Keith Hart (2001:188–89) reminds us that the founders of economic anthropology, Malinowski and Mauss, were both influenced by Durkheim's approach to the division of labor, which privileged the "social background to individual acts of exchange, 'the non-contractual element in the contract,'" and emphasized that "the point of division is to increase the cohesion of the whole" and "to unify on the basis of complementary difference." The influence of this approach on substantivists from Polanyi to Sahlins is palpable.

8. Hornborg (2001:39), who correctly emphasizes that the "operation of human economies . . . can be understood only in terms of the *interfusion* of objective, material conditions and subjective, cultural constructions," imaginatively extends the understanding of commodity value beyond the economy into the process of economy/technology/ecology "interfusion" where energy transfer/dissipation becomes the ultimate value determinant (2001:40–48). This approach is most convincing at the global level of value flows/relations but also applies to intrasocietal class analysis. It implies that the subordination of nature to humanity through the economy may be illusory: ultimately, nature takes its revenge on humanity ecologically for economic "progress" (cf. Cook 1973:42). More specifically, it focuses on injustice and inequality in the human use of renewable and nonrenewable natural resources.

9. I employ the term "agency" in this study to refer to individual subjects' or agents' capacity to make informed decisions or choices that translate into actions in their own perceived material interests. The assumption is that such decisions or choices involve both intentionality and rationality (cf. Little 1991:18). A further assumption is that agent decisions/choices are situationally influenced by social structures and may, when aggregated in patterned ways, effect change in those structures. According to Little (1991:19), "Institutions and other aspects of social organization acquire their causal powers through their effects on the actions and intentions of the individuals involved in them—and *only* from those effects. So to affirm that an institution has causal powers with respect to other social entities, it is necessary to consider how typical agents would be led to behave in a way that secures this effect." Needless to say, the connection between agency and rationality, attributes of all subjects, must be operationally related to a concern with representativeness of subjects in given circumstances. For me, claims or assumptions about subject/agent representativeness are most reliable when supported by well-defined procedures of disaggregation (that is, recognition of social differentiation) and sampling (Cook and Binford 1990:113–23, 243–49, 251 n. 1). In short, a focus on agency must be wedded to analysis involving disaggregation of social subjects/agents into meaningful categories and attentivness to circumstances limiting representativeness. My argument regarding the

hypothetical origins of commodity production is compatible with Gramsci's thesis that "there is no human activity from which all intellectual intervention can be excluded—homo faber cannot be separated from homo sapiens" (1957:121).

10. It was in the context of writing a book on the border brick industry that I elaborated the linkage between commodity production and culture through the concept of "Mexican brick culture" (Cook 1998:288 n. 2). I defined "brick culture" as "all the systematic knowledge, skills, experience, and behavior required to produce handmade brick" (1998:288 n. 2) but fleshed this out more fully in discussing its Mexican variant (1998:17–22). My thinking has evolved since then in the direction of broadening the focus beyond production to embrace all categories of the economy and, most particularly, to more systematically and explicitly encompass all dimensions of commodity value (that is, use, exchange, and sign/symbolic).

11. I use the term "NAFTAmerica" as a shorthand way of referring to the transborder space objectified and regulated by NAFTA as it involves primarily U.S.–Mexico relations. My use of the term also implies acceptance of Orme's (1996:313) prediction that "NAFTA will restructure the continent, with lines of people and goods running north-to-south as well as east-to-west, and once-fixed borders blurring in overlapping spheres of economic influence and political power" and that "because of NAFTA, the twenty-first century will be marked by the consolidation of a new North America, an economic community with common goals and standards, and one of the richest unified markets in the world."

12. This paragraph evokes a need to clarify a concept mentioned earlier, namely, "political economy," which until the late nineteenth and early twentieth centuries was the "common name for economics" (Seldon and Pennance 1965:328). This common usage became uncommon under the influence of Alfred Marshall's *The Principles of Economics* published in 1890. Subsequently, the term "political economy" has tended to be understood as referring to Marxist and other approaches to economics that incorporate an "analysis of government action and of the mechanisms and prevailing philosophies of political life" (Schumpeter 1950:22). The recent term "anthropological political economy" refers to a "political economic approach to history and culture" and has developed to address cultural differentiation, social and political inequalities, and the "historical formation of anthropological subjects within processes of uneven development" (Roseberry 1989:3, 13–14). As I conceive it, economic anthropology differs from "anthropological political economy" by having a stronger concern with core issues of "economics," which implies a heightened degree of analytical concern with processes internal to the economic field or economy.

1

Economic Otherness South of the Border: The Twentieth-Century Foundations and Formation of the Economic Anthropology of Mexico

As was customarily the case elsewhere in the world, U.S. business interests penetrated Mexico's economic landscape before academics began to study it. Even before the period of dictatorship of Porfirio Díaz (that is, the Porfiriato, 1876–1911) U.S. investors had significant investments in Mexico. It was during the Porfiriato, however, that U.S. capital was established by invitation and concession as a senior partner in the development and operation of the Mexican economy (Hart 2002). Although by 1910 American anthropologists like Frederick Starr (1900–1902, 1908) had begun to survey and write about the exotic Indian inhabitants of this economic landscape, it was during the 1920s aftermath of the revolution and the phase of its early institutionalization that American academic scholars came to Mexico and "quietly joined their artistic and literary counterparts" in cultural production—often in collaboration with Mexican colleagues (Hart 2002:368; cf. Delpar 1992).

Both the U.S. and the Mexican branches of the sociocultural anthropology of Mexico were incubated in this early twentieth-century setting, but with regard to economic studies in particular, the beginnings of specialized knowledge production are in the 1930s—at a time when both branches had passed their formative stages. The resulting body of knowledge—accessible in a variety of publications, including monographs, reports, and articles—is uniquely delimited by combining a substantive focus on economic activity with empirical data from fieldwork among indigenous peasant artisans. Some nonanthropologists have subsequently contributed to this literature, and research has also been conducted among rural and urban mestizos.

A SELECTIVE OVERVIEW OF ECONOMIC ANTHROPOLOGY IN MEXICAN STUDIES

The growing pains of economic anthropology in twentieth-century Anglo-American anthropological discourse, epitomized by the formalist–substantivist controversy (Wilk 1996:4), were experienced in Mexican studies through the travails of *indigenismo* and a variety of reactive theoretical currents focused on producing knowledge about village-based indigenous peasantries in a mestizo capitalist national economy (Hewitt de Alcántara 1984; Medina 1996). Many of the contentious issues central to the development of economic anthropology as a comparative field of study did not resonate with the crosscurrents of *indigenismo*. Consequently, contributions to the economic anthropological field in Mexican studies developed more in response to the *indigenista*-generated agenda (driven, for example, by a concern with agrarian and rural industry questions among peasant Indians), often filtered through the broader lens of sociocultural anthropology, than to the specialized academic agenda of discourse in economic anthropology. This is especially true of contributions by Mexican anthropologists but also of contributions by many American anthropologists. One of the peculiarities of this history is that an anthropologically inclined writer, B. Traven, produced stories and novels that lend themselves to an economic anthropological reading and had a significant role in shaping views about economic otherness in Mexico.

Arguably, economic anthropology in Mesoamerican/Mexican studies was never constituted in any collectively coordinated way by specialists attuned to the agenda of general, comparative economic anthropology. Rather, it took shape on the basis of early contributions by nonspecialists and grew during the second half of the twentieth century through the combined contributions of specialists and nonspecialists. This mixed formational trajectory is exemplified by the fact that the most widely influential twentieth-century study of economic otherness south of the U.S.–Mexico border, *Penny Capitalism*, was authored by an anthropologist, Sol Tax, who never identified himself as a specialist in economic anthropology. To my knowledge, there is only one major twentieth-century publication prior to the encyclopedic volume 6 of the *Handbook of Middle American Indians* published in 1966, namely, the chapter "Economy and Technology" in the Viking Fund Seminar's *Heritage of Conquest* (Tax et al., 1968), which directly addressed the general subject matter of economic anthropology, took stock of the state of knowledge, and pointed to directions for future research through focused collective discourse. Of the anthropologists participating in the Viking Fund Seminar, none were primarily career specialists in economic studies or made specific theoretical contributions to the development of the comparative field of economic anthropology. Three of them—George Foster, Julio de la Fuente, and Ralph Beals—were, nonetheless, at various times in their careers, involved in the production of monographs of a specifically Mexican economic content.

It was not until the 1960s and early 1970s that anthropologists who were career specialists in economics used data from Mexican fieldwork to address theoretical issues current within the general field of comparative economic anthropology, which, at that time, was fueled by reactions to the publication of the substantivist magnum opus by Karl Polanyi and his associates *Trade and Market in the Early Empires* (Polanyi et al. 1957; see also Cancian 1965, 1966, 1972; Cook 1966a, 1970; Dinerman 1974; Durston 1976; Isaac 1965; Nash 1961). By the late 1970s, Mexican research was stimulated by and contributed to the discussion of new sets of issues generated by Marxist discourse regarding the fate of petty agricultural and industrial production under conditions of capitalist development (Bretón and Labrecque 1981; Cook 1984a, 1984b; Littlefield 1976, 1979; Novelo 1976; Stavenhagen 1978; Stromberg 1985; Warman 1976, 1980; Young 1978).

In short, the interplay between Mexican research agendas and comparative economic anthropological discourse has been irregular but has produced a substantial and diverse literature that is the joint product of generalists and specialists. For the most part, like the sociocultural anthropology of Mexico in general, this literature has been produced through regional particularism (by specific states and/or groups of states) and is further fragmented along lines of ethnicity (Zapotec, Maya, Nahua, Tarascan, and so on) and of research interest (for example, craft production, markets, agriculture, development, gender relations, and so on). This makes for quite a mixed and disjointed, if invaluable, repository of knowledge.

For purposes of the present study, selection from the literature was made on the basis of my own judgment about the importance of particular contributions to understanding the problems of small-scale enterprises and their agents in Mexican and continental capitalism. The studies I chose also have relevance to the wider field of comparative economic anthropology, although many of them—especially those written during the past two decades—are, in fact, products not of comparative economic anthropology but of a culturally anthropologized political economy that is more focused on the study of political culture and power, ethnic relations, ecological degradation, or family, community, and ethnic group survival than on core matters of economic concern.[1]

THE CURIOUS CASE OF GEORGE FOSTER AND THE SCARCITY POSTULATE

George Foster was the first American sociocultural anthropologist/ethnographer to stake out a special interest in the rural Mexican economy, as evidenced by his early study of Popolucan peasant artisans in Veracruz (1982) and by his subsequent work among the mestizoized Tarascan peasant artisans around Lake Patzcuaro in Michoacan (1948a, 1948b; 1965, 1972, 1988). His first monograph, *A Primitive Mexican Economy* (1982), was submitted as his doctoral dissertation and was framed as a contribution to the emerging subfield of comparative economic anthropology; it was informed primarily by the work of Melville Herskovits (1940), with whom Foster had studied as an undergraduate; Raymond Firth (1939); and neoclassical economics. This study positioned Foster as a de facto founder of the Anglo-American branch of economic anthropology in Mexican studies and created the likelihood that he would continue to contribute to the development of this subfield as his career progressed.

Foster was defensive regarding his classification of the Popoluca economy as "primitive" (1982:2–3), but his usage conformed to precedents set by Firth (1939) and Herskovits (1940). He insisted that the analytical use of general categories of neoclassical economics was not tantamount to forcing noncapitalist economies into a capitalistic mold (1982:3, 98) and that means–ends rationality shared by different types of economies placed a high premium on understanding the nature of differing sociocultural matrices into which the substantive economic process was carried out. As he expressed it, "The student of primitive economics . . . cannot accept as 'given' or 'known' the factor of cultural background . . . without a general understanding of its social context the study of an economy will prove sterile" (1982:2). Foster also clearly expressed his understanding of the exceptional nature of capitalism in the history of the human economy: "The development of capitalism and the machine age have had such far-reaching consequences as to give the economy thus engendered a stamp peculiar unto itself" (1982:3). He did not elaborate on this thesis.

Perhaps Foster's most original contribution, and the one that was potentially the most significant for setting the course of development of economic anthropology in Mexican studies, was with regard to issues of commodity circulation, or, as he phrased it, "the handling of that portion of the family produce to be exchanged for outside products . . . involving such phenomena as trade, the market, price, value, exchange and barter" (1982:45). In rereading Foster, I was most struck by the originality of his discussion of the thesis that "Popoluca values cannot be entirely explained in terms of Western economy . . . unless scarcity and utility give an object power in exchange, or exchange value, it is of little economic importance" (1982:51). More specifically, he proposed that "beyond the local area, including most of southern Veracruz, there existed a 'super market' composed of Mexico and the entire world" on which coffee is the "export product most markedly dependent" (1982:52).

Next Foster turned to the topic of "money versus barter," where he observed that beans "have constituted the principal cash crop since time immemorial, and before the advent of money were exchanged almost exclusively for desired articles not produced at home" and in large quantities [together with lesser quantities of maize] in the late 1930s were still "bartered to individual small scale traders who are in many cases the ultimate consumers" (1982:53). The study includes intriguing data on barter and exchange ratios for six products that were commonly bartered for specific quantities of beans and of four products that were commonly bartered for specific quantities of maize. Foster observed that with the introduction of money, there was a year-to-year variation in the value of other items without a concomitant change in the exchange rate. For example, the price of 1 arroba (11.5 kilos) of lime had an average price of 1.25 pesos but that of beans fluctuated from a low of 1.035 to a high of 2.07 pesos. Regardless of fluctuations in the price of beans, they were regularly bartered at the customary rate of 1:1 arrobas (beans:lime). One of Foster's Popoluca informants explained this by asserting (1982:56), "Exchange is exchange. It doesn't matter if beans are worth more" (Cambio es cambio. No importa si frijoles valen más).

The logic behind this apparent indifference by the Popoluca to losses or gains in money-measured value intrigued Foster (1982:56–57), leading him to observe, "Uncertainty is the lot of the Popoluca producer, who one year must give more labor, as expressed in a larger proportion of a poor crop, for his necessary lime, salt and pots than he will the next" (1982:57). Since lime was produced in Jaltipan outside the Popoluca area (1982:45–46), Foster's explanation assumed relative demand inelasticities for both parties to the barter transaction but emphasized how the logic of any system of exchange is tightly bound up with a division of labor and specialization and a corresponding division of material "lacks or 'wants'" (1982:45), which, in the long run, is more fundamental than short-term market fluctuations measured in money terms (cf. Cook 1976:416, 422).

This point was driven home by Foster with an example of day laborers from Mecayapan who "often accept less maize in payment than they demand in money. Their needs in maize are fixed and known; if what they consider to be a fair amount can be obtained for working, they are less interested in money wages. Cash means greater uncertainty as to where the maize will come from, and at what price, and hence, what quantity" (1982:57). Foster's explanation of this point makes sense from the perspective of chronically maize-short households that have low-yielding or no land for maize growing and, therefore, prefer to acquire it as a wage in kind rather than buy it from merchants at elevated prices. It also recognizes the role of corn as a local/regional commodity money (Cook 1982:121–22). It should not go unnoticed here that the common thread in both of Foster's examples was a conception of equivalency in Popoluca commodity exchange implying a prudently rational trade-off between the value of labor time and of food staples based on a rank ordering in terms of relative scarcity or need.

Foster's data on money and barter in the Popoluca economy suggested that a monitoring or continuing study was certainly justified. Regrettably, not only did Foster not do this, but he made no attempt whatsoever to compare his Popoluca findings with those from his later work on the Tzintzuntzan economy—even, as we will see, when his findings on money and barter in the later study directly contradicted those from his Popoluca study. The astute economic anthropologist of the Popoluca was to eventually vanish down another path in the Michoacan village of Tzintzuntzan.

Foster identified Tzintzuntzan as "a *mestizo* and not an Indian village" (1948a:31) but also endowed it with a "primitive" economy, like the Popoluca (1948a:52)—a village economy he also recognized was inserted in international capitalist markets. This taxonomic conundrum reflected Foster's underlying belief in the dual economy thesis.

From the standpoint of the development of economic anthropology in Mexican studies, Foster's first Tzintzuntzan ethnography (1948a) represented a step backward from his Popoluca study. A purely descriptive, topical organization consisting of four main headings ("Earning a Living," "Commerce and Finance," "The Domestic Economy," and "Wealth and Property" —1948a:52–188) and a plethora of loosely related subheadings replaced the general categories of economy framework of the earlier study, and there was a corresponding lack of systematic, theoretically integrated discussion. For example, after an initial overview of the economy under the subheading "General Considerations" (1948a:52–58), the reader is hard-pressed, given the maze of subheadings, to sift out specific from general discussions. Under the heading "Credit Facilities and Price Structure," the reader is informed that "the general forms of production and the mechanics of the exchange of goods have now been discussed" (1948a:143); this is nearly 100 pages after the general overview and separate discussions boxed under a total of five major subheadings under the general heading "Earning a Living" ("Agriculture," "Pottery," "Fishing," "Domestic Animals," and "Secondary Occupations") and fifty-five additional minor subheadings.

Then, under the heading "Credit Facilities and Price Structure," the reader is further instructed that "certain additional data are necessary to further explain the basic nature of the economic system of Tzintzuntzan" (1948a:143). This statement is followed by an all-too-abbreviated discussion of money and barter—again without mentioning his Popoluca findings on this topic even though his Tzintzuntzan findings contradict them. Foster found that "barter ratios fluctuate as the monetary values of the items in question fluctuate" [compare with the previous statement on the Popoluca] and that "practically speaking, people in the entire area produce, exchange, and consume on the basis of a money economy. Even the common Mexican Indian practice of cooperative work exchange is almost unknown. The individual knows the amount of money his work is worth, what it will produce, and how much it will cost him to live" (1948a:143). In short, the important economic anthropological content of Foster's Tzintzuntzan I text seems to be randomly scattered throughout a maze of ethnographic boxes—with the reader being forced to infer from the descriptive headings and subheadings which set or subset of boxes might hide such content. Moreover, we are left to wonder why Foster did not compare his different findings on money and barter among the Popolucans and the Tarascans to achieve further insights or, at least, the identification of problems for further consideration.

Also appearing in 1948 in what would prove to be his last publication focused exclusively on economics was an article in which Foster (1948b) summarized his findings about the Tzintzuntzan economy and reclassified it under the "folk" rubric, which really was a euphemism for "peasant"—a term that he used by 1960. This folk stage in his "taxonomic conundrum" from primitive to peasant economy went hand in hand with a dualistic characterization of Tzintzuntzan as an "economy within an economy"—a rural agroindustrial form of economy based on a simple technology of low productivity within the urban, higher-tech industrial capitalist national and world economy (1948b:154). This article was more coherently organized than his ethnography and showed that something still remained of the economic anthropologist who wrote so perceptively about the Popoluca economy—especially regarding markets and pricing but also on the topic of the impact of inflation on peasant producer–sellers which Foster may have been the first to address (1948b:161).[2] It also made his economic dualism explicit.

Foster's biographers, Eugene Hammel and Laura Nader, overlook the unevenness of his contribution to economic anthropology and emphasize, instead, a common thread of "scarcity" providing theoretical continuity to his work in peasant studies, economic development, and applied anthropology (Hammel and Nader 1979:160–61). The Hammel–Nader thesis that Foster's theorization of Tzintzuntzan society derived from his study of economics and economic culture, while unsubstantiated by them, is plausible.

Foster's approach to models, his interest in predicting behavior, his fixation on equilibrium, his functionalist approach to systems, his view of social relations as if they were exchange relations, and his refashioning of zero-sum gamesmanship into a "limited good" worldview all point to an origin in neoclassical scarcity economics. Indeed, in retrospect, Foster was the first sociocultural anthropologist to interpret Mexican peasant society in the image of its commodity economy—an image or model that Foster presumed to be applicable to peasants everywhere (1988:6). Still, it was rather late in the post–World War II trend in anthropological discourse initiated by Kroeber (1948:284) when, in the 1960s, Foster finally removed the people of Tzintzuntzan from the "primitive" and "folk" categories and reclassified them as "peasants" who represented a "generic style of life" (1988:6): half of the world's people . . . peasant villagers who eke out a bare subsistence from exhausted soils . . . [and] uneconomic handicrafts. . . . Envious of the more fortunate peoples they see and hear about, they are nonetheless bound up in a cocoon of custom where the traditions and values of earlier generations still are seen as the safest guideposts in life" (1988:3).

As expressed in Tzintzuntzan II (1988), Foster's approach epitomized the apex of the convergence of uncritical positivism, economic dualism, developmentalism, and culturalistic psychologism in anthropology. He was convinced that the rationale for long-term intensive ethnographic study of a community like Tzintzuntzan was that the "real behavior of people can be recorded and worked into theoretical models which explain their behavior" (1988:5). He also confidently asserted that "cultural models which explain and predict dynamic processes with some accuracy are . . . enormously useful in planning specific developmental strategies" (1988:5).

Foster was not satisfied with positing cognitive models that corresponded to different fractions or groups of peasant-artisan villagers or that were situationally limited. Rather, his intent was to depict the "cognitive orientation" of entire communities by means of an ideal–typical model that "accounts for a very wide spectrum of behavior . . . and relates basic values and attitudes to . . . diverse institutions" (1988:123). Consequently, his model of the "Image of Limited Good" encompassed Tzintzuntzeños's social, economic, and natural universes, that is, their "total environment," which they see "as one in which almost all desired things in life such as land, other forms of wealth, health, friendship, love, manliness, honor, respect, power, influence, security, and safety exist in absolute quantities insufficient to fill even minimal needs of villagers" (1988:123). Moreover, people themselves were viewed as lacking the power to increase the available supplies of scarce items (1988:124). The scope of Foster's project was all-embracing. The "Image of Limited Good" was a zero-sum game writ large (Foster 1988:370, 385).

Indeed, one need not read Tzintzuntzan II for very long to realize that Foster's model also epitomized that school of thought that saw the source of peasant underdevelopment within peasant culture itself. Echoing the complaints of extension agents, governmental promoters, and developmentalists, Foster was troubled by Tzintzuntzeños's "irrational" "behavior in the modern world . . . under [which] . . . lie reason and thought, however unsoundly based they may be . . . patterns of reason and thought which are a major barrier to modernization of village life" (1988:16). From today's postmodern perspective, it seems embarrassingly obvious that a substantial combination of hubris and cojones was required to assume, as Foster did in a quintessentially patronizing way, that his "scientifically objective" practice of ethnography laid bare the cultural bases of maldevelopment among Mexican villagers.

Incredibly, the repertory of negative cultural baggage with which Foster burdened the Tzintzunteños (1988:chap.5) includes a entire section of his book devoted to their "Relative Absence of Foresight," in which we learn that they "take relatively few steps that can be thought of as influencing the future" (1988:114). Foster did not even consider their decisions to migrate as negating his characterization because he judged the people of Tzintzuntzan to be "so woefully equipped for another life, and understand so little of the wider world, that they simply cannot compete with other Mexicans" (1988:274). Earlier in the same chapter, Tzintzuntzeños were characterized as being ruled by gossip and rumor (91, 93), distrustful and suspicious (94–95), inordinately sensitive to real and imagined slights and insults (96), fearful of the known and the unknown (103–8), deceitful and manipulative (108–9), lacking standards of moral appropriateness (110), and unable to critically evaluate evidence (114). In short, Foster portrayed Tzintzuntzeños and, by implication, all Mexican peasants as being collectively sociopathic.

In the 1979 reissue of Tzintzuntzan II, Foster did express second thoughts about his model but only in terms of its applicability to the younger generation of Tzintzunteños, which had matured since 1965. In the 1979 preface, he admitted that younger Tzintzunteños were "no longer bound by the psychological shackles of the Limited Good outlook" (1988), and in an epilogue he essentially reviewed the post-1965 history of economic development and cultural change in the village that, if his model had been correct, could not have occurred. He insisted that his model did not preclude the possibility of change but does not begin to explain how, in a relatively short period of fourteen years, the fundamental changes he documents in his epilogue could have occurred among a population as cognitively crippled as were the Tzintzuntzeños portrayed in his Limited Good model (1988:384–87). In short, the inapplicability of the theory to the younger generation of 1979 suggests that it was an ill-conceived model in the 1960s.

The Image of Limited Good versus the Reality of Commodity Culture

How does the work of George Foster resonate with my notion of commodity culture(s)? His early work, from 1942 to 1948, is quite compatible with it, but his quest for a definitive, comprehensive, predictive model that assumes a uniformly shared cognitive orientation or worldview, namely, that of the "image of limited good" elaborated in Tzintzuntzan II, is not. In the first place, Foster's model greatly overextends and distorts the operational significance of the scarcity postulate in rational, culturally appropriate decision making. Scarcity in neoclassical economic theory is a relative not an absolute concept; the scarcity of any commodity is always relative to the demand for it—hence the need to schedule or make decisions that imply sacrifice or deprivation (that is, in order to get more of a given commodity, a quantity of some other commodity must be relinquished; or, in order to allocate labor time and effort in one direction, its allocation in another must be forgone) (cf. Cook 1966a:334). It is simply illogical to assume, as Foster does, that an assumption that "all things in life . . . exist in absolute quantities insufficient to fill even minimal needs" could possibly "subsume and explain concisely . . . the infinite forms and relationships of [economic] behavior that can be observed" among people, like the Tzintzuntzeños, who are participants in historically deep commodity cultures. In reality, Tzintzunteño wants were (and are) relative, not absolute. The pursuit to satisfy them evokes the exercise of prudent rationality, not zero-sum gamesmanship.

In the second place, I do not share Foster's positivistic faith in the capacity of anthropological interlopers to produce authoritative ideal–typical models that purport to explain subjects' behavior according to principles that operate outside their conscious powers of comprehension or awareness (Foster 1988:122–23). I think that our time is better spent in trying to systematically record and understand what subjects actually do and how they situate, interpret, and explain what they do and, perhaps, to expose some unintended consequences of this activity—nothing more, nothing less. In short, I do not propose a commodity culture(s) and labor alienation framework as a putatively comprehensive, predictive Fosterian model like the image of limited good. Rather, it is simply a theoretical departure point for analyzing and understanding Mesoamerica's (and Mexico's) historical indigenous capitalist development and interaction with external capitalism.[3]

Other Founders: Othón de Mendizábal, Marroquín, Beals, and de la Fuente

Andrés Medina must be credited with calling our attention to the pioneering role of Miguel Othón de Mendizábal in the definition and study of the "economic problem" among Mexico's indigenous peasant artisans (Medina 1996:147–58). As Medina points out, Mendizábal's ethnographic work, and especially his study of craft industries in Otomí villages in the Mezquital valley that provided a basis for Medina's own work (Medina and Quesada 1975), was informed by a cultural materialist approach in which fundamental importance was assigned to the relations between natural environment and level of technology and their close connection to the rest of culture (1996:138). This approach was best exemplified in a series of studies by Mendizábal of the pre-Colombian and colonial periods, one of which focused on the production and consumption of salt (Othón de Mendizábal 1946, 2) and others on the evolution and organization of the textile industry (Othón de Mendizábal 1946, 3:340–45; see Medina 1996:170 for complete bibliography). Mendizábal's functionalist analysis of salt production and consumption linked the physiological importance of salt for human survival to the geography and economics of its production and consumption and, ultimately, to broader dimensions of culture (Othón de Mendizábal 1946, 2:185) through the innovative key concept of "género de vida" (type of life). Medina (1996:138–39) is right to suggest that Mendizábal's study merited scholarly accolades such as those expressed by Malinowski regarding the pathbreaking work of Audrey Richards (1932:x) on nutrition. In any case, Mendizábal's study anticipated research findings by subsequent generations of scholars documenting that salt was unquestionably an object of the development of commodity culture(s) in Mesoamerica centuries before the arrival of the Spanish (Andrews 1983; McKillop 2002).

Mendizábal's ethnographic studies of the hard-fiber (*ixtle*, derived from varieties of agave, such as maguey and *lechuguilla*) weaving/twining industries of the Mezquital valley (1946, 6:153–99), together with several essays on contemporary peasant-artisan industry (1946, 4:205–11, 212–14) and economy (1946, 6:508–21), merit consideration as foundational contributions to the economic anthropology of Mexico. First and foremost, Mendizábal's ethnographic reports included systematic, detailed descriptions of technology, work organization, and labor processes industry by industry and product by product. They incorporated corresponding quantitative case study data on production costs in labor time and money, together with accompanying comprehensive tabulations of data on a village-by-village and industry-by-industry basis. Exemplifying his innovative presentation of the results of data analysis was a "Calendario Semanario" (weekly calendar) for a family of nine *ayateros* (rope twiners) that summarizes in tabular form the work contribution of each family member for every day of the week to the total average weekly output of fifteen *ayates* (lengths of rope) (Othón de Mendizábal 1946, 6:insert, 162–63).

In addition, Mendizábal presented the reader with important generalizations derived from his observations and data analysis. For example, he noted that the division of labor and specialization in a region like the Mezquital valley disclosed a pattern of greatest concentration and dependency on craft production in areas without irrigation agriculture (1946, 6:153–54; cf. Cook 1978:300–2; Cook 1984b:17; Cook and Binford 1990:43; Medina and Quesada 1975). The gender dimension of production and its implications for women's status caught his attention. In the processing of *ixtle,* according to which the maguey leaves were roasted prior to being scraped to expose the stringy inner pulp (following a pre-Hispanic pattern), he referred to the unique role of women: "This system permits the Otomí to unload [*descargar*] the roughest part of the work on women, who realize it with ease by adopting a technique that involves movements analogous to those to which they are accustomed to execute in grinding *nixtamal* [shelled corn soaked in lime] on the metate" (1946, 6:159).

Finally, Mendizábal's (1946, 4:205–11) essay titled "Small Indian Industries and Popular Manufactures" (Pequeñas Industrias Indias y Manufacturas

Populares) was presented to the Mexican legislature and made six recommendations for legislation pertaining to craft industries (including proposals that were eventually realized in the establishment of agencies such as the Museo de Artes e Industrias Populares as a subunit of the Instituto Nacional Indigenista and Fondo Nacional para el Fomento de las Artesanías) (1946, 4:210–11; Novelo 1976:50–80). In this essay, he astutely classified and reviewed the economic status of craft industries in Mexico and distinguished three forms of small-scale production that involved both Indian and mestizo men, women, and children (1946, 4:206–7): 1) domestic production for family use, 2) commercial domestic manufacture, and 3) small popular industries (with four subcategories: industries of practical utility, artistic industries of practical utility, decorative industries, and entertainment industries). Mendizábal emphasized the importance of the first form of production to the national economy because they "remove an elevated number of individuals from the consumption of products of small and large industry" (1946, 4:206) and recognized that the second form was participated in by indigenous and mestizo families, so that the income complemented their economic needs fundamentally provided by agricultural or other activity but with a potential for developing into full-time occupations (1946, 4:206–7). Most significantly, he recognized that "small industries and popular manufactures constitute a very important line of business in the economy of our large urban and rural masses, from the viewpoint of production, as well as distribution and consumption" (1946, 4:208) and are of "decisive importance as a complement of the economy of our rural population" (1946, 4:209).[4]

Mendizábal's legacy in economic studies was, perhaps, most directly influential in the work of Alejandro Marroquín (1957a, 1957b, 1978). In a separate article published in the same year (1957a) as his well-known monograph *La Ciudad Mercado (Tlaxiaco)* (1957b), Marroquín acknowledged Mendizábal's influence in rejecting the functionalist approach (that relied on a solar system metaphor and the principle of equal benefits to all participants, regardless of ethnoclass or residential identities, in regional Mexican market economies) in favor of an approach that emphasized exploitation and unequal exchange between town-dwelling mestizos and village-dwelling Indians (Marroquín 1978:43–44; Othón de Mendizábal 1946, 2:433–40). We also learn from Drucker-Brown (1982:6) that Marroquín's study was "explicitly based on the earlier work of Malinowski and De la Fuente" (see Marroquín 1978:33).

Although conceding that Marroquín's market project had many merits, Beals was critical of its short duration in terms of field research, its almost exclusive focus on the urban center of Tlaxiaco, and its reliance on a "simplified and rather doctrinaire Marxist interpretive framework" (1975:3). The latter judgment undoubtedly derived from Marroquín's repeated emphasis in *La Ciudad Mercado* on the systematic exploitation of Indian peasant artisans by mestizo intermediaries through unequal exchange (1957b:207–14, 222).

On the basis of the same source and evidence, Diskin and I cited Marroquín favorably as one among several students of "blatant Ladino exploitation of the Indian" (Cook and Diskin 1976:20) and emphasized his pioneering contribution to the study of indigenous markets. If we had read Marroquín's article then, we would have also extended his pioneer status to include a thoughtful Marxist interpretation of the articulational complexities between regional market economies like Tlaxiaco and the national and international capitalist system (Marroquín 1978:32–33, 37–43). Beyond that, the article reveals that, through a careful reading of the relevant comparative literature, Marroquín fashioned a critical economic anthropological approach to the "study of indigenous Mexican reality" to confront "institutions in a stage of transition, that constitute links" between the capitalist and precapitalist epochs (1978:31).[5]

Marroquín grappled thoughtfully, from a materialist rather than an idealist perspective (1978:38–39), with the problem of conceptualizing the town-based market of Tlaxiaco in the context of its interethnic regional economic matrix and locating the region in the developing national capitalist economy (1978:37–43). This effort was partially hampered by his inability to resolve contradictions between process, system, and structure and to appreciate the nuanced interplay between different types and scales of enterprises in the regional commodity economy. He was unable to reconcile a posited coexistence of separate economic systems in Mexico (underdeveloped capitalist, semifeudal, and indigenous precapitalist; 1978:41) and his tripartite classification of the indigenous market (semicapitalist, intermediate, and local traditionalist; 1978:42–43) with the notion of inexorable capitalist development that "will disintegrate the precapitalist economic system that still exists in indigenous communities, so as to integrate it definitively and categorically within the more vast and developed national economy" (1978:40). Despite these shortcomings, Marroquín's commodity value orientation enabled him to gain unprecedented insights into the dynamics of equivalency reckoning under market conditions "that tend to eliminate the use of money as a general equivalent, but make articles that are exchanged [to have been] previously valorized in money terms" (1978:46). This, in turn, provided the basis for an important series of observations regarding price formation in the indigenous market (1978:46–47).

Still, Marroquín's book lacked systematic analysis of the complex relations between indigenous peasant-artisan labor, indigenous village-based as well as mestizo town-based merchant capital, and value, price, and profit in the Tlaxiaco regional economy. He tended to waver between emphasizing the rural–urban ethnoclass divide on the one hand and symbiosis between rural indigenous labor and mestizo town-based capital on the other. This contradiction emerges clearly in his summary characterization of Tlaxiaco's economic structure (1957a:240–41) and is highlighted in his conclusion that "the economy of Tlaxiaco, *without* its own production base, is a parasitical economy that rests on the exploitation of indigenous labor" (1957b:241; emphasis added). His sophisticated theoretical understanding of the evolution of commodity value (1978:33–34) seems disconnected from his empirical discussions of price determination in the market (1978:207–11) and of industrial production for the market (1978:109–26). By not clarifying the differences between merchant, commercial, and small industrial capital, Marroquín precluded an analysis of how they might have overlapped in particular enterprises. In short, he did not systematically address the complexity of capitalist enterprises in the regional economy.

To his lasting credit, however, Marroquín built on the strengths of Mendizábal's and Malinowski–de la Fuente's prior work on regional market systems to advance our understanding of the mechanisms that "provoke the hypertrophy of small local economies or their maintenance at a accentuated level of backwardness, in order to satisfy the parasitical demands of the dominant regional center" (1978:43). In doing so, he achieved insights that anticipated those by scholars like Aguirre Beltrán (1967), Frank (1969), and Stavenhagen (1969:193–264). Thus, the most lamentable aspect of Marroquín's project is that there was never a sequel to build and improve on the original.

Beals (1975:277) was the only member of the Viking Fund Seminar (Tax et al. 1968) who subsequently undertook a major economic anthropological project involving extensive fieldwork that was explicitly concerned with ongoing debates in the broader subfield of economic anthropology and economics proper (1975:1–5). He found that Foster's notions of the principle of limited good (1988) and of institutionalized envy, or *envidia* (1972), were either absent or of little importance in inhibiting individual enterprise in Oaxaca (Beals 1975:277). Indeed, if any single generalization resulting from his Oaxaca markets project can adequately sum up Beals's view of the relation between culture and economy in the everyday lives of rural Oaxacans, it is the following: "Clearly, the rural-born Oaxaqueño does not function as a tradition-bound automaton but uses current economic criteria in his decision making" (1975:25).

This insight grew out of Beals's encounter with economics and economists from the early days of his project. In a letter to me dated October 13, 1965 (prior to my affiliation with the project in 1967–1968), Beals conceded that initially he had resisted the notion that economists "have developed perhaps the most powerful tools in the social sciences" due to "a certain hostility toward economic theory because I felt most economists gave inadequate consideration to the totality of social and cultural phenomena in which economic events occur." Nevertheless, as work proceeded on the project, he came "to the view that formal theory is not what is so culture-bound but [rather] it is the assumptions and variables considered or taken for granted by some economists that are culture bound . . . what we are studying is . . . a situation where market considerations must have operated for a very long time." Once recognizing that present-day market orientation in Oaxaca has a deep history, it followed that he would be "impressed with *the evidence that the calculations on which economic decisions are based are essentially those one would expect in our own society—providing one takes the social situation into account*" [emphasis added]. Thus, by 1965, Beals had moved into the vacuum in neoclassical economic anthropology in Mexican studies created by Foster's post-1948 refocus on what he viewed as dysfunctional cognition at the core of Tzintzuntzeño economic culture.

In this same letter, Beals elaborated on what he called "two distinct orientations" by sellers in the markets of Oaxaca: the orientation of the market personnel that makes its living from the market and the orientation of many of the producers selling in the market. He emphasized that many of the latter actually rely on consumption; that is, "their sales are governed by their need to obtain certain consumption goods rather than toward maximizing their profits through timing their sales to take best advantage of conditions of scarcity and advantageous prices . . . these consumption demands involve many social and ritual requirements rather than subsistence requirements . . . in the actual selling procedures, within the limits that he has to sell a certain quantity of goods by a certain time, the producer is acting like any other vendor in trying to get the maximum price." Beals qualified this statement to account for the effect of market "modernization" by observing that the producer–seller "is always making a calculation involving the best use of his time and labor . . . he may sell wholesale rather than retail because he believes he can more profitably invest his labor and time in production activities rather than in selling retail even though the latter may produce more money. In other words, he is making a choice in the direction of greater specialization because he thinks it will be more profitable in the long run."

Generalizations of this type expose both the strengths and the weaknesses of a functionalist and neoclassicalist approach to market process in economic anthropology. The focus is exclusively on prudent decision making by individual economic agents to the exclusion of the social relations of value production and distribution between and among economic agents.

Turning to the topic of reciprocity and ceremonial exchange, Beals (cf. 1970) emphasized that reciprocity involves many aspects of more generalized economic behaviors. Accordingly, for him, the Zapotec reciprocity principle known as *guelaguetza* "can be viewed as a credit mechanism or savings mechanism in which obligations are created which will assist in meeting future consumption needs" (1965, letter). Referring to the ritual giving of turkeys in accordance with *guelaguetza*, Beals observed that "it is not enough to have a turkey returned on the appropriate occasion. The turkey must be of exactly the same weight or else the giver or the recipient pays a cash consideration to make up for the difference in value. I have come to the conclusion . . . that *ignorance of cost accounting in an accurate sense must not be taken as evidence that an economic decision is of a different qualitative order. The same calculations are there; they just are less informed*" (1965, letter; emphasis added).

In a subsequent publication, Beals noted that as far back as the 1930s, ethnographers like Elsie Clews Parsons (1936:12–13), writing about the Zapotec community of Mitla, commented on peoples' "preoccupation . . . with prices . . . even though no immediate purchase or sale is contemplated" (1975:186). Such commentaries, reinforced by findings from his Oaxaca markets study, suggested to him that the "society of this region clearly is market oriented and has been so for a very long time" (1975:2). He clarified that "market oriented" "does not mean that all economic activities are controlled by the market . . . it means that the majority of the population involved are aware of market considerations and that this influences their economic decisions" (1975:2 n. 1). Thus, in Oaxaca, a peasant who is engaged primarily in the production of foodstuffs for his own consumption usually does so as the result of an evaluation of the market and has decided that subsistence farming is the best use of his available time and resources. Beals's recognition of a common thread of prudent rationality in both market (utilitarian) and reciprocal (ritual) exchange, as expressed previously, is suggestive of an implicit preconcept of commodity culture(s) in peasant-artisan regions of Mexico that reflects a long participation in market and nonmarket exchange—a "market orientation."

In his critique of Marroquín's Tlaxiaco study, Beals acknowledged but underestimated the importance of unequal exchange (that is, merchant appropriates surplus value as profit through resale of peasant-artisan products that are bought cheap and resold dear) between intermediaries and their peasant-artisan clients in Oaxaca markets (Cook 1982:354–57). He recognized the "potentiality" for it to occur but emphasized that its actual occurrence was "far outweighed by the function of the market—particularly in its traditional aspect—in the distribution of goods, which serves important economic and social ends" (1975:269). Diskin and I, while not rejecting Beals's functionalist interpretation, downplayed it in favor of a Marxist approach to commodity circulation in which "the deeper significance of the market lies in the class relationships it reinforces in its capacity as a social mechanism that facilitates the appropriation of surplus-value" (Cook and Diskin 1976:255).

Even though Beals's project incorporated into its design results from the earlier study of Malinowski and de la Fuente (1957; cf. Beals 1975:4; 1976:27–28), it failed to critically reconceptualize the nature of the articulation between "traditional" and "modern" forms within the Mexican economy (1975:13). His project was also disappointing for not engaging the earlier Malinowski and de la Fuente study of the Oaxaca market system in a more direct, systematic dialogue, so that it could have produced results that were derived from a comparative research strategy using the Malinowski–de la Fuente study as a baseline for comparison (cf. Drucker-Brown 1982:44–46). Diskin and I diplomatically alluded to this failure in the collection of essays we edited to supplement Beals's (1975) study: "In the synchronic, functionalist, empiricist tradition of the Malinowski–de la Fuente study, the Beals project held out the possibility of an eclectic, integrative, macroscopic approach to the Oaxaca marketing system, while necessarily devoting much effort to collecting and analyzing an extensive corpus of data dealing with sections or aspects of that system" (Cook and Diskin 1976:5–6). In retrospect, our statement could have been more explicit in pointing out that more than one "possibility" was unrealized in the project (cf. Cook and Diskin 1976:247–80; Smith 1976).

Julio de la Fuente, a participant in the Viking Fund Seminar, had a unique role in the development of economic studies in Mexican anthropology by virtue of his joint study with Bronislaw Malinowski of the Oaxaca marketing system, a Spanish translation of which was published in 1957. Susan Drucker-Brown (1982:3) reveals that de la Fuente "had been a student of Marxism . . . for most of his adult life," but her review of his contribution is not equally revealing about how his Marxism specifically impacted the jointly written monograph. This is not apparent from de la Fuente's running commentary in the original English version of the monograph, which was not published until 1982. Perhaps this impact was reflected in the study's attentiveness to production as a "principle of order" (Malinowski and de la Fuente 1982:115; cf. 111–13), to its thesis that the "function of the market is closely related to the hand-to-mouth existence of the poorest Indians" (1982:68), to its general concern with inequality, to its several references to social class and class relations (1982:118, 124–25, 133, 182), and, finally, to its concluding concern with labor value (1982:136, 147, 191). In any case, his collaboration with Malinowski in the Oaxaca study represents de la Fuente's most important contribution to economic anthropology in Mexican studies.

THE MARGINAL ROLE OF ECONOMISTS: MICHAEL BELSHAW IN HUECORIO

For better or worse, the intervention by economists in the development of economic anthropology in Mexican studies has been quite rare. Although there may be others, I can think of only one full-length monograph by an economist on a village economy—that by Michael Belshaw (1967) on Huecorio in Michoacan. Also worth noting is Ralph Cassady's invited participation in Beals's Oaxaca market project that resulted in one unique publication on marketplace haggling as a form of "double auction" (Cassady 1968; cf. Beals 1975:ix, 188–97).[6]

Belshaw's study was heavily concerned with issues of applied developmentalism and sponsored technoeconomic change a la CREFAL (Centro Regional de Educación Fundamental para la América Latina sponsored by UNESCO; Foster 1988:327–47) rather than with issues of theoretical economic anthropology. Nevertheless, his study provides a good illustration of how an economist goes about studying a Mexican village economy. In addition, it takes on added significance because it was published in the same year as Foster's Tzintzuntzan II and dealt with a village less than ten miles away from Tzintzuntzan with which it shared common pre-Columbian origins in Tarascan culture.[7]

Unlike Foster, who burdened Tarascan villagers with cultural baggage that essentially made them misfits in a commodity economy, Belshaw characterized them (based on evidence from the analysis of survey questionnaire results as well as from follow-up interviews and observations) quite differently: "Long contact with the realities of production gives them a thorough awareness of the relationships between production, income, and consumption. They are aware that, if they are to enjoy a better material life, they must produce more" (1967:338). In addition, he found widespread evidence that "Huecorianos are preoccupied with the business of making a living and that they consciously and constantly express a desire for a higher level of material well-being" (1967:334). Belshaw paid tribute to Foster's Tzintzuntzan I (1948a) as providing models and inspiration for his own work but emphasized that "despite the physical proximity of the villages, one must infer that until recently the villages lived as worlds (hence cultures) apart from each other in the Mexican cultural galaxy, and evolved diversely from what was once a common denominator" (1967:xiii). Surely, Foster's Tzintzuntzan II left Belshaw doubly satisfied with this judgment.

Belshaw also distanced his study from studies conducted by Foster and other anthropologists (Beals 1946; Lewis 1951) by recognizing that while the latter "contained substantial economic data," they lacked "economic analyses, since it was at least equally important to the researchers to record information on religion, folklore, ceremonials, the life cycle, the quality of interpersonal relations, and so on" (1967:xiii–xiv). By contrast, his study was "built upon an analysis of the classic factors of production—land, labor, capital, and entrepreneurship" plus "observations on population, the social and political situation and . . . the level and standard of living" (1967:xvi). In short, he tried to "account for all the internal circumstances that impinge upon the economic condition of the people of Huecorio and to suggest some of the external factors, such as the migrant labor policies of the United States government, that play their role" (1967:xvi).

In marked contrast to Foster, who produced generalizations about everything in Tzintzuntzan's culture, including their cognitive structure, Belshaw, with considerably less hubris and more sensitivity to heterogeneity, admitted that "at very few points is it possible to indulge in unqualified generalizations" because "Huecorianos are individuals of very different circumstances and outlooks, and this diversity must be acknowledged" (1967:xvi). It is precisely this capacity of economists to keep their focus on the economic field, with a selective and accessory focus on economically relevant phenomena in other fields and an assumption of socioeconomic heterogeneity, that needs to be emulated by economic anthropologists to avoid losing their focus on material reproduction in a quest for sociocultural embeddedness.

Aside from issues of approach and method, Belshaw's project set high standards for the qualitative and quantitative study of land use and agriculture worthy of emulation by economic anthropologists. Many of us can sympathize with his generalization that "the analysis of land distribution is a morass of unknowns surrounded by a swamp clogged with the roots of hidden assumptions" (1967:16) but will also appreciate his sample data that showed a uneven distribution of holdings by size (1967:18), their fragmentation and dispersion, and the acute shortage of good quality land and that "illegal dealings . . . frustrated the egalitarian intent of ejido legislation" (1967:25). His analysis of the planting of subsistence versus cash crops raises some unanswered questions regarding the rationality in income terms of growing cash crops rather than corn on irrigated land when, in fact, cash crop earnings are used mainly to buy corn at high prices since they produce only about half their annual corn needs (1967:35–40, 46). Furthermore, even farmers who do grow corn are regularly forced to sell it before harvest to merchants at a low price in order to meet preharvest fiesta expenditures, only to buy it back later from the same merchants at an elevated price.[8]

There are other noteworthy findings in Belshaw's study, for example, regarding capital accumulation as voluntary saving (for example, through self-employed labor [1967:175–76]) and entrepreneurship (for example, Huecorianos know little about the accounting of costs but are very much aware of profits [1967:206]), which he approached through several case studies (1967:20827). There was, unfortunately, no systematic treatment of the role of unwaged or undervalued labor in these case studies, and one of the cases—a textile workshop with dependent ties to another enterprise in a neighboring community—cried out for further analysis (1967:221–27). The same can be said for his abbreviated treatment of the returning braceros' repatriation of one-third of their U.S. earnings "toward capital in the form of sewing machines, irrigation pumps, tools, and inventories of merchandise for sale" (1967:338).[9]

CONCLUSIONS

There are important examples of continuity in the published record of economic anthropology in Mexican studies where later studies acknowledge and are partly designed to follow up and build on previous ones, for example, Medina and Quesada (1975) vis-à-vis Othón de Mendizábal (1946, 6) in the Mezquital valley, Marroquín vis-à-vis Mendizábal and Malinowski–de la Fuente in Oaxaca, Beals (1975) and Cook and Diskin (1976) vis-à-vis Malinowksi and de la Fuente in the Oaxaca valley, and Cook (1970) vis-à-vis Nash (1961) on price and output variability. Nevertheless, the overall record of publications in the subfield shows unevenness and discontinuity that limits its significance from the perspective of comparative economic anthropology. George Foster's failure to compare commodity circulation and equivalency in Veracruz (Popoluca) and Michoacan (Tzintzuntzan) set a precedent in this regard. There was subsequently more evidence of continuity, but even the previously mentioned series of projects on regional markets were lacking in systematic substantive integration.[10]

By 1970, economic anthropology in Mexican studies was dominated by the ascendancy of interdisciplinary peasant studies with a strong infusion of Third Worldist theory and including a focus on capitalist development and rural class differentiation. Many sociocultural anthropologists who took up peasant studies, however, did so from perspectives that ignored or downplayed class analysis and, often, ignored Chayanovian analysis as well (Cook and Binford 1986, 1990:15–34; Hewitt de Alcántara 1984).

It is clear from today's perspective that the formalist–substantivist debate had relatively little impact (as measured by the published record) on economic anthropological knowledge production in Mexican studies and that sifting through the literature of "rural otherness in postrevolutionary Mexico" (Hewitt de Alcántara 1984:178) with a particular focus on economic anthropology yields uneven results and suggests the need for a new, refocused agenda for twenty-first-century inquiry. The concept of commodity culture(s) is proposed as one possible axis around which such an agenda can be constructed.

NOTES

1. Symptomatic of the marginal position of economic anthropology in the Mexican branch of sociocultural anthropology is the paucity of articles on this topic in the journal *Nueva Antropología*. Since its inception in 1975, there has been no issue on this subfield and only one article that I could identify that addressed a topic of comparative interest, namely, Paré's piece on "*Tianguis y economía capitalista*" (1975). By contrast, there have been several issues devoted to the field of political anthropology, ethnic studies, and medical anthropology. This same trend characterizes anthropological collections like, for example, the Palerm Festschrift (Glantz 1987). There is no simple explanation for this neglect, but it may reflect the widespread impact of *indigenismo* and of Marxism in Mexican anthropology and, therefore, a judgment that comparative economic anthropology had little relevance to understanding Mexico.

2. David Kaplan (1965) attempted to exoticize the same Patzcuaro market studied years earlier by Foster through emphasizing "traditional" constraints on pricing, the absence of any precise notions of costs of production, failure to treat labor as a commodity, and the lack of long-term cost accounting so that the "worth of a good becomes somewhat indeterminate" (1965:88–90). This still left him with the impression that the Patzcuaro market approximated Joan Robinson's exchange-economy model in which "groups of producers depend for their living upon the sale of a particular commodity" (Robinson 1958:168). It should also be noted that, aside from his confusing and data-free discussion of pricing, Kaplan also argued in favor of economic dualism (1965:84–85) and, inexplicably, never cited Foster's (1948) article.

3. Robert Redfield, apparently referring to Manuel Gamio's discussion of his distinction between "objective" and "subjective" observation and his methodology for indirectly eliciting from informants' testimonials given in a "state of voluntary eloquence" (Gamio 1971b:xi–xii), proposed that "people act, not only because things are so, but because they think them or assume them, to be so" (Redfield 1971:xiii). Implicit was an opposition between informant opinions as rationalizations and "objective truth" and a warning that the former are not to be confused with the latter but are useful in explaining or anticipating conduct. He concludes by arguing that generalizations derived from testimonial or conversational data have "some of the value in understanding and anticipating behavior that there is in literature or art" (1971:xiv). This seems to reflect the same positivistic faith in social scientific method expressed by Foster.

4. In the second paragraph of this essay, Mendizábal anticipates a theme raised much later in the "crafts in world markets" literature (Nash 1993): "Many of these manufactures, due to their artistic quality and for the ingenuity of their conceptions and the primitivism of their technique, that constitutes a powerful attraction for individuals who live under the standardizing influence of mass production by large industry, have surpassed the radius of original action, as a function of recent national and international demand" (1946, 4:205). This theme, as well as another that Mendizábal addresses, namely, that of the unequal exchange between mestizo middlemen and indigenous producer–sellers in local and regional markets, is also addressed in Traven's work (see chapter 2).

5. In direct contrast to the 1957 edition of *La Ciudad Mercado*, which had neither source references nor bibliography, the 1957 article includes extensive references to the relevant literature in Mexican studies, economic and cultural anthropology, and economic sociology (1957a). Beals's (1975:3) criticism of the "limited degree of field research" underlying Marroquín's Tlaxiaco market study was in reaction to information provided in the front matter of the original edition (1957a:6) of that monograph, where we learn that "the research was conducted in the last week of July and the first of August of 1953" with the collaboration of four anthropology students (presumably *licenciatura* students from ENAH). In view of this time constraint, the quantity and quality of the Marroquín team's observational and conversational data are truly impressive and clearly reflected efficient planning, training, organization, and dedication. What remains a mystery is why Marroquín's thoughtful article was published separately months before his book (Báez-Jorge 1978:10) and not as an introduction to the book. As Báez-Jorge observes, fewer "theoretical limitations and disassociations" (1978:11) occur in the article than in the book.

6. The important study of four Mexican communities by Sergio de la Peña (1981) also merits mention here.

7. CREFAL is an acronym for Centro Regional de Educación Fundamental para la América Latina, established in the Lake Patzcuaro region in 1951 on an estate donated by Lázaro Cárdenas, former president of Mexico. Devoted to community development training, it is sponsored by the United Nations through UNESCO and by the Mexican government (see Foster 1988:328–47; cf. Belshaw 1967:xi–xii).

8. This situation is referred to as "*el trinquete del 8 de diciembre*" (1967:47).The word *trinquete* is generally used to denote a person (*acaparador*, or buyer-up) who does not act in good faith, but in this context it refers to a person who takes advantage of others who have an urgent need for money by buying unharvested crops at less than the market price (Belshaw 1967:181–82).

9. Another example is David Kaplan's (1965) article on the same Patzcuaro market studied years earlier by George Foster (1948b) in which Kaplan fails to cite Foster, much less compare his findings or interpretations with Foster's.

10. With special reference to commodity circulation, I will use the term "equivalence" throughout this book to refer to the state or property of approximating "equivalent" or "equal" amounts. Foster approached this issue exclusively through a focus on barter, emphasizing the quantitative determination of rates of exchange between commodities (and labor) with a monetary common denominator (implying only use and exchange components of commodity value). He avoided addressing the issue in the context of reciprocal exchange where commensurateness (and, therefore, equivalence) is less precise. I favor an approach to equivalence that accommodates the symbolic/sign component of commodity value so as to facilitate an understanding of commodity circulation in contexts of reciprocity as well as of barter. The guiding principle of commodity exchange is "good enough" rather than "exactly equal"—even when labor time or monetary common denominators are used without strict capitalist cost accounting. There is always a mutual adjustment between use, exchange, and symbolic elements of value in the determination of equivalence in commodity transfers among peasant artisans.

2

Commodity Culture(s), Capitalism, and the Economic Anthropology of Mexico: The Case of B. Traven

Many of the issues of central concern to *indigenismo* dating from the 1920s addressed in the work of anthropologists were woven into the widely read stories of B. Traven, an ethnographically inclined writer who studied anthropology at the Universidad Nacional Autónoma de Mexico (UNAM) in the late 1920s. Indigenous village life and its engagement with external markets and power provided materials and themes for much of Traven's work. Most recently, his realistic fictional narratives have resonated with postmodernist currents in cultural anthropology that accentuate the "translocal" nature of the Mexican craft circulation (Wood 2000b). It is a tribute to the resilience and ingenuity of Mexico's peasant artisans, as well as to the complexity and adaptability of market economy and commodity-producing enterprises, that the same issues addressed by B. Traven in short stories and novels during the first half of the twentieth century will necessarily be addressed by economic anthropologists and others in the twenty-first.[1]

June Nash's *Mayan Visions* (2001), inspired and informed by her fieldwork in Chiapas, calls to mind B. Traven's "Assembly Line" story set in rural Oaxaca in its attempt to come to grips with the clash between capitalist and indigenous peasant-artisan commodity culture. Nash's book exemplifies that at the beginning of the twenty-first century, the political economy of ethnocultural survival in Mexico reconfronts the same contradiction that bedeviled prior generations of writers, including Traven, between the "principle of sufficiency for existence" (Sombart 1967:17), which was the presumed modus operandi of "precapitalist" peasant-artisan economic activities, and capitalist accumulation. Polanyi expressed this as the clash between the "provision of material means of want-satisfaction" and the "economic principle of formal rationality [economizing]" (1968a:122, 132). In broader terms, it was a clash between capitalist and peasant-artisan commodity culture and their contrasting modes of producing, exchanging, and consuming commodities.

Through my interviews with Antonio Reynoso, the owner and foreman of a small-scale brickworks (*ladrillera*) near the banks of the Rio Bravo in Reynosa, Tamaulipas, in 1993, I was able to show how Traven's story detailing an ill-fated business relationship in the 1920s between a New York City merchant and a peasant-Indian basket maker from a Oaxaca village was relevant to understanding business relationships decades later between small-scale brick producers in Reynosa and their Texas-based clients (Cook 1995). My analysis explored the similarities and differences between artisanal production in peasant Oaxaca and brick making in Reynosa. I also examined the different constraints affecting their market performance. Antonio first became familiar with Traven's story in its Mexican movie version, and he alluded to it during our first conversation in responding to my question about the problems of his brick export business.

TRAVEN'S "ASSEMBLY LINE" IN OAXACA AND REYNOSA

According to the story, a New York City businessman, Mr. E. L. Winthrop, traveling as a tourist in the state of Oaxaca, arrives one day in a peasant-Indian basket-making village that Traven names Huehuetonoc. Attracted by the uniquely designed baskets he observes one peasant making, Winthrop buys up the basket maker's entire inventory of sixteen baskets for forty-five centavos (about four cents) each (Traven 1993:75, 78). After returning to New York and discovering a potential market for such baskets, Winthrop negotiates a trial order with "one of the best-known candy-makers in the city" for 10,000 baskets to be used as "fancy packing" for French pralines (Traven 1993:78–79). The negotiated price is $1.75 each, delivered in the port of New York (80–81). Winthrop rushes back to Oaxaca to work out a deal with the peasant basket maker. To his chagrin, he finds that the basket maker is willing and able to make only three dozen baskets over a two-month period. Winthrop, obsessed by the prospect of handsome profits if the deal can be closed as negotiated in New York, urges the basket maker to reconsider the possibility of making more baskets and to do so at a wholesale price per 1,000 pieces. The basket maker agrees to rethink the matter overnight and the next day responds to Winthrop as follows (Traven 1993:84): "If I got to make one thousand canastitas, each will be three pesos. If I must make five thousand, each will cost nine pesos. And if I have to make ten thousand, in such a case I can't make them for less than fifteen pesos each." Winthrop, who Traven implies views economics through the lens of capitalist commodity culture of mass production through wage labor, is dumbfounded by the logic of this response—larger volume, higher cost—and desperately probes for a further explanation, which the basket maker provides (Traven 1993:84–85): "Bueno, patroncito, what is there so difficult to understand? It's all very simple. One thousand *canastitas* [little baskets] cost me a hundred times more work than a dozen. Ten thousand cost me so much time and labor that I could never finish them, not even in a hundred years."

Next, at Winthrop's insistence, to clarify the reasons why village basket production capacity is so limited, the basket maker explains in some detail the elements of the typical Oaxaca villager's livelihood strategy, combining agricultural production for own use with craft production for raising cash for additional household needs and embodying logics that in today's academic discourse are known as subsistence "safety first" (Scott 1976:15–26) and simple "opportunity cost." In a display of Traven's recognition of the peculiar constraints influencing Oaxaca villagers' decision making, Winthrop pointedly asks the basket maker why he does not recruit relatives or other villagers to help out with agricultural or basket production and elicits the following reply: "They might, patroncito, yes, they might. Possible. But then you see who would take care of their fields and cattle if they work for me? And if they help me with baskets it turns out the same. No one would any longer work his fields properly. In such a case corn and beans would get up so high in price that none of us could buy any and we all would starve to death" (Traven 1993:85–86). In short, Mr. Winthrop returned to New York empty handed, frustrated, and cursing the stupidity of Mexican peasant-Indian artisans for their lack of business acumen.[2]

It can be inferred from this synopsis that Traven was well informed about political economy, was knowledgeable about the realities of daily life in southern Mexican peasant-Indian villages, and had a good grasp of factors that mattered in peasant-artisan decision making regarding participation in subsistence agriculture and/or craft production for cash and/or wage labor. He understood that these factors would not be appreciated by a New York City businessman.

Why is Traven's Oaxaca tale, written more than a half century ago, relevant today to a small-scale capitalist brickworks owner–boss (*ladrillero*) in Reynosa, far removed in time, place, and level and type of socioeconomic development from rural Oaxaca of the late 1920s? Its relevancy hinges on Antonio's perception of a parallel between Traven's explanation of why the peasant-Indian basket maker could not supply enough baskets to meet Winthrop's business needs and Antonio's own understanding of a similar incapability of his brickworks to make enough bricks to supply the export market.

Traven's explanation of why the New York City–Oaxaca village basketry business was not viable struck Antonio as being applicable to his own difficulty in conducting a viable export business because it highlighted constraints on labor productivity. In conventional economics, this issue evokes the marginalist model of dual sector economies in which, to quote from an economics textbook, "With the assumed fixity of wants an individual's supply curve of effort to the exchange sector turns back for rates of reward above a certain point; beyond this point the quantity of effort offered varies inversely with the reward per unit" (Bauer and Yamey 1957:85). In essence, the cases of Oaxaca basketry and Reynosa brick making exemplify the "backward bending supply curve of effort" so familiar to neoclassical development economists but by no means applicable only to developing Third World economies.[3]

The labor productivity issue was central to Antonio's explanation of his relations over the years with an Anglo-Texan broker, Bill Cypert, from Houston. On his periodic visits to the Reynosa *ladrilleras*, Cypert always complained about their lack of output capacity and irritated Antonio by making invidious comparisons between his *ladrillera* and another one in the same area who Cypert wrongly claimed was producing 100,000 bricks monthly with only four brick makers. Antonio knew these claims to be wrong through his own periodic observations of what was going on in his neighbor's *ladrillera*. He knew, too, that during any given week, eight to ten brick molders (*hechureros*) were at work in his own *ladrillera* and that his average output of 50,000 bricks monthly was at least equivalent to—and often exceeded—his neighbor's. Yet Cypert apparently never got his output estimates in line and caused Antonio even more disgruntlement by telling him on one occasion that he lacked the will to make his *ladrillera* more productive ("El decía que yo no tenía ánimo de trabajar").[4]

Antonio tried, in vain, to explain to Cypert the reasons why it was impossible to regularly produce 100,000 or even 50,000 handmade bricks monthly in either his or his neighbor's *ladrillera*: "There are weeks that we make twenty odd thousand; then there are weeks that it is only make, make, make and we produce 30,000. But then a week comes along when we have to get, load, and unload firewood, or load unfired brick into the kiln, fire it, unload it from the kiln and stack it or load it on a trailer. And then there are rainy days. It is not pure make, make, make. So I have the desire to work, what I don't have is the desire to lie about the nature of the work. I am not able to tell you that X number of workers on any given day can make me, say, 8,000 bricks. Today, perhaps, but tomorrow they will work at a different pace and they will make me only 2,000. And day after tomorrow, a trailer drives up and has to be loaded so they make me only 2,000 again." Antonio's dealings with Cypert were asymmetrical and tensely miscommunicative because of their irreconcilable perceptions of economic reality and proved ultimately abortive. This parallels the relationship portrayed by Traven between the anonymous Oaxaca basket maker and Mr. Winthrop. Cypert was Antonio's Mr. Winthrop.

During another conversation, Antonio was even more explicit in explaining to me why Traven's story was meaningful to him as a small brickworks employer. "One has a two-sided problem. The customers, since they speak about large volumes, demand a very low price. That's where the case of the baskets [in Traven's story] is relevant. If I supply the client with, say, 10,000 bricks weekly, I can do so at a price of thirty-five dollars per thousand pieces. But, if I supply him with 20,000 logic says that I would sell at a lower price per thousand. But that is not the case. The price tends to go up due to the little problems we have with the workers. With three or four hours work daily, they want to earn an eight-hour salary. When they see that I have an order, they will ask me for a raise, not to work more hours but to work less for the same salary." It is as if Antonio had complied with a request from me to provide an example of the academic economists' backward-bending supply curve of labor.

In the nonwage situation depicted by Traven, the rescheduling of labor time from subsistence agriculture to basketry led to higher opportunity costs for the peasant artisans. The use of wage incentives by Reynosa brickworks employers like Antonio to increase productivity may also lead to cost increases as well as to possible decreases in output. Thus, a worker who had to work five hours to produce 1,000 bricks prior to a wage increase may be able to earn the same income after a wage increase by working one hour less and producing only 800 bricks. Despite its many differences with peasant-artisan basket making in Oaxaca, petty capitalist brick making in Reynosa also confronts a series of constraints on labor input that inhibit the expansion of output for the Texas export market.

Although the common condition in the two situations is that labor input/productivity is constrained, it is important to understand that the specific constraints are different and that the subsistence risk/cost-benefit factor to labor is higher in the Oaxaca case. For purposes of his story, Traven assumed the relative absence of a rural proletariat and a predominantly independent peasant-artisan population where the typical household engages in subsistence agriculture. Under such conditions, the opportunity cost of neglecting subsistence agriculture for cash-earning craft production would be higher than the potential income from basketry. A comparable opportunity cost factor is not operative among the Reynosa brick industry proletariat, which lacks the option of subsistence agriculture. In their case, the choice is between leisure and work but is constrained by the physically punishing nature of brick-making labor (hence a high "drudgery" factor) and by a level of earnings targeted to meet an acceptable standard of living. This is why their response to wage incentives is not open ended.

A caveat is in order here. Whereas Antonio is correct to emphasize the parallel between the constraints operating on labor performance and productivity, it is important to point out that these constraints can be (and have been) overcome in the border brick industry by an increase in the number of small *ladrilleras*, either as new independent enterprises or as satellites of already existing enterprises. The satellitization strategy is known as the "*campero*" (field boss) system, and the satellite brickfields are known as "*campos*." Nevertheless, only the largest brickworks have the capital required to implement the satellite field strategy, and its successful implementation implies an employable pool of brick-making labor available either locally or through off-border recruitment (Cook 1998:207–16).

COMMODITY CULTURE VERSUS MORAL ECONOMY

Traven was deeply concerned that the more that peasant artisans played the market game, the faster the commodity culture–social relations dialectic moved away from the intimacy of household- and community-based petty commodity production toward the impersonality of market-dominated, money-mediated capitalist production. It was clearly Traven's belief that as capital penetrates peasant-artisan production, typically through a combination of credit and piece-rate payment from sources external to the local community, the artistic soul of that intimate production system dissipates.[5]

In the very title of his Oaxaca tale, Traven implicitly set artisanal production in opposition to large-scale capitalist mass production. His metaphor of the "assembly line" was employed ironically to expose Winthrop's ethnocentrism, but as the narrative unfolds, the metaphor serves to highlight that artisanal production is prevented in two ways from meeting the demand of a mass market: first, because the artisans are also peasant agriculturists with a subsistence-first and opportunity cost orientation who are culturally and emotionally tied to the soil and, second (and here is where Traven succumbs to a romantic, nostalgic, essentialist, and utopian vision of bucolic, nonindustrial, small-scale production), because each and every product of artisanal labor is unique not only in design and appearance but also because it embodies a piece of the cultural soul or essence of the artisan.[6]

For Traven, artisans were artistic and, therefore, were artists. Regarding the basket maker, he wrote that "[this craftsman] had made in his life several hundreds of those exquisite baskets, but so far no two of them had he ever turned out alike in design. Each was an individual piece of art and as different from the other as was a Murillo from a Velásquez" (1993:76). And speaking through the basket maker, Traven (1993:87) waxes even more poetic regarding the nature of artisanal labor: "I've to make these *canastitas* my own way and with my song in them and with bits of my soul woven into them. If I were to make them in great numbers there would no longer be my soul in each, or my songs." From the standpoint of the ethnographic record, the voice of the Oaxaca basket maker here is not representative of most twentieth-century Mexican peasant artisans who have found a way to reconcile their culturally embedded sense of artisanry with their commercial market participation.[7]

In taking this extreme position vis-à-vis the conflict of economics against morality or technique against art, Traven placed himself in the company of cultural purists or essentialists who contend that systematic production for sale inevitably results in the debasement of the aesthetic or artistic quality of craft products. In addition, he joined company with many radical intellectuals whose romantic, utopian vision leads them to see worker anomie as a necessary concomitant of mass production and capitalist development (cf. Sancíprián 1991:10). These beliefs, together with Traven's special dislike of the U.S. brand of capitalist massification of production and consumption (that is, his anti-Fordism), resonate in the moving and sardonic concluding lines of his Oaxaca tale (1993:88): "And in this way it happened that American garbage cans escaped the fate of being turned into receptacles for empty, torn, and crumpled little multicolored canastitas into which an Indian of Mexico had woven dreams of his soul, throbs of his heart: his unsung poems."[8]

An anecdote from Panajachel (Guatemala) told by Sol Tax in a lecture at the University of Chicago attended by June Nash (1993:18) in her student days to illustrate his concept of "penny capitalism" (Tax 1963) strikes me as more closely approximating the ethnographic reality (what Nash refers to as the "ingenuity of entrepreneurial artisans") of most twentieth-century Mexican peasant artisans than Traven's statement. According to Nash (1993:18), "A Panajacheleño weaver-entrepreneur who had sold him [Sol Tax] and his wife Gertrude so many pieces that they had no need or desire left . . . continued to return with offerings, each time pegged so much lower in price that they felt forced to take advantage of the offer. Finally, Sol asked the man how he could sell at a price so much reduced from the first items he had sold. The man told him to bring those earlier sale items out, and then he pointed out the progressive reduction in size and complexity of design that made the lower price possible."

In other words, the market orientation of peasant-artisan petty commodity producers in most branches of artisanal production usually conflicts with their practice of any form of aesthetic or artistic extremism in their craft (that is, practices that result in the maintenance of high but costly quality standards). Their need for cash and their market experience encourage most peasant artisans to look for ways to ensure the competitiveness of their products through a measured sacrifice of artistic or aesthetic quality for economic gain. This does not mean that Mexican peasant artisans are necessarily moneygrubbing philistines or cultural adulterators who knowingly deceive an aesthetically concerned but naive clientele, even though the principle of caveat emptor is very much operative in markets where peasant artisans sell their own commodities. Rather, it simply highlights a cultural circuit in the system of commodity production and market economy: involvement in production for sale teaches that time is money and that money lost or time squandered will inevitably lead to reduced sales and income for the noblest and most moral of peasant artisans. Once again we are vividly confronted with expressions of indigenous Mexican commodity culture.

It is, I would contend, the same "entrepreneurial ingenuity" referred to previously by June Nash that facilitates artisanal production for the mass market or that enables small-scale, labor-intensive producers to find ways to work more efficiently and, if necessary, to expand output well beyond levels conceived as possible by Traven and moral economists. Peasant artisans manage to do this as independent petty commodity producers by working harder, working longer hours, employing additional household members, working more efficiently by making technological innovations that do not involve mechanization, and so on. Or they may do it in association with intermediary capital or small-scale industrial capital (such as hiring pieceworkers)—still, it must be emphasized, without machinofacture or significant degrees of mechanization. Most typically, they achieve efficiency independently through the formulaic conception and execution of their work. Successful artisanal production for the market is predicated on the routinization of effort and the standardization of form and style. In sum, artisans economize by producing as efficiently as they can one product after another in serial and replicated fashion. For Traven (and also for Othón de Mendizábal 1946:205), by contrast, the assembly-line metaphor represents mass production as an exclusively machine-driven, large-scale capitalist process in which artisans are absent.

The ethnographic record in Mexican studies suggests that when output expansion is the goal in particular craft industries, productivity-enhancing processes inevitably lead to the recruitment of neophyte labor previously uninvolved in craft work. Two illustrative cases in the Oaxaca valley are the embroidery and the treadle-loom weaving industries. In the case of embroidery, a sort of mushrooming spin-off process has occurred in which the industry leapfrogs from household to household and village to village under the sponsorship of merchant capital and a network of commission agents and outworkers. Embroidery units are replicated as nonembroiderers become embroiderers, embroiderers become commission agents, and commission agents become independent merchant engrossers. It is a competitive, market-driven cycle that seems to be capable of expanding up to the limits of the available labor supply. In treadle-loom weaving, three processes occur: the establishment of new, independent weaver enterprises; the expansion of existing weaver enterprises by the exploitation of household and wage labor to develop multiloom workshops; and the intervention of intermediary capital to establish putting-out/buying-up systems in which outwork weavers are exploited through credit arrangements (Cook and Binford 1990:esp. chap. 4; Waterbury 1989).

There are, admittedly, branch-specific upper limits on the expandability of output in craft industries—ecological, technological, demographic, and economic in nature. What is true for treadle-loom weaving is not necessarily true for embroidery or brick making, backstrap-loom weaving, metate making, and so on (see Cook and Binford 1990). Nevertheless, it is the mass-production capacity of artisanal industries to turn out relatively uniform products in sufficient quantities to meet market demand, as well as the ways in which they realize it, that is noteworthy from the standpoint of economic anthropology. This is diametrically opposed to the aestheticists' focus on the debasement of "authentic" crafts through the practice of artisanal mass production.[9]

Indeed, if artisans, in combination with merchant capital, did not practice their version of mass production, then the entire *Crafts in the World Market* (Nash 1993) and *Ethnic and Tourist Arts* (Graburn 1976) themes would most likely not exist, and craft scholars today would be debating more esoteric themes dealing entirely with high-priced, made-to-order, scarce luxury crafts. In other words, the secret to the persistence, and especially to the growth, of craft production in the contemporary world market lies in the capacity of labor-intensive, artisanal forms of production to flexibly adjust output to fluctuations in demand and, when necessary, to increase output geometrically through innovative labor organization and, perhaps, with appropriate technological improvisation.

The later decades of the twentieth century, especially the 1990s, were characterized by a boom in Mexican crafts generated not only by tourism but also by their entrepreneurial insertion into the burgeoning "interior decoration/adornment" market in the United States. This, in effect, translated into a proliferation of Traven's "Mr. Winthrops" wheeling and dealing their way across the spectrum of Mexico's craft industries—from ironware, pewterware, glassware, woodworking and furniture making to basketry, weaving, pottery, embroidery, and, yes, bricks. But unlike Mr. Winthrop, many of these new entrepreneurs are also designers attuned to the fluctuations in styles, fashions, and fads in the retail home adornment market who, through websites and other forms of electronic communication and mail-order catalogs, maintain nationwide ties with retailers in markets ranging from lowbrow to upscale. They traffic primarily in a series of new craft commodities rather than in the traditional lines of ethnified crafts. The constant information flow from the demand side of the market enables these new entrepreneurs to keep their production closely tied to market fluctuations. In addition, unlike Mr. Winthrop, these new entrepreneurs have direct involvement in production either through the operation of production facilities in Mexico or through a variety of subcontracting arrangements.[10]

More often than not, these new entrepreneurial craft businesses are located along the U.S.–Mexico border in cities like Brownsville, McAllen, Laredo, and El Paso, Texas, or San Diego, California—but some may be in off-border locations, like Santa Fe or Albuquerque, New Mexico, or San Antonio, Houston, or Dallas, Texas. Much to the dismay of handicraft aestheticists or indigenous cultural reproductionists, the commodities targeted by these new entrepreneurs reflect markets saturated with traditional ethnic art and with a craving for innovative designs, whether contemporary, neotraditional or pseudoethnic (for example, Navajo by Zapotecs or Zapotec by Chinese or Philippinos). This implies the culmination of a long-simmering crisis in the popular arts-and-crafts sector of Mexican life and agencies directly concerned with it like FONART between the preservation of traditional "ethnic" styles and economic progress in the lives of artisans (Amador Tello 2002; cf. Cook 1981).[11]

Despite the empirical support in the ethnographic record from contemporary Mexico for the decline in the quality of particular crafts for reasons of economic or market expediency (Stromberg 1976), it is by no means so widespread as to warrant one-sided, alarmist, and elitist concerns about the proliferation of "ethno-kitsch" (Graburn 1976:6). Indeed, there is sufficient contrary evidence of artistic creativity and improvement in product quality among capitalist market–involved artisans to support the thesis that international market participation has been a boon to artisanal production not only from a narrow economic perspective (for example, the resuscitation of the use of vegetable and insect dyestuffs and the use of natural wool in the weavings of Teotitlán del Valle [Cook and Binford 1990:89; cf. Stephen 1991:131]) but also in the case of the *amate* bark painting industry of Guerrero, where Stromberg (1976:162) points to a decline in artistic quality associated with competitive participation in a mass market and concludes that "it is still possible to see . . . artistic forces at work." Furthermore, it should not be overlooked that this entire industry started only in 1959 as an innovative response to economic need among artisans and cash-earning possibilities generated by capitalization of the labor and design process that tapped new markets (Stromberg 1976:148–49). It should also not be overlooked that this particular line of artisanal commodities may be representative of a relatively high degree of market saturation, especially in the United States.[12]

Against Traven's romanticist positioning of the peasant artisans' creative souls in a battle for survival against the juggernaut capitalist market, I would argue that, by the time he observed and wrote about them, most Mexican peasant artisans had long since been preconditioned by participation in commodity production and market economy to willing, if calculated, involvement in capitalist markets. It must be noted, nevertheless, that not all Mexican peasant artisans today appear to display the degree of commercial participation or the lack of commitment to ethnified forms of cultural expression as do many of those in Oaxaca (Carlsen 1993; Eber and Rosenbaum 1993; Nash 1993). A special exception in Oaxaca is the proactive, Zapotec reethnification movement associated with the so-called Tlacolula weaving production complex (WPC) centered around the community of Teotitlán del Valle that reflects a long tourist and international market involvement (Stephen 1991, 1993; Wood 2000a, 2000b).

TRAVEN'S ANTHROPOLOGICAL AND POLITICAL ECONOMICS

In reading Traven as an economic anthropologist, it is necessary to read him first as a political economist of capitalism. He came to Mexico fully prepared to view its economy as neocolonial capitalist and to view its rural peasant-Indian peoples as at least partial participants in capitalist markets for labor and its products. In everything Traven wrote about rural Mexico that significantly deals with economic themes, capital is a powerful presence in the lives of indigenous peasants. It is this awareness and understanding of capital, combined with a fascination with its multiple activities and relations and their compelling implications in exotic hinterlands of provincial Mexico, that makes Traven's economic anthropology so unique for its time and still relevant today. That Traven was able to convey so effectively and sympathetically the participation of peasant-Indian villagers in this capitalist relational process, as well as in those domains of life where capitalism was peripheral or absent, with insights only mildly tainted by ethnocentrism, accentuates the uniqueness and relevance of his legacy.

Traven was a severe critic of capitalism and statism. He sided ideologically with labor in its historic struggle against capital and with civil society (the people) in its (their) struggle against the state. Although critical of the Communist Party (Stone 1977:31–32, 47, 52–53) and not a Marxist, he shared with many Marxists a view of capitalism as an international class struggle in which capitalists' profit is derived from their exploitation of a proletarian class that embraces rural and urban workers in both the Old and the New World. For Traven, Mexican peasant-Indian ranch or forestry workers, like workers in all colonial and neocolonial countries, were as much a part of the proletariat as were European or U.S. factory workers (Guthke 1991:186, 263–64). Raskin (1980:179) makes this point succinctly: "For Traven the Indian is a proletarian, a worker. To understand the Indian, Traven says, we have to understand labor." Traven's labor-centered approach to capitalist production carried over to his approach to peasant-artisan production.

In his novel *The White Rose*, Traven presents a short course on the political economy of capitalism, the central theme of which he expresses as follows (1969e:165–66): "Workers do not work because they are stupid . . . but because they are so compelled by the iron laws of the capitalist system. No matter how much workers do and plan within this social and economic system to which they belong and of which they form part, the only result will be to strengthen capitalism. As long as the system lasts, labor will be inevitably coupled with capital, without possibility of escape. Unions are of greater value to capitalism than to the workers. Workers find themselves tied to the monster of capitalism, no matter whether its end represents death and disaster or life and the culmination of our culture. . . . The active produce, the inactive suffer. Inside this system capitalists are active, workers are inactive because they must receive orders from those who are active. The capitalist knows what he is after. Money, and after money, power. Workers are after only their share, and if this turns out to be sufficient to more or less maintain them and permit them certain comforts, they are satisfied and appreciate the current system." This is a realistic assessment by an ambivalent anticapitalist who had come to the conclusion that, like it or not, the hegemony of capital will persist because "the Worker, in the present system . . . at heart is as capitalist as the proprietor of a bank" (Traven 1969e:166). In short, this passage presents us with the gist of Traven's trenchant thinking about capitalist hegemony.[13]

An important pillar in Traven's understanding of political economy and in his economic anthropology emerges clearly in his Tamaulipas period novels. There are several passages in *The Treasure of the Sierra Madre* (Traven 1969f:96, 236) and in another Tamaulipas period novel, *The Cotton-Pickers* (Traven 1969a:22, 111), that directly invoke the labor theory. Admittedly, in *Treasure* when he writes about the value of gold, Traven (1969f:56; cf. p. 210) emphasizes more than once the importance (and risk) of transporting it to market (for example, "No gold has any value if it cannot be transported to a place where people need it"). Nevertheless, even in one version of this thesis, the role of labor is highlighted (1993:19–20): "Oil, like gold, is worthless in its natural state. It obtains its value only by handling and being taken where it is needed." In short, my limited search of his Tamaulipas period publications yielded significant textual evidence for Traven's belief in the labor theory of value but also for his appreciation of the importance of marketing in the realization of labor-created exchange value.[14]

How does Traven's labor-centered approach carry over from his critique of capitalism to his representation of peasant-artisan production? The answer is through the linkage of cost–price to work or labor time and effort. This linkage emerges clearly in the haggle between Winthrop and the artisan basket maker, but Traven, as the storyteller, makes the connection explicit earlier (1993:75): "Each basket cost him between twenty and thirty hours of constant work, not counting the time spent gathering bast and fibers, preparing them, making dyes and coloring the bast. All this meant extra time and work." The same connection is explicitly made more than once by the basket maker when he explains to an incredulous Winthrop why the price has to jump so high if he buys more than a hundred baskets (1993:84–85). Traven's emphasis on the relationship between the cost of artisanal commodities like baskets calculated in labor-time units and market price is paralleled and substantiated in my analysis of the Oaxaca valley metate industry (Cook 1976). This relationship in my judgment and, I think, Traven's as well is critical to the functioning of the peasant-artisan branch of Mexico's commodity economy (cf. Cook and Binford 1990:32–34). It is, in short, a critically important element of indigenous Mexican peasant-artisan commodity culture and serves them well in their ongoing market engagements with North American capitalism.

Together with his critical, labor-centered view of capitalism and commodity economy in general, the non-Marxist Traven implicitly shared a Marxist concern with class and social relations of production. He tended to view the underdeveloped rural sector of developing capitalist countries like Mexico as straddling the divide between capitalist and petty commodity culture on the one hand and production for own use on the other. In the rural branch of commodity economy, for Traven, the allocation of labor time was influenced more directly by sociocultural structure (such as community and kinship obligations) and the forces of nature (such as rainfall patterns and seasonality in general) than it was in metropolitan urban-industrial capitalism.

Like many who wrote before and after him, Traven flirted with the view that underlying the perceived "backwardness" of economic life among peasant artisans was their ignorance and illiteracy vis-à-vis the cost-accounting rationality of capitalism. Hence, in his Oaxaca tale, the Indian basket maker is portrayed as a slow and limited calculator in comparison to Mr. Winthrop. Interestingly enough, this was how Malinowski and de la Fuente in their Oaxaca markets study tended to view "Indians from outlying districts . . . who cannot manipulate figures" (1982:140–41). Fortunately, the overall thrust of Traven's story is to highlight the contextual appropriateness of the basket maker's rationality, leaving the reader with the impression that, given the conditions of life in a Mexican village at that time, including the lack of formal schooling, the villager's decision making was the same as the reader's would have been (cf. Beals 1975:263–65; Cancian 1972). In the end, the prudentially rational logic of the Indian peasant artisan wins out over Winthrop's formal capitalist logic.[15]

This interpretation is borne out by the way in which Traven presents the negotiations between Winthrop and the peasant-Indian basket maker as representing a commodity economy dialectic between an exchange value–driven advanced (that is, capitalist) form and a use value–driven simple (or petty) form (cf. Cook 1981). For Traven, both are commodity forms of business, organized for producing wealth and related through markets; the difference between them lies in their scale, in the type and quantity of wealth they are organized to produce, and in how and why they produce it. In his view, gringo big business, motivated by greed and profit, mass-produces commodities through machinofacture to generate money capital. Mexican peasant-Indian petty business, both its agricultural main branch and its subsidiary craft branch, soulfully produces commodities on a small scale without machinery for livelihood. Traven's peasant-Indian artisan produces with his heart as well as with his head and his hands. It is clear from Traven's text, nevertheless, that the basket maker did not lack the desire to increase his earnings by expanding his output of baskets but that he was prevented from doing so by a variety of structural conditions.

It bears mentioning that Traven did not fall into the "natural economy" trap that vitiated much European economic thought of his time and that was recently resurrected in Mexican studies by June Nash (2001:5–6). He did not assume that the peasant economy was autochthonous, marketless, and commodityless and that its peasant-artisan agents blithely ignored material cost–benefit logic, the market–cash nexus, and exchange value as they went about satisfying their culturally circumscribed consumer wants (Cook 1984b:5–15; Roseberry 1989:chap.8). Traven did not mistake peasant artisans in Oaxaca for participants in autochthonous primitive communes who were naive regarding exchange value, money, or the market. Still, in contrast to his portrayal of peasant-Indian plantation workers in Tamaulipas and forestry workers in Chiapas who are heavily involved in the wage system, Traven (1993:85; cf. 1956:25), through the dialogue between Mr. Winthrop and the basket maker, envisages the possibility of expanding basket output by additional labor recruited through kinship duty, not wage payment.[16]

To Traven's credit, he accurately (if figuratively) portrayed Oaxaca's peasant artisans as petty commodity producers, combining subsistence agriculture with craft production for sale in the periodic town market, to make and earn their livelihood. In his words (1993:74-5), "His principal business . . . was not producing baskets. He was a peasant who lived on what the small property he possessed . . . would yield. . . . Baskets he made when there was nothing else for him to do in the fields . . . the sale of his baskets . . . added to the small income he received from his little farm. . . . Whenever the Indian had finished about twenty of the baskets he took them to town on market day."

Traven (1956:11–12; 1993:75–76) realized that when the peasant-Indian basket maker came into town, he was in hostile territory in both the ethnocultural and the economic sense. The town, both in and out of the marketplace, was mestizo turf, where the peasant-Indian producer–seller was subjected to patronizing discrimination that robbed him of human dignity as well as of a significant portion of the exchange value embodied through the expenditure of his artisanal labor time and effort in his baskets. In the marketplace haggle, the basket maker ended up receiving less than half of the eighty centavos (equivalent to ten U.S. cents) he originally quoted for a basket that embodied fifteen to twenty hours of his labor (not including procurement and preparation of the fibers and other raw materials). Not only is the peasant-Indian basket maker compelled to, in effect, give away his embodied labor, but he also had to suffer the verbal abuse and belittlement from mestizo hagglers.[17]

The situation worsened when the peasant Indian peddled his baskets in town but outside of the marketplace. As Traven (1993:76; cf. 1956:12; cf. Marroquín 1957b:207–8) wrote, "Naturally he did not want to take those baskets which he could not sell at the market place home with him again if he could help it. In such a case he went peddling his products from door to door where he was treated partly as a beggar and partly as a vagrant apparently looking for an opportunity to steal, and he frequently had to swallow all sorts of insults and nasty remarks." This shabby, patronizing treatment is exemplified in the encounter between the basket maker and a mestiza town resident (Traven 1993:76–77; cf. 1956:12–13): "In many instances he would actually get no more than just ten centavos, and the buyer, usually a woman, would grasp that little marvel and right before his eyes throw it carelessly upon the nearest table as if to say, 'Well, I take that piece of nonsense only for charity's sake. I know my money is wasted. But then, after all, I'm a Christian and I can't see a poor Indian die of hunger since he has come such a long way from his village.'" In short, when one contrasts Traven's depiction of the international cross-cultural encounter between the basket maker and Mr. Winthrop (a representative of the gringo branch of the world market) with his depiction of the intranational ethnocultural encounter between the basket maker and town mestiza buyers, the latter situation is portrayed in more extreme terms vis-à-vis the quality and magnitude of discrimination and exploitation. This provides a basis for inferring that if he could have started doing business with Mr. Winthrop, the basket maker probably would have experienced some improvement in his economic condition and, possibly, less exposure to ethnic discrimination in the market town. Maybe it is more significant that Traven's material lends itself to such an interpretation than it is to definitively determine that this is the interpretation Traven wanted the reader to make.

TRAVEN'S LEGACY FOR ECONOMIC ANTHROPOLOGY

In Traven's work, the "economic other" in Mexico is variously depicted as a subaltern Indian ethnoclass, as peasants tied to the land and agriculture, as artisans producing artistic crafts to reproduce ethnocultural identity, as petty commodity producers with market habits, and as exploited workers in a world capitalist economy. Perhaps this varied depiction is one reason for his appeal among a diverse readership. In retrospect, it is impossible to determine to what extent Traven's work was influenced by specific Mexican academic anthropologists or, in turn, influenced them. It is clear, for example, that Othón de Mendizábal's (1946, 4:205–11) approach to popular industries in the national economy had parallels with Traven's views, which, in any case, were echoed widely in *indigenista* discourse. It is also clear that Traven's "single economy" thesis, like Sol Tax's (1957a) regarding Guatemalan Indians and Ladinos (as will be argued in the next chapter) had little notable impact in changing the "dual economy" thinking of his contemporaries.

The significance of Traven's (and Mendizábal's) approach becomes clearer when measured against George Foster's (1982) study of Popoluca peasant artisans in Veracruz where the reader finds a dualistic conceptualization that inserts Mexican peasant artisans in a "primitive" non-Western economy separate and distinct from what is referred to as "our own Western European economy" (Foster 1982:2–3). Moreover, in other anthropological studies completed in the 1940s or 1950s, with the previously noted exception of Tax (1957a), one finds an indigenous regional economy conceived as separate and distinct from the national economy (Drucker-Brown 1982; Malinowski and de la Fuente 1957) or as precapitalist yet coexisting with an underdeveloped capitalist system (Marroquín 1978:41). In the 1960s and 1970s, a neoclassical approach emerged that had the merit of emphasizing a common logic of rational decision making that cross-cuts all economic behavior without violating cultural specifics, but it still retained the residual notion of a separate "peasant economy" within the wider capitalist economy (Cancian 1972). Finally, during the 1970s and into the 1980s, an effort was made to address capitalist development in peasant-artisan regions. Whether or not the authors of these studies did (Cook 1982: esp. chaps. 1 and 8; Cook and Diskin 1976c:chaps. 1 and 12) or did not (Greenberg 1981:chaps. 5 and 7) highlight the significance of petty (or simple) commodity production, they still clung to dualistic discourse by inserting the corporate peasant community into a precapitalist (or noncapitalist) mode of production articulated with the dominant capitalist mode.

Only in the past decade or so has dualistic discourse been seriously challenged in the economic anthropological branch of Mexican studies. Presented as an alternative to the "peasant-economy-in-capitalist economy" concept is that of a single market-integrated commodity economy comprised of multiple forms and scales of enterprises differentially located in the national economic space (Cook and Binford 1990:esp. chaps. 1 and 7; Foladori 1981; Kearney 1996:90–98, 108–12). With regard to this fundamental conceptual problem, then, only recently is economic anthropology finally catching up with Traven.[18]

On the other hand, Traven's essentialist thesis linking artisan to artifact in a process of cultural transmission was not new with him. In the context of Mexican studies, the same thesis was presented in the book *Las artes populares en México* by Geraldo Murillo (Dr. Atl) (1980), first published in 1922, and by many other *indigenistas* during the 1920s and 1930s. The popularity of this thesis reflected the pursuit of a key strategy in the postrevolutionary nation-state project to build hegemony for the mestizo bourgeoisie. Flora Kaplan (1993:120) and Lynn Stephen (1991, 1993), along with several others (García Canclini 1982; Martínez Peñalosa 1978; Novelo 1976), have elaborated on this political ethnification of Mexican crafts. Traven, as I have pointed out, did not address these issues but, rather, was more concerned with the moral economics of a worldwide struggle between two different approaches to livelihood through commodity production.

As previously noted, Traven showed considerable insight into ethnoclass relations in rural Mexico and gave us a description of the dynamics of asymmetrically discriminatory and exploitative peasant-Indian/mestizo relations in market towns that anticipates later contributions in economic anthropology (Marroquín 1957a, 1957b). At the same time, he presented the peasant-Indian artisan as also involved in the tourist market (Winthrop made his purchase of baskets as a tourist) and, potentially (through Winthrop's failed deal), in an international mass-merchandising market for craft commodities, once again in anticipation of a direction that economic anthropology would subsequently take (Nash 1993) and that only a few of Traven's anthropologist contemporaries noted (Othón de Mendizábal 1946).

Despite my criticism of his emphasis on the idea that mass production is incompatible with artisanal production, Traven deserves credit for exposing the role that ethnocentrism plays in economic relations between representatives of developed and underdeveloped economies. Mr. E. L. Winthrop from the pages of his Oaxaca tale, along with Mr. C. C. Collins from the pages of *The White Rose*, should occupy permanent places in the literary museum of unsavory capitalists and "ugly Americans." Traven also presented an ethnographically grounded explanation of why peasant-artisan simple commodity producers and capitalist entrepreneurs often cannot do business together. There are, indeed, many such cases, and he recognized the importance of the problem and provided an explanation for it long before any economic anthropologist did.

Given his status as a fiction writer rather than a social scientist, Traven's work has not had an acknowledged influence in the publications of anthropologists studying Mexico's economy. This is especially unfortunate for the economic anthropology of Mexico because Traven imaginatively combined local cultural knowledge with an understanding of the political economy of capitalism in a way that few of his anthropological contemporaries did. This enabled him to make one of the first coherent statements of the conflict between capitalist and peasant-artisan commodity cultures and their social relations in Mexico. The major conceptual themes in his work, most of which remain important in anthropology and political economy today, were creatively woven into his storytelling in terms that were both original and popularly accessible.

NOTES

1. B. Traven was the pen name of Otto Feige, born in 1882 in Germany (Schwiebus, Pomerania), who also used the pseudonyms Ret Marut, Traven Torsvan, and Hal Croves at various stages of his life (Schürer and Jenkins 1987:5-8; Wyatt 1980). As a political refugee from Europe, he took up permanent residence in Mexico in 1924 via the

port of Tampico, Tamaulipas. It is possible that he visited Oaxaca between 1926 and 1928 on his way to or from Chiapas (Schürer and Jenkins 1987:360), although Zogbaum doubts this (personal communication, 1995).

According to his biographer Karl Guthke (1991:188–89), in 1927, 1928, and 1929 Traven took a series of six-week summer courses at UNAM in Mexico City in the Spanish language and Mexican cultural history. Specific course themes included the Mexican Revolution, Mexican archaeology, Mexican folklore, the geography of Mexico, Mexican history, and Mexico's political and social problems. Thus, Traven was not unschooled regarding Mexican economy, society, and culture and also surely learned about rural Mexico from ex cathedra discussions with anthropologists and other Mexican intellectuals.

It is always possible, as Wood (2000b:192, 199), following Zogbaum (1992:98) implies, that Traven's Oaxaca tale was derived from his Chiapas experience and information garnered from anthropologists. After all, he was first and foremost a fiction writer. Wood's discussion of this topic, however, reveals a tendency in postmodern dialogical anthropology to reduce literature and oral testimonials/conversations from all genres and sources to a series of equivalent "texts" ignoring the implications of their different modes of production and flirts with epistemological anarchism if not nihilism. For more on Traven's identity and background, see Cook (1995:77–78).

2. "Safety first" is the logic of calculating cost by the sacrifice of the alternatives forgone in producing a given commodity or service. For example, the cost of making ten baskets is the five bushels of corn that might have been harvested in their stead by the peasant-Indian basket maker. The direct production of foodstuffs is accordingly of higher priority than the acquisition of cash to buy foodstuffs.

3. My interviews with Antonio regarding Traven's story were conducted after he had an opportunity to read a copy of the story in Spanish that I gave him a few days after our first meeting.

Benjamin Higgins (1959:286–87) was among the first to argue that the backward-sloping supply curve of effort "appears in any society which stagnates (or slows down) long enough to weaken the 'demonstration effect' provided by people moving from one standard of living to another, as a result of their own extra effort, directed specifically toward earning additional income." He argued further that "the truth may well be that, in a static world, supply curves of effort and risk-taking are normally backward sloping. Where no other changes are taking place, most people would probably like some additional leisure, or some additional safety and liquidity, when rates of pay for effort and risk-taking are increased, so that the extra leisure, safety, and liquidity can be had without a reduction in material standard of living" (1959:287 n.).

Economic anthropologists will also associate this kind of marginalist logic with Chayanov's (1966:esp. pp. 70–85) analysis of the "drudgery of labor" in the context of the Russian peasant farm. Though operationally dependent on marginal utility analysis, Chayanov's approach does not actually view the peasant household as an enterprise but as something different whose output decisions require special explanation in terms of sociocultural or demographic/life cycle factors peculiar to the household (Durrenberger 1984, personal correspondence). This makes Chayanov's approach particularly relevant for economic anthropology. It is possible that Traven read Chayanov's work since the German translation of *The Theory of Peasant Economy* was published in 1923 (Thorner et al. 1966:287).

4. I interviewed Bill Cypert in 1993 at his place of business in Tomball, Texas (near Houston). His recollections of the period when he regularly visited the Reynosa brickworks do not contradict Reynoso's reconstruction on any important detail (Cook 1998:201, 260). Still, Reynoso's memory for detail regarding their meetings is more vivid, thus biasing the reconstruction of his conversations with Cypert in his favor.

5. In more literal Marxist terms, this subordination of peasant-artisan production by capital could occur during the stage of "formal subsumption" without necessarily involving the subsequent stage of "real subsumption" (see Cook and Binford 1990:23–24; see also Chevalier 1982:151–70; Foladori 1981:143–54; Marx 1977). This process may also be conceptualized in Marxist discourse as a transition from a use-value to an exchange-value regime (see Cook 1981).

6. Wood's translation of the tale's Spanish title as "Batch of Little Baskets" (2000b:190) misses the intended meaning of "*en serie*," which is captured in the tale's English title, "Assembly Line," a matter that would not have escaped Traven's attention (cf. Cook 1995:77–78 n. 3).

The importance of the bucolic, quasi-Thoreauian image of the simple, close-to-nature life of the independent tiller of the soil is highlighted in Judy Stone's interviews with Traven (as Hal Croves) (1977:58–59) when he is quoted as saying, among other things, "This nearness to the soil . . . is the most frequent and most important element in Traven's books" (59). Nevertheless, Baumann's (1987:253–54) perceptive analysis of Traven's Chiapas-based *Caoba* (mahogany) Cycle works (Traven 1928, 1969b, 1969c, 1969d, 1994a, 1994b) suggests that the author had "no romantic illusions about traditional agrarian society" and "In *Land* . . . warns readers against idealizing Indian communes, and . . . considers conditions even in the worst industrial slums preferable—for everyone but the Indians themselves—to the harsh living conditions in Indian villages." In *Land*, continues Baumann, Traven "also argues that not the agrarian reform but only industrialization could offer a better future to rural Mexicans. In the *Caoba* Cycle, Traven makes us aware of how difficult it was in traditional agrarian society to scrape together a living that would mean more than having the sheer necessities for survival." The contradiction here between Traven's statement to Stone's and Baumann's interpretation of Traven's views in the *Caoba* Cycle probably boils down to a fundamental split between Traven as observer/analyst or amateur ethnographer and Traven as imaginative writer and visionary.

7. Traven's soulful vision of artisanal production (and even his wording) is paralleled in the following statement by my comadre Teodora Blanco, a renowned potter from Santa María Atzompa in the Oaxaca valley, recorded by representatives of the Fondo Nacional para el Fomento de las Artesanías (FONART) sometime prior to her premature and tragic death: "Es necesario tener, este, amor al trabajo y ponerle sentido y todo. Nuestro barro o nuestro trabajo tienen un sentido y en ese sentido es el gusto que tenemos, ahí se queda un pedazo de nuestra vida, o sea de nuestro corazón" (Becerril Straffon and Rios Szalay 1981:77). This rings true in comparison with other statements I heard from Teodora during the years that I knew her as an inventive, imaginative, and even dream-inspired artisan. It is pertinent to note that during her own lifetime, her imaginative and dream-inspired images were "borrowed" and produced "*en serie*" by many other potters in her community. A sizable portion

of these Teodora Blanco–inspired products were (and still are) mass-merchandised by FONART and by private sector intermediary capitalists. It is probable that Traven's "soulful vision of artisanal production" was influenced by his reading of Sombart (1967:17; cf. Roseberry 1989:204).

8. The themes of "economics and morality" and "technique and art" were provocatively discussed in a thoughtful little book by Godfrey and Monica Wilson (1945). They perceptively argue that "all co-operative actions must be both efficient in their use of material resources—time, energy, tools, material environment, and objective social relations—and have moral value for the people concerned." In a similar vein, they argue that technique, which is "concerned with the overcoming of the inherent stubbornness of material, which resists human shaping," and art, the "expression of intrinsic quality," are always dependent on each other. As they put it, "There is a certain intrinsic quality manifest in every product of craft" (1945:76–78). Of course, it is necessary to operationalize this notion of "intrinsic quality" in order to avoid essentialism, but it is an early expression of the sign or symbolic exchange value of artisanal commodities.

9. As I have pointed out elsewhere (Cook 1984b:35 n. 18), Herman's (1956) argument that mass production, standardization, and assembly-line organization are not only possible but also characteristic of some branches of nonfactory industrial commodity production has unfortunately escaped the attention of many writers on craft production.

10. García Canclini was well ahead of most of the rest of us in applying the "social life of commodities" approach to Mexican crafts in his discussion of "la 'migración' de los productos de la culturas indígenas" (the migration of the products of indigenous cultures) or "el itinerario mutante de las artesanías" (the mutating itinerary of crafts) and his analysis of the displacement and exile of crafts from their native space—indigenous life, the rural market—to another scene—bourgeois culture, the urban shop, the museum, and the boutique (1982:134–35)—through capitalist development or the opportunistic intervention of capital in craft commodity production and circulation (1982:126).

11. This paragraph reflects ethnographic as well as personal knowledge derived from familiarity, through family ties, with the operations of a large interior decorative arts/crafts emporium, including Mexican products, among others from around the world, in Asheville, North Carolina. Over the years, the inventory of the Mexican crafts unit (El Gallo del Sol) in this emporium (Interiors Marketplace) has transitioned from traditional ethnic crafts (such as lacquerware, *amate*/jute paintings, and masks from Guerrero; *tapetes* from Teotitlán del Valle; and Talavera ceramics from Guanajuato) to, among other things, neo-ranch-style pine furniture from Aguascalientes; decorative wrought-iron lamps, mirrors, and furniture from San Miguel de Allende; pewterware from León, Guanajuato; and model motorcycles made of scrap iron from Monterrey. Generally, the customers in this emporium are less interested in the provenience of craft commodities than in a combination of their price, utility, appearance, and style. Only in the case of higher-priced goods, say over $100, does provenience become an issue (that is, the buyer will want an authentic craft from with a particular provenience).

12. Scholars like Graburn (1976:6) who accentuate the inevitable debasement of the artistic/aesthetic/cultural quality or integrity of so-called traditional crafts via "souvenirization" in the capitalist market seem to overlook the fact that the com-

moditization of crafts long pre-dates capitalism and also occurs under conditions of simple commodity production. Decisions by peasant artisans and full-time artisans, pitting economic considerations against artistic or aesthetic ones, have been made about and have affected crafts long before the emergence of an international tourist market. Incidentally, there is every reason to believe that there was no community of shared meanings about craft commodities, either under precapitalist or underdeveloped capitalist market conditions, that cross-cuts the dividing line between producers and consumers and makers and users of craft commodities in a way that would negate the caveat emptor type of decision making implied here. Finally, the entire debasement argument overlooks the fluctuating and differentiating nature and impact of capitalist intervention in commodity economy as well as its multidirectionality and cyclicality. In short, new market niches for high-quality artistic artifacts are created along with those for varieties of souvenirs.

Gobi Stromberg was apparently in error when she credited Xalitla with originating bark painting. Good (1988:30) presents a convincing case for its origins in the more isolated community of Ameyaleptec, where potters traditionally painted their pottery (see chapter 5).

13. Traven (1969e:167) makes clear that Mr. Collins has learned the secret of capitalist hegemony without the help of formal study of economics, that "he was unfamiliar with anything that could help him to analyze the ups and downs of capitalism," and that he "came only by instinct to understand the laws according to which this very complicated system works." According to Traven, "That same instinct had led him [Collins] to discover the fact that presently no branch of the capitalist system has greater influence over public opinion than the struggle, or if you wish sporting event, commonly called capital against labor or labor against capital. Labor does not benefit much materially from its positive opportunities, nevertheless, it achieves something by impressing the conscience and opinion of the public." There are substantial differences between the Spanish (Traven 1969e) and English (Traven 1979) translations of the original German edition of this novel. I prefer the longer Spanish edition, from which I translated the quoted passages.

14. Joel Kahn (1997:69–75) has another take on Traven and gold inspired by Taussig's (1980) study of commodity devilization in South America.

15. The most explicit statement in the tale illustrating Traven's posture is in a paragraph involving his voice directly as commentator and indirectly through the basket maker: "That figure was too high for the Indian to grasp. He became slightly confused and for the first time since Mr. Winthrop had arrived he interrupted his work and tried to think it out. Several times he shook his head and looked vaguely around as if for help. Finally he said, 'Excuse me, jefecito . . . that is by far too much for me to count'" (1993:83; cf. pp. 78, 82). Traven (1993:86) later reinforces this theme of the Indian's deficiencies in quantitative reasoning by characterizing him as being awestruck "as Mr. Winthrop wrote down . . . long figures, executing complicated multiplications and divisions and subtractions so rapidly that it seemed to him the greatest miracle he had ever seen."

16. It seems likely that Traven's views on peasants and artisans was influenced by Sombart (1967:17), who contended that "economic activities in the pre-capitalist period were regulated solely in accordance with the principle of a sufficiency for existence . . . peasant and craftsman looked to their economic activities to provide them

with their livelihood and nothing more." He continues in a passage that resembles Traven's statements quoted previously from his Oaxaca tale: "As for work itself, for the peasant and the craftsman alike it was lonely, patient effort. Man lost himself in his work. He lived in it, as the artist does, he loved it so, that he would much rather not have parted with his handiwork . . . the potter strove hard not to be tempted by the trader's offers for his pipe. But if it had to be sold, then the commodity was to be worthy of its maker. The peasant, like the craftsman, had put something of himself into his product; and in its making the rules of art were obeyed"(1967:18–19).

17. Traven (1956:11; cf. 1993:77) indicates knowledge of the periodicity of the marketplace system in Oaxaca when he writes, "Al tener listas unas dos docenas de ellas [canastitas], el indio las llevaba al pueblo los sábados, que eran días de tianguis." This bit of information also reinforces the hypothesis that the "pueblo" (as opposed to "pueblito"), or "town" (as opposed to "village"), is indeed Tlaxiaco in the Mixteca Alta, where the "día de plaza [*tianguis*]" is Saturdays (Marroquín 1957b:168).

18. Wood (2000b:19) contends that I attempt "to use the 'Canastitas' tale as proof of the validity of what economic anthropologists say about peasant petty-commodity producers." This is a strange contention that has nothing to do with my "use" of Traven's tale. I would never look to a piece of fiction as a source of proof for measuring the validity of work in economic anthropology—which would even be a greater exercise in futility than attempting to do so from within that field. Rather than viewing the tale as "proof" in any sense, I viewed it (in the spirit of my *ladrillero* informant) as a useful source of explanation/interpretation of the complexities of small-scale commodity production within capitalism and suggested that it precociously anticipated later economic anthropological discourse.

Wood also mistakenly claims that "what makes Traven's contribution and relevancy to studies of peasant economy so important" to me (vis-à-vis Traven's Oaxaca tale) was the fact that in that story Traven overcame "his earlier proclivity for romanticizing the Indian" (2000b:198). Wood supports this claim by citing a footnote in which I quote Zogbaum as attributing to Traven views that confuse biology and culture in understanding Mexican Indians in his pre-Oaxaca tale writings. As I concluded that footnote, "The absence of these views from his Oaxaca tale may reflect the fact that Traven's first encounter with Oaxacan peasant-artisans was during his second or third trip to Chiapas in 1927 and 1928, a period when he became aware of errors in his earlier understanding of Indian life and Indian-Ladino relations thanks to course work at the National University and additional thought and experience" (Cook 1995:93–94 n. 18). Wood (2000b:199) correctly implies that I recognize the possibility that anthropological sources "may have influenced the framing" of Traven's Oaxaca tale. Still, the happy omission in his Oaxaca tale of biology/culture confusion, though welcome, is not why Traven's contribution to peasant-artisan studies is important to me—as explained in my 1995 article and in this chapter.

Finally, Wood asserts that "Cook fashioned Traven's basket weaver as a peasant," somehow implying that this was my authorial appropriation of a nonpeasant discourse (that is, that of the "Indian problem") that was Traven's own. Unfortunately for Wood's argument, Traven himself referred to his Mexican protagonist as "Indian," as "basket-maker," and as "peasant" (Traven 1966:74–75). The main problem with Wood's entire interpretation of Traven is that it ignores his political economy of capitalism, which informed his entire corpus. As I argued in my 1995 article and in this chapter, reading Traven as an economic anthropologist must be subordinated to reading him as a political economist of capitalism. Mexican Indians, for Traven, were first and foremost idiosyncratic workers in the arena of world capitalism. The "Indian problem" in Mexico was interpreted by Traven through his political economic understanding of capitalism.

3

Rereading *Penny Capitalism*: The Paradox of Poverty in a Land of Enterprise

In the lead sentence of his preface to *Penny Capitalism*, Sol Tax admitted that he chose the title because it was catchy but also because it conveyed something fundamental about the nature of the society he was writing about: it was "'capitalist' on a microscopic scale" (1963:ix). What did Tax mean by this? A partial answer to this question can be pieced together from what Tax states either explicitly or implicitly in his preface and elsewhere in his book. A more complete answer requires going back to 1938–1939 during one of Tax's field seasons in Guatemala in the Carnegie Institution's Maya Project on ethnography headed by Robert Redfield. Apparently, what began as a request for information on Panajachel economics from F. W. McBryde (1945), a topic of peripheral interest for Tax, evolved into his only book-length work on Guatemala (Rubinstein 1991:26, 233). Long before the book was completed, Tax's draft paper and his correspondence with Redfield about it clearly influenced Redfield's (1962) seminal article "Primitive Merchants of Guatemala," which, for the first time, poignantly described pervasive, impersonal, money-based relations in the context of a "folk society."[1]

Subsequently, Tax's selective reading in the field of economics and discussions with colleagues like the economist Bert Hoselitz (1964) helped him revise his book-length manuscript, which was finally published in 1953 as *Penny Capitalism*. Even though many principal research findings of the Carnegie Project's economic research in Guatemala were summarized in Redfield's article, the publication of Tax's book was significant not only for its oxymoronic title but also for its presentation of a huge corpus of ethnographic data regarding economic attitudes, conduct, and the tabulated, quantitative results of the latter as well as for its probing analysis of complex problems like socioeconomic differentiation under the rubric of "The Significance of Wealth Differences" (1963:191–207). Thanks to Redfield's article and to prepublication leaks of Tax's work, "enough was known of the . . . Tax achievements to prompt debate in the graduate seminars of the late '40s" (Belshaw 1979:70) and to make the publication of *Penny Capitalism* a much-anticipated, if anticlimactic, event in Mesoamerican economic studies.

Tax's lack of specialized knowledge of economics and economic anthropology; his compulsive empiricism; the prolonged period of research, write-up, and revision of the manuscript until its final publication; and the fact that it represented his only book-length contribution to Guatemalan ethnography combine to complicate understanding *Penny Capitalism*'s significance—but also make an attempt to do so more challenging and worthwhile.

SITUATING TAX AND *PENNY CAPITALISM* IN ECONOMIC ANTHROPOLOGY

Penny Capitalism occupies a special niche in the history of economic anthropology because its clever title won enduring recognition as a metaphor for enterprising economic behavior by unlikely subjects in unexpected places. Given its 1953 publication date (fieldwork conducted between 1936 and 1941), Tax's work was at the chronological border of several transitions in the practice of ethnography: from "primitive" to "peasant" as the unified subject of study, from greater to lesser naïveté about economic and social theory, and from compulsive data collection that viewed the universe as the sample to more theoretically focused data collection that employed sampling methodology. By today's standards, in a community of 157 households that Panajachel had in 1936, it would be considered unjustified to collect as much data from every household as Tax did. A sampling interval of no larger than 33 percent would now be considered adequate to make statistically valid generalizations about the universe regarding fundamental socioeconomic and demographic variables. Thus, Tax's inclusive household sample did not produce a deeper understanding of Panajachel life than would have been achieved from analysis of a smaller sample. Instead, he would have been better advised to have spent less time in villagewide surveys and more time in researching important issues more intensively through a combination of selective interviewing and case studies to achieve deeper understanding.

The shortcomings in Tax's research reflect the lingering influence of the Boasian culturalist approach, in which careful, meticulous, and exhaustive empirical description took precedence over any explicit concern with theory—the assumption being that meaning or understanding was implicit in and/or would emerge from the empirical facts themselves. A careful reading of *Penny Capitalism* and Tax's other economic writings (1952, 1957b), however, reveals that his empiricism was tempered by a selective concern with theory—especially as it related to understanding the paradox of poverty in a market economy of industrious, rationally calculating subjects.

Mixed Reactions to *Penny Capitalism*

Soon after its publication, John Gillin praised the "felicitous title" of Tax's book as covering "perhaps the most detailed account of the economic activities of a single community ever made by an anthropologist" (1955:631). Even prior to its publication, Tax's manuscript was available to Melville Herskovits, who summarized it in the 1952 revised edition of his classic textbook *Economic Anthropology* as follows (1960:235–36):

> [An] example of how a pecuniary standard makes for modes of determination of values that are in line with canons of economic theory derived from the presence of money is available in the economy of Panajachel of Guatemala. The people of this village, who "enter in minor ways, into the capitalistic world economic system" have, as far as they and their neighbors are concerned, what is described as "a domestic money economy with a strongly developed market which tends to be perfectly competitive." The unit of production is the family, and the local specialization in certain agricultural products makes it necessary to sell these so as to obtain, by purchase in the market, all subsistence and production goods. Buying and selling is for cash; credit can be extended and interest is known, but these are rarely found. What is important is that "the price of a product in a given market is fixed by the law of supply and demand." Sales, moreover, are made on the basis of cost estimates which empirical analysis shows to be remarkably accurate. Endowed with "the spirit of business enterprise," this example shows how, in a nonliterate but pecuniary society, we may encounter an almost classical economic system.

Herskovits's summary highlights the principal findings of Tax's research that provided an empirical basis for his concept of penny capitalism and would establish the book's place in the literature of the subfield as a exemplary ethnographic case supportive of what would become identified in the 1960s as the "formalist" approach in economic anthropology (Cook 1966b).[2]

If John Gillin found the title of Tax's book to be "felicitous," it was decidedly infelicitous from the perspective of Angel Palerm (1954), who was the first critic of Tax's concept and his approach to indigenous Mesoamerican economic life. Palerm was unimpressed by Tax's Oscar Lewis–like exercise (1951) in using Redfield's ideal–typical "folk–urban" continuum as a framework for situating Panajachel comparatively because the "contradiction between its real economic life . . . and the 'ideal type' of 'folk' society is palpable" and "the real life of human communities escapes and evades being squeezed into conventional typologies" (1954:205). He also objected to Tax's usage of capitalism in the book's title because of ambiguities surrounding its meaning and to his decision to apply the terminology and concepts of economics to the indigenous economy of Panajachel. In his words, "The extent to which the application of the terminology and concepts of western economics 'colors' the description of Panajachel's economy is something that surely will be discussed and disputed. The phenomenon that we call 'capitalism' is surely neither economic nor social in a straightforward sense as Weber, Sombart and Tawney, among others, have shown. Even employed as a 'catch word,' its usage seems very debatable" (1954:205–6).

Palerm's critique went further in showing from Tax's own findings the inappropriateness of calling Panajachel capitalist when in fact such a label was more appropriate for the larger town of Chichicastenango, which displayed a crystallized overlapping of economic class, social status, and political power. "In Chichicastenango," Palerm notes, "the most important posts are won by the richest families, who can better withstand the expenses, and the less important posts are destined, in practice, to poor families. In this way, the tendency toward the formation of social classes is intensified in Chichicastenango. Wealth and power tend to remain in the same families generation after generation. By contrast, the difficulties for the development of an analogous tendency in Panajachel are better appreciated" (1954:206). Thus, according to Palerm, the results of Tax's own analysis "particularly illuminate the problem, at the same time that they increase our doubts regarding the necessity and the utility of the author's insistence on defining the economic phenomenon of Panajachel as 'capitalist' in character" (1954:207).

Daniel Fusfeld (1957:351), a contributor to *Trade and Market in the Early Empires*, critiqued Tax from that perspective: "The fundamental institutional bases of the market economy and the tremendous differences between market and non-market institutional patterns are not understood. The underlying difficulty is Tax's use of the conceptual framework of the economics of the market and analysis of the economy of Panajachel in terms of the maximization and allocation principles . . . a distorted picture and improper conclusions emerge." Even Tax's meticulous empiricism, his exhaustive documentation of an indigenous market culture, and his attempt to conceptualize a market economy embedded in a village-based, peasant-Indian society was not enough, from Fusfeld's perspective, to excuse his flirtation with Smithian economics and his discovery of a market mentality on the fringes of Western capitalism.

Penny Capitalism would present a challenge to the peasantist approach to economics that was to be elaborated in a series of publications by Eric Wolf (1955, 1956, 1959a, 1959b, 1966). Partly echoing criticisms of Palerm and Fusfeld, Wolf (1959a:224–30) contested Tax's emphasis on peasant householders' businesslike economic performance motivated by a quest for material gain as misrepresenting the simple reproductive realities of life in Mesoamerican Indian communities. According to Wolf, such communities were historical precipitates of asymmetrical development with defensive sociocultural structures that encouraged redistributive and reciprocal relations between households. Wolf's critique will be explored more fully in chapter 6.

George Dalton, long enough after his 1961 opening cannonade in the substantivist attack on formalism to enable him to moderate his radical stance in response to formalist critics (and in marked contrast to Palerm, Fusfeld, and Wolf), viewed Tax's phrase "penny capitalism" as being appropriate in highlighting an important difference between primitive and peasant economies. According to him, in peasant economies "most people depend for the bulk of their livelihood on production for market sale or selling in markets; purchase and sale transactions with cash are frequent and quantitatively important; and, frequently, resource markets are present: significant quantities of labor, land, tools, and equipment are available for purchase, rent, or hire at money price"(1969:74). Dalton also admitted that "traditional" peasant economies may more closely resemble "primitive" ones (for example, small scale, simple technology, narrow-range and low-level output, and poverty and material insecurity) or appear "incomplete and underdeveloped compared to market organization in a modern national economy" (for example, some markets, like those for land or labor, may be absent or minimal; production for use is quantitatively important). But even in these cases, the rudiments of capitalist (market) economy are present and of sufficient importance to justify referring to them appropriately with Tax's phrase (Dalton 1969:74–75).

June Nash, who as a graduate assistant had the thankless task of retyping the second and third drafts of Tax's book "with its endless tables of products and earnings," earned the right to label him "the ultimate empiricist" (1997:14). But Tax's empiricism aside, Nash recognizes that "he taught us to appreciate the complex inner workings of Panajachel onion-growers who rejected the ox and plow, and other colonial innovations based on a rational calculus of the greater returns from intensive cultivation of cash crops, in favor of fodder for animals on land whose value had been driven up by tourism" (1997:13). Moreover, Nash credits Tax, along with others of his generation, with having "proved the rational allocation of resources that was in his time denied to a peasantry whom most developmentalists saw as mired in traditional patterns" (1997:13–14). In her recent book, Nash parts company with the legacy of Tax's lessons about the market-attuned rationality of the Guatemalan Maya to view the economic behavior of the Chiapas Maya as "governed by kinship or communalistic considerations" (2001:2). Polanyi has displaced Tax in Nash's thinking about Maya rationality.

Richard Wilk, unlike Nash, has nothing favorable to say about Tax in his 1996 textbook on the foundations of economic anthropology. He devalues *Penny Capitalism* as representing the "just-the-facts thread of economic anthropology," which "rarely makes its assumptions clear, because they are taken for granted. He then quotes Tax's disavowal of influence by "economic theory" that he was simply "describing the way a people live, picking out those elements to describe that I understand fit under the rubric of economy" (Wilk 1996:120; cf. Tax 1963:ix) as evidence (together with ethnographies by Pospisil and Wagley) of the limitations of a "neo-Boasian" approach that assumed that the facts speak for themselves—a trivial pursuit in which "cultural economics became simply the documentation of all the wonderful ways that cultures shape production, consumption, and exchange" (1996:120). Wilk failed to probe beneath the surface of Tax's own description of his work to look for the origins of his understanding of what fit under the economy rubric. He also overlooked Tax's argument that, more often than not, culture did not as much shape as it was shaped by the economy in the western highlands of Guatemala (1963:16, 19).

Tax and Economics

The bibliography of *Penny Capitalism* includes four sources that influenced Tax's thinking about economics: F. H. Knight (1941), Oscar Lange (1945–1946), Adam Smith (1937), and Max Weber (1947). His preface (pp. ix–x) and a section called "The Kind of Economy" (1963:13–19) in chapter 1 are where the theoretically relevant aspects of his study are explicitly discussed—notwithstanding his disclaimer that "there is no economic theory in this book" (1963:ix). It was, of course, the classical–neoclassical tradition of economics that informed his ethnography, supplying him with the descriptive categories in which to organize and interpret economic facts, and supported his assumption that "the Panajachel economy is like ours." Nevertheless, by 1957, when his last two articles on Guatemalan economics were published (Tax 1957a, 1957b), his bibliographic references to the economics literature had expanded to include publications by J. H. Boeke (1942), Benjamin Higgins (1956), Bert Hoselitz (1956), Simon Kuznets (1953), and Sanford Mosk (1954), among others. This expansion reflected his increased attention to problems of economic development and wealth distribution.

Curiously enough, Tax did not consciously situate his work in the subfield of economic anthropology or directly cite any of its foundational literature (Firth 1939, 1946; Goodfellow 1939; Herskovits 1940, 1952; Malinowski 1921, 1961; Thurnwald 1932). In his prefatory dialogue with economists, an awkwardly worded sentence alludes to the subfield by mentioning "Firth and Herskovits" as anthropologists from whom economists can learn "something about anthropologists" who study community economies (Tax 1963:x). This is about as close as Tax came to acknowledging the existence of economic anthropology.

Tax's admission that "my own work falls short of an ideal because I had no model" (1963:x) may reflect his relative lack of familiarity with the economic anthropological literature of his day but to a larger degree probably reflected a belief that his study of a "money economy" like Panajachel was, in fact, pioneering and had no precedent in the ethnographic literature. Tax did have at least one unconscious economic model in his head, namely, that of the "market" or a "conception about an idealized form of buying and selling" (Carrier 1997:vii). As it turns out, notwithstanding his statement to the contrary, he also had some conscious models—albeit not derived from his study of the economic anthropological literature. Whatever the reason for Tax's failure to explicitly situate his *Penny Capitalism* project in economic anthropological discourse, it was destined to be situated there for him by virtue of its subject matter.

Adding to the paradox of Tax's distancing of his work from economic theory and economic anthropology—and to the problematic status of *Penny Capitalism* as canonical—is Herskovits's acknowledgment in his preface of Tax, among others (including Edward LeClair Jr.), "who have read and commented" on his rewritten manuscript of the 1952 second edition of *Economic Anthropology: A Study in Comparative Economics*. This acknowledgment by Herskovits makes Tax's distancing of his ethnography from economic anthropology even more puzzling. Yet it provides more direct evidence, in addition to Tax's own citations of the economics literature, that he was not uninformed about economic theory or about economic anthropology.

It is a mistake, then, to interpret the paradoxical and idiosyncratic elements in Tax's approach to economics exclusively as either economically naive Boasianism (Wilk 1996:120) or an atheoretical contribution to economic anthropology's database through "pioneering ingenuity in obtaining figures and using them to discover relationships and back up propositions" (Belshaw 1979:70). For one thing, Tax's recognition of the historical type of economy Panajachel represented limits the applicability of the thesis that he operated on the assumption that "each culture is different and that economic behavior is therefore different in every setting" (Wilk 1996:120). He explicitly viewed Panajachel as representative of a type of Indian economy found in the highlands of Guatemala, Chiapas, and Oaxaca in Mesoamerica and, implicitly, as representative of small-community market economies elsewhere in Mexico, Latin America, and other Third World regions (1957a, 1968:66, 1963:ix–x; cf. Hoselitz 1964; Mosk 1954).

Moreover, his concern with capitalism and its economics yields information that helps to more firmly situate Tax's *Penny Capitalism* project in economic anthropological discourse. To a greater degree than Malinowski (1961:60–61), Tax conducted his ethnography as a dialogue with economists. Malinowski's more dramatic (and hostile) attack on the "primitive economic man" model of the economics textbooks (1961:60–61; cf. LeClair and Schneider 1968:3–5), was paralleled by Tax's friendly challenge to the core of Smithian liberal economic thought. Tax did not share Malinowski's antieconomics since, unlike Malinowski in the Trobriand Islands, Tax was ethnographically immersed in a money- and market-integrated economy that prima facie shared some common elements with the economy that he referred to variously as "capitalist," "modern," (1963:ix), the "world economy of firms" (1963:13), or the "wider world economy" (1963:15).[3]

Departing from the Smithian theory that "it is the free-competitive economic system that makes for the production of wealth and the high standard of living," Tax (1963:28) posed the following challenging question: "Why is it that this region of Guatemala, which has so close an approach to the ideally free competitive economy—where rugged individualism is not bothered by governmental red tape or by labor unions or trusts—why is it, then, that the region is so poor and the standard of living so abysmally low?" Tax documented in Panajachel that the pursuit of self-interest will not increase the wealth of a society lacking in technological means (1963:29), a finding that he believed countered 200 years of economists falsely crediting to "free competition the glory that progress in technology has deserved." Tax concluded that Adam Smith's thinking about the relationship between the division of labor and technological progress was unclear but acknowledged that Smith made the linkage (1963:27–28 n. 21; cf. Smith 1937:9–15, 246). In addition, Tax shared the concern of classical economics with development and, in contrast to the early Malinowski, ended up using economics not as a foil but as a sounding board for understanding economizing behavior and economic development. Regrettably, the soundings were channeled so as to preclude an understanding of unequal exchange, exploitation, and other "market" sources of maldevelopment.

REDFIELD'S "PRIMITIVE MERCHANTS" AS PRECURSORS OF TAX'S "PENNY CAPITALISTS": CONTRASTING OXYMORONS, SAME COMMODITY CULTURE

It is clear from their correspondence that Redfield had read and commented on Tax's Panajachel economics paper within a month of its completion in late January 1939. His comments are worth quoting here in extenso (Rubinstein 1991:261–62):

> I have read with a great deal of interest your paper on Panajachel Indian Economics. It is an extraordinarily thorough and painstaking investigation of this aspect of community life. There is probably no study of a simple native economy that compares with it as a cost-accounting analysis. I assume that it will form a part of your *opus* on Panajachel. Its value will be enhanced if it is presented together with discussions of the social organization and of the religious, moral and ideological aspects of life, and if you then show the extent to which the eco-

> nomic life is or is not conditioned by these other aspects of life, and how these, to what extent, are conditioned by the economic life. That the Indians are neither capricious nor stupid in their business life you certainly show, and that they are largely motivated by desires to better themselves economically. You also show the free character of the capitalistic, individualistic, pecuniary economy.

It can be concluded from these comments that Redfield approved of the economic analysis in Tax's draft manuscript ("incomparable as a cost accounting analysis") but disapproved of its lack of noneconomic analysis ("serious deficiencies as sociocultural analysis"). Redfield must have been sorely disappointed that Tax never produced a broader sociocultural study of Panajachel life.

Redfield makes no mention in his published letters to Tax for the remainder of the 1939 field season that he is either planning or writing a manuscript of his own on economics that was, in fact, published in late 1939 as "Primitive Merchants of Guatemala." The irony of this situation is that Tax published no major opus on his Guatemalan fieldwork other than the long-delayed *Penny Capitalism* itself and that Redfield's article does not cite Tax's unpublished paper but does incorporate data from Panajachel (as well as from San Pedro, Chichicastenango, and Agua Escondida, which was Redfield's base). Apparently, Redfield's article was written to address most of the sociocultural deficiencies that he had identified in Tax's paper.

Redfield's term "primitive merchant" is less catchy than Tax's "penny capitalist," but it has the same literary effect and highlights the same thesis: contrary to the logic of an ideal–typical model of the civilizational process like the folk–urban (primitive–modern) continuum with a primitive or undeveloped or simple society at one pole versus a modern, business or commercial, developed society at the other, a mixed society is possible. Redfield's opening sentence evokes the binary logic of the model: "We do not usually think of primitive people as businessmen, or of businessmen as primitive people" (1962:201). He elaborates, "The Indian peoples of western Guatemala show us that a combination of tribal life and highly developed commercialism is possible. These are preliterate people and agricultural villagers, practicing a simple technology, but they are also merchants and travelers, and commercialism, the measurement of values in terms of money, profit-making and a general secular hardheadedness are their outstanding characteristics" (1962:201).

In Redfield's extraordinary essay, we have a full description of the Indian penny capitalist in all but name. Even though his letter credited Tax for successfully describing the "capitalistic" behavior of the Panajacheleños, Redfield (1962:205) qualified this by referring specifically to the most enterprising individuals who had achieved relatively high levels of capital accumulation and who regularly employed hired hands, implying that entrepreneurial householders who did not do so were not capitalistic. From the standpoint of Max Weber's definition of capitalist enterprise, which clearly influenced Redfield's thinking (1962:206), two important criteria were not met anywhere in the Guatemalan highlands: businesses were not separated from households, nor was there evidence of rational bookkeeping (Weber 1958:21–22, 1961:207).

Redfield's sardonic prose—illustrated by his observation that the *cofradía* (confraternity; see Tax 1963:220) in Chichicastenango operates a profitable meat market to help defray its expenses (1962:208) and by his revelation that the Indian rituals performed in clouds of incense and with kneeled incantations in the dark nave of the Chichicastenango church involve "hired specialists" (1962:208)—gives the impression that he was miffed at these "tribal" Guatemalan Indians for being so damned businesslike and secular—even commodifying, hence profaning, the sacred spheres of their culture. He seems to have been disillusioned with these "primitive folk" whose moneygrubbing market habits exposed them as "economic men" in Indian disguise—the only exception being their "retention of an animistic or anthropomorphic view of nature" (1962:210; cf. pp. 202–3). Redfield's succinct summing up of his (and Tax's) research findings, by contrast, is dispassionate and matter of fact (1962:209): "From the above survey, one conclusion seems plain: A preliterate life with a local culture and the personal and magical attitude toward nature which is characteristic of the primitive world is quite compatible with commercialism and a pecuniary economy." Redfield, in this passage, seems to resist arguing that "market mentality" is an integral part of indigenous Guatemalan culture.

Redfield (1962:210) concluded his essay with a paragraph that would have served nicely as a summary of the final chapter of *Penny Capitalism* if he, not Tax, had been its author:

> The fact that these Highland Indians have displayed relatively little technological improvement in many centuries, and that they retain a simple set of tools practically without artificial power or shop-organized industry, indicates that a money economy and a secular viewpoint are not necessarily directly dependent upon great technological advance. In the history of our own society, science, secularism, and an enormous expansion of money and commerce were approximately synchronized with the great technological advance of the industrial revolution. We are so accustomed to thinking of these elements of modern life as being naturally inseparable that we contrast "technological society" with "primitive" or "folk society." The Guatemalan case indicates that a stable society may exist which exhibits to some degree the commercial spirit and pecuniary economy of our own society, as well as some of its secular attitude, but which has a simple technology. These Guatemalan tribes are not "technological societies" and certainly not "industrialized societies" as we use that word to imply factories and mass production. But neither are they primitive societies in the

> typical sense conceived by Henry Maine. They are a mixed yet self-consistent social type: primitive merchant societies.

Here Redfield unequivocally views economizing and market behaviors as integral elements of Guatemalan indigenous culture.

The statement just quoted is vintage Redfield and represents a privileging of ideal–typical positioning of societies that ran counter to Tax's privileging of the empirical and was an exercise Tax was certainly less adept at performing than Redfield. By classifying highland Guatemalan Indian societies as underdeveloped mercantilism rather than downsized capitalism, Redfield was adhering to a stricter interpretation of Weber's scheme according to which industrial organization and commercial enterprise in the Guatemalan highlands more closely approximated "craft work" (Weber 1961:97–101) and "merchant" forms of organization that were "precapitalistic" because of the absence of "the separation of household and business accounting" (1961:170–72). In contrast to Redfield, Tax's immersion in Guatemalan economics reflected his pragmatic and empirical bent and his genuine commitment to apply his research so that it would be of material benefit to his Guatemalan subjects. Given the direction his career was taking by 1953 and the evolution of his concern with economics, Tax's article "The Indians in the Economy of Guatemala" (1957b) is the culmination of his contribution to the economics literature and clearly separates him from the Redfieldian approach.

PENNY CAPITALISM AND DOLLAR CAPITALISM

Even though Tax used different terms to refer to capitalism or the capitalist economy, it is a mistake to characterize his approach to defining these concepts as taking assumptions for granted, as "unhinged from controversies" (Wilk 1996:120), or as innocent of economic theory as Tax himself would have us believe. Despite his 1939 admission that "I am not at all up on current economic ideas" (Rubinstein 1991:273), it is clear that Tax did some reading on the subject between then and the 1953 publication of *Penny Capitalism*. The delay in publication partly reflected his "desire to revise the manuscript," which was "fortunate, both because in the intervening years I learned much from colleagues at the University, and because the long delay permitted a fresh approach to the manuscript" (1963:x). One of the colleagues Tax consulted with was the economist Bert Hoselitz, who got him to read Oscar Lange (and probably to reread Weber) and who wrote a perceptive introduction to the Spanish translation published in Guatemala in 1964. Hoselitz, among his other contributions, located *Penny Capitalism* in the field of economic anthropology (Hoselitz 1964:14) as one of the few studies focusing on "problems of economic conduct and decision-making" (1964:14). He elaborated this thesis as follows: "That means that the basic nucleus of economics, as much in its application to modern, advanced societies as to the simplest preindustrial ones, is the systematic analysis of decisions in the fields of production, distribution, and consumption; the study of the processes by means of which diverse goods and economic actions are evaluated, and the forms of individual behavior to earn a living and plan for the future" (Hoselitz 1964:14–15).

Although the concept of "penny capitalism" was introduced and discussed by Tax in a theoretically unsystematic way, his basic argument was clear: the difference between the peasant-Indian economy of communities like Panajachel and the Guatemalan national economy is one of scale, not type—although he confusingly described the former as a "rural," "primitive underdeveloped," "community," or "primitive money" economy (1963:x). Moreover, like the contemporary capitalist economy, for Tax, the economy of the western highlands region of Guatemala was relatively autonomous vis-à-vis social institutions. As he expressed it, "Social institutions and cosmology . . . are as separated from the processes of making a living as are our own" (1963:ix). This relative autonomy justified in his mind the use of capitalist economic terms to describe the Panajachel economy (1963:ix) and is consistent with his empiricism. Yet it was the premium placed on economizing in the daily behavior and conversations of the people of Panajachel and their ethical commitment to hard work, investment of savings, and profit seeking, albeit of small sums, that for him sealed their identity as penny capitalists and "urged upon Tax the kind of precisely cost-accounted analysis he made of their activities" (Peattie 1979:85).[4]

It was in the context of rejecting the applicability of J. H. Boeke's "dual economy" model to Guatemala that Tax made his clearest statement of his intended meaning of penny capitalism (Tax 1957a:416–17):

> It so happens . . . that the Indians of highland Guatemala have, to a degree that would be considered high for any society, many of the characteristics of western capitalism. Accompanying a community and regional division of labour resulting in a free-competitive, monetary system of market exchange, the Indian culture stresses (1) individualism; (2) striving for economic gain that is reinforced rather than limited by social-ceremonial considerations; and (3) an ethic similar to that which accompanied the development of capitalism in Europe. The characteristics so impressed me when I studied the economy of Panajachel and its environs that the title *Penny Capitalism* seem appropriate for the book in which I described it.

This is a much more thoughtful and theoretically informed explanation of his catchy title than the one given in his 1963 preface. Item 2 is a clear statement of the thesis elaborated later by Frank Cancian (1965; 1967) that eventually compelled Eric Wolf to modify his emphasis on fiesta-cycle expenditures as a social leveling mechanism (1955; cf. 2001:164). The thesis is also a building block in my concept of commodity culture(s).

There is little else that Tax explicitly says about capitalism, but it is possible to negatively infer a few more characteristics from what he attributes to penny capitalism (that is, capitalism on a microscopic scale). Capitalist firms are business enterprises established to make a profit and employ formal bookkeeping and cost accounting. Wage labor, freely contracted in a labor market, is pervasive. Tax does not identify capitalism as a mode of production, but he associates it with corporately organized, machine-driven factories; a commercial credit system; competitive markets; and enormous wealth-generating potential because it encourages technological progress. When examining Panajachel in the western Guatemalan highlands against this ideal model of capitalism, Tax found it lacking with regard to elements of scale and organization but not enough to exclude it from the capitalist type. The essence remains: "An ethic . . . that encourages individual industry, acumen, and enterprise in a struggle to gain wealth" (1963:19), which he identified as "the spirit of business enterprise" (1963:18).

The basic unit of the penny variety of capitalism is the household as a production–consumption unit, which Tax, following Lange (1945–1946:30), viewed as displaying the rationality of firms because "their preferred allocation of resources among different wants can be ordered along a scale" thus facilitating the "maximization of a magnitude" (1963:17). Even though Tax found only primitive, unsystematic forms of bookkeeping, he did find much evidence of businesslike calculations and behavior among Panajacheleños and, for all practical purposes, considered the household to be an informal business unit.

A major logical flaw in Tax's view of penny capitalism as simply a downscaled version of capitalism proper is that, with "single households being both consumption and production units" (1963:13), it violates the criterion of "social institutions . . . as separated from the processes of making a living as are our own." Since the household is the home base for a family and the latter is a fundamental social institution, Tax's separation criterion is violated. In capitalist society, the major site of commodity production is the factory, not the household, thereby sustaining Tax's thesis of "separation" of the processes of making a living from social institutions. In Panajachel society, on the other hand, according to Tax's own analysis, the major site of commodity production is the household, thereby negating his "downscaled capitalism" thesis.

The upshot of this critique is that an economy like that of Panajachel is best studied by a method of analysis that considers the household as both a social unit and an enterprise. This implies that household demographics, family life cycle, consumer–worker ratios, and so on must be examined as necessary elements in any attempt to understand the household as an economic enterprise. This was precluded in Tax's work since it pre-dated the availability of the writings of A. V. Chayanov (1966), who pioneered this analytical method.

Wage labor was common in Panajachel, almost exclusively in agriculture, and was essentially freely contracted (Tax 1963:108). Penny capitalism, accordingly, had no manufactories or workshops and lacked machine-driven technology and a commercial credit system.[5] "The idea of borrowing money either to buy merchandise for resale, or to rent land and hire agricultural labor," says Tax, "is virtually nonexistent" (1963:14). Even though it has competitive markets, it generates limited wealth—enough to meet subsistence (food, clothing, and shelter), replacement, and social–ceremonial needs. "With good luck and hard work," says Tax, "a poor family can in a generation become a rich family; but the largest fortune can as quickly be frittered away" (1963:12).

Tax was silent regarding the class structure of capitalism proper in *Penny Capitalism*, but in his 1957 article he acknowledged that Guatemalan Ladino society is divided into classes (1957a:415–16). In *Penny Capitalism*, he devoted several pages to a theoretically weak yet suggestive empirical analysis of the "'class' aspects of differences in wealth" (1963:187) and the "functions of wealth" (1963:186–207). His analysis yielded no evidence of social classes in Panajachel but revealed "a tendency toward the formation of what approximate social classes in Chichicastenango" (1963:207). Tax's concept of social class, however, was formulated not around relations of production but around indices of wealth, status, and power that is intergenerational in particular family lines (1963:206–7). He concluded that Panajachel did not have social classes in this sense because "any family . . . in the course of two or three generations, has its important ups and downs, and the rich and poor are soon scrambled genealogically" or "there is no such thing as a 'wealthy family' of two or more generations' standing" (1963:202). This can be construed as Tax's version of a Chayanov-like peasant household cycle that inhibits class polarization and promotes the reproduction of a middle peasantry (Chayanov 1966; Cook and Binford 1990:15–20; Shanin 1972).[6]

Nevertheless, Tax found a definite socioeconomic differentiation in Panajachel in terms of landholding and employer-versus-employee status: those owning most land hire labor, and those who own little or no land hired themselves out (1963:196–97). On this basis, an argument could be made for the existence of incipient class differentiation in Panajachel (Cancian 1989; Cook and Binford 1986, 1990:15–22, 113–51; Smith 1984), but for Tax, class relations, whether interethnic or not, were not explicitly associated with exploitation or unequal exchange (cf. Hewitt de Alcántara 1984:66).

PENNY CAPITALISM'S CULTURE OF DIFFERENCE AND GUATEMALAN ECONOMIC DEVELOPMENT

Tax was interested not only in documenting and classifying the highland Indian economy but also in understanding its potential contribution to the development of the Guatemalan national economy. This is why he insisted without equivocation that "Indians and Ladinos form part of a single economy" (1957b:417) regionally and nationally. Regionally, for Tax, the economy was penny capitalistic, but nationally it was capitalistic and integrated with international capitalist markets (1957b:416). In his words (1957b:417; cf. Hewitt de Alcántara 1984:65; Mosk 1954:22):

> Indians and Ladinos are in all ways part of a single network of direct economic relations. *Much more than they are part of a single social, political, or religious system do Indians and Ladinos form part of a single economy.* If the Guatemalan national economy is part of the world commercial economy, then so also is the Indian economy, for on any general measures of economic interconnection, Indians are related more closely to Ladinos than Ladinos are, say, to North Americans.

This clear statement of the "single economy" thesis was unfortunately either not understood or ignored by most anthropologists who, largely under the influence of Eric Wolf's paradigm or Foster's (1948b:154) "economy within an economy" thesis, persist to this day in viewing the indigenous peasant economy of Mesoamerica/Mexico as separate and distinct from the enveloping advanced commodity economy of capitalism (Cook and Binford 1990:chap. 1).

Beyond his concern with the type and place of Guatemala's regional economy in the national and international system, Tax raised the question of the origin of the relative poverty of the regional economy, given its penny capitalistic culture, and was motivated to make policy recommendations that would integrate it into the national development process. Hoselitz (1964:18) succinctly expressed the essence of Tax's diagnosis of the reason for Panajachel's poverty as residing in inferior technology and a lack of capital, not in economic ethics or cultural values, and his remedy is that "a bettering of the position of the Indians with respect to capital could carry them to a higher level of economic performance and a gradual elimination of the worst forms of poverty" (1964:18). Their commitment to a cost–benefit calculus leads the Panajacheleños to adopt new technologies, like motorized transportation and new crops, but these, as well as new inputs of capital, must come from the outside, that is, from Guatemalan Ladino society and from the international economy. But Tax insisted on an approach to development that avoided imposition of inflexible, inappropriate models and that included "the widest possible range of alternatives encouraging [the Indians] to choose freely, and to learn from their choices the directions in which they are developing so that more and more realistic choices can be offered" (1957b:423).

Tax's insistence on the indigenous Guatemalan point of view was based on his extensive familiarity with the indigenous culture of difference, which, for him, was indigenous people's source of identity (that is, in opposition to the hegemonic Ladino identity) and something that classified and ordered their material needs, wants, and expectations or, in his words, "their own pattern of needs and tastes" (1957a:152). Tax anticipated the consumption-oriented study of the "social life of things" (Appadurai 1986) in his recognition of the symbolic importance of useful objects and that "even when a difference is not a symbol of social identification, there are resistances related to the cultural difference . . . differences of taste" (1957a:150–51). In his analysis of changes within indigenous patterns, he emphasized three findings: 1) "Indians like what they have and simply want more of it" (for example, they like more meat but with even more corn) (1957b:152); 2) "not only is it the case that Indians tend to use more of everything as they become richer, but change itself is not at all slow" (the example of clothing in Panajachel and Cantel [1957b:152–55]); and 3) "like us the Indians operate in terms of a complex of competing values, but the results are different partly because their ordering of the values is different from our own, and partly because the arena in which the values compete is different" (1957b:155). Thus, for him, the social relations of small-community life structured indigenous decision making but not so rigidly as to preclude agency, difference, and change.

Tax drew two important messages from his analysis of consumption: first, peasant Indians in Guatemala are no slower than we are in accepting realistic choices that seem to be in their own interest—they are not "averse to accepting alternatives that are clearly (and by their own definition) advantageous" (1957a:147). Second, regarding external approaches to internal economic development, the key obstacle to increasing levels of living, rates of saving, and capital formation is failure to privilege the indigenous perspective in determining realistic alternatives so that the people themselves can "work their own way to their own solutions" (1957a:156). There was no hint in Tax's perspective that class relations are sources of maldevelopment in commodity economy.

EVALUATING TAX'S CONTRIBUTION TO THE ECONOMIC ANTHROPOLOGY OF MESOAMERICA FIFTY YEARS AFTER *PENNY CAPITALISM*

The fact that the term "penny capitalism" coined by Sol Tax in 1953 is still found in academic discourse today suggests that it remains expressive, at least in some general, metaphorical sense. Strangely enough, the term was never rigorously conceptualized by Tax and never became the focus of systematic attention in economic anthropological discourse. In short, the meaning of penny capitalism is apparently viewed as self-evident and unproblematic and the term itself as analytically undeserving of attempts to conceptualize or theorize it. It continues to be used ambiguously as a catchy way to refer in general to small-scale market economy.

Implicit in Tax's approach was acceptance of the thesis that the abstract concept of "economy" encompassed those social processes necessary to secure the material requirements of everyday life, among which food, clothing, and shelter were most prominent. In other words, the economy was the proper focus of an economic study and was not reducible to other cultural fields or institutions. His approach also demonstrated that economic acts, consisting of production, exchange, and consumption and their distributive results, can be systematically observed and counted because they reflect planned, rational decision making in pursuit of certain goals. Moreover, Tax correctly emphasized that material gain was an important motive in economic performance and, when possible, did result in savings and capital accumulation in a minority of household enterprises that could be destined either for business expansion or for increased social–ceremonial expenditures. Indeed, his thesis that striving for economic gain in the Guatemalan highlands is reinforced rather than limited by social–ceremonial considerations clearly set the stage for important contributions to the understanding of socioeconomic dynamics of highland Maya societies by Frank Cancian (1965, 1967), Manning Nash (1958), and others (such as Smith 1977).

Tax was also critical of the concept of dual economy and advocated a single-economy approach for developing countries like Guatemala. This meant that the penny capitalist culture of Guatemala's highland Indians, which made them upwardly mobile and progressive in attitude, was conducive to their acceptance of technological change. Yet he recognized that their commitment to "traditional" culture (such as civil–religious hierarchy) and commodity/market economy was not incompatible—that the two were interrelated. Rather than viewing the relationship as mutually constitutive, however, he argued that, more often than not, culture did not as much shape as it was shaped by the economy in the western highlands of Guatemala (1963:16, 19). This set an unfortunate precedent for economistic explanations of sociocultural process and encouraged the elaboration of a model of narrow economic rationality that makes "overly restrictive assumptions about the role of norms in rational behavior" (Little 1991:153). Preferable—and analytically more productive—is a model of "broadened practical rationality" that "needs to incorporate a decision rule that represents the workings of moral constraints and commitments as well as goal-directed calculation" (Little 1991:153; cf. Cook 1974a:842–46). Such a model presupposes that a prudent regard for self, family, and community welfare are potentially of motivational importance in economic behavior and that patterns in that behavior can be understood as an "aggregate consequence of individuals" acting according to such a model (Little 1991:150).

Evon Vogt, in his critique of Tax, argued that the Zinacantecos (Chiapas, Mexico) like the Panajacheleños are "penny capitalists" in the marketplace but that they are simultaneously "tribal ritualists" who "have very astutely adapted . . . market pricing . . . to express, measure, and keep close track of their reciprocal obligations in the ceremonial round of life" (Vogt 1974:162). The thrust of Vogt's argument is to emphasize the complementarity of economizing and symbolic values in the daily lives of Mesoamerican Indians (cf. Heath 1974:158), whereas Tax (and Redfield 1962) emphasized the pecuniarization of the ritual sphere as a manifestation of Panajachel's penny capitalism. Vogt's point is well taken and is also applicable to the Valley Zapotec in Oaxaca, where obsessive concern with market pricing extends into commodities reciprocally exchanged or gifted in ceremonial or ritual contexts (Beals 1970; Cook 1982:107–15). Again, Vogt comes close to recognizing that economizing is part of indigenous commodity culture(s) and that the latter operates both within and outside the economic field. Still, Tax came closer to recognizing that both market production and ceremonial circulation are encompassed by commodity culture(s) and that the circulatory destination of commodities does not alter their value composition or how it is reckoned.

Tax's *Penny Capitalism* inspired a study of nineteenth-century English working-class entrepreneurs by economic historian John Benson (1983) even though Benson recognized that the oxymoronic concept "has never been clearly defined." He turned this lack of precise definition to his advantage by asserting that the basic contention of his book is that "the very difficulty of defining penny capitalism is fundamental to an understanding of it" (1983:4). Benson borrowed the concept from Tax because of its wide acceptance as denoting "small-scale entrepreneurial activity" (1983:1–2) and argues that it is "conceptually and historically impossible to distinguish clearly penny capitalists from wage-labourers below and from the petty bourgeoisie above" (1983:3), so that "the very difficulty of defining penny capitalism is fundamental to understanding it" (1983:3). His research disclosed the part-time, shifting, informal, casual nature of small-scale entrepreneurial activity (1983:128–29). Benson defined penny capitalism in terms of four criteria: 1) responsibility for the whole process, however small—from acquiring the necessary capital, choosing a site, bargaining for raw materials, deciding the working methods, providing the tools, and finding a market for the finished product; 2) like the capitalist proper, assuming risks in the hope of making profits; 3) working-class origin; and 4) small-scale operation.[7]

As can be inferred from these criteria, Benson was not concerned with small-scale industrial production since most of the cases he identified historically were not in the primary or the secondary sector of the economy but in the tertiary, or service, sector. In any case, I think his study would have benefited by his addressing the discourse surrounding petty commodity production, especially regarding the issue of household-enterprise reproduction strategies. Whereas it may be "historically impossible to distinguish clearly penny capitalists from wage-laborers below and from the petty bourgeoisie above" as Benson contended, it is not impossible to do so conceptually or ethnographically as my own work in Oaxaca (and work by others) demonstrated.

Unlike Tax, Benson avoided arguing that penny capitalism is just downscaled capitalism but also fails to rigorously define capitalism proper. To the extent that Tax's concept implied an *identity* between capitalism proper and penny capitalism, it was wrong: penny capitalism, defined as synonymous with petty commodity production, is not the same as either petty capitalism or capitalism proper. Tax was right, however, to associate penny capitalism (as embracing small-scale enterprises) and dollar capitalism. They are two asymmetrically articulated forms, at different levels of development, within a single commodity economy.

CONCLUSIONS

Whereas the term "penny capitalism" has the advantage of implying rational choice for potential material gain in small-scale market settings, it has the disadvantage of evoking a false analogy with advanced forms of commodity production that have developed in conjunction with mass markets and large-scale machinofacture—forms that are unequivocally capitalistic. Penny capitalism is most usefully understood as a metaphor for two distinct forms of economic activity that need to be conceptualized separately: the petty commodity form and the petty capitalist form. The essential difference between these two forms of enterprise, which are typically household based, is that the former employs wage labor only casually, if at all, to supplement family labor and is geared toward simple reproduction or household maintenance—although not to the exclusion of exchange value deliberations, realization, or accumulation. The latter, by contrast, regularly employs wage labor, either as a supplement to or in lieu of family labor, and is geared toward capital accumulation (Cook and Binford 1990:8–11, 127–30). It is important to note that both of these forms share rational decision making and even material gain (that is, earnings in excess of costs) as a motive. But only in the petty capitalist form does the material gain motive regularly result in profit or capital accumulation to facilitate enterprise expansion through the systematic exploitation of wage labor.

Tax's catchy term wrongly implied that small-scale commodity production and exchange was "capitalistic" just because it involved rational decision making by individual producers or traders in competitive markets and was motivated by the possibility of realizing cash returns in excess of costs. These are necessary but not sufficient criteria to define capitalism. According to Weber (1961:207), the sine qua non of capitalist enterprise identity is formal capital cost accounting. According to Marx (1967, 1:509), it is the repetitive appropriation by capital of surplus value (processional value) from the engagement of labor in an ongoing process of commodity production. In short, penny capitalism is an ambiguous term that, for analytical purposes, must be redefined as petty commodity production as separate and distinct from petty capitalism.

Tax's theoretical deficiencies were offset by his pioneering role in correcting a popular misconception that indigenous people in countries like Guatemala lacked the inclination, capacity, and rationality to participate in the market economy. Beyond his exhaustive empirical contestation of this misconception, Tax's contribution included some imaginative thinking about important issues, like the sociocultural dimensions of economic choice, poverty and progress, "realistic" or "appropriate" economic development attuned to the needs and wants of its subjects, and a unified Ladino-Indian economy.

His sensitivity to cultural particularities was counterbalanced by an appreciation of deliberative decision making in Guatemalan indigenous economic life, which, for him, pointed to the shared humanity between them and us. The pragmatic empiricism of Tax and his Boasian predecessors provides us with mountains of data boxed according to the everyday categories devised by the foundational scholars of capitalist market economy, namely, the classical economists who used the categories of production, distribution, exchange, and consumption to describe and analyze economic behavior, just as every twentieth-century economics textbook has done. Tax, at least, felt the need to justify his use of these categories by explaining that, in the part of Guatemala where he was collecting data for analysis and write-up, social institutions and worldview were "as separated from the processes of making a living as are our own" (1963:ix). It never occurred to many other anthropologists that the use of these categories in situations where such a separation was lacking made them vulnerable to charges of Eurocentrism. Tax seemed to be aware of this vulnerability and probably would not have used (or advocated the use of) an economizing approach in a nonmarket setting. In this sense, then, Tax was really not a formalist; the use of classical economic categories was, for him, dictated by his study of a market-integrated economy.

The main shortcoming of his work, aside from his lack of theoretical discipline, was to fail to appreciate the dark side of commodity economy, namely, how its market processes can maldistribute economic value through class relations and, in the specific case of Guatemala, through ethnoclass relations. His work also failed to anticipate the dark side of economic development under external sponsorship that would transform the localities of Guatemalan penny capitalism into Cold War killing grounds during the second half of the twentieth century (Carmack 1992).

NOTES

1. The Carnegie Institution's Maya Project was extended from Mexico to Guatemala in 1934—the same year that Tax completed his doctoral study at the University of Chicago (Hinshaw 1979:762). Robert Redfield was director of the ethnographic portion of the project.

2. Herskovits's reference to the "family as unit of production" and Tax's references to both "family" and "household" in *Penny Capitalism* with regard to both production, consumption, residence, and kinship and marriage ties (1963:154–55, 195–207) established both good and bad precedents in economic anthropology—good in calling attention to the social composition of fundamental economic units and bad in lack of systematic analysis of that composition and its ramifications. I agree with Michael Kearney (personal communication) with particular reference to rural Mexico and especially Oaxaca (and including the role of migration, remittances, and nonresident members) that "patrilineal and patriarchal kin groups made up of senior fathers and their brothers and sons are . . . important" and that these "larger families" regularly subordinate "households" (cf. Cook 1982:46–53; Cook and Binford 1990: 251 n. 1).

3. It bears pointing out that the Malinowski who wrote about economics in *A Scientific Theory of Culture* (1960:126–28) and coauthored, with Julio de la Fuente, *The Economics of a Mexican Market System* (1982) had a different posture toward classical/neoclassical economics than Malinowski in the Trobriands. In *A Scientific Theory of Culture*, he defined economics as "the study of the production, exchange, distribution and consumption of wealth" (1960:126) and argued that, for purposes of cross-cultural studies, the "general structure of classical theory is applicable, with modifications" (1960:127). The Oaxaca markets study is replete with applications of this theory.

4. She goes on to sum up his study as follows: "Tax (1953) showed that monetization and market rationality of a classicism hard to find nowadays in the New Industrial State could exist in societies otherwise displaying characteristics of the societies my father, Robert Redfield, was calling 'folk'" (Peattie 1979:86).

5. Tax (1963:26 n. 20) was curious about women foot-loom operators in San Pedro Sacatepequez shops. If he had investigated this further, he would, indeed, have identified penny capitalism as a petty form of industrial capitalism.

6. This is not to imply that Tax was consciously making a Chayanovian or neopopulist interpretation. The bibliography for *Penny Capitalism* suggests otherwise.

7. A 1979 book by James J. Hester, under the pseudonym of Algernon Horatio, was titled *The Penny Capitalist: How to Build a Small Fortune from Next to Nothing* (New Rochelle, N.Y.: Arlington House Publishers) and presumably takes its title from Tax's 1953 book, although Hester does not acknowledge this. In any case, the subtitle shows that Tax's catchphrase opened a Pandora's box of contested meanings.

4

Rereading Canonical Texts and Revisiting the "Great Debate": A Retrospective View from the Trenches through a Twenty-First-Century Lens

Long after it became passé among economic anthropologists, a prominent philosopher of social science, Daniel Little (1991:136–58), turned his attention to the formalist–substantivist controversy and drew lessons from his case study that are pertinent to economic anthropology today. Little's attention formed part of his review of attempts in recent social science to "explain a pattern of social behavior or an enduring social arrangement as the aggregate outcome of the goal-directed choices of large numbers of rational agents" (1991:136). Formalists can feel somewhat vindicated by Little's sophisticated and independent review since, on balance, he is less critical of their approach than of substantivism. His thesis that "humans are rational, goal-directed beings whose goals include the satisfaction of material needs" (Little 1991:149) is surely more attuned to formalism than substantivism but, more important, provides a key operating assumption for future inquiry in economic anthropology that can build on its best work of the past century.

A recent textbook in economic anthropology by Richard Wilk (1996) does not cite Little's work but, in recognizing the importance of the formalist–substantivist debate in shaping the subfield's development, provides welcome dissonance to the chorus of voices portraying it as misguided polemic, without significant theoretical or methodological content (Isaac 1993; Plattner 1989). Little's contribution, together with Wilk's, provides all would-be participants in twenty-first-century economic anthropological discourse with an opportunity to revisit important, unresolved issues of epistemology, theory, and method raised by the twentieth-century debate and to develop a defensible position on the perplexing issues it raised. To not do so is to risk repeating or perpetuating past mistakes in theory and method.

While not declaring a winner in the debate, Little presents a strong case for a "wide range of potential applications for the rational choice framework . . . to explain patterns of social behavior and social arrangements in a variety of social settings" (1991:157). He warns that the substantivist approach, to be viable, need not deny the "workings of means-end rationality in traditional societies" but simply insist on "the essential importance of norms, values, and worldview in constraining and propelling individual action" and "requires a richer and more culturally detailed conception of individual agency" (1991:157). Even more significantly, Little's analysis demonstrates that the radical substantivist argument associated with Polanyi and Sahlins, namely, that rational choice approaches impose an ethnocentric conception of rationality, is simply wrong in view of the impressive work in area studies conducted on the basis of the central assumptions of the rational choice framework. Moreover, he contends that the radical substantivist approach, which assumes that "each society works according to forces that are unique to it," condemns social science to a "purely descriptive chronicling of concrete phenomena" (Little 1991:155). By contrast, according to Little, the concept of "prudential rationality" developed by formalists "allows us to construct parsimonious explanations of a wide variety of social phenomena in various non-Western cultures" (Little 1991:155).

A CONTRADICTORY CONJUNCTURE

The "Great Debate" (Wilk 1996:13) was initiated in 1961 with the publication of a lead article in *American Anthropologist* by the economist George Dalton that aggressively rejected the prevailing approach in economic anthropology associated with the work of Herskovits (1952) and Firth (1939; 1951:chap. 4), among others, and advocated its replacement by the approach developed by Karl Polanyi and his associates (1957). The debate "thread" triggered by this article burned out in the 1970s, when, according to Wilk's tabulations "most publications were no longer concerned with the formalist-substantivist debate" (Wilk 1996:4).

In 1983, Barry Isaac took over the editorship of the annual review that George Dalton started, *Research in Economic Anthropology*, and promptly discouraged 1960s-style polemics and encouraged empirical studies. He speculates, rather dramatically, that his change of editorial policy may "have contributed to the death of the destructive formalist-substantivist debate" (1993:215)—which is wishful thinking more than fact. Isaac himself seems to admit as much when he notes that "the debate simply fizzled out in the late 1970s, to the relief of practically everyone" (1993:229). It should be noted, however, that under his editorship the journal provided a supportive venue for two articles by Rhoda Halperin (1984; 1985): one an examination of

Polanyi's relationship to Marx and Marxism (1984) and the other on Polanyi as an interpreter of Weber (1985:359, 360). Both articles, with some notable exceptions, were well documented and fair, if not impartial, in their interpretation of the literature. Moreover, one gets the impression from Isaac's postmortem that the aftermath of the debate has left economic anthropology without a raison d'être (Isaac 1993:229–30).[1]

None of the debate's postmortems has captured a sense of the unlikelihood of its occurrence, given the academic circumstances prevailing at the time. In 1960, no subfield of anthropology had a more authoritative and comprehensive sourcebook than *Economic Anthropology: A Study in Comparative Economics*, authored by Melville J. Herskovits (1952), one of American cultural anthropology's leading scholars at the peak of his career, or a more rigorous and sophisticated ethnographic case study than *Primitive Polynesian Economy*, authored by Raymond Firth (1939), the prize student of one of the subfield's founders, Bronislaw Malinowski, and in his own right one of British social anthropology's premier scholars. Needless to say, both Herskovits and Firth were strong advocates of the selective applicability of neoclassical economics to the study of so-called primitive, tribal, or noncapitalist economies.[2]

Moreover, there was a broad consensus in support of the selective applicability of neoclassical economics to the entire Third World, a position implied in judgments like the following by two Africanists that "those economic activities organized on the market principle are expanding with a concomitant attenuation of redistribution and reciprocity" and that "economies are becoming like our own in the sense that the sectors dominated by the market principle are being enlarged" (Bohannan and Dalton 1962:24–25). This widespread recognition of worldwide economic change seemed to reinforce rather than weaken the formalist approach advocated by Herskovits and Firth. Ironically, the coauthor of this statement was the same George Dalton who in 1961 argued so forcefully to restrict the applicability of Western economic theory to "market industrialism" or "industrialized market systems" (1968:164–65), which, for all practical purposes, was tantamount to eliminating its use by economic anthropologists in their studies of the nonindustrial economies of the Third World. Consequently, the contradictions between changing realities and change-resistant theories in economic anthropology in the early 1960s meant that complex issues had to be worked out through debate. At stake was how the subfield should approach the comparative, cross-cultural study of past, present, and future economies.

The formalist–substantivist controversy was nurtured by the peculiar nature of anthropological discourse and knowledge production—its liminality vis-à-vis the sciences and the humanities, its tension between generalists and specialists, its penchant for interdisciplinary cross-fertilization, and its internationally fragmented organization. The controversy was bound to have originated in American cultural anthropology, where the profession's demographics, organization, communication structure, and social dynamic created a context for democratic, if not anarchic, discourse involving many voices that were differentially enculturated in the knowledge subcultures of the undisciplined subfield. It was inevitable that British social anthropology would be dragged into the fray, given the substantivists' targeting of contributions by Raymond Firth, Richard Salisbury, and other British-trained social anthropologists and the American formalists' defense of them. Six years after Dalton's opening gambit and following a cycle of rejoinders in the American literature, a major British response was published (Firth 1967).

REREADING POLANYI AND RECONSIDERING THE SUBSTANTIVIST PARADIGM

A good starting point in reexamining substantivism is Morton Fried's succinct introduction to an essay by Karl Polanyi (1968a) first published in Fried's reader (Fried 1968).[3] According to Fried (1968:215–16):

> Among economists, there was one whose denunciations of the application of modern economic theory to all economies in general attracted considerable attention among anthropologists. Arguing that modern economic theory is designed for the analysis of systems in which values are determined through market transactions, this economist contended that neither primitive cultures nor the societies of classical antiquity operated according to such a system. He suggested, instead, that there are three fundamental kinds of economic system, two in addition to the market type. Simplest of these is the reciprocal economy in which goods move from one person or group to another and back, each pair of participants constituting a complete and independent unit. The other is the redistributive economy which sees goods and services flow into a central store, then redistributed (though not necessarily in equivalent repayments to contributors so as to exhaust the central store).

Fried was himself so taken with Polanyi's scheme that he used it as the framework for his study titled *The Evolution of Political Society* (1967).

My rereading Polanyi's essay titled "Anthropology and Economic Theory" in the Fried reader disclosed explicit arguments for three specific positions not mentioned by Fried: 1) the elimination of rational action and means–end decision making from the realm of nonmarket economy as his solution to what he called the "economistic fallacy" (that is, the "artificial identification of the economy with its market form" [Polanyi 1968a:218]); 2) the contention that social structure compels, causes, or dictates individual behavior, thus denying the significance of human agency in social process; and 3) the subordination of or fragmented approach to production in the economic process. Fried, in his statement, raised economic value as an issue of concern to Polanyi and, more specifically, implied that Polanyi posited different sources of economic value in primitive, nonmarket societies than in market-integrated societies. This is a dimension of Polanyi's contribution that also merits further consideration.

A necessary implication of Polanyi's argument that formal economics is both a creature of and exclusively applicable to the capitalist market economy is that the latter's emergence in Western Europe and North America represented the epitome of humanity's expression of the "logic of rational action" and that the affairs of humanity outside that institutional framework lacked the organized expression of such logic.[4] Polanyi equated "formal economics" with "rules governing choice of means" and "the logic of rational action" (Polanyi 1968a:216). Then he asserted, "The last two centuries produced in Western Europe and North America an organization of man's livelihood to which the rules of choice happened to be singularly applicable . . . a system of price-making markets . . . [that] could be reduced to a pattern that lent itself to the application of methods based on the formal meaning of economic" (1968a:217; cf. 1957:244). Finally, Polanyi concluded, "Outside of the institutional system of price making markets economic analysis loses most of its relevance as a method of inquiry into the working of a definite economy" (1968a:220; cf. 1957:247). This latter view was asserted less subtly by George Dalton (1968:144)—"economic theory cannot be fruitfully applied to the study of primitive communities"—and was escalated from polemic to hyperbole by Marshall Sahlins (1972:xiii)—"Embodying the wisdom of native bourgeois categories, formal economics flourishes as ideology at home and ethnocentrism abroad . . . it draws great strength from its profound compatibility with bourgeois society."[5]

Perhaps sensing that their approach was bordering on the exclusion of rational choice-making behavior from much of humanity's economic life, Polanyi and his coeditors of *Trade and Market in the Early Empires* (1957:xvii) argued that in "marketless economies where there is no 'economizing,' i.e., no institutional framework to compel the individual to 'rational' and 'efficient' economic activity. . . . Economizing action may be present in various aspects of behavior, e.g., in regard to one's time, energy . . . but the economy need contain no institutions of exchange to reflect these principles in the individual's daily life as they have done in our own day." Despite this tortured effort to rescue some modicum of rational choice in nonmarket settings, the syllogistic die was already cast for substantivist economic anthropology by Polanyi's forceful and extensive arguments in *The Great Transformation* (1957) and his essay "Our Obsolete Market Mentality" (1947): formal economics was not applicable outside of the capitalist market economy of Western Europe and North America because only the latter operated by a "set of rules referring to choice between the alternative uses of insufficient means"

(Polanyi 1968a:217; cf. 1957:246–47). By implication, means–end logic and choice-making behavior was marginalized by Polanyi to the point of irrelevance in nonmarket economies.

If further proof of this marginalization is still required to convince remaining skeptics, consider the following: in the context of a discussion elaborating his contention that a "broad reason for the absence in primitive society of an integrating effect of the economy is its lack of quantitativity" (Polanyi 1957:73), Polanyi reviewed Malinowski's seven categories of "gifts, payments, and transactions" in the Trobriand economy. With regard to the type of transaction "where the gift is expected to be returned in an economically equivalent manner," Polanyi emphasized that any resemblance between this and utilitarian trade is misleading because "occasionally the same object is exchanged back and forth between . . . partners" (1957:74). This fact alone, for Polanyi, deprived the "transaction of any conceivable economic purpose or meaning" (its sole purpose being to tighten social relations by strengthening the ties of reciprocity). And he went further: "By the simple device of handing back, though in a roundabout way, the pig to its donor, the exchange of equivalencies *instead of being a step in the direction of economic rationality* [emphasis added] proves a safeguard against the intrusion of utilitarian considerations" (1957:74). Having deprived Trobrianders of the exercise of economic rationality in their practice of balanced reciprocity, Polanyi failed to explicitly acknowledge that they did exercise it in utilitarian barter, which he characterized merely as displaying "at least a pretence of higgling and haggling" (1957:74). Polanyi was simply unable to come to grips with the reality of commodity circulation in nonmarket economies.

Moreover, when Polanyi turned his discussion in this same essay to the "probings" and writings of Aristotle, who was an "eye witness . . . of some of the pristine features of incipient market trading at its very first appearance in the history of civilization" (1957:67), he does not address the issue of economic rationality at all, preferring instead to emphasize Aristotle's sociological approach to the economy (1957:79) and his interpretation of barter (that is, the exchange of equivalencies) "as an obligation of householders to give of their surplus to any other householder who happened to be short of that definite kind of necessary" (1957:90). Consequently, Aristotle, according to Polanyi, viewed exchange "as part of reciprocity behavior in contrast to the marketing view which invested barter with the qualities which are the very reverse of the generosity and grace that accompanied the idea of reciprocity" (1957:90–91).[6]

Thus, not only Malinowski's Trobrianders but also Aristotle's ancient Greeks were, according to Polanyi, not presented with economic situations requiring the exercise of rational calculation and decision making. These economies are "embedded" in noneconomic institutions, which was Polanyi's shorthand way of saying that their economic process is instituted through kinship, marriage, age-groups, and so on. The term "economic life" has no obvious meaning in or with reference to these societies, and the individual is simply not aware of any pervading interest in regard to his livelihood that he could recognize as economic (Polanyi 1957:70–71). Consequently, there is no justifiable need by the participants in such economies to exercise the logic of rational action. It must be noted that Polanyi's interpretation contradicts Malinowski, who explicitly noted the role of haggling in Trobriand barter, or *gimwali*, which is distinguished from other forms of exchange in Trobriander economic discourse (Malinowski 1961:189): "They [Trobrianders] state correctly and clearly its general conditions, and they tell readily which articles may be exchanged by *gimwali*" (1961:190).

A second point, related to the first, that emerges from rereading Polanyi's essay is his (and his colleagues') defensiveness regarding the problematic status of individual behavior in a human economy "embedded and enmeshed in institutions, economic and non-economic," which were understood to "compel" (1968a:222; Polanyi et al. 1957:xvii), "cause" (Polanyi 1957:247), or "dictate" (Dalton 1969:67) individual activity. Polanyi insisted that his posited forms of integration—reciprocity, redistribution, and exchange—did not merely reflect "aggregates of the respective forms of individual behavior" on the personal level but that the "integrative effect was conditioned by the presence of definite structural patterns . . . such as symmetrical arrangements, central points and market systems"(1968a:223; cf. 1957:251). Then Polanyi (1968a:223) posed a question—"can these structures be accepted as independent variables . . . do they not represent merely a form of the self-same personal behavior pattern the eventual effects of which they are supposed to condition?"—and answers it—"the significant fact is that they do not." Sensing that he had evaded answering the question of what produces structural patterns if individual behavior does not, Polanyi (1968a:224; cf. 1957:251) defensively demurred, in a classic example of circular reasoning, "We do not wish to imply . . . that those supporting patterns are the outcome of some mysterious forces acting outside the range of personal or individual behavior. We merely insist that if, in any given case, the societal effects of individual behavior depend on the presence of definite institutional conditions, these latter conditions do not for that reason result from the personal behavior in question." Hopkins's (1957:297–99) use of sociological systems theory to attempt to answer the question Polanyi evaded was equally convoluted and evasive.

In this discursive exercise, the Achilles' heel of the removal of means–end rationality and human agency from the economic life of precapitalist humanity, exposed earlier, is enlarged. The entire edifice of intermeshed social structures facilitating economic process, according to Polanyi's approach, does not drop from the sky and is not a product of individual or interindividual behavior. So where do the structures, institutions, or patterns that allegedly "cause" (Polanyi 1957:247) behavior in such economies originate?

What is the precise relationship of living subjects to these structures? Unfortunately, these questions were never answered by Polanyi and his group, although Conrad Arensberg (1957:97–113) laid out a potentially productive framework for answering them in what I think is by far the most operationally coherent, if overlooked, contribution to the theory and method of substantivism. According to Arensberg, it requires the anthropologist "to spell out in faithful, empirical detail all observable and checkable dovetailing of transmitted action, interaction, meaning and context which makes up any culture pattern" (1957:102). Here was a promising formula for an operational method that was stillborn in substantivist discourse.

A third issue raised by rereading Polanyi was his tendency to insert production into his scheme as a subordinate concern to his main focus on "locational" and "appropriational" or "goods-handling" and "goods-receiving" activities. Polanyi rightly emphasized that a focus on economic process necessarily involves "analysis in terms of motion" (1968a:220), but his conceptualization of the process was inconsistent, awkward, and unclear in addressing production and activities of transformation (that is, manufacture).[7] Production, juxtaposed with transportation, was viewed by Polanyi as involving locational movement and technology in manufacturing and as an essential element of the substantive economy supplying producers' and consumers' goods for consumption (1968a:221). Polanyi (1968a:222; 1957:249) saw production as a natural process of interaction between ecology and technology or, more poetically, as a "jig-sawing of human and non-human movements" (1968a:221). These "bare bones of production" (1968a:221) become coherent and historical only through insertion in a social or institutional process, resulting in an integrated economy dominated by a form that "integrates the factors of production, land and labor, with the rest of the economy" (1968a:223). The dominant forms that identify three different types of economies are reciprocity, redistribution, and exchange (1968a:221–23), but "substantivism," as Jenkins demonstrated, "cannot . . . provide any theoretical basis or necessity for these 'mechanisms'" (1977:87). In short, reading Polanyi to ascertain the precise status of production in each of his posited economies is complicated by his disjointed and brief discussion of the topic in his major essays (cf. Cook 1974a:815–16).[8]

Specifically, regarding the issue of peasant production in market economies, Polanyi had very little to say, and the substantive approach to production in peasant economies seems to rely mostly on a combination of Chayanov and cultural ecology/cultural geography (Halperin 1977:19, 269–97). Production aside, substantivism has more potential in peasant studies, and greater success has been achieved, in building on Polanyi's work on institutionalized patterns of product movement, especially reciprocity (Orlove 1977). Yet under conditions of international capitalist economy and internal and external capitalist development of peasant economies, it seems anachronistic and analytically counterproductive to follow substantivism in conceptualizing the integration or general coordination of peasant livelihood in a way that precludes addressing relations of distribution as class relations or that assumes that no single form of integration is dominant and that peasant economies are integrated by institutional structures involving a combination of reciprocity, redistribution, and market exchange (Halperin and Dow 1977:185). A more realistic assumption for twenty-first-century peasant studies is that reciprocity and redistribution are subordinated to market exchange and that all economic transactions, because of the circulation of all-purpose money, have a significant degree of quantitativity and, hence, accountability (cf. Polanyi 1957:73).

A fourth and final issue, one raised in Fried's commentary, is the role of economic value in Polanyi's approach, which was overshadowed by his emphasis on the instituting of the economic process and the social embedment of the economy. For him, the locus of economic value in all economies of record lay in circulation, not in production. Regarding value in capitalist economies, Polanyi rejected the Ricardian–Marxian labor theory of value and, it seems, agreed with mainstream economics in looking for the value of objects exchanged in the transaction itself (that is, what was given for what was received). This led him to focus on the media and mechanisms of exchange, especially money or in-kind equivalences, rather than on the cultural origin of the valuation of products and services. For example, price, in his scheme, is "that form of equivalency which is characteristic of economies that are integrated through exchange" (Polanyi 1957:269). The useful distinction between "all-purpose" and "special-purpose" money was one of Polanyi's many contributions to the study of the esoteric field of "catallactics," or exchange (Polanyi, in Dalton 1968:178–80). Walter Neale, an original member of the Polanyi group, perhaps sums up the findings of substantivism on this subject: "There are no universal rules for relating value, treasure, utility, and money uses: what appears to be a reasonable relationship in one place or time turns out to be wrong in another" (1976:11).

Strangely enough, Polanyi and the substantivists, by the very logic of their approach, should have made significant contributions to our understanding of barter. Yet a recent important collection on the topic (Humphrey and Hugh-Jones 1992) suggests that Sahlins is the only substantivist worth citing, mainly for his concept of barter as "negative reciprocity" and as an "archaic prototype of capitalism" (Humphrey and Hugh-Jones 1992:7). It could be argued that Polanyi did advance our understanding of the formation of equivalencies or the quantitative aspect of barter—how much of this for how much of that. But overall, the contribution of Polanyi and other substantivists to the dynamic or processual aspects of barter and to gifting has been disappointing, amounting to little more than the "equation of 'reciprocity' with 'gift exchange'" (Gregory 1997:922; cf. Ingold 1997:749).

This "equation" had already been made by Mauss (1954) and could be interpreted as a step backward from Malinowski's ethnographically thick categorization and discussion of gifts, payments, and commercial transactions (1961:177–94) as well as from Mauss's more sophisticated attempt to theorize the commodity through a focus on reciprocity and to shed light on the "emergence of advanced commodity economy out of a social order that was at first constituted according to other principles" (Hart 1982:45). With the lone exception of Sahlins's provocative contribution (1972), the substantivist approach has never come to grips with the common element in the thought of Marx and Mauss that tends to dissolve the boundary between products given and commodities circulated in the sequential history of exchange or the growth of commodity economy (cf. Hart 1982:45–47). Nor have they coped with newer approaches that are extending the significance of commodity circulation into domains precluded in classic Marxism and in Mauss's *The Gift* (Appadurai 1986; Baudrillard 1981; Bourdieu 1977; Humphrey and Hugh-Jones 1992).

THE "'ECONOMY PLUS SOCIETY' SYNDROME" AND THE EMBEDMENT MUDDLE

This syndrome was defined by LeClair and Schneider (1968:8–9) as a "preoccupation with social and cultural factors in the economic equation" and was correctly attributed by them to "new economic anthropologists" like Raymond Firth and Manning Nash (1961), who viewed the "decision-making process as strictly circumscribed by the social structure" (LeClair and Schneider 1968:9). They also associated this syndrome with economic sociology as represented by the work of Parsons and Smelser (1956) that viewed the economy as a subsystem of the social system and emphasized the priority of a state of equilibrium for the entire system over that of the economic subsystem considered in isolation (cf. LeClair and Schneider 1968:9). LeClair and Schneider contrasted this syndrome with the approach that typically prevails among economists who employ the ceteris paribus (other things remaining equal) assumption to eliminate a concern with "possible social and cultural constraints in studying Western industrial economies" (1968:9). This can be labeled the "economy minus society" syndrome.

It is noteworthy that under the rubric of the "economy plus society syndrome," LeClair and Schneider failed to explicitly discuss Polanyi and substantivism. Possibly one reason they failed to do so was the challenge presented by Polanyi's separation of the formal and substantive meanings of "economic," which, in effect, permitted him to study the economy without economics or, more specifically, to study "substantive economy plus society minus formal economy." That LeClair and Schneider were uncomfortable in dealing with paradoxes of this order is suggested by their interpretation of the "anti-economics of Bronislaw Malinowski" (1968:3–5). According to them, "Malinowski did not consider the *kula* exchange to be an economic activity, though what he did consider to be economic activity was associated with it on occasion" (1968:3–4). This conflicts with Malinowski's insistence that despite the fact that the "fundamental aspect of the *Kula*" is the "ceremonial exchange of . . . two articles" (1961:83), it is "concerned with the exchange of wealth and utilities, and therefore it is an economic institution" (1961:84). He supported this interpretation by emphasizing that the institution encompassed "associated activities and secondary aspects," including the building of canoes, the provisioning of the expedition, and secondary trade (1961:99) or barter (*gimwali*) involving haggling to determine equivalences (1961:189).

Malinowski (1961:60) was against the universal applicability of the classical–neoclassical Economic Man model but, at that early stage of his career, was merely naive about economics rather than being "antieconomics" in the substantivist sense. He studied the Trobriand Islands as an exemplar of the "substantive economy plus society" syndrome without economics. Polanyi made selective and strategic use of Malinowski's ethnography, downplayed the latter's discussion of "associated activities and secondary aspects" referred to previously, and emphasized his sociocultural contextualization of economic activity—or, to use Polanyi's terms, how it is "embedded" or "instituted" (1957:68–71).

Plattner's assurance to his readers that some years after the formalist–substantivist debate we now take the "substantivist truth for granted that all economies are embedded which means that the economy is an aspect of social life rather than a segment of society" (1989:14) not only is cryptic but also begs the question of the operationality of social embedment that was at stake in the debate, preferably through a focus on production as suggested at the time by Walter Neale (1964:1304).[9] Wilk also considers the notion of embedment (or "embeddedness") to be the "strongest substantivist position" apparently because it views the economy as a "type of human activity, embedded in different social institutions in different kinds of societies" (1996:11).

Wilk questions the "truth" status of the substantivist embedment proposition by listing five equally plausible alternatives, heuristically speaking: 1) the economy is not embedded at all but is an autonomous subsector of society; 2) society is embedded in the economy; 3) economy is only partially embedded in social institutions; 4) the economy is embedded in every single society in a different way, so there are no types; and 5) the economy is not a sector of society or a type of behavior at all but, rather, is omnipresent in human activity. This exercise, however, assumes the meaning of embedment to be unproblematic. It is no substitute for a rigorous critique of the type undertaken by Jenkins (1977), who, while noting that "substantivists stress the absolute necessity of an understanding of the relation between all economies and their existent supporting social environments" (1977:73), demonstrated their failure to formulate a theoretically rigorous "concept of the integration of economic and non-economic" that specified the "conditions and modes of articulation of each sub-set of movements/actions (locational and appropriational) with a determinate sphere of the non-economic" (1977:76).[10]

Polanyi's embedment thesis was the theoretical basis for his classification of "*societas* economies" (Cook 1974b:360 n. 1) as either redistributive or reciprocative but was not clearly or systematically formulated by him (Polanyi 1957:71). Terence Hopkins (1957:297–303; cf. Jenkins 1977:72–77) was more systematic in his elaboration of the embedment thesis but admitted that the "theoretical underpinnings of the 'forms of integration' have not been clearly stated—so that at times the 'forms' are used to refer to locational changes of objects, at other times appropriational changes and occasionally to both—and need to be developed if the concepts are to be basic tools as well as pragmatically useful designations" (1977:302). It still remains true, as Jenkins pointed out, that "since these lines were written it cannot be said that this advice has been taken. Substantivist economic anthropology has . . . failed to develop theoretically in this direction" (1977:77).

The potential for refining the substantivist taxonomy of precapitalist economies implied in the previous quote by Polanyi was partially realized by Dalton's (1969:71) tentative schematization of "traditional economies" through his useful analytical distinction between "organization" and "performance" and ensuing discussion (1969:72–74). Such taxonomic exercises, however, generate little enthusiasm and much controversy (Dalton 1969:80–95).[11]

Dalton must also be credited with making the most intelligent statement ever by a substantivist about the embedment concept, needless to say one that has been ignored by substantivists and their fellow travelers ever since. In 1971 he stated, "Certainly since Malinowski and Mauss wrote, we have known that social organization (e.g., kinship) and cultural practices (e.g., religion) are inextricably part of labor and land allocation, work organization, and product distribution. I would change Polanyi's catchphrase by saying 'economy' and 'society' are 'embedded' in each other, and that it is impossible to attribute primacy to one over the other, for traditional societies" (1971:11). He then refers to the "interleaving of economy and society" (1971:11). Dalton's statement anticipated the dialectical conceptualization of the economy–society relationship disseminated through the writings of Raymond Williams (1981:12–13) and, in the field of anthropological political economy, by Roseberry (1989:42). In short, according to Dalton's unintentional dialectics, his perceptive reconceptualization of Polanyi's thesis of the mutual embeddedness or "interleaving" of economy and society does anticipate a dialectical view of the economy as both socially constituted (it is a product of present and past activity) and socially constitutive (part of the context in which activity is imbued with meaning) (cf. Roseberry 1989:42).[12]

With regard to the specifics of how economies are embedded in their social matrices, Polanyi's effort was overly concerned with integrative patterning in systemic terms and too little concerned with patterned behavior or activities that were counterintegrative—a good example of this being his handling of utilitarian barter, or *gimwali*, in the Trobriand economy (1957:74). With this important qualification, together with my critique regarding the removal of means–end rationality/human agency and taking the heavy reliance on structuralist–functionalist discourse *cum grano salis*, Godelier's criticism that "at no point does Polanyi . . . ask himself why it is that the economy occupies a particular position in a given society, and why it functions, 'embedded' or not, within kinship or political or religious relations" (1986:189) is on target. The inescapable implication is that Polanyi's theoretical inflexibility and his empiricist method precluded his posing the right questions and providing adequate answers regarding the "underlying processes which generate the social types" he posited (Salisbury 1968:479).

The fact that Godelier's critique (1986:189–93) did not question the meaning of Polanyi's concept of embedment is symptomatic of an appropriation of the term by Marxists, especially those who advocate a social reproductionist and livelihood-focused approach. Susana Narotsky (1997) and June Nash (2001) are cases in point. Given the ambiguity surrounding the meaning of the verb "to embed" (for example, to submerge, enclose in a matrix, circumscribe, surround closely, introduce as an integral part of, and so on) and Polanyi's nondialectical, holistic conceptualization of the relationship between economic and noneconomic fields, the reason for its appeal among Marxists is puzzling. This is especially true in view of Polanyi's belief that the embedment of the economy in nonmarket-integrated societies in other social institutions is matched by its putative disembedment in market-integrated societies and of his unilineal evolutionary view of a progression in economic history from a condition of sociocultural embedment in precapitalism to one of sociocultural disembedment in capitalism (1957:68).

POLANYI WAS NOT A MARXIST

One of the cardinal tenets of Marxism is that the behavior of commodities in the capitalist economy is inextricably bound up with social relations. Indeed, Marx emphasized the social nature of economic process from the beginning of our species' history and never conflated ontology with epistemology as Polanyi did with his murky concept of embedment. Rather, Marx emphasized that the notion of a market economy detached from society was a creature of classical political economic thought (and popular perceptions), not of the actual history of concrete capitalist formations. He also recognized that this epistemological fiction, which did appear to have some ontological support, was historically unprecedented and had important implications for knowledge production about the economic process. Unlike Polanyi, who never really explained the transition in economic history from embedment of the economy under feudalism to its putative disembedment under capitalism, the process he labeled the "Great Transformation" (cf. Jenkins 1977:83–84), Marx did provide a sophisticated explanation as a concomitant of his elaboration of his theory of surplus value and the industrial capitalist mode of production (Dobb 1963; Mandel 1971:79–99; Meek 1956:chaps. 4 and 5).[13]

Perhaps the best news regarding what Rhoda Halperin labels as the "now infamous formalist-substantivist debate of the 1960s" (1985:359) is that "since the beginning of the 1970s, issues raised by Marxism have taken center stage in the discipline . . . [and] the Marxian focus . . . on systems of production and the pursuit of power by social groups . . . [is] an approach that is neither purely formalist nor substantivist" (Wilk 1996:13). The main rationale for privileging production is not as much because it is the beginning of the economic process but because, by virtue of encompassing technology, it is strategically located in any society's economic relationship with its physical environment; and, by virtue of its encompassing of the labor process, it is a principal nexus of articulation between the entire economic process and the sociocultural structure of any society.[14]

The economic anthropological study of this nexus proceeds in accordance with the following assumptions: 1) that the sociocultural relations dominant in a given society tend to determine the integrative principle of the economy without precluding the simultaneous operation of other less integrative principles; 2) human agency expressed through individual exercise of rational choice is omnipresent—not just in market-organized societies; what differs between market and nonmarket economies is the range of choice, not its presence or absence (cf. Wilk 1996:6–8, 12; Godelier 1986:192–94; cf. Cook 1974a:842–46); and 3) the economic process necessarily involves interpenetrating relationships between production, exchange, consumption, and distribution—no one of these components or phases counts heavily in the absence of mutual relations with the others.

Halperin (1984) made a case for viewing the relationship between Polanyi and Marx as "complex" by claiming that Polanyi's work was simultaneously an interpretation, an elaboration, and a critique of Marx (1984:268). She also insisted that the "issue is not, simply, whether or not Polanyi was a Marxist" (1984:268), implying that in a "complex" sense Polanyi was a Marxist. My argument is that in neither a simple nor a complex sense was Polanyi a Marxist, but I agree with Halperin, albeit for different motives, that a consideration of the relationship is enlightening.

Halperin contended that "substantivism, as formulated and elaborated by Karl Polanyi, derives from Marxian origins and . . . contains fundamentally Marxian concepts" (1984:246) and that the "questions Marx and Polanyi asked about the economy and the methods they proposed for studying it are strikingly similar, although there is little doubt that Polanyi went beyond Marx" (1984:268). These claims are sweeping and, perhaps, shocking to those with more than a passing familiarity with Marx's and Polanyi's work. They run contrary to my own interpretation of these two scholars' approaches to economic knowledge production. In this section, I explicitly address certain specific arguments made by Halperin over the course of her attempt to substantiate the sweeping claims quoted previously. A broader, implicit refutation of her claims emerges in subsequent sections of this chapter and in the next chapter.

Halperin cites Polanyi's dominance criterion as evidence that he "gave production an important place in his analysis of the economy" (1984:262).[15] Then she takes out of context a 1944 statement by Polanyi to falsely imply that his "almost exclusive emphasis on distribution came only later," namely, in *Trade and Market in the Early Empires*, which was "more widely read by anthropologists" (1984:262). In fact, Polanyi's emphasis did not change between 1944 (*The Great Transformation*) and 1957. The 1944 statement Halperin emphatically misquotes as an asseveration was in fact an interrogative: "But how, then, is order in production and distribution ensured?" Polanyi (1957:47) immediately responds to his own question: "The answer is provided in the main by two principles of behavior not primarily associated with economics: *reciprocity* and *redistribution*."[16]

Not being satisfied with misquoting Polanyi, Halperin (1984:362) fails to paint him with the brush of ethnocentrism with which she paints Marx. Her argument strains credibility on several counts. First, here and earlier in her essay (1984:261–62; cf. Halperin 1977:87), she oversimplifies Marx's exegesis of the categories of conventional economics by leaving exchange out of the equation, a practice that reflects the substantivist tendency to conflate distribution and exchange as locational movements. This conflation distorts the real nature of distribution in classical and Marxist economics as rewards or payments to the factors of production for the role they perform in the production process. Defined in this manner, the process of distribution results in patterned relations that mirror relations of production or class relations.

Next, Halperin fails to mention Marx's well-known statement of caveats regarding the application of bourgeois economic categories to noncapitalist social formations (Marx 1970:211–12). Finally, she completely misses the real significance of Polanyi's dominance criterion, namely, that it was derived from his recognition that liberal, market capitalism, with its emphasis on the individual economic agent's practice of the logic of rational action, was historically and culturally unique. According to this criterion, socially organized humanity outside of liberal, market capitalism was free of the necessity of practicing means–end rationality in supplying themselves "with the means of material want satisfaction" (Polanyi 1968a:216). Polanyi's position was a major issue of contention in the formalist–substantivist controversy and is considered by some to reflect a peculiar strain of reverse ethnocentrism that probably grew out of Polanyi's rejection of the naturalistic economism of post-Smithian classical or liberal economics, that is, the belief that a socially disembedded, separate economy of individual actors who seek material gain is a natural condition of humanity (Polanyi 1957:125–26, 269–73).

Marx (1970:211) viewed liberal, market capitalism as a historically developed formation embodying elements or relations of earlier formations. Marx's position is controversial, even among Marxists, because it appears to contradict his critique of political economy as well as his conceptualization of precapitalist economic formations and is vulnerable to the charge of Eurocentrism. Marx rejected liberal socioeconomic theories arising with capitalism for reifying the individual and society, thereby obscuring linkages between actual living persons and social institutions (cf. Wessman 1981:76). Unlike Polanyi, however, Marx did not view individuals "as being totally subsumed by social forces, unable to move for [themselves]" (Wessman 1981:75), but as possessing agency and the capability of devising strategies for social change.[17]

Both classical Marxism and substantivism limit the role of commodity production and market exchange in precapitalist formations and emphasize how the process of producing and circulating material wealth in such formations is differently organized, both socially and ideologically (culturally), than in capitalist formations. Perhaps as a consequence of their critique of formal economics, substantivism (and to a lesser extent, Marxism) gives too little weight to individual agency, to decision making, and to commodity value in the precapitalist and mixed-capitalist economic process.

RATIONALITY, ECONOMIC PROCESS, AND COMMODITY CULTURE(S): POLANYI AND WEBER

Polanyi's conflation of capitalist rationality with means–end rationality emerges most clearly in his narrow interpretation of Max Weber. According to Polanyi (1968b:136), Weber

> asserted that "economic" meant provision for the means of material want-satisfaction, but also insisted that the intrinsically "economic" behavior was of "pure rationality" (*zweckrational*), the most typical form of which we encounter on the stock exchange. Owing to this ambiguity, Weber's terms proved a very useful instrument of inquiry into capitalist economy, in which the same conjunction of meanings prevails. However, outside of capitalism, the inclusion of pure ra-

> tionality into the definition of "economic behavior" made that term unsuitable for general economic history.

It is unclear from this source which specific Weber text Polanyi had access to, but my assumption is that it was a pre-1956 (fourth edition) German edition of the two-volume *Wirtschaft und Gesellschaft: Grundriss der verstehenden Soziologie.*

In any case, my source is the 1978 English translation of the 1956–1964 German editions published in two volumes as *Economy and Society: An Outline of Interpretative Sociology* (Weber 1978). In chapter 2 of volume 1 of this edition, titled "Sociological Categories of Economic Action," Weber's discussion of rational economic action is at odds with Polanyi's interpretation, especially in view of Weber's specific insistence that the general concept applies to primitive economies (1978, 1:64). Nor is Polanyi's interpretation consistent with Weber's well-known emphasis on capital accounting, formal bookkeeping, the method of enterprise, or the "formal rationality of economic action" as the sine qua non of capitalism (Weber 1961:207; 1978, 1:85–86, 90–100).

In short, it was Polanyi, not Weber, who conflated capitalist rationality with means–end rationality. It appears that Polanyi rejected Weber's approach because he judged him to be "an economic liberal and a strong believer in the vitality of the capitalist economy" and the market system as well as for his heuristic acceptance of the "primacy of the economic factor" (Polanyi 1968b:135–36). But Weber, unlike Polanyi, did not make the mistake of conflating the cost-accounting form of rationality found in capitalism with the prudent means–end rationality or a "rational attitude" (Schumpeter 1950:122; cf. Bottomore 1985:39) exercised by humanity in all economies of record.[18]

Another point that needs to be clarified regarding Polanyi's interpretation of Weber is that Polanyi cleverly redefined Weber's distinction between "formal and substantive rationality of economic action" (1957:71–72) as the "substantive and formal meaning" of "'economic' in all the social sciences" (Polanyi 1968b:139). What this redefinition enabled Polanyi to do was to appropriate Weber's terms without his focus on the "degree to which the provisioning of given groups or persons (no matter how delimited) with goods is shaped by economically oriented social action under some criterion (past, present, or potential) of ultimate values . . . regardless of the nature of these ends" (Weber 1978, 1:85). In other words, Polanyi consolidated all of Weber's rational action concerns under the "formal meaning" rubric and reduced the "substantive" rubric to material provisioning without rational action. Sahlins, in his sequel (1976) to *Stone Age Economics*, managed to provocatively address the rationality question, only to outdo Polanyi by removing both the economy and practical reason from the realm of observable social conduct into the arcane and ethereal domain of symboling—much to the delight of cultural interpretivists everywhere who want to sever the dialectical connection between the mental and the material.

With regard to defining the economy or economic field of activity, Polanyi and his associates were right to emphasize the importance of a substantive concept focused on material want satisfaction or "the livelihood of man from the material angle" (Polanyi et al. 1957:241) but wrong to preclude economizing behavior or economic calculation from premarket or nonmarket economies. Godelier correctly reminds us that "there exists in all societies an empirical knowledge—which is often very advanced—of society's productive capacities, together with rules for a measured use of these resources so as to ensure their reproduction, and with it the reproduction of social life" (1986:198; cf. Cook 1974a:819–20; Little 1991:148–49). "Measured use" implies reasonable decision making.

Does this mean that substantivism has nothing to offer economic anthropologists who study nonmarket integrated economies? No, because considering the writings of Polanyi and *Trade and Market in the Early Empires* alone, there is still much to be mined regarding organization and process in such economies. Does substantivism have anything useful to say about market-integrated economies? Yes, because substantivists, including Polanyi, have a lot of interesting ideas about market organization and process that await empirical application. Despite the muddling of popular and scientific meanings of "market" in Polanyi's work (Cook 1968a:968; cf. Cook 1968b:32–47), Carrier (1997:27) may be right to note that in one sense Polanyi's main point was that "the market is a conception of the world rather than the world itself" (even though Polanyi himself never expressed it so succinctly as a general proposition). Still, substantivists, especially Polanyi, were prone to conflate ontological and epistemological objects and did so regularly regarding locational, transactional, and allocational meanings of the market.

Weber is a better source on the notion of "substantive rationality" than is Polanyi—simply because Weber is more explicit theoretically regarding the cultural or value component than is Polanyi. As I pointed out in 1974 (Cook 1974a:843–44), both Godelier (1972) and Sahlins (1969) made important contributions toward operationalizing substantive rationality. Still, Little may be right that Weber's formal-versus-substantive rationality distinction is "infelicitous" (1991:158 n. 1) and that a focus on rationality that is "prudent" (a term that Little may have borrowed from Weber [1978, 1:65], who declared that "the most essential aspect of economic action for practical purposes is the *prudent* choice between ends") is more analytically rewarding.

METHOD, KNOWLEDGE PRODUCTION, AND THE CAPITALIST ECONOMY

Neither Marx nor Polanyi's approach to the society–economy relationship is understandable in terms specific to the previously mentioned framework, but it does provide a general point of departure toward such an understanding. In one sense, Marx and Polanyi espoused different versions of a "society plus economy" approach that places emphasis on prioritizing social relations in the study of the economic process. Marx's approach—because it privileges production over circulation—facilitates a more direct study of the economic process in precapitalist or noncapitalist societies than does Polanyi's. Furthermore, Marx and Polanyi had significantly different methods of knowledge production. Marx made use of bourgeois economic categories in a limited but important way that was precluded by Polanyi's extreme cultural relativism and aversion to the heuristic method and dialectical reasoning.

Whereas for Marx (with appropriate caveats) (1970:211), "bourgeois economy . . . provides a key to the economy of antiquity," for Polanyi, the historical disembedding of capitalist economy from its social matrix and the consequent privileging of the economic sphere made capitalist economic categories inapplicable to precapitalist, premarket economies embedded in their social matrices, where "the needs of livelihood" are organized mainly through noneconomic channels (Polanyi 1957:70). By implication, for Polanyi (1968a:218), Marx's approach was tainted by economism.

Ironically, one of Polanyi's leading spokespersons, George Dalton, advocated an approach to precapitalist economies that conforms to the logic of Marx's "key rule." In taunting anthropologists for their lack of understanding of economics and in explaining "why theory in economic anthropology remains underdeveloped" (1968:x), Dalton asserted, "In order for anthropologists to see what is analytically important in Trobriands' economy they must first understand the structure of industrial capitalism; to understand the special usage of pig-tusk and cowrie money, they must first understand the organization and usage of dollars and francs." This almost reads like a paraphrase of Marx's discussion of his "key rule" (1970:211; cf. Dalton 1968:xi).

Marx qualified his "key rule" immediately by warning that "it is quite impossible to gain this insight in the manner of those economists who obliterate all historical differences and who see in all social phenomena only bourgeois phenomena. If one knows rent, it is possible to understand tribute, tithe, etc., but they do not have to be treated as identical" (1970:211). For Marx, as Terrell Carver points out, "the most abstract categories, though valid (in the sense that they are logical universals) for all forms of society, are nevertheless very much the products of a long historical process of development. They can only be formulated at a late historical stage when social life has become diverse and complex, and only in a developed society do they posses their 'full validity,' their full range of connotations and denotations" (Carver 1975:147–48). Thus, the simple categories of "labor in the abstract" or "money in the abstract" emerge only in a particular sort of society, as expressions of practical social relations in modern, complex societies (Carver 1975:146–47). Such categories are formulated and are fully valid only in such societies.

Given their long period of development, these simpler yet more developed categories can express insights into more complex, less developed forms of the past. For Marx, historical development implies that "past economic forms are 'really' those of the present, but in an undeveloped way, whereas 'objective' understanding only develops when scholars see their own societies critically . . . hence only after criticism of the present (i.e., seeing its 'positive' aspects, and those leading to its negation) do we understand the past" (Carver 1975:149).[19]

Marx's "key rule" appears to invert evolutionary logic. Yet Marx had a complex theory of the evolution of socioeconomic formations as stages in the general development of human society and as an expression of the "unity of the global historic process," which also took into account the distinctive histories of discrete societies (Semenov 1980:40; see also Gellner 1980). As the premier dialectical thinker, Marx's understanding of diachronic processes involving past–present–future relations and of synchronic processes involving part–whole relations was predicated on complex logical principles, such as that the unity of concrete reality is a unity of contradictions (Edgley 1985:143; see also Bhaskar 1991a). Keith Hart has summed up the perspective underlying Marx's "key rule" as follows: "The universalization of capitalist commodity production makes it possible for the first time, according to Marx, to see the simple, general categories underlying human economy. So the most primitive forms are entailed in the most developed expression of commodity economy; and his main analytical effort is directed, teleologically, at the most recent part of a historical process of evolution. In taking his position, Marx is not alone: most of us, self-consciously or otherwise, derive our concepts from the emphases most apparent in our day" (Hart 1982:44–45; cf. Godelier 1986:149).

Polanyi shared Marx's understanding of the counterpoint between the process of capitalist development and the development of economic thought. The removal of production from households to manufactories and factories, the growth of land and labor markets, the subordination of labor to capital, the spread and intensification of machinofacture, and so on represented the rise to dominance of organized economic activity in society and created the necessary material conditions for making the economy an object of thought—hence the inevitable rise of economic theory. Nevertheless, this intersection of espistemology and ontology is more complex in Marx's work than it is in Polanyi's. Both Marx and Polanyi were morally and politically appalled by the human consequences of the rise of capitalism, but, given Marx's more profound methodological engagement with dialectics and empirical social science, his approach is at once more intellectually challenging and analytically productive than Polanyi's.

Polanyi's historicoempirical approach was indifferent to the heuristic method, dialectical or nondialectical, whereas Marx's sophisticated alternation between empirical social science and the dialectical method of political economy translated into a process of knowledge production that was more accommodating of the contradictions in moving between the abstract and concrete, the subjective and objective, and the diachronic and synchronic. Marx could, therefore, integrate the classical economists general concept of economy into his analysis of modes of production, combining approaches that Polanyi labeled as either economistic or societal, to the overall enrichment of his contribution.

Polanyi (1957:125–26, 269–73), on the other hand, opted for a societal approach that left him without the capacity to identify specific substantive economic activities that were all embedded in their societal matrix. In falsely associating all economizing with formal capitalist rationality, Polanyi was also deprived of any rationale for addressing rational choice and human agency in the process of provisioning material needs in non- or precapitalist economies.

In short, if Marx and some Marxists are vulnerable to the charge of Eurocentrism for using formal categories for analyzing precapitalist economies and for assuming that their agents exercise means–end rationality, what is to be said of Polanyi and the substantivists who conflate capitalist rationality with means–end rationality and banish the latter from precapitalist economies?[20]

Polanyi, in effect, recognized that the shifting role of economy in society is institutionally fixed at given historical conjunctures by a particular form that integrates the factors of production (1957:255). Having said that, however, neither Polanyi nor other substantivists have empirically demonstrated in specific cases precisely how a particular form like reciprocity or redistribution actually integrates the factors of production with the rest of the economy. This "dominance criterion," aptly described by Jenkins as the rule that "in the last analysis one mechanism in particular will tend to exert a dominant integrative effect" (1977:79), was derived from Polanyi's earlier (1957) study of historical capitalism and of the classical–neoclassical tradition of economic thought (formal economics). Polanyi traced the emergence of market exchange as the uniquely dominant integrative institution in capitalism and inferred from his analysis that precapitalist economies would have comparable dominant integrative institutions (such as reciprocity and redistribution). Thus, Polanyi's "dominance criterion" exemplifies Marx's rule that "bourgeois economy provides a key to the economy of antiquity" (1970:211), albeit with less profound analytical implications for the origins of commodity circulation. There is no better illustration of the marginal presence of Marx's influence in Polanyi's work than Polanyi's apparent lack of insight into the epistemological origins of his own approach to the "economy of antiquity."[21]

Unquestionably, Polanyi's view of capitalism, not as a mode of production but as an economy dominated by the market, even to the point of transforming land and labor into commodities with a price, determined his circulationist approach to precapitalist economies. Redistribution and reciprocity as described in the anthropological literature were, for him, the likely sources of integrative mechanisms (functional equivalents for the market in his model of capitalist economy) in precapitalist economies. Since the market assumed dominance in capitalism by integrating land and labor into the economy, so would reciprocity and redistribution assume dominance in precapitalist economies. In other words, Polanyi's privileging of circulation over production in his approach to capitalism set a precedent for doing the same in his approach to precapitalist economies. This was an inventive, if ill-fated, exercise in economic typologizing from which Polanyi deviated in his posthumous work on Dahomey (1966), where reciprocity, redistribution, and market exchange were considered as principles operating together, each within a separate sphere and within a single economy—none was considered to be integrative of the entire economy (cf. Salisbury 1968:480). The ethnographic record of primitive and peasant economies is replete with similar cases.[22]

Polanyi accepted the validity of formal economics in the study of market-integrated economies (1957:241) and rejected Marxism, "which seemed to him to lead to an erroneous conception of value and prices" (Godelier 1986:182; cf. Polanyi 1957:126). He also rejected Marxism for "defining classes in economic terms" (Polanyi 1957:151), for a "crude theory of social development" (Polanyi 1957:151–62), and for overstressing the "influence of the economic factor generally, at all times and places" (Polanyi 1968b:134). The latter charge seems also to have eliminated Marxism, in Polanyi's eyes, from contributing to the production of knowledge about the place of economies in noncapitalist societies, something that is confirmed by the paucity of references to Marx in the substantivist magnum opus *Trade and Markets in the Early Empires*.[23]

Polanyi strongly rejected Marx's appreciation of David Ricardo's (1911) theoretical innovations regarding the value aspects of the labor–capital relationship and was adamant in his rejection of Marx's own labor theory of value. Ricardo, according to Polanyi (1957:126), "in a mistaken theorem of tremendous scope . . . invested labor with the sole capacity of constituting value, thereby reducing all conceivable transactions in economic society to the principle of equal exchange in a society of free men." In the context of Polanyi's overriding concern with the place of economies in societies and with an economistic or societal approach to that concern, Ricardo ranks higher than Marx on Polanyi's hit list. Ricardo defined the place of the economic system in society by combining "the hunger and gain motives with the profit motive as a general incentive determining human behavior" (Polanyi 1968b:131). This was instrumental in establishing "the modern concept of a separate autonomous economic system, governed by economic motives, and subject to the economic principle of formal rationality [economizing]" (1968b:132).

DALTON'S GAMBIT AND ITS MUTATIONS

Despite the controversial reactions, principally by nonanthropologists (Rottenberg 1958; Smelser 1959), to the 1957 publication of *Trade and Market in the Early Empires*, it was economist George Dalton's 1961 lead article in *American Anthropologist* "Economic Theory and Primitive Society" that framed the content, tone, language, and the polemical strategy and tactics of the "great debate" (LeClair and Schneider 1968:11–12). My article in the same journal (Cook 1966b) was a direct response to Dalton, as were previous articles by Burling (1962) and LeClair (1962), and was written to turn his provocative polemical style against him. Critics of "pithiness" in the language of the debate will find ample precedent in Dalton's article as exemplified by assertions like "primitive economy is different from market industrialism not in degree but in kind" (1961:164; cf. Polanyi in Dalton 1968:67) or sweeping categorical imperatives like "economic theory cannot be fruitfully applied to the study of primitive communities" (1961:144). In short, Dalton directly challenged the prevailing practice of economic anthropology as demonstrated in its best studies of "primitive" economies, including Raymond Firth's (1939) canonical *Primitive Polynesian Economy*. Given the nature of the challenge embodied in Polanyi's writings from 1944 to 1957, controversy was inevitable and justifiable.[24]

In a perfectly screened universe of discourse, Dalton's 1961 manuscript would not have been published until he was editorially compelled to substantively address the canonical texts in economic anthropology that disproved his thesis of the nonapplicability of formal economic theory to the study of primitive economy. From this perspective, it is troubling that Dalton's article was published without the journal requiring him to demonstrate exactly how Raymond Firth's application of neoclassical economic theory in *Primitive Polynesian Economy* (1939) distorted Tikopian economics and why Herskovits's application of it in his *Economic Anthropology* distorted our understanding of comparative economics. The fact that Dalton or, for that matter, Marshall Sahlins (1969, 1972)—himself a Polynesianist who took up the Polanyi–Dalton antieconomics banner—never produced a point-by-point refutation of Firth's selective application of neoclassical economics speaks volumes about substantivism and about the lax standards governing anthropological discourse in the United States at the time.

Aside from the controversial content of Dalton's programmatic statements as chief substantivist spokesman, the main reason why passions ran so high on the formalist side of the debate, even in such mild-mannered, even-tempered souls like Richard Salisbury (1969:89), was in reaction to provocatively unfair discursive tactics engaged in by Dalton (cf. Cook 1966b:334). The most egregious of these, the utter disregard of studies like those of Firth and Herskovits that contradicted his main thesis, has already been mentioned.

Three additional examples from his 1969 article will suffice to make my case: 1) a tortured attempt to define the meaning of the applicability of formal economics to primitive economies so as to eliminate its successful application by anthropologists like Salisbury (1962), whose study he cavalierly dismissed as illustrating a "simplistic notion of what 'applying economic theory' means" [1969:67–68]; 2) misrepresenting opponents' arguments (for example, Dalton wrote (1969:68) that "Cook (1966) criticizes Polanyi and myself for analyzing in detail the structure of traditional subsistence economies such as the Trobriand Islands in Malinowski's time"; I actually stated, "It is undeniable that anthropology can still profit from the study of extinct societies as well as from the study of extant 'primitive' societies; and, in the field of economics, substantive theory offers one meaningful approach to such studies" [Cook 1966b:325]);[25] and 3) accusing anthropologists who selectively applied neoclassical economic theory to the study of primitive or peasant economies of misunderstanding or oversimplifying economics without providing any specifics as to where their analyses went wrong or what an alternative substantivist analysis might be (Dalton 1969:67–68; cf. Sahlins 1972:xi).[26]

The published record indicates that Dalton did subsequently moderate and partially revise some of his extreme views. Only one year after the publication of his 1961 article, he went on record as accepting evidence of the expansion of "economic activities organized on the market principle" (Bohannan and Dalton 1962:24) in Third World economies. By the mid-1960s, he admitted that "small-scale peasant societies . . . can be considered analytically with the concepts and questions from large scale American and European market economies" (1965:122), a position he later reiterated in slightly different terms: "those of the thousands of economies studied by anthropologists that are underdeveloped, small-scale market systems—peasant economies . . . can be fruitfully analyzed with the concepts of conventional economics" (1969:66). This reiteration was accompanied by Dalton's clarification that Polanyi's approach was limited to "primitive and archaic economies in which market organization is absent or confined to petty transactions" (1969:79). He also conceded that "conventional economics is relevant to the commercialized sectors of peasant economic organization (i.e., where dependence on purchased land, wage-labor, and the market sale of produce is quantitatively important) and useful in quantifying economic performance—the amounts and composition of produce—for any economy, primitive, peasant, industrial capitalist (1969:65), but he continued to insist that "interesting questions about the organization of traditional, primitive economies" require "conceptual categories different from those used in conventional economics" (1969:66).

Compared with his 1961 views, and even with those of most substantivists in 1969 and long after, Dalton clearly made important clarifications and concessions to his critics. Even so, in the early 1970s (1971:7), he combatively rejected Firth's thesis that the exercise of choice by nonmarket subjects like the Tikopia reflected the principle of rationality. Dalton to the end remained under the spell of Polanyi's idiosyncratic interpretation of Weber's concept of formal rationality.[27]

It is noteworthy that writing several years after the debate had waned, Lisa Peattie, in the context of characterizing Sol Tax's analysis of "penny capitalism" in a Redfieldian "folk" society, asserted that "Firth's monumental studies showed that even non-monetized societies, in which 'social elements interpenetrate and overlay the economic organization' [quoting Firth 1939:352], could be analyzed according to the major categories of economics and could follow basic principles of maximization" (1979:86). To the extent that her view was representative of postdebate discourse in economic anthropology, the substantivist thesis of the nonapplicability of neoclassical economics to nonmarket/noncapitalist economies won few converts.

WHITHER ECONOMIC ANTHROPOLOGY? A CRITIQUE OF THE "GREAT DEBATE'S" POSTMORTEMS AND BEYOND

With the notable exception of the discussion in Richard Wilk's (1996:3–13) clearly written and carefully researched textbook, most postmortems of the great debate fall short of adequately representing its nature, substance, relevance, and outcome. Stuart Plattner's postmortem trivializes the debate as a combination of "theoretical pronouncements and polemics" in which the "argument was hot and heavy, and generated a good bit of heat in proportion to the light" (1989:14). Plattner may be right that "neither side won the argument" (1989:15; cf. Dalton 1971:6), but he glossed over viewpoints from the sociology of knowledge and epistemology that were brought to bear against Polanyi and the substantivists to expose the romantic and ideological underpinnings of their approach (Cook 1966b, 1974a). He criticizes both camps equally for failing to "put their approach to empirical test" and asserts that "the formalists felt they were carrying the social scientific flag because their approach was nomothetic and generalizing" (1989:14).

This line of criticism reflects confusion about the history of economic anthropology and oversimplifies formalist discourse about scientific method. The overriding issue was not empirical testing of hypotheses but rather supporting explanations with rigorous empirical evidence to rule out alternative explanations. The record is clear that Firth, Salisbury, and other selective appliers of conventional economics had followed this procedure in their studies of nonmarket or "primitive" economies and that Polanyi, Dalton, and Sahlins in their critiques of formalist economic anthropology never falsified the empirical applications of conventional economics by their own application of substantive economics. The extreme cultural and historical relativism of substantivist discourse inevitably led to a formalist defense of the quest for general theory of cross-cultural sets of societies—but this was only one of the reasons formalists carried Plattner's "social scientific flag."

Richard Wilk's appreciation of the role of controversy in affecting knowledge production and discourses about it served him well in situating the formalist-versus-substantivist debate in the history of economic anthropological and philosophical thought. In his words (1996:4), "Economic anthropology as a sub-discipline was at least partially created by the formalist-substantivist debate; to this day, this is the part of economic anthropology that most other anthropologists, economists, and sociologists know about, the part that appears in introductory anthropology textbooks." Whereas Wilk's characterization of the debate as "largely philosophical and academic" and focused on issues relating to "human nature" (1996:12–13) downplays issues of method and discursive standards it raised, he recognized, to his credit, that the debate also raised "wider questions about social change and evolution" and about "how the economy relates to other classic objects of anthropological study like kinship and ritual" (1996:12). These issues and more were at stake in formalist attempts to support the selective use of neoclassical theory and to place limits on the substantivist approach with regard to the peasant market economies of the capitalist world (Cook 1966b:324–25; 1969:398–99; cf. Cancian 1966:465; Fried 1968:239–40).

Despite the tendency among recent commentators on the formalist-versus-substantivist debate to declare it a draw (Isaac 1993:229; Plattner 1989:15; Wilk 1996:13) as well as the boost in popularity for Polanyi and the substantivist approach derived from the surge in culturally focused studies and an interest in trust-generating embedment (Sayer 1997:19–20), the fact remains that, if economic anthropology embraced substantivism with its belief that each economy works according to unique cultural meanings and principles, then cross-economy generalizations would be impossible, and anthropologists would be limited to a "purely descriptive chronicling of concrete phenomena" (Little 1991:155). Scientific inquiry would be held hostage to the bizarre contention that to assume reasonable and prudent decision making in human affairs before the rise of capitalism (or on its periphery) is to eth nocentrically impose a bourgeois business outlook on them (Sahlins 1972:xi–xiv; cf. Cook 1974b:355–58).

CONCLUSIONS

Like it or not, issues that were at the heart of the formalist–substantivist controversy in the 1960s and 1970s remain alive in economic anthropological discourse today because of 1) persisting claims for the relevancy of Polanyi's concept of "embeddedness" (Granovetter 1992; Narotsky 1997; Sayer 1997:19–20), 2) references to peculiar subsistence logics implied in Polanyi's emphasis on the substantive meaning of the "economic" (Nash 2001), and 3) references to corresponding counterclaims in favor of a universal rationality postulate and a rejection of extreme forms of cultural relativism (Little 1991:chap. 7; Wilk 1996:esp. chap. 2). There is also an eclectic approach that places limits on all three major approaches—formalist, substantivist, and Marxist—and advocates a sort of ad hoc, opportunistic or selective application of competing paradigms to situations or time frames where they seem to make optimal heuristic or explanatory sense (Donham 1990; Wilk 1996:esp. chap. 6).

Within this discursive context, I have reconsidered the contributions of Marx, Weber, Polanyi and others from the perspective of retaining a sharp focus on the economic process of commodity production, circulation, and distribution—and the critical role of individual agency in it—and have found Polanyi's to be especially limited. In contrast to both Marx and Weber, who do not deprive subjects in precommodity economies of the exercise of means–end rationality, Polanyi for all intents and purposes does so in his extreme formulation of Weber's distinction between formal and substantive rationality and his identification of means–end rationality with market economy. Unlike Marx and, to a certain degree, Weber, whose method promoted a view of the interplay between the economic and the noneconomic as mutually constitutive, Polanyi was adamant in viewing the economy (or the "economic") as being constituted by society (or the "noneconomic"). Polanyi shared with Marx and Weber a fundamentally substantive view of the economy as a process of provisioning of material wants but, unlike them, lost sight of individual human agency in this social process. In effect, Polanyi's thesis of the "economy as an instituted process" is one-sided in emphasizing the "noneconomic" origins and meaning of the "economic" in a way that privileges structure over agency to the point of precluding any role for enculturated subjects beyond following the rules.

Polanyi was right to emphasize the close fit between conventional economics and the substantive economies of market capitalism and on that basis to question the comparative applicability of conventional economic knowledge. Classical and neoclassical economics were (and are) largely indifferent to the empirical record of precapitalist, non-Western economies. Nevertheless, these limitations do not, ipso facto, make conventional economics inapplicable to nonconventional economies. As the best work of the formalists demonstrated, the question of applicability is one that must be answered operationally through empirical analysis. Moreover, acceptance of the fundamental unity of humanity's economic experience and of a multilineal civilizational process from a common (or similar) species' origin implies that the interplay between the general and the specific, or the universal and the particular, are complex in each specific historical or ethnographic case so that no approach to knowledge production can legitimately be excluded or rejected a priori—especially on grounds of Euro- or ethnocentrism.

Unlike Weber and Polanyi, Marx's privileging of use, exchange, and abstract labor/money value provided his approach with a method for studying the economic process in all social formations. His position that use value is realizable in the absence of exchange as a regular condition in the so-called natural economy and in precapitalist formations generally undermined the recognition of the role of commodity production before the emergence of intercommunity division of labor and specialization. Nevertheless, Marx's dialectical linking of use, exchange, and abstract value in the commodity concept provides a basis for understanding how the reckoning of value emerged from subjective origins through progressively objective determinations that facilitate more accurate labor-time calculations of equivalence.

Marx's historical relativism, like Weber's but unlike Polanyi's, was limited methodologically by his recognition that the study of capitalism (and theoretical approaches to it) provided tools for understanding its precapitalist origins and, consequently, the economic life of our species. Marx's emphasis on relations of production as the organizing principle of historical economies—a conceptual insight gained from his analysis of the capitalist mode of production—enabled him to expose the crucial differences between the latter and various precapitalist modes in a more precise way than either Weber's focus on cultural superstructure or Polanyi's on transactional modes. This has been borne out in the study of so-called Third World or developing economies during the second half of the twentieth century where approaches derivative from Marx or creatively combining Marx and Weber have proven to be more significant in economic knowledge production than those derived from Polanyi.

NOTES

1. One notable exception to this trend is the thoughtfully provocative contribution by Susana Narotsky (1997). Richard Wilk (1996) also deserves credit for an imaginative, eloquent, and eclectic effort to propose new directions for the subfield.

2. The combination of sound reasoning, clear writing, and astute comparative ethnographic analysis in Herskovits's (1960) textbook is impressive. His qualified acceptance of Polanyi's (1957:46) thesis that "man's economy . . . is submerged in his social relationships" provided a solution for the formalist–substantivist debate before it began. Herskovits recognized that the "process of economizing . . . is essentially based on the broader organization of society" but emphasized that "All choices . . . however they may be influenced by considerations of social standing, social claims, and social assets, are ultimately the choices of individuals" (1960:7). For him, individual choices were necessarily informed by cultural values, by the "cultural definition of wants and the conventions that dictate how and when they are to be regarded as adequately satisfied" (1960:8).

An earlier, valuable survey of the subfield was Richard Thurnwald's *Economics in Primitive Communities* (1932), which was ethnographically comprehensive, thoughtful, and pioneering for his comparative approach to sociopoliticoeconomic evolution with an emphasis on stratification. Although Thurnwald anticipated Polanyi in rejecting both the applicability of conventional economics to the study of "primitive" economies (1932:285) and an "abstract *homo economicus*" in favor of "several *homines oeconomicos*" (1932:4), the "spirit of primitive economics" was, for him, not incompatible with the presence of market exchange (p. 159), private property (p. 276), and the "accumulative process" (pp. 287–88). He emphasized the familial, communal, and kinship organization of precapitalist economic life but did not deny a role for the "plans and calculations of the individual" (1932:xi–xii) and also had much to say about the evolution of money and value (pp. 252–65). Whereas Thurnwald emphasized a predominant concern with concrete use and/or symbolic value and the lack of concern with abstract value and material gain in precapitalist societies (pp. xiii, 179), he did not hesitate to identify economic activities in such societies that "suggested the idea of productive possessions and of interest on capital" (1932:205).

3. This essay was published earlier in a revised form as "The Economy as Instituted Process" in *Trade and Market in the Early Empires* (Polanyi et al. 1957:243–69).

4. This means that Godelier's (1972:17–21) devastating critique of Oskar Lange's argument that the principle of economic rationality is a historical product of capitalism is equally applicable to Polanyi.

5. It is instructive here to compare the fair and reasoned appraisal of the best formalist studies like Firth's *Primitive Polynesian Economy* by Daniel Fusfeld (1957:352–53) in his contribution to *Trade and Market in the Early Empires* (note 2) with the following blanket indictment by Sahlins (1972:xi): "'Formalism . . .' amounts to . . . . [applying] the ready-made models of orthodox Economics, especially the 'microeconomics,' taken as universally valid and applicable *grosso modo* to the primitive societies . . . it is . . . the perspective of Business, for the formalist method must consider the primitive economies as underdeveloped versions of our own." Aside from completely misrepresenting the careful and selective use of economics by Firth, Salisbury, and other formalists, Sahlins avoids seriously addressing the ethnocentrism/Eurocentrism issue, which would have required him to show why "unorthodox" economics is not as tainted by this accusation as is the orthodox variety.

6. Marx, on the other hand, interprets Aristotle differently as stating "quite clearly that the money-form of the commodity is only a more developed aspect of the simple form of value, i.e., of the expression of the value of a commodity in some other commodity chosen at random" (1977:151). Moreover, for him, "Aristotle's genius is displayed precisely by his discovery of a relation of equality in the value-expression of commodities" (1977:152).

7. Halperin (1977:18), in an effort to develop a substantive approach to production, admits that "the focus of Karl Polanyi's work is distribution" but adds that "he was also concerned with problems of production . . . although much less explicitly." Jenkins (1977:72–73) incisively exposed the shortcomings of the substantivist attempt to deal with production as locational and appropriational movements as exemplified in George Dalton's discussion of production processes and their mode of organization in primitive African economies which "provided . . . no conceptual specification of the nature of internal economic production processes" (1977:85).

8. Polanyi (1957:255) expresses the dominance criterion as follows: "Traditional groupings of economies which roughly approximate a classification according to dominant forms of integration are illuminating. What historians are wont to call 'economic systems' seem to fall fairly into this pattern. Dominance of a form of integration is here identified with the degree to which it comprises land and labor in society. . . . The rise of the market to a ruling force in the economy can be traced by noting the extent to which land and food were mobilized through exchange, and labor was turned into a commodity free to be purchased in the market." This statement highlights the origin of Polanyi's dominance criterion in his study of the rise of the capitalist market economy. Nevertheless, in this same paragraph, Polanyi refrains from assigning reciprocity or redistribution the role of dominant forms of integration—rather, "ties of kinship," "ties of fealty," and "temple or palace" are assigned that role in "savage society," "feudal society," and "floodwater empires," respectively. This mode of classification is considered by Polanyi to represent an alternative to the "historically untenable" Marxist approach to societal classification "which flowed from the conviction that the character of the economy was set by the status of labor."

9. This is the approach I proposed (1974a:815–23) to redefine the formal-versus-substantive problem in economic anthropology and to shift the theoretical focus in the subdiscipline away from a privileging of exchange and distribution in the sense of product-handling and product-receiving processes and toward a privileging of production.

10. The concept has recently invaded the discourse of economic geography, much to the dismay of Martin and Sunley (2001), who are critical of the trend toward "vague theory" that includes terms and notions "cherry-picked" from this or that branch of cultural or social theory, rapidly accepted, and "assigned an unquestioned profundity before they have been adequately defined and conceptualized" (2001:153). According to them, the term "embeddedness" typifies this trend.

11. In his comments on Dalton's article, Lorenz Löffler observes that "a classification of 'economies' and an outline of types is no substitute for a general theory of economics" but goes on to say (1969:86) that "Dalton himself denounces any claim in this direction as unrealistic. For him there can be nothing but theories relating to special segments of the economic field, and, in consequence, he has to reduce all attempts to frame a suprasegmental theory to the level of segmental theories or to an even lower level where their value is to be judged against folkviews; the theories of Western economists, on the other hand, are exempt from any such 'proof.'" Löffler then draws on a similar dispute in sociology that clarifies the formalist–substantivist controversy (1969:87): "There are sociologists who cumulate segmental theories but denounce any quest for a theory of society as modern metaphysics. The trouble with anthropologists is that they have folkviews (and ethnography) on the one hand and a yearning for meta-theories (and general anthropology) on the other hand, while segmental theories are at best in the making and generally start either from the folkviews (new ethnography) or the general theories (old ethnology). Whatever the foundations of a general theory—behaviorism, functionalism, structuralism, etc.—its results are not to be measured against folkviews, but only against the possibility of deducing from its set of axioms the fundamentals of the different segmental theories. And in order to yield this possibility, the notions of any suprasegmental theory must, as a matter of fact, be more comprehensive. It is useless, therefore, to maintain that the proponents of such theories have misunderstood the conceptions used by West-

ern economists: it will be necessary to 'misconceive' them in order to proceed. In this sense, e.g., economizing and maximizing may be principles of any economic system, irrespective of whether they are consciously employed (and hence traceable to folkviews) or even calculated (and hence a subject of 'higher' economics)."

12. As I have noted, the 1961 Dalton was not the same Dalton encountered in 1969, 1971, and later. He became less aggressive and intransigent in his dissemination of Polanyi's views and less combative and more eclectic in expressing his own views on many issues. I like to think that this process of change was aided by Dalton's recognition that his polemical adversaries had made some good points. Nevertheless, Jenkins expressed a larger truth in his judgment that many years after Polanyi et al. laid out the substantivist position, "the leading protagonist of substantivism, George Dalton, is unable to achieve a higher degree of theoretical rigor in conceptualizing the economy" (1977:71–72).

13. Granovetter's approach to embedment, which distinguishes between "undersocialized" and "oversocialized" views, is a step in the direction of operationalizing the concept, but he still resorts to statements that describe his approach as threading his way between these views "by analyzing how behavior is embedded in concrete, ongoing systems of social relations" (1992:22). As far as I am concerned, Granovetter's language should be "disembedded" to add clarity and precision to this analysis.

14. Without citing names (though he is probably referring either to Godelier or to Keith Hart), Isaac asserted that "some Marxists argue . . . that Marxian analysis in its various forms renders a separate economic anthropology both obsolete and unnecessary" (1993:229). I certainly have never argued for the subfield's demise on these grounds, nor do I sympathize with such views.

15. There are, for example, nine separate page citations for "Marx" in the author index in Polanyi's *The Great Transformation* (1957:314). The most important of these involve Polanyi's rejection of the Ricardo–Marx labor theory of value (p. 126), Marx's economic class analysis (pp. 151–52), or his politics. Polanyi did seem to have a favorable view of Marx's early writings focused on "the totality of society and the noneconomic nature of man" (p.151); however, his definitive judgment was that Marx's "societal approach . . . was sapped by the economistic element inherited from the classics" (1968b:134).

16. Halperin's emphatic misquote is as follows (1984:262): "In *The Great Transformation* [1957:47], Polanyi clearly stated his concern for discovering 'order in *production* and *distribution* processes in pre-industrial societies'" (Halperin's emphasis). Even though Halperin goes out of her way to criticize what she considers Dalton's misrepresentation of Polanyi, this episode demonstrates that she borrowed Dalton's penchant for misquoting sources to bolster specious arguments.

17. Little carries this a step further in asserting that Marx's "materialism incorporates the core elements of rational choice theory. It postulates that individuals will act to serve their material interests" (1989:21).

18. It seems clear from these statements by Weber that Schumpeter's emphasis on the prevalence of a "rational attitude" (1950:122) or "rational habit" (1950:123) in noncapitalist economies is not incompatible with Weber's views as Bottomore implies (1985:45 n. 1). Elsewhere, however, Weber made references to "types of action which, though actually oriented to economic considerations, do not know calculation" (1978, 1:107). Here Weber seemed to have in mind hunters and gatherers with

a traditional orientation or whose economic action is "affectually determined," by which he seemed to imply semi-instinctual (1978, 1:107). Weber also referred to societal conditions where economically oriented action is dominated by religious faith, warlike passions, or attitudes of personal loyalty as exhibiting "a very low level of rational calculation" (1978, 1:107). He also posits money as the "propagator of calculation," but his long discussion of calculations in kind showed that he really meant to emphasize that money was a propagator of *formal* calculations. In any case, Schumpeter made important and welcome clarification and extension of Weber's position by proposing that "the rational attitude . . . forced itself on the human mind primarily from economic necessity; it is the everyday economic task to which we [*Homo sapiens*] . . . owe our elementary training in rational thought and behavior . . . the economic pattern is the matrix of logic" (1950:122–23). Schumpeter further contended that this primordial role was due to the "inexorable definiteness and, in most case, the quantitative character that distinguish the economic from other spheres of human action, perhaps also to the unemotional drabness of the unending rhythm of economic wants and satisfactions" (1950:123).

19. A concise statement of the meaning of simple versus complex concepts in Marxist analysis was made by Zbigniew Kowalewski in his comments on Dalton's article in *Current Anthropology* : "Marxian analysis shows that the simplicity of economic categories is the result of a complex process, that simple categories appear on the highest levels of a society's development, in extremely differentiated social wholes, while on the lower levels of development the categories are more concrete, more complex" (1969:85).

20. Sahlins also finds himself mired in self-contradiction on this point. In his 1972 book, he proclaims the reprehensibility of any application of bourgeois economics to the study of nonbourgeois economy but in 1974 writes, "Yet as Marx said truly, the anatomy of man is the key to the anatomy of the ape. The more developed economic system makes an explicit differentiation of categories that remain combined, ambiguous, or only virtual in the less-developed one. In the same way, the implications foreshadowed in a given intellectual perspective become explicit only in more evolved versions of it" (1976:87). He cannot have it both ways.

Godelier also contradicts himself on this issue. First, he ignores Marx's qualified argument supporting selective use of the general categories of economic analysis in the study of precapitalist economies and emphasizes instead that Marx "disputed the possibility of 'generalizing' the theorems of political economy to pre-capitalist modes of production" (1986:179–80). For some reason, he chose not to apply his earlier critique (1972:17–22) of Lange to Polanyi since he seems to accept Polanyi's critique of Weber and Parsons for viewing the market as a prototype of all rational economic institutions (1986:184–85) and credits Polanyi for seeking to "jettison every ethnocentric a priori" (1986:186). On the other hand, he rightly criticizes Polanyi for holding that "only the modern generalized market economy renders economic 'calculation' both possible in a formal sense and necessary in a practical sense. In fact . . . there exists in all societies an empirical knowledge—which is often very advanced—of society's productive capacities, together with rules for a measured use of these resources so as to ensure their reproduction, and with it the reproduction of social life" (1986:198). Just like Sahlins, Godelier wants to have his cake and eat it too regarding Polanyi's position on rationality and irrationality in economics.

21. Polanyi probably had Marx's "key rule" in mind when he accused him of making "a grave mistake" in allowing "the discovery of the importance of the 'economic' under a market economy" to induce him "to overstress the influence of the economic factor generally, at all times and places" (1968b:134). Polanyi seemed to be unconcerned (or unaware) that his "dominance criterion" for structuring and identifying nonmarket economies was, in fact, his own version of Marx's rule.

22. Rather than ignoring production in his analysis of the economic process and of economic integration through exchange, reciprocity, and redistribution (Cook 1969:385; 1974a:815–16), Polanyi underprivileged it.

23. The only substantive reference to Marx in the main body of the text is one paragraph in Harry W. Pearson's chapter "The Economy Has No Surplus" (Polanyi et al. 1957:333–34).

24. For some reason, the favorable view of Daniel Fusfeld about Firth's work seemed to fall on deaf ears among his colleagues in the original Polanyi group and every other substantivist. He recognized that Firth's "study of the economy of the Polynesian island of Tikopia makes use of the concepts of modern economics" but that he "never allows those concepts to obscure the relationship between economic life and kinship, magic, ritual and chieftainship, nor to obscure reciprocal or redistributive forms of economic activity" (1957:352). Moreover, Fusfeld (1957:353) argued, "While the weaknesses of Herskovits' and Goodfellow's work arise from a largely uncritical acceptance of economic theory, Firth's success is due in large part to this selective use of its concepts and principles. His awareness of the methodological pitfalls involved in economic theory is typified by the statement that 'the anthropologist accepts as valid the body of economic doctrine' but 'he can absorb only a very small part of it into his conceptual apparatus for the study of primitive society.'" If this fair interpretation of Firth's contribution would have been shared and communicated by Polanyi and Dalton and caused them to modify their inflexible position regarding the nonapplicability of formal economics, then there would have been less justification for a "great debate."

25. As in this instance, it was Dalton's tendency to fail to cite page numbers when he was intentionally misrepresenting an opponent's views in the published record. Like Dalton, Marvin Harris (1980:234–35) was also skilled at misquoting targeted opponents. He distorted my definition of the economy, which I carefully constructed (1974a:808–12), by quoting my 1966 summary of the standard definition of economists (1966b:335) as if it were my own definition. This kind of willful misrepresentation of scholarly work precludes any possibility of progressive knowledge production.

26. Rereading the first two formalist responses to Dalton's article, by Burling (1962) and LeClair (1962), I remain impressed by their muted, dispassionate tone. Even LeClair, who had been an associate of Herskovits, admitted that the time was ripe for a "systematic reexamination" of his position and credits Dalton with presenting a "revolutionary case" for the "substitution of a new basic premise" (LeClair and Schneider 1968:188). LeClair's critique of Dalton's position was incisive, but I felt that the substantivist position needed to be approached in the more passionate and ideologically charged terms that characterized Dalton's and especially Polanyi's discourse. At the time, still another dispassionate critique would have been redundant.

27. My critique (cf. Cook 1966b:324–25) may have stimulated Dalton in subsequent publications to restrict the applicability of Polanyi's economics to primitive and

archaic economies and to reiterate the applicability of conventional economics to the study of peasant economies in his 1969 article. In any case, together with the thesis of Polanyi's romanticism (which Dalton acknowledged [1969:79] but never refuted), the applicability thesis was the core of my 1966 critique and, according to Isaac, was "the major reason it attracted so much initial and enduring attention" (Isaac 1993:227).

My 1966 contribution to the controversy reflected my background as an undergraduate economics major; I did graduate work in economics before I took my first course in anthropology. Nevertheless, I am sure that I was among those economic anthropologists who were chided for their "naive economics" (Sahlins 1972:xi; cf. Dalton 1969:63, 67). In retrospect, it is ironic that several years after I discontinued graduate study in economics, when I finally realized that I was more interested in social science than I was in the mathematical/statistical sciences, I became a defender of the use of economics by anthropologists. By all odds, given my background as a defector from the economics field, I was a prime candidate for embracing Polanyi's substantivism when I first began to study economic anthropology. Nevertheless, I found the selective use of economics by anthropologists like Raymond Firth and Richard Salisbury and their rationale for doing so more convincing than the rationale for its nonuse offered by Polanyi and Dalton. Even so, I never shared the view of extreme formalists, like Schneider (1974) and Belshaw (1969), whose commitment to the means–end rationality principle translated into a social exchange approach to all behavior.

5

Commodity Value, Culture, and Economy

A cursory review of the history of economic thought verifies that "the theory of value has always been regarded as the corner-stone of economic analysis" (Fraser 1947:56). There are four senses in which value is understood in economics discourse: as 1) cost value, 2) use value, 3) exchange value, and 4) esteem value (Fraser 1947:59). Of these, only the latter two meanings regularly concern conventional economists (Fraser 1947:60), whereas cost value, exchange value, and, to a lesser extent, use value are concerns in the Ricardo–Marx tradition of analysis (cf. Fraser 1947:123). Indeed, L. M. Fraser views the concern with cost value as being the Achilles' heel of the Ricardo–Marx school of thought. He contends that the "attribution of ultimate 'value' to labour . . . is . . . an act of 'valuation' on the part of the attributer" and that the "concept of cost value has its source in a valuing subject"—hence, it is unscientific (1947:123). It escaped Fraser's attention that the same critique could be made of conventional economic analysis about the role of capital vis-à-vis exchange value.

Succinctly, to paraphrase Fraser, cost value hinges on the question "what it costs to make" (1947:56); use value refers to an object's usefulness or utility, apart from its cost of production or its rate of exchange; exchange value is synonymous with an article's "exchangeable worth" or its value in terms of other articles or money, that is, its rate of exchange; and, finally, esteem value reflects not merely an object's usefulness but also the ease of acquiring it, whether by exchanging other things for it or by assigning one's own time and energy to its production (Fraser 1947:57–59)—in other words, an object acquires esteem value only because it is both useful and scarce. The cultural origins of esteem value and its incorporation into the mutable funds of knowledge of agents/subjects in particular economies is a topic not addressed in conventional economics except through mathematical modeling of the market economy.

There should be little disagreement that, in comparison with conventional economics, economic anthropology has approached value in all four senses posited by Fraser but has done so less theoretically and more empirically and has probed much more systematically and deeply into the cultural origins and permutations of value than has economics. It is also accurate to say that economic anthropology, like economics, has privileged the exchange and esteem dimensions of value, but in a way that has been more prone to either downplay or confuse the commodity identity of valued things. In contrast to economics, however, anthropology has been much more focused on understanding the structural conditions in particular sociocultural formations under which individual subjects/agents make decisions and engage in social action for economic purposes, customarily defined in terms of physical and social reproduction and as wedded to noneconomic logics. Thus, whereas the question of value in economics generally assumes the submission of society to economy, in anthropology it generally assumes the submission of economy to society. My approach to value in this chapter assumes that the relation between society and economy, like that between subject and object, is dynamic and interactive; the focus is relational rather than causal.

The connection of commodity value to culture is implicit when we focus on the rates at which one commodity exchanges for another (exchange value) but more explicit when we focus on the importance that a given commodity or commodities has for valuing subjects (absolute esteem value) or on their "rates of indifference" between commodities (relative esteem value). All these senses in which exchange has traditionally been understood in economic discourse refer to relations, not to qualities or quantities. According to Fraser (1947:75), "Absolute esteem value is more naturally to be thought of as a quality of the esteemed objects," but exchange value and relative esteem value are perhaps best expressed "either as the (purely relational) qualities of 'purchasing' and 'preference' power, or else quantitatively in the form of exchange and indifference 'equivalents'" (1947:55). The study of the cultural permutations of commodity value is challenging enough to merit scrutiny from a variety of approaches in economic anthropology. A focus on esteem value clearly dovetails with marginal utility analysis or indifference analysis favored by the formalist approach (Schneider 1974; cf. Fraser 1947:chap. 5) or with the symbolic, sign-value approach favored by Baudrillard, Bourdieu, and Sahlins. By contrast, a focus on exchange value intended to understand its wider socioeconomic implications inevitably leads toward Marxist analysis. There are sufficient analytical problems bedeviling the explanation of economic value to be shared by all comers.

There should be widespread recognition in scholarly discourse that, regarding the economy, all truths are relative and that its conceptualization is purely an ad hoc, heuristic matter. There is broad consensus among scholars regarding the general contours of the economic field as involving the provision of physical needs that are transhistorical and specieswide (such as food, tools, clothing, shelter, and old-age security) yet, at the same time, geohistorically specific in culturally peculiar ways (cf. Sayer 1997:17). There is less consensus about the specific content of economic reality or about prioritizing particular moments or phases in the economic process and about its relationship to other sociocultural fields.

The fact remains, however, that there is a huge body of literature written about the economy, from a variety of disciplines and perspectives, defining it substantively (and with varying degrees of abstraction) by employing the categories of production, exchange, distribution, and consumption. Expediency does have its place in economic knowledge production, and, in the case of the categorical approach to the economic field, it seems to have resulted in explanatory progress.[1]

MARX'S VIEW OF THE GENERAL CATEGORIES OF ECONOMY AND THE PRIVILEGING OF PRODUCTION

A rationale in favor of the general categories approach to the economy that takes it a step beyond the level of documentation and description (Wilk 1996:28–29) comes from the pages of Karl Marx's introduction to *The Grundrisse* (1970:188–217; 1971:16–46; 1973:83–111). Marx justified the surface delimitation of the economic field in general categorical terms because he wedded it to a dialectical method of explanation that treated concepts as, at once, organic, relational, and temporal. He employed the classical categorization in an experimental search for a launching pad into his radical study of capital. As Althusser (1970:109–10) pointed out, "Neither this (abstract) description of economic behavior nor its supposed foundation in the mythical *homo economicus* interested Marx"—his concern was the dialectic of the mutations of the anatomy of this world of individual economic behavior. Marx, according to Althusser, understood "abstract economic reality . . . as the effect of a deeper, more concrete reality: the mode of production of a determinate social formation" and for the first time measured individual economic behavior "according to its conditions of existence" (1970:110). Consequently, between the *Grundrisse*, where the production-in-general scheme is discussed, and volume 1 of *Capital*, where it is not, the basic concepts for Marx and Marxism became the degree of development of the forces of production and the state of the relations of production (Althusser 1970:110).

Because of the circulationist influence of Polanyi, Dalton, Sahlins, and other substantivists, together with the emergence of anthropological political economy as a separate field, Marx's profoundly original substantive view of the economic process as the transformation of the natural environment through the exercise of labor to make products for satisfying wants (that is, the "labour-process" [Marx 1967, 1:177]) has been analytically sidetracked in economic anthropology. Marx's imaginative interpretation and use of the classical general categories approach to the economy, as a point of entry into the conceptualization of the internal structure and dynamics of the substantive economy as a generalized labor process, with few exceptions (Cook 1974a; Godelier 1972) has been largely ignored by economic anthropologists. Accordingly, it is important to review Marx's approach that enabled him to expose how the economic process articulates with its enveloping society and culture and to analyze those elements or activities internal to its functioning.

The concepts Marx employs in his theoretical exercise are organic, relational, and temporal. Their designation as "organic" means that they must be viewed as one-sided moments in a process of mutual interaction, different sides of one process (for example, production is consumption, and production is consumption). They are "relational" because they embody many ties to other necessary moments in a process (for example, wage labor implies capital, exchange value implies use value, and so on).

Finally, Marx's concepts must be understood as "temporal" because they have material origins in the past and possible trajectories in the future. They did not drop from the sky and are not pure ideas or mental constructs; they are processual and componential, meaning that they germinate temporally (evolve from single elements into complex unities) (cf. Ollman 1971:3–19). Ollman, paraphrasing Marx, emphasized that "no production is possible without an instrument of production, even if this instrument is simply the hand. It is not possible without past, accumulated labor, even if this labor is only the skill acquired by repeated practice and concentrated in the hand" (1971:3–19). This temporality is explained by Marx himself regarding his general concept of production, production in general, which is "a multifarious compound comprising divergent categories. Some elements are found in all epochs, others are common to a few epochs. The most modern period and the most ancient period will have [certain] categories in common" (Marx 1970:190).

Marx's method requires treating any one concept in this quartet in relation to each of the others rather than in isolation. It is the relations between production, exchange, consumption, and distribution that are critical, not their role in isolation. To paraphrase Harvey's (1982:2) rendition of Ollman's (1971) metaphor, Marx sees each relation as a separate "window" from which we can look in on the inner structure of the economic process. Thus, in his own exposition of these abstract categories and their connections,

Marx observes that "production is the decisive phase" since the entire "process always starts afresh with production" (1970:204–5); but production itself is "determined by the demands of consumption," which "exerts a reciprocal action on the point of departure" to initiate the whole economic process once again (1970:194). According to Harvey, "The view from any one window is flat and lacks perspective. When we move to another window we can see things that were formerly hidden from view. Armed with that knowledge, we can reinterpret and reconstitute our understanding of what we saw through the first window, giving it greater depth and perspective" (1982:2). In reading Marx on the relations between the general categories of economy and by moving from the production window to the exchange window and on to each of the other two windows, "we come closer and closer to understanding" the economic process and "all of its inherent contradictions" (Harvey 1982:2).[2]

Whereas these categories reflect necessary general conditions for social production at all times and places, they remained for Marx "abstract conceptions which do not define any of the actual historical stages of production" (Marx 1970:193). For him, discourse about production must focus on a "definite stage of social development" or must refer to the production by individuals in a specific social formation (1970:189–90); this sociohistorical awareness is the proper starting point for materialist analysis. As another commentator has expressed it, "There is no simple relation between production and the rest of the economy, mode of production, or social formation," but "production and its related moments are always social in a specifically historical form and . . . these must be studied to extract the specific forms of determination and definition that they involve" (Fine 1991:447–48).

An important point for economic anthropology regarding production-in-general is that "the proper beginning is not with the dawn of history but rather with that category which occupies a predominant position within the particular social formation being studied" (Nicolaus 1973:37). Such a beginning for the critique of the capitalist economic categories (and system), according to Nicolaus, would not be material production in general but capital or production for exchange since these are the "categories which rule this historic society" (1973:37).

A perusal of the early sections of *Critique of Political Economy* published in 1859 and volume 1 of *Capital* published in 1867 confirms that Marx chose the category "commodity" as the starting point of his analysis of the capitalist mode of production. The rationale for this starting point is explained by Nicolaus as follows: "It is . . . at once concrete, material, almost tangible, as well as historically specific (to capitalist production); and it contains within it . . . a key antithesis (use value v. exchange value) whose development involves all the other contradictions of this mode of production" (1973:38; cf. Harvey 1982:1–4). It was, in short, a "truly dialectical beginning" (1973:38), which it would not have been if Marx had started with the simple, general, abstract relations between universals like production, distribution, exchange, and consumption.

In arguing that the commodity category is historically specific to capitalist production, Nicolaus precludes the possible contribution of Marxism to understanding precapitalist commodity production. It is one thing to argue that only in capitalism is the commodity form integrative of the entire economy (and society) but quite another to historically limit the commodity form to capitalist economy and society. This places an arbitrary limitation on the capacity of Marxism to best employ Marx's own methodological dictum that "bourgeois economy . . . provides a key to the economy of antiquity" (1970:211) in the comparative study of the economy.

It is clear that the study of capitalism and the theorization of the capitalist mode of production enabled Marx to identify the commodity as the fundamental concept in economics precisely because it highlighted the critical role of labor in the production of value and the reproduction of society. "Labour," according to Marx, "as the creator of use-values, as useful labour, is a condition of human existence which is independent of all forms of society; it is an eternal natural necessity which mediates the metabolism between man and nature, and therefore human life itself" (1977:133). Labor is useful as the source of use value through production but is also expressed as exchange value when one useful product is exchanged for another—the only common denominator between two different products that provides a basis for their exchange is the socially averaged amount of socially divided labor power they embody, that is, abstract human labor (1977:126–31, 150). In short, Marx's privileging of production in the categorical segmentation of the economic process reflects his identification of the dual character of labor as the source of use value (the natural form) and of exchange value (the value form) that constitutes commodities (1977:138).

For Marx, anything possessing utility or use value that is realized through exchange is a commodity. Many such things are tangible, material products fashioned through a process involving the expenditure of human labor in the employment of a given technology (tools and/or equipment plus the knowledge to employ them) on a given set of raw materials. Other such things, like land and labor itself, can become commodities simply by virtue of their potential capacity to produce other commodities. In the case of labor, which is the most unique commodity category (the only one, in fact, that has the capacity to conceptualize, plan, and produce other commodities and realize their use values through exchange), commoditization was a multiple-stage process of long evolution culminating in the development of general-purpose money (Hart 1982:40). Marx recognized that "the invention of socially recognized standards of measurement for the quantities of . . . useful objects" (1977:125), culminating in general-purpose money, was necessary to the predominance of commodity circulation in a given economy, but his imaginative, nuanced, and abstract discussion in the first chapter of volume 1 of *Capital* certainly leaves the door open for a consideration of the role of commodities in precapitalist economies without general-purpose money.[3]

WEBER'S VIEWS OF THE "ECONOMIC," THE "ECONOMICALLY RELEVANT," AND THE "ECONOMICALLY CONDITIONED"

Max Weber's discussion of the definition of the economic field remains seductive, even though his method needs to be subordinated to Marx's in order to maintain a research focus on the "economic" without being seduced into quixotic searches for far-flung or possible connections in other fields of a sociocultural formation. Weber, in effect, attempted to articulate a view that combined Marx's emphasis on "need-meeting interaction with the natural environment" (Marshall 1998:401) with the means–end logic of neoclassical formalism. This is evident in the following statement: "In the widest sense, 'social-economic' is constituted by the fact that our physical existence and the satisfaction of our most ideal needs are everywhere confronted with the quantitative limits and the qualitative inadequacy of the necessary external means, so that their satisfaction requires planful provision and work, struggle with nature and the association of human beings" (Weber 1949:64). Unlike Marx, Weber was insistent that the "social-economic" is an epistemological, not an ontological, category—that is, the "quality of an event as . . . 'social-economic' . . . is not something which it possesses 'objectively'"—rather, it is "conditioned by the orientation of our cognitive interest, as it arises from the specific cultural significance which we attribute to the particular event in a given case" (1949:64). He did not privilege labor in the economic process as Marx did and, unlike Marx, provided an operational formula for distinguishing between economic and noneconomic cultural activities and for relating cultural activities not directed to reproduction to those that are (for example, as economically relevant or economically conditioned) (cf. Sayer 1997:17–18).

Within this wide range of the "social-economic," Weber recognized the analytical usefulness of delimiting a narrower range of phenomena (such as events, institutions, and norms) as "economic," namely, those that "were deliberately created or used for economic ends" (1949:64). The examples he gave are the stock exchange and banks. He distinguished these from "economically relevant" phenomena, which, like religion, are not primarily of interest for their economic significance but which acquire such significance because "they have consequences which are of interest from the economic point of view" (1949:64). Finally, he posited "economically conditioned phenomena," which are neither economic nor economically relevant but are "influenced in certain important aspects by economic factors" as exemplified by "the social stratification of the artistically interested public" (1949:64–65). He illustrates these three aspects of "economic" through the example of the "state," which in its fiscal aspects is an "economic" phenomenon. To the extent that it influences economic life through legislation, it is "economically relevant," and it is "economically conditioned" to the extent that "its behavior in non-'economic' affairs is partly influenced by economic motives" (1949:65). Finally, Weber summarized his discussion as follows: "It is self-evident that: firstly, the boundary lines of 'economic' phenomena are arguable and not easily defined; secondly, the 'economic' aspect of a phenomenon is by no means only 'economically conditioned' or only 'economically relevant'; thirdly, a phenomenon is 'economic' *only* insofar as and only as long as our *interest* is exclusively focused on its constitutive significance in the material struggle for existence" (1949:65).

Weber accepted as inevitable and emphasized that the economic domain "extends naturally . . . through the totality of cultural life" (1949:65) but recognized that immaterial factors can play a constitutive role in the material life struggle. Given his fondness for the scarcity postulate, Weber was drawn toward the study of economic motives wherever these operate. For him, this was everywhere in society and culture that human wants exist, are scarce in relation to the demand for them, and are satisfied. These wants or needs may be material or immaterial but, if scarce, become economic objects (1978, 1:339–40). Weber was explicit in rejecting the thesis that every instrumental action among organized social groups was economic (1978, 1:339). The limits of economic action were set by the interaction of needs and scarcity. In his words, "We shall speak of economic action only if the satisfaction of a need depends, in the actor's judgment, upon relatively *scarce* resources and a *limited* number of possible actions" (1978, 1:339). Thus, Weber's substantivist conceptualization of the economic as material struggle was ultimately overtaken by the expansivist method derived from the scarcity postulate. The latter postulate inevitably widened the focus of economic inquiry to the "totality of cultural life" (1949:65) wherever scarcity is subjectively perceived to exist and that perception orients behavior (1978, 1:339).

For Weber, then, the "organizing principle of economic activity" did not lie "outside of the economic subject with his individual ends, subjective capacities for definition of means, but through an expansion of these capacities as ideal forms" (Jones 1977:32–33). Still, it is possible to use Weber's guidelines for delimiting the "economic" as a cultural process of material life struggle or of activities directly related to the production, exchange, consumption, and distribution of "scarce material means" (Weber 1949:65) and to be selective in the application of his expansivist method and combine it with Marx's method of political economy.

THE ISSUE OF ECONOMIC DETERMINISM

A charge often leveled against the tendency to privilege the economy in the study of society, whether from a Marxist or from a non-Marxist perspective, is that such privileging is tantamount to exaggerating the importance of the economic field, both synchronically and diachronically, in shaping the social process of life (or the historical process). It allegedly does this by downplaying the possibility of the "relatively independent influence of ideology, class consciousness, and political action seen as a manifestation of human agency" (Bottomore 1991:168) or of other specific dimensions of culture, such as religion (Weber 1958). Weber, in opposition to Marx, seemed to favor an approach that highlighted the economic without being materialist (that is, advocating the material struggle for existence as a prime cause of historical change). Yet there is ambivalence in his position. On the one hand, Weber asserted that "the economic determination of social action is ambiguous—contrary to the assumption of so-called historical materialism," while, on the other, he admitted that "at some point economic conditions tend to become causally important and often decisive . . . for social groups . . . which have major cultural significance" (1978, 1:341).

Under societal conditions, such as those existing in contemporary Mexico, in which the commodity dimension of culture has evolved to assume pervasive influence, there is less ambiguity surrounding the economic determination of social action. Even so, this is not a license to embrace economic determinism. Neither Marx nor most Marxists are guilty of an exclusive preoccupation with economy or material production as prime movers. As Ben Fine has pointed out, "Marx is clear that society produces its political, ideological as well as its economic relations, whereas there is a tendency under capitalism . . . to identify production with capital alone or more generally with wage labour" (1991:448). Marxism has also shown that ruling classes must produce ideological means to legitimate their rule and that many of the activities that reproduce the working class at the domestic or household level are both material and ideational in content. Indeed, according to Marx, peoples' ideas are produced by the activities and relations in which they participate "as much as, if not more than, by the act of thinking itself" (1991:448).

This is the central thesis of an early book by Marx and Engels, *The German Ideology*, which was a critique of philosophical idealism and a profound assertion of human agency. Their often-quoted summary of this thesis concludes with the well-known proclamation, "Life is not determined by consciousness, but consciousness by life" (1947:14–15). Marxists are now less inclined, and rightly so, to avoid emphasizing, as Marx and Engels sometimes did, the one-sided determinism of this proclamation but, rather, to emphasize the interactive, interpenetrating nature of the relationship between life and consciousness (Godelier 1986; Roseberry 1989; Wessman 1981:21–22; Williams 1981). In short, despite rhetorical flourishes in Marx's writings that can be construed as deterministic (such as the "thesis that for everything that happens there are conditions such that, given them, nothing else could have happened" [Bhaskar 1991b:139]), there is considerable evidence from his and subsequent writings that makes it implausible to interpret most contemporary Marxist theory as deterministic in the sense of determinate or dated future outcomes (conditions, states of affairs, events, and so on) being inevitable.[4]

Regarding predictability, for the most part Marx's (and Marxist) predictions are typically conditional (reflecting tendential laws) and are "subject to the operation of *ceteris paribus* clauses" (Bhaskar 1991b:140). Arguably, an emphasis on the role of technoeconomic forces in general sociocultural evolution or the civilizational process that spans millennia yields a coherent sequence of general societal transformations of a cumulative and directional nature. The main proviso regarding this thesis is that over shorter periods of development in specific social formations, there are many situations in which the action of technoeconomic factors is "conditioned by social constrictions and advanced or retarded by ideological factors" (Ribeiro 1970:428; cf. Cook 1974a:819). Althusser's "overdetermination" thesis remains persuasive in this context: "it is the economy which determines which relatively autonomous level of the superstructure is conjuncturally or epochally dominant" (Bhaskar 1991b:139–40; cf. Althusser 1970:89–116; Godelier 1972:xiv, 86–92).

In any case, rigid hierarchical and oppositional structurations of process should be avoided. The best approach is one that is flexible and accommodating of the interpenetration of economy and culture (or the technoeconomic and the ideological). Roseberry's (1989:30–54) thesis that culture is at once socially constituted (as a product of present and past activity) and socially constitutive (part of the context in which activity is given meaning) neatly resolves the problem of determinism without invoking structuralist notions. This analytical principle is an overdue corrective to and safeguard against rigid, one-sided deterministic reasoning. The only drawback to transforming this principle into a research canon is that its application might then become ritualistic and rhetorical rather than representative of inquisitive application of dialectical method.[5]

NATURAL ECONOMY AND THE PRIVILEGING OF USE VALUE

The concept of natural economy is undertheorized and inconsistently defined in Marxist thought. There is no entry for it in the *Dictionary of Marxist Thought*, and it is absent from many basic introductions to Marxist political economy (such as Leontyev [1975], Eaton [1966], and Mandel [1969]). The precedent for the lack of systematic elaboration of the concept was set by Marx. In *Capital*, Marx opposed natural economy to money economy and noted that the latter is common to all commodity production (1967, 2:116), so, in effect, natural economy is opposed to commodity economy. One necessary condition for its existence is "when no part of the agricultural product, or but a very insignificant portion, enters into the process of circulation . . . [and] . . . encompasses equally well the products of industrial labor" (1967, 3:786). He also observed that "domestic handicrafts and manufacturing labor, as secondary occupations of agriculture, which forms the basis, are the prerequisite of that mode of production upon which natural economy rests" and that "the capitalist mode of production completely abolishes this relationship" (1967, 3:786–87). Finally, as implied in what has already been said, Marx was explicit about natural economy being an autarky—a completely self-sufficient or self-reproductive economy: "the conditions of the economy are either wholly or for the overwhelming part produced by the economy itself, directly replaced and reproduced out of its gross product" (1967, 3:795).

Thus, for Marx, the natural economy seems to correspond to a generalized precommodity, premoney mode of production that was constructed in opposition to the tandem of simple and advanced commodity economy, the latter being synonymous with the capitalist mode of production, but both of which presume the presence of general-purpose money and the monetized calculation of exchange value as abstract labor. Although Marx's general discussion of the commodity as a material bearer of use value and exchange value (1977:126) seems to present the possibility of its universal presence in the human economy, in fact there seems to be no place for it in his precapitalist economic formations where the purpose of labor "is not the *creation of value*" but the "maintenance of the owner and his family as well as of the communal body as a whole" (1965:68).[6]

Baudrillard (Poster 1988:98) puts Marxist political economy in the same boat with all other schools of political economy regarding the acceptance of the philosophical assumption that human existence is an end for which humans must find the means. In considering this as the "wildest and most naïve postulate about the human race," Baudrillard dramatically and definitively rejects, for his purposes, the entire project of political economy (and, of course, of economic anthropology). Ironically, however, in his prolegomenon to his nonpolitical economic project, Baudrillard incisively laid bare the core logic of Marx's labor theory of value by critiquing his deconstruction of labor into a double concept of commodity labor power: abstract social labor (exchange value) and concrete labor (use value). In the course of his critique, Baudrillard tacitly provided the means for exposing an unresolved contradiction in Marx's method, namely, his failure to conceptualize natural economy as on the distant "horizon of exchange value" (Baudrillard 1988:101), the complex nature of which was shown by his study of capital.

Baudrillard correctly characterizes the outcome of Marx's dialectical analysis of the commodity labor power as "the final precipitate of the law of value" (1988:100). Regarding Marx's dialectic of quality and quantity vis-à-vis concrete labor and citing a specific statement by Marx (1904:33), Baudrillard "rediscovers" a concrete, differentiated, and incommensurable moment of the use value of labor (1988:101). This is the basis for his thesis of the incommensurability of labor power under precapitalist conditions. Baudrillard's thesis accords with the main thrust of Marx's analysis of capital but does not accord with the spirit of the application of Marx's "key rule" and related texts, which suggest that cultural means for circumventing this incommensurability were present and evolving in prebourgeois and preartisanal (or simple commodity) forms. The key to understanding equivalence and commensurability in these forms resides in extending Marx's concept of abstract social labor as a common denominator to include the cultural matrix of the valuing subject and to recognize that the transfer of commodities need not always and everywhere depend on precise, objective criteria for reckoning value.[7]

Such an approach would seem to find justification in Marx's contention that simple economic categories like use value and exchange value lead "an antediluvian existence" (Marx 1904:294). The point is that if humanity is reduced in Marx's political economy to a "producer of value," it makes no sense for him to insert early human populations into a natural economy in which the seeds or germs of commodity economy are absent. In the spirit of Marx's "key rule" and his general concept of "commodity," it is reasonable to extend the ontological boundaries of its application to a "primitive" or "original" form of economy as a precursor of petty commodity production.

Appropriately, the ideal–typical concept of "natural economy" (*Naturalwirtschaft*) is elaborated by Weber in his discussion of "Calculations in Kind" (1978, 1:100) and is defined as an "economy where money is not used" (1978, 1:100). To underline his point that the concept is imprecise, Weber notes that it may mean either an economy without exchange or a barter economy. It is the latter type that is of most interest to my proposals regarding "primitive" (or original) commodity economy. According to Weber, there are two types of natural economies of the barter type that have been common in the empirical record: those dominated by exchange in kind with no calculation in money terms and those "where there is exchange in kind, but where calculation is occasionally or even typically carried out in money terms" (1978, 1:100). It is not so much Weber's assertion that calculation in kind is concerned mainly with consumption or want satisfaction that is most noteworthy in his discussion but, rather, his positing of the realization and possible accumulation of exchange value in barter economies ruled by calculation in kind. To quote him in extenso (1978, 1:101):

> Calculation in kind is in its essence oriented to consumption, the satisfaction of wants. It is . . . quite possible to have something analogous to profit-taking on this basis . . . in a barter economy, goods may be disposed of and acquired by exchange, perhaps in systematically repeated barters, though strictly without the use of money. Such action would be systematically oriented to securing a supply of goods which, as compared with the state which would exist without these measures, is judged to establish a more adequate provision for the needs of the unit. It is, in such cases, only when quantities of goods which are qualitatively similar are compared that it is possible to use numerical terms unambiguously and without a wholly subjective valuation. It is possible . . . to set up a system of in-kind wages consisting of typical bundles of consumer goods . . . such as were the in-kind salaries and benefices particularly of the ancient Orient (where they even became objects of exchange transactions . . .).

It is precisely a value regime of this type operating through calculations in kind to arrive at approximations of equivalences, or even of what I would call "superior equivalences"—which imply profitlike increments of exchange value for quantities of qualitatively similar commodities transferred between producers—that I have speculated was operating in pre-Columbian Mesoamerica as a concomitant of repetitive labor alienation.[8]

Roseberry (1989:197–232) examined the foundations of the persisting allure of the natural economy construct in Marxist and non-Marxist thought. He found that non-Marxists contrast natural economy with money economy and have viewed the difference as one between a relative lack of exchange and a prevalence of exchange (1989:239). Marxists, on the other hand, contrast natural economy with commodity economy and have viewed the difference from the perspective of production and its orientation (which may not correspond exactly with product destination). More specifically, according to Roseberry, "The basic opposition for the Marxist distinction . . . is not production for use versus production for exchange but production for use value versus production for exchange value" (1989:239). I think the opposition between exchange value and use value, when linked back to producer intent, precludes understanding the origins of commodity consumption through exchange and confounds understanding that the relationship between exchange and use value is as inseparable as that between production and consumption. This opposition also blurs the relationship between use and exchange value (both of which are phenomenal forms of value) on the one hand and abstract value on the other.

Viewing the entire history of humanity's economy from the perspective of economic anthropology, product circulation (that is, use-value realization only) is the exception and commodity circulation (use- plus exchange- plus abstract-value realization) the rule. Rather than emphasizing the separation between exchange value and use value, an epistemological refinement that is defined ontologically, a more appropriate emphasis is the difference between the *accumulation* of use/exchange value and the *realization* of use/exchange/abstract value. In the history of humanity's economy, the "great transformation" (Polanyi 1957) revolved around the ascendancy of the quest for the accumulation of use/exchange value through the production of commodities with commodities, not its simple realization, which was accomplished in history wherever a useful object was exchanged to be consumed by someone other than its producer.

Roseberry's point regarding the transgression of the boundaries of natural economy through product exchange raises questions at the interface of economic anthropology and Marxism that may not be definitively answerable on the basis of analysis of the archaeological and historical records of extinct economies or through the ethnographic record of extant economies. Suffice it to say that the empirical record suggests that natural economies in the sense of local group autarkies probably never existed or, at most, are extremely rare. But in the sense of production geared to consumption needs of the producers, with production for the possible accumulation of exchange value being subordinate, so-called natural economies are more common in the precapitalist record.[9]

A concomitant of the convergence of economic anthropology and Marxist political economy beginning in the 1960s was the introduction of conceptual distinction that has served to inhibit rather than advance knowledge production in economic anthropology: product versus commodity. Traditional Marxist political economy defined a product (or good) as embodying only use value and defined a commodity as embodying both use and exchange value (Eaton 1966:22–23; Mandel 1969:9–10). This oppositional conceptualization of product and commodity should be abandoned in favor of a uniform definition of all artifacts of human labor, in any economy, as commodities that embody *potentially realizable* use, exchange, and abstract labor and/or money value from the point of their physical inception. It is clearly a matter of empirical determination as to the specific situational details of the value realization of given commodities.[10]

The realization of exchange value as a concomitant of transfer-facilitated consumption (that is, the realization of use value) extends deep into the history of the human economy into Sahlins's (1972) "Stone Age" of so-called original affluency. Even in the absence of special or general-purpose monies, it is perfectly plausible to assume that the origins of commodity production lie in the practice of barter, in which equivalences can be ultimately determined by calculations of embodied labor time or simply as objectively incommensurate results of alienated labor (that is, you get what I produce for whatever you produce that I, for whatever reason, do not or cannot produce), or, for that matter, in gifting and reciprocity, where equivalences are delayed and may also be objectively incommensurate. However, this objective incommensurateness does not preclude the realization of abstract labor value and symbolic values that are within the use value of given commodities (and can make exchanges *subjectively* commensurate). Thus, in the situation Roseberry describes regarding exchange of products in a natural economy, the important point is not so much boundary transgression as it is labor alienation and the opening up of a sphere of commodity circulation within the natural economy—for once products regularly produced are exchanged (presumably via barter) with nonproducers, they in effect become commodities, not products, since their exchange, use, and abstract/symbolic values are all being realized. Once this opening occurs, the accumulation of exchange value also becomes possible.

The relationship between natural economy and simple (or petty) commodity economy raised by Roseberry is pertinent if only because of a persisting tendency in anthropological discourse to interpret petty commodity production through the lens of natural (or subsistence) economy in analyses of the detrimental impact of international capitalist development on indigenous economies. Even when more than subsistence needs are taken into account in their consideration of the simple reproduction of indigenous peasant household enterprises, anthropologists often downplay the possibility of value accumulation, investment for productivity expansion, or the benefits of participation in the market economy. It is important to emphasize the linkage between commodity circulation and consumption, but it is a mistake to subordinate commodity circulation (and exchange-value realization and possible accumulation) to consumption.

THE LABOR THEORY OF CULTURE

An analytically fertile point of departure for understanding differences and similarities between the economic life of Mesoamerica and of other areas of world culture combines the labor theory of culture and of commodity evolution (that is, commoditization) with the writings of scholars like Saussure, Baudrillard, Sahlins, Bourdieu, and Little, focused on the intersection of commodity culture, economic value, and rationality. A beginning assumption in such an inquiry is that human labor is paradoxical: it is an inalienable property of the human individual that creates alienable things. Although labor is "an inalienable bodily and mental function," it represents an alienable capacity (Braverman 1974:54).

It is impossible for one human being to endow another with one's own capacity for work. But it is possible for one to transfer or exchange to another one's capacity to perform work (that is, labor power) for a specified length of time or the embodiment of that capacity in a particular commodity or set of commodities. The repetitive transfer or exchange of labor power in either of these two ways creates and re-creates alienated labor. In this fundamental sense, alienation certainly pre-dates capitalism. It was part and parcel of the Neolithic division of labor and specialization and, in a more randomized form, was present during earlier stages of human economic development. Just as a plausible case can be made for the dialectical relationship between labor and culture and its role in creating *Homo sapiens* (Engels 1972; Woolfson 1982), so can another be made for the origins of alienated labor in the Paleolithic trade of artifacts documented by archaeologists.[11]

This raises the question of the temporal relationship between production and consumption or supply and demand. The best answer is that they coevolve or codevelop. With regard to the abbreviated time frame of production cycles, it is also logical to emphasize the close functional linkage between the two "moments" in the economic process. Nevertheless, there is evidence derived from the study of modern, advertising-dominated, consumer society to support Baudrillard's thesis that needs are "produced as a force of consumption" to fuel production (Poster 1988:41). If this thesis is correct, and if Marx's "key rule" is followed (that is, Bourgeois economy . . . provides a key to the economy of antiquity [Marx 1970:211]), then consumption can also be privileged over production in the study of the precapitalist economy. This is essentially what Baudrillard implies in his interpretation of the relationship between needs, objects, and agents as tautological, rendering the subject–object dichotomy problematic (1981:45, 70–71). His interpretation reduces to the proposition that a system of needs that reflects social institutions determines behavior "before even being considered in the consciousness of the social actors" (1981:31).

At work here is a posited "unconscious social logic" (Baudrillard 1981:63), an "unconscious logic of social structures" (1981:72), or a "fundamental level. . . . of unconscious structures that organize the social production of differences" (1981:74). Concomitantly, Baudrillard posits a differentiation of human subjects into partners bound by rules of exchange and of exchange material, goods, and products (1981:75). Individual agency is irrelevant. Just as language "cannot be explained by postulating an individual need to speak . . . [s]imilarly, consumption does not arise from an objective need of the consumer, a final intention of the subject towards the object; rather, there is social production, in a system of exchange, of . . . a code of significations and invidious values. The functionality of goods and individual needs only follows on this" (1981:75). Hence, "there are only needs because the system needs them" (1981:82).

This thesis calls to mind Sahlins's (1972) "structural substantivism" (Cook 1974b), which was elaborated in *Stone Age Economics*. Such posited structures and processes, unfortunately, do not lend themselves readily to direct empirical study. The subconscious or unconscious is simply posited to fill a gap between conversational and observational data about what subjects think or how they claim to behave and the actual results, intended or unintended, of their actions. In other words, such an approach should be viewed skeptically by economic anthropologists who select theories on the basis of the quantity and quality of their empirically verified content.

For purposes of economic anthropology and in the evolutionary context, the only way to resolve the structure-versus-agency dilemma of the triumvirate of needs–objects–agents is to start with the recognition that both "toolmaking and speech represent indirect or mediated interventions in the natural and social world" (Woolfson 1982:73) and that both evolved interactively in a "new temporal dimension of existence" (1982:73). Woolfson (1982:73–74) proposes that "speech . . . brought with it 'release' from the shackles of time present, and for evolving hominids the entry into a new temporal dimension of existence increasingly governed by the 'economy of time.'" Thus, according to Woolfson, the "economy of time . . . becomes identical with the inauguration and development of artificial productive forces . . . the proper proportional distribution of labour . . . becomes a necessity even in the earliest forms of society" (1982:73–74).

The economy of time is not to be confused with the "subjective form of the early consciousness of time directly 'imposed' by nature" (Woolfson 1982:101 n. 37). It is plausible to assume, from the standpoint of general economic and sociocultural evolution, that agent consciousness of labor time was present before the development in class society of a distinction between free time and labor time (cf. Woolfson 1982:101 n. 37). In other words, consciousness of labor time is most likely to have arisen in preclass society as a concomitant of labor alienation and primitive commodity circulation.

On the basis of Woolfson's compelling scenario, then, commodity culture(s) can be posited to originate with the systematic recognition by producers that their own knowledge and energy embodied and expended in useful things for their own domestic group could also be exchanged for other useful things. Thus, the practice began of producing things for other use so that other things for own use could be acquired through exchange. It is precisely around this interplay between labor alienation and commodity consumption (that is, the prerequisite of labor reproduction) that commodity culture began to be constituted as a way of creating, monitoring, realizing, and accumulating economic value. As long as commensurateness of values embodied in commodities was determined subjectively, objective standards for measuring value were superfluous to the process.

The capacity for this development was brought from the Old World to the New World with the early wanderers who eventually populated Mesoamerica. That capacity evolved interactively with the division of labor and specialization as well as with the social relations of production and distribution so as to constitute and be constituted by differentiated labor processes and social relations and also by noninstrumental culture or "norms and values . . . according to which actions are seen as good or bad in themselves rather than in terms of their consequences" (Sayer 1997:17). Through these relations and interactions, commodity culture coalesced around the reckoning and privileging of exchange value to satisfy various reproduction and/or accumulation purposes and possibilities. There is no doubt that the reckoning of equivalency in commodity value terms was subjective and imperfect until money evolved as a general standard of commensurateness—but the subjectivity and imperfection of the process clearly did not preclude the reckoning of exchange value bundled together with use and symbolic/sign value.[12]

Baudrillard refers (1981:140) to "the obscure mysticism of commodity value" and questioned Marx's failure "to examine his own use of the Crusoe myth" to the degree that his use of it is tantamount to his acceptance of the bourgeois "natural law of needs" (1981:141). Baudrillard overlooks Marx's insistence that social demand can be understood only in terms of particular time and place formations, not as abstract needs in an economy in general. He is unjustifiably dismissive of interdisciplinary, neohumanist efforts to define "needs" or demand structures in terms of historical/sociocultural context (1981:72–73). In any case, the scenario outlined in the preceding paragraph does imply that ancient Mesoamerican agents were, by virtue of their involvement in the labor alienation and commodity culture nexus, transformed simultaneously into productive forces and people with needs and that through their labor they became use values for a system of production just as goods and products became use values for them, assuming meanings as functions of their needs (cf. Baudrillard 1981:141). By implication, I do not consider this to be an unnatural set of conditions or one linked to any fictional Robinson Crusoe.

Marx viewed commodities as having a dual nature, as objects of utility and bearers of value. He defined objects as commodities only because they have a double form—a natural form as physical objects, produced by social labor, "with coarsely sensuous objectivity," and a value form. The most familiar value form of commodities is the money form (1977:138–39). According to Marx, "To show the origin of this money-form, we have to trace the development of the expression of value contained in the value-relation of commodities from its simplest, almost imperceptible outline to the dazzling money-form" (1977:139). Commodity circulation was present throughout a long process of evolution of exchange value, characterized by a dialectical interplay between two inseparable but mutually exclusive forms of exchange-value expression: the relative (from the perspective of the commodity whose value is being expressed) and the equivalent (from the perspective of the commodity in which value is being expressed) (Marx 1967, 1:49; cf. 1977:139–40). Commodity circulation is implied whenever one object is exchanged for any other object—that is, when to the "elementary relative value-form" of an object there "corresponds the single equivalent form of one other" object (1967, 1:62), and as one object enters into exchange with several other objects, "we get for one and the same" object "different elementary expressions of value" (1967, 1:62). This "embryonic form . . . must undergo a series of metamorphoses before it can ripen into the price-form" (1977:154).

Even though Marx insists that "it is only at a definite historical epoch in a society's development that [a product of labor] becomes a commodity, viz., at the epoch when the labour spent on the production of a useful article becomes expressed as one of the objective qualities of that article, i.e., as its value" (Marx 1967, 1:61; cf. 1977:153–54), he refers to objects involved in preprice form exchanges as commodities. This contradiction mirrors his contention that the "magnitudes of different things only become comparable in quantitative terms when they have been reduced to the same unit . . . a common denominator, and are therefore commensurable magnitudes" (1977:140–41). For Marx, qualitatively, the common denominator—human labor—was objectively present in all commodity exchanges (1977:151–52).

Therefore, there is a basis in Marx's work for considering social relations of production as synonymous with commodity social relations. When human labor cooperatively produces objects for consumption by others outside its own cooperative unit, it follows that the objects so produced are commodities and that the social relations facilitating the production, distribution, and realization of the value embodied in said objects are commodity social relations. This necessarily implies some degree of social consciousness of labor time/labor product. Given such consciousness, the subjective conditions are present for products to be objectively considered as commodities by virtue of their implicit exchange value content, which, of course, would be realized in the event of their transfer for use by other than their own production units.

Jacques Chevalier's rule regarding "subsistence commodities" (1982:117–19), formulated to apply to peasant economies subsumed by capitalism—namely, that in value terms there is a formal equivalence between subsistence goods and wage goods (or, expressed differently, that producers for own use realize the use as well as the exchange value of the goods/crops they produce to consume themselves)—should be extended to apply across the spectrum of human economies. All products are commodities whose potential exchange value is consumed as use value by their direct producers. A parallel argument was advanced earlier in Fraser's excursus on language and thought in economics where he stated that "so long as a commodity can be exchanged at given rates with other commodities we shall almost certainly regard these rates as representing its value even though they are not often put to the test of actual purchase and sale . . . it is evidently of the essence of purchasing power that it should belong to a commodity even when that commodity is not in course of being offered for sale" (1947:66–67).

SAHLINS, SIGN VALUE, AND THE FRENCH CONNECTION

A major challenge to the heuristic deployment in economic anthropological knowledge production of Marx's dialectical approach to understanding economic process through the optic of general categories comes from Marshall Sahlins (1972, 1976) and Jean Baudrillard (1981). They are critical of Marx for offering no independent consideration of the cultural construction of consumption, reducing the latter to the logical outcome of prior production cycles and submitting it to a commodity value logic that ignores sign value and a pregiven cultural structure, "order," or "scheme" (Sahlins 1976:205–21; cf. Miller 1991:48).

Regarding the issue of consumption, this critique of Marx is valid but can readily be corrected without following Baudrillard and Sahlins onto their divergent paths of rejecting the study of practical reason, instrumental culture and its outcomes, and the entire "phenomenological" approach to understanding human cultural activity (Ingold 1997:332). To accept Sahlins's (and Baudrillard's) critique is to opt for a "cognitivist" economic anthropology that converts economics into a branch of Saussurean linguistics and privileges the search for "a stable system of received conceptual categories" over the theoretically informed empirical study of performance (cf. Ingold 1997:332; Sahlins 1976:214–15).

Sahlins draws on Saussure's analogy between linguistic value and economic value or, in his words, of Saussure's "use of exchange-value to illustrate the conceptual value of the sign" (Sahlins 1976:214). Sahlins finds Saussure's exercise to be supportive of the proposition that the pursuit of material gain by agents in capitalist market economy is "mediated by the symbolic" and that "exchange-value is acquired by producing objects that are not the same as other products; objects that have a differential meaning in the society as organized" (1976:215). He elaborates, "Rational production for gain is in one and the same motion the production of symbols . . . because, (1) in order to be exchanged for something else (money), the goods produced must (2) contrast in one or another original property with all other goods of the same general kind" (1976:215).

Sahlins's oppositional thinking pits capitalism against precapitalism—or the "West against the rest" (1976:165). He puts a semiological slant on Polanyi's thesis of the "institutional dominance of economy" in Western capitalism, emphasizing that 1) the traditional functional relation between cultural series and natural series is reversed—"rather than serving the differentiation of society by a differentiation of objects, every conceivable distinction of society is put to the service of another declension of objects" (1976:215)—and 2) the relations of production compose the main classificatory grid for Western society. This fits in with his opposition between Mauss and Marx. Mauss, focusing on the Maori notion of *hau* (1954:8–10), posited a fundamental rule for *societas* (kin-based societies) economy: exchange of things equals exchange of persons. Marx's theory of commodity fetishism, according to Sahlins, posits the rule for capitalist society that the bond of persons is a relation between things and, as applied to non-Western, primitive economy by formalist economic anthropology, the "idea that custom is fetishized utility" (Sahlins 1976:x). In another version of this fundamental opposition, Sahlins states, "If, as is frequently noticed of 'primitive' exchange, every transaction has a social coefficient, a relationship between the participants of one kind or another that regulates the material terms of their interaction, of ourselves it seems true that every transaction has a material term that supplies important dimensions of the social relationship" (1976:215).

The fact remains that the Maori gift, inhabited by the spirit of the *hau*, "strives to bring . . . some equivalent to take its place" (Mauss 1954:10). Neither Mauss's nor Sahlins's interpretations preclude the unspoken presence of exchange value and the quest for a replacement of alienated labor lurking beneath the spirit of the *hau*.[13]

Sahlins does not address crucial statements by Saussure comparing linguistics/language and economy/economics. For example, Saussure states, "As in the study of political economy, one is dealing with the notion of value. In both cases, we have a *system of equivalence between things belonging to different orders*. In one case, work and wages; in the other case, signification and signal" (1986:80). Regarding method, Saussure (1986:80–81) insists that the study of values must take into account two axes—of simultaneity (synchronic) and of succession (diachronic). He identified an important difference between sign value and commodity value, namely, that natural connections have no place in the determination of the former but do have a place in the determination of the latter. Sahlins seems to make two interpretations of Saussure: one for the West and another for the rest. In other words, in Western market capitalism, the "ostensible quest for the material is mediated by the symbolic," whereas in non-Western precapitalism, the quest for the material is determined by the symbolic and submitted to the social.

The Saussurean thesis—embraced by Baudrillard, Bourdieu, and Sahlins—that symbolic production is material production is axiomatic. It inevitably follows from Saussure's proposition that linguistic signs are tangible—or that "a language is a repository of sound patterns, and writing is their tangible form" (1986:15). It is also axiomatic that language informs all other human cultural pursuits, including economy and commodity culture(s).

The dividing line between language and the economy is not identity as cultural or material, which both share, but that language produces sign value, whereas the economy produces use and exchange value. It is also clear that language and economy not only share identity as cultural and material (that is, in the sense that their products can be perceived as materially existent) but also interact as separate fields. Human economic activity, like all cultural activity, is predicated on language and the concepts, classifications, and distinctions it makes possible. Put differently, the economic is always mediated by the symbolic (cf. Godelier 1986:150–53).

This was the point of Leslie White's example of the stone axe as a "culture trait . . . meaningless without an idea, a conception of its nature and use" (1959:15; cf. Cook 1975:381)—implying a dialectical way of dissolving the antimony between material and immaterial or ideal culture and avoiding the reification of technology and its products (Cook 1975:380–81) and emphasizing that the "economy is a culturally mediated field" of human activity (Cook 1974a:810). Mediation is one thing; determination is another. The language of commodity culture is fashioned and refashioned through human experience in the labor process, that is, in the interplay among human subjects in their transformative and instrumental interaction with the physical environment. There is a dual symbolic element in the labor process, one of which is instrumental and the other expressive. Both elements constitute social reality, but one of them, the instrumental, plays a predominant though by no means exclusive role in the production of commodity value (cf. Godelier 1986:150).

Saussure's (1986:113–14) thesis that all values, sign and exchange/use, always involve 1) something dissimilar that can be exchanged for the item whose value is under consideration (such as a five-franc coin for bread) and 2) similar things that can be compared with the item whose value is under consideration (such as the one-franc coin or dollar) makes sense only when the commodity values in question are commensurable in general-purpose money terms (token value). In the absence of token value, as opposed to sui generis value, Saussure's reasoning does not apply—even in situations like New Guinea, where a particular commodity like salt serves as a general, if not universal, equivalent (Godelier 1971:66). All that is required for exchange/use value to be operative in the circulation of objects is that they be dissimilar and recognized as useful. The requirements become more complex for commodity money value (see Godelier 1971:65–66)—but fall short of Saussure's stipulations for token value. Commodities produced in premonopolistically competitive market economies, unlike signals vis-à-vis significations (or signifiers vis-à-vis signifieds), are not arbitrarily interchangeable, nor does the realization of their use and exchange value depend on their commensurateness with token value (in the same way as words must be contrasted with other words [Saussure 1986:114]).

The creatively destructive work of Jean Baudrillard exemplifies the radical current of contemporary thought that in bursts of dialectical logic consumes even its own products in a sort of hypercritical, nihilistic inevitability (cf. Kellner 1989:53). In a tandem of unquestionably brilliant studies, Baudrillard critiqued Marx's critique of political economy and then outdid himself by critiquing his own critique and leaving empirical social science, philosophically speaking, with an empty toolbox. There is no denying that Baudrillard's contribution should be confronted and addressed by any scholar working in the Marxist tradition of political economy. Our approach to commodity value can be strengthened by addressing his challenging analysis of sign value, but in a way that avoids replacing the study of the production of economic value with the study of the symbolic production of tastes as Sahlins (1976) did (cf. Wessman 1981:94–97).[14]

Sahlins's critique of practical reason was inspired generally by Saussure but parallels Baudrillard's (1981) approach to sign value (*valeur d'echange/signe*) glossed by Sahlins as "symbolic exchange value" (1976:166). Sahlins's (1976:161) very large claim that "the species to which Marx's 'species-being' belongs is Homo economicus" derives from Habermas (1971), among others (see Sahlins 1976:161–65). This enables him to put Marxist economics in bed with the formalists' neoclassical economics through a common acceptance of instrumental logic, a connection made quite explicit from the early days of Marxist economic anthropology (Cook 1969:380–81). Ironically, this convergence between conventional and Marxist economics is viewed by many of us as a source of the latter's analytical strength, whereas for Sahlins (1976:166) it is viewed as reprehensible for "concealing the meaningful system in the praxis by the practical explanation of the system." This reflects his unremitting defense of Polanyi's arguments against the role of means–end rationality and labor value in the study of the human economy.[15]

The danger of Baudrillard's positing of four mutually exclusive object logics in his privileging of use value and consumption as a mirror of production is reflected in his footnoted admission that "there is also a question of price" (1981:52 n. 32). This occurs in his prelude to an elaboration of the distinguishing and discriminating functions of objects, where price and the economic logics of use and exchange value are subordinated to the eminently sociocultural logic of sign value. Distancing of the economic is understandable, perhaps even justifiable, given the nature of Baudrillard's radical critique of Marx, which, after all, need not be carried to the extreme taken by its author (that is, the total disarming of Marxist political economy).

There are analytically sound reasons for revising the political economy of commodity value to include a consideration of sign value as a supplement to the study of use and exchange value. From my perspective, the ambivalence and difference implied to Baudrillard's symbolic exchange and sign value logics are not mutually exclusive of the practical operations and equivalence implied in the logics of use value and exchange value. Price or equivalency is partly subject to indirect influence by sign-value logic, just as the ambivalence of symbolic exchange may, in the long run, turn out to reflect the logic of equivalence. Sign value, however, can never displace exchange and use value in economic studies. It is, however, a potentially fruitful conceptual tool for exploring the foundations of "esteem value" in different cultural economies, that is, the importance that given commodities have for valuing subjects and, more important, of their preferences for this commodity or that (Fraser 1947:72–73, 75).[16]

BOURDIEU'S "HABITUS," ECONOMIC VALUE, AND COMMODITY CULTURE(S)

June Nash has recently appropriated Bourdieu's concept of habitus together with Polanyi's substantive meaning of the economic and the concepts of natural economy that are conducive to her positing of a Maya culture-specific, antimarket, use-value logic. There is clearly support in Bourdieu's work, especially related to his elaboration of the concept of "symbolic capital" (1977:171–83), for Polanyi's substantive meaning of the economic conceptualized as the "good-faith economy" (1977:173–74; 1998:chap. 5) and for interpreting all precapitalist economies in terms that accentuate the subjectivist cultural suppression of the practical logic of exchange posited in the objectivist model (cf. Bourdieu 1990:23). For Bourdieu, economism is the reduction of the "economy to its objective reality," that is, as a "system governed by laws of interested calculation, competition, or exploitation" (1977:172)—a reduction that is "socially repressed" in precapitalist formations. This, in effect, limits the epistemological tendency of economism to the study of the precapitalist economy since capitalist development implies, for Bourdieu, the economization (or desocialization or disembedding) of the economy. Presumably, for Bourdieu, economism distorts a proper understanding of the precapitalist economy but not of the capitalist economy.

Bourdieu's interpretation of precapitalist exchange based on fieldwork in Algeria (among the Berbers of Kabylia) and his accompanying critique of Lévi-Strauss on reciprocity are problematic in the Mesoamerican context. I am referring specifically to his contention that "the interdependence of gift and counter-gift destroys the practical logic of exchange, which can only function if the objective model (every gift requires a counter-gift) is not experienced as such . . . this misconstrual of the model is possible because the temporal structure of exchange (the counter-gift is not only different, but deferred) masks or contradicts the objective structure of exchange" (1990:23) through the "sincere fiction of disinterested exchange" or acts of generosity without calculation (1977:171). Bourdieu also seems to imply a contradiction or incompatibility between commodity transfers that occur in accordance with ceremonial pretexts and that reproduce established social relations and those made for economic reasons or that "explicitly acknowledge . . . economic ends in relation to which [the economy] is objectively oriented" and reproduce the economic bases of the economy's existence (1977:171). It is unclear to me why "functions" of the former type of transaction need to be concealed for the entire system of commodity transfers to operate.

My study of Valley Zapotec gifting and reciprocity culture in two villages found that agents' behavior is consciously planned in accordance with their own clear understanding of the difference between market exchange, gifting, and reciprocal exchange, which includes separate lexical labels for these as well as related discourse regarding corresponding social personality types (1968b:120–32; 1982:91–116; cf. Beals 1970). The Zapotec villagers' understandings of the linkage between wealth accumulation, redistribution, and prestige/honor or between economic and symbolic capital are compatible with their reasonable decision making. These villagers recognize a category of commodity transfers as gifts that do not carry an expectation of reciprocity and that are appropriately given when one attends an event, like a wedding or a funeral, to which no formal invitation was extended (Cook 1982:108–9). The empirical record, regarding both agent representations and the results of their performance, is inconclusive regarding the extent to which implied claims that such commodity transfers are motivated exclusively by generosity mask an expectation of deferred reciprocity that is confirmed by practice. All ceremonial transfers in Valley Zapotec village economies are made according to a pretext of complying with "*costumbre*," or local cultural traditions, and their socially and economically reproductive consequences are both unintended and unrecognized.

My reading of Bourdieu also suggests that his approach to the economic field is compatible with an attempt like mine to link prudent rationality and commodity culture together as comprising elements in the Mesoamerican habitus.[17] In the first place, the analytical attractiveness of the twin concepts of prudent rationality and commodity culture lies in their status as dialectically straddling objectivist and subjectivist moments—that is, between the outside analyst's constituting of structural constraints that bear on agents' interactions and the subjective representations of the agents themselves regarding their interactions (Bourdieu 1990:125). Like Bourdieu's questioning of Berber informants as to why particular "customs" were practiced, a line of anthropological fieldworkers in Mesoamerica, among many others (including myself), Redfield, Tax, Malinowski and de la Fuente, Manning Nash, Ralph Beals, and Frank Cancian, have intensively questioned Mesoamerican agents about their practice of economic and marketing customs and have collectively produced a "theory of this non-theoretical, partial, somewhat down-to-earth relationship with the social world that is the relation of ordinary experience" (Bourdieu 1990:20) that is implicit in references to a businesslike demeanor. The twin concepts of prudent rationality and commodity culture(s) are posited with the intention of advancing our understanding of economic life in Mesoamerica/Mexico beyond the level associated with the notion of "penny capitalism" (Tax 1963) or "market culture" (Goldin 1996).

In Bourdieu's terms, the practice of prudent rationality and commodity culture by Mesoamerican subjects may be understood as a "strategy" that is neither conscious, calculated, nor mechanically determined but is exercised through a "feel for a particular game"—be it one involving symbolic capital (honor, reputation, or prestige), social capital, or economic capital (1990:22–23, 62–63). On the other hand, it may also be understood as what I would call a "tactic" that involves a certain degree of conscious, calculated decision making, although not to the extreme demanded by the canons of formal rationality. I favor the latter approach since in the study of the economic field, the unintended is more pertinent than the unconscious. To the extent that the "feel for the game" leads to unintended consequences, it reflects some degree of subject consciousness.

In the context of Mesoamerica, Bourdieu's many economies (such as the economic, the religious, the honorific, and so on), it seems that the weight of ethnographic evidence points toward a merging of temporal and objective structures of exchange as well as a tendency to subjectively privilege the "economic" economy so that agents have no illusions about understanding or recognizing the linkage between gift and countergift as specifically costed equivalences (cf. Bourdieu 1990:22–23, 92–93). Accordingly, a metate presented as a gift by godparents to their goddaughter on the occasion of her wedding (which occurs because of the coparent relationship between two separate households) will inevitably be matched by an equivalently valued countergift in the future (or is given as a countergift). Although empirical data is lacking, it is reasonable to suppose that over the life cycles of Valley Zapotec households or intergenerationally between their descendants, commodities transferred in any particular ceremonial or ritual context will inevitably be reciprocated in kind (and probably with incremental exchange value) in the same or another ceremonial or ritual context. Such commodity exchanges are both socially and economically reproductive.

Unlike Bourdieu's "agents that have emerged from precapitalist societies" who are "thrown into a capitalist economy" and who possess a "discordant" habitus (1990:90), the habitus of today's Mesoamerican agents includes predispositions derived from historical experience in commodity culture(s) and markets. This, in turn, means that Mesoamerican agents, if not like "fish in water" (Bourdieu 1990:90) in the capitalist world, are, at least, like amphibians whose habitus embodies elements from their deep historical experience in the stream of commoditization (Hart 1982; cf. Appadurai 1986). In short, Mesoamerican agents have a "feel for the game" of commodity circulation that is part of their "second nature (Bourdieu 1990:62–63)—it has served them in the *tianguis* and *plaza* as well as in gifting, reciprocity, barter, and business within the *pueblo*. The game is regulated by "*costumbre*" in many contexts but by codified rules in other contexts.

This implies a subtle, nuanced, situational understanding and recognition, in substantialist and relational terms (Bourdieu 1990:125), of the "criterion of value" (1990:89). It opens, in some respects, a Pandora's box simply because Mesoamerican economies, like all others, have histories in which different "regimes of value in space and time" (Appadurai 1986:4) have developed and are part of a repertory of commodity culture that can be drawn on situationally or contextually by agents to give meaning to commodity transactions. Each value regime employs different criteria for determining value in exchange in both a proximate and a more remote sense, and these criteria vary in terms of agent negotiability and recognition. Among peasant artisans in the central valleys of Oaxaca in the second half of the twentieth century, for example, exchange value of commodities transferred inside or outside of marketplaces—and whether sold, given, or bartered—tends to be determined, at least indirectly, in money terms. Nevertheless, the equivalency in a "close enough" sense may be in kind—that is, a particular quantity of labor time or a particular quantity of corn or other commodity (Cook 1982:chap. 3).

With regard to commodities regularly produced by peasant artisans for exchange in the regional marketplace or *plaza* system, I have argued that "value is a property of commodities . . . something that attaches itself to them like 'utility' and is reflected in their market price . . . [and] in the socially necessary labor-time they embody" but also that "the "labour-value embodied" in them "is realized through exchange in the marketplace; and that the latter is where the inter-village division of labour is regulated to meet social demand, and integrated to facilitate social reproduction" (1976:421). Through an analysis of one particular set of commodities—metates and manos—I attempted to show how the involved agents, the *metateros*, conceive of the value of the commodities they produce and how their understandings and recognitions of value creation and realization affect their conduct (Cook 1982:chaps. 6, 7).

Needless to say, the value question has another side, namely, that of value in use or the demand side of commodities produced for sale. Bourdieu reminds us that "economic production functions only in so far as it first produces a belief in the value of its products" (1990:89). Appadurai elaborates, "Demand is thus neither a mechanical response to the structure and level of production nor a bottomless natural appetite. It is a complex social mechanism that mediates between short- and long-term patterns of commodity circulation" (1986:40–41). The use-value elements of commodity culture(s) imply not only knowledge by producers that impacts on the production of commodities but also knowledge by consumers as to the proper use of particular commodities, that is, how to consume them (1986:41). Moreover, as I discuss in chapter 8 regarding the significance of the metate in the Oaxaca valley, the consumption, demand, use, and symbolic value dimensions of commodities inevitably lead into critical areas of culture that lie beyond the economic field proper.

CONCLUSIONS

Thanks to Little's perceptive contribution, we can add to Roseberry's (1989:31–33) "grid of analogous oppositions" another antinomy, namely, economic anthropology versus anthropological/cultural economics. Although we may choose to dissolve this contradiction, as Roseberry does, by emphasizing an intersection of concerns by proponents of these opposed approaches around the theme of "meaningful action" and a common recognition that "[economic] action is shaped by the [cultural] meanings people take" to it "even as [cultural] meanings are shaped by people's [economic] activities" (1989:33), to do so in my opinion risks collapsing the economic into the cultural. My resistance to this dialectical dissolution of the "economic" is founded on a heuristic premise of the analytical benefits derived from rigorously defining the empirical field of study in broad substantive terms and then, more specifically, by using the general categories of production, distribution, exchange, and consumption. I am convinced that the analytical advantages of this approach, especially when focused on economic value issues, far outweigh the disadvantages—especially in the context of contemporary studies within the boundaries of capitalist market economies.[18]

Given the pervasiveness of exchange in the ethnographic record of precapitalist economies, it is realistic to assume that every useful artifact is a commodity since the potential exists for it to be exchanged at any time before it is consumed. In addition, exchange value and abstract/symbolic value realization often either occurs in the absence of uniform standards of measure to facilitate the precise calculations of equivalences or is deferred beyond the time of transfer (as in gifting or delayed reciprocity). The value returned may be in the form of an indeterminate (hence incommensurate) or "close enough" equivalent quantity of useful artifacts or services. In any event, a strong logical case can be made to get rid of the confusing natural economy concept (and with it the illogical distinction between product and commodity) and replace it with a less abstract, more realistic concept like original commodity economy (Cook 1976:399–400).

The implication that in early twenty-first-century capitalism, crises in simple household reproduction, resulting in reallocations of labor to production for own use, may reflect the resuscitation or strengthening of "natural economy" is misleading on several counts. It misrepresents the past in implying that "self-sufficiency" was a viable option in peasant economies built on commodity production (that is, division of labor and specialization). Moreover, it misrepresents the present in underestimating the extent to which local economic life is penetrated by external and internal market processes and, therefore, the extent to which products or goods produced by households for own consumption are, in reality, "subsistence commodities" (Chevalier 1982:chap. 4) whose exchange values can be reckoned objectively in monetized, labor-time terms and reflect a "calculative pursuit" of "tangible increases in levels of consumption" Chevalier 1982:115). In today's international economy, the boundaries of local economies that could conceivably be construed to approximate the "natural" model have been violated everywhere by commodity forms—and the question becomes one of how household and community needs can be served at all by economic activity that bypasses commodity circuits. There is, indisputably, a growing need and plenty of economic space for the performance of unwaged labor in households and communities differentially dispersed throughout the international commodity economy. Two points are critical. First, the reproduction of local economies is increasingly dependent on the sale of their labor power and material commodities in external markets, transactions that inevitably result in the acquisition of other commodities. Second, whether or not labor power and material commodities are sold or directly consumed, the use and exchange value embodied in them are realized. The objectification of value (that is, its commensurability in money terms) is simply an inevitable concomitant of capitalist market penetration. In both precapitalist and mixed economies, however, there is no question that commodity value is less objectified; that is, the degree to which commodity circulation is dependent on strict (and quantifiable) standards of commensurateness is reduced. The cultural construction of demand or material needs and of sign/symbolic exchange value that consumptionists justifiably privilege in their analyses of contemporary capitalism is also at play in precapitalist and mixed economies in the reckoning of equivalence. The relative impreciseness of measuring equivalency as "close enough" in product (or service) transfers in the latter type of economy, however, is by no means sufficient cause for depriving them of generic commodity status.

NOTES

1. Godelier (1971:69) expressed this forcefully: "Economic anthropology can only exist if it takes as its own the standard definition of economic activity as consisting of production, distribution, and consumption of material goods. This definition is the only one which delimits the field of inquiry to subjects proper to economic science. It in no way prejudges the nature of the relations existing in each type of society between its economic structure and other institutional sub-systems."

2. Marx's discussion of the categories of economy can be interpreted as an exercise in idealist dialectics (that is, "the dialectical balancing of concepts") to critique the mechanistic or empirical materialistic use of these categories in classical political economy from Adam Smith through John Stuart Mill (Nicolaus 1973:36; cf. Marx 1971:23). However, this does not diminish the relevancy of the exercise in promoting our understanding of how Marx moved beyond these categories to historical materialist categories of social formation, mode of production, and so on.

3. In his otherwise insightful and comprehensive exegesis of Marx's approach to commodity value, David Harvey (1982:15), like Martin Nicolaus, emphasizes its exclusive applicability to the capitalist mode of production. Consequently, he circumvents Marx's "key rule" and the critical issue (for economic anthropology) of extending Marx's approach to the study of precapitalist economies or to local/regional peasant-artisan economies within present-day capitalism. Even so, Harvey's review of Marx's value theory yields many generalizations (for example, "the commensurability of commodities achieved through exchange renders the labor embodied in them equally commensurable" [1982:14]) that are suggestive of the possibilities of such an extension. Still, there is no question that determinations of equivalency/commensurability in nonmoney economies are less objectified than in those with special-purpose monies and that economies with general-purpose money set the standard for precise determinations of equivalency in commodity transfers.

4. In the spirit of reclaiming "the facts of determination, structure and essentialism in social life" from the "current intellectual vogue," Michael Watts has eloquently reminded us that "it was Marx, who after all pointed to the fact that not everything was negotiable or contested—or that there are quite different sorts of determinations operating within the circumference of lived realities" (2002:45).

5. Roseberry's thinking was influenced by his reading of Raymond Williams's discussion of the contemporary convergence between the anthropological/sociological senses of culture according to which "a distinctive 'signifying system' is seen not only as essential but as essentially involved in all forms of social activity" and "the more specialized, if common sense of culture as artistic and intellectual activities" (Williams 1981:13). In his discussion of idealist and materialist approaches to culture, Williams wrote about the latter, "'Cultural practice' and 'cultural production' . . . are not simply derived from an otherwise constituted social order but are themselves major elements in its constitution. It then shares some elements with [the idealist] in its emphasis on cultural practices as (though now among others) *constitutive*" (1981:12–13; cf. Wessman 1981:68-72).

6. This exemplifies the tension between Marx as theorizer of the commoditization of labor as "labor power" and, hence, as discoverer of "surplus value" and Marx the evolutionist and comparative economic historian. The first role inevitably exceptionalizes capitalism or the capitalist mode of production and emphasizes the discontinuity, in terms of the organization of economic value production, between it and all previous economies/modes of production. The latter role, subordinated to the former, inclined Marx toward an emphasis on origins/connections/continuities between capitalism and precapitalist forms of economy/society. This tension or contradiction is palpable in discourse about the labor theory of value and the concept of simple commodity production (Cook 1976:398–404). Keying in on the critical distinction between wage rates (or the price of labor power) and the value of labor power (in terms of wage goods), Harvey argues that Marx's overall strategy was "to see value as an expression of social necessity under the class relations of capitalism and to assert that values (including that of labor power) become the regulators of economic life only to the degree that the capitalist mode of production becomes hegemonic within a social formation" (1982:52). The challenge is to explore how Marx's approach to commodity economics can be extended to pre- and noncapitalist formations without losing sight of the conditions

that make capitalism exceptional.

7. According to Harvey (1982:1), "Marx considers the commodity as a material embodiment of *use value, exchange value* and *value.*" In premonetary barter economies, only an "equivalent form" of value operated according to which the value of goods being acquired by a community or bargaining agent is measured against the single value of a good being disposed of. Under such conditions, "abstract human labor" is the only "common denominator between two different products that provides a basis for their exchange" (Marx 1977:126–31, 150). As such economies evolve, one commodity or set of commodities emerges as a universal equivalent (that is, general-purpose commodity money) facilitating the operation of a "relative form" of value according to which "the relative values of all other commodities can . . . be expressed in terms of this money commodity" (Harvey 1982:11). Hence, the money form of value is born, and the true historical seedbed of capital is in place. Under the money form, of course, labor value becomes quantifiable in money terms. Abstract value in the senses just mentioned differs from Sahlins's concept of "symbolic exchange value" derived from the Saussure/Baudrillard notion of "sign value" (Sahlins 1976). It is obvious that in the premonetary stage described here, the determination of equivalency in goods transfer relies on the valuing agent and leaves open a role for symbolic exchange value together with abstract human labor (through labor alienation). Meek (1956:294–95) argues plausibly for labor value as a fair or natural "method of exchanging commodities" in the precapitalist period.

8. Although Weber does not use "natural economy" as an example in his explanation of the heuristic and expository purposes of the "ideal type" of procedure, it is clear from his discussion that like, for example, the "city-economy" or "handicraft," it is a "unified analytical construct" that "cannot be found empirically anywhere in reality" (1949:90). As Roseberry points out, it is clearly such a construct in Marxist theory as well.

9. Rosa Luxemburg (1968:368–69) viewed natural economy as distinct from "a system of simple commodity production both in agriculture and trade" or "commodity economy," which, she noted, "exists mainly in an environment of peasants and artisans" (1968:368). She recognized, together with Lenin (1964), that peasants can also participate in natural economy. But her conceptualization encompasses several precapitalist modes of production in which peasants are direct producers and "production only goes on because both means of production and labor power are bound in one form or another" (1968:368–69). Luxemburg also contended that "the general result of the struggle between capitalism and simple commodity production is this: after substituting commodity economy for natural economy, capital takes the place of simple commodity economy" (1968:416). Thus, she gave an original slant to Marx's ideas about natural economy and to the global struggle between capital and noncapitalist forms through her understanding that the latter were essential to capitalist accumulation. She failed to understand, however, that subsumption by capital did not necessarily entail "progressive disintegration" (1968:416) of subsumed noncapitalist forms.

10. A careful reading (and rereading) of Marx (esp. 1975:198) supports the interpretation that he clearly separated the notion of a useful thing, which he called a "labour-product" or good, from the notion of a commodity. In addition, it supports the interpretation that he did conceive of a commodity as having use value and exchange value but emphasized the latter as being a phenomenal form or "appearance" of "value" that, itself, is a potential representation of use value. In his words, "[The

commodity] . . . is, on the one hand, in its natural form, a *useful thing*, alias a *use-value*; on the other hand, it is a *bearer of exchange-value* . . . but exchange-value is only a '*form* of appearance,' the autonomous mode of presentation of the *value* contained in the commodity. . . . I do not divide *value* into use-value and exchange-value as antitheses into which the abstraction 'value' splits, rather [I divide] the *concrete social form* of the labour-product; '*commodity*' is, on the one hand, use-value, and on the other hand, 'value,' not exchange-value, since the mere form of appearance is not its proper content . . . the 'value' of a commodity is neither its use-value nor its exchange-value" (1975:198–99). For Marx, "value" refers to an "abstraction from use value . . . one and the same sort of labour . . . human labor in the abstract . . . the common substance that manifests itself in the exchange-value of commodities, whenever they are exchanged, is their value . . . the labour . . . that forms the substance of value is homogeneous human labour, expenditure of one uniform labour-power" (1967, 1:38–39).

11. The concept of labor alienation is related to Marx's general theory of alienation regarding the impact on humanity of the transformation of society to capitalism: "In capitalist society . . . the process of appropriation of nature has lost its creative character and has become. . . . 'direct one-sided gratification—merely in the sense of possessing, of having'" (Wessman 1981:82; cf. Ollman 1971:91–95). It refers specifically to the production of objects for other use in order to acquire objects for own use through exchange—a process that, for Marx, implied that the product of labor is an alien object that exercises power over its producer (Marx 1964:111). The process also implied, for Marx, that such products are reciprocally alienated from their producers in separate communities by exchange as a necessary condition of social reproduction (Marx 1977:182). As exemplified in the work of Mauss (1954) and Sahlins (1972, 1976), anthropologists "have exaggerated the totalizing holism of small-scale social groups, often ignoring contradictions and feelings of alienation" derived from a "simple distinction between persons and things" (Miller 1997:416–17). It is a small step from that distinction to a recognition that work embodied in a thing endows it with value that gives it the potential of being transferred and reciprocated.

12. Mandel's elaboration of the classic Marxist thesis of the origin of commodity exchange in intergroup trade and not in intragroup reciprocity exposes a fundamental contradiction. On the one hand, he emphasizes that reciprocity "does not depend on any expectation of a precise reciprocal payment" and that "*a measured reciprocal payment is what constitutes the essential characteristic of exchange*" (1970:49). On the other hand, he admits that "exchange, the most precisely 'measured' operation in modern economic life, was born in material conditions that *excluded any possibility of precise measurement*" (1970:49; emphasis added). As far as I am concerned, the most logical way to resolve this contradiction is to drop the dichotomization of product versus commodity and reciprocity versus exchange and assume that, from the perspective of economic value, labor alienation is the precipitating material condition that creates the possibility of the valuation of alienated things.

13. The implication of Sahlins's linkage of dominance of the economy in capitalist formations to the predominance of the relations of production as a classificatory grid begs the question of the nature and function of relations of production in precapitalist formations where, presumably, according to substantivist logic, the economy is not dominant and noneconomic institutions or domains are. Sahlins's position on this

question was more clearly staked out in *Stone Age Economics*, where he rejected the thesis that, for example, kinship functions as relations of production in such societies. He had to reject this thesis because it points to the economic determination of the dominance of kinship in *societas* societies that he would rather attribute to the cultural or symbolic order, which, for him, constitutes the pregiven conditions from which all else follows (cf. Cook 1974b:377–78; Godelier 1972:92–97; 1986:147–48). Rather than being satisfied with the thesis that there is an element of the mental in all social reality, Sahlins's embrace of semiotics reflects his belief that everything in reality worth investigating is mental (cf. Godelier 1986:151).

14. I use the term "dialectical" with some trepidation—given the controversy and complications surrounding it. For me, its meanings are relatively straightforward. In the metaphysical/ontological sense, it implies change, process, becoming; conceptually, it precludes stasis or static equilibrium and emphasizes a moving or shifting process of equilibrium and disequilibrium. Put differently, it accentuates becoming over being. Epistemologically, it implies a method of reasoning by negation combined with an insistence on interpenetration of opposites and of a necessary interplay between empirical inquiry and abstract conceptualization and of subject and object, always with a view toward promoting more approximate understandings of changing, shifting reality. It seeks to produce understanding of change in a framework that connects past, present, and future while trying to avoid the pitfalls of teleological or historicist thinking. In my opinion, the best example of dialectical reasoning in the economic anthropological literature is Keith Hart's essay "On Commoditization" (1982).

15. To my knowledge, Sahlins, unlike Dalton, has never expressed in print any second thoughts, qualifications, or differences of interpretation, much less criticism, regarding Polanyi's writings.

16. Consequently, I agree with Baudrillard's insight that "in the correlation: EV/UV = Sr/Sd use value and signified . . . have a tactical value—whereas exchange value and signifier have strategic value. . . . Absolute preeminence redounds to exchange value and the signifier" (1981:137). But rather than using this a justification for embracing a new theory that breaks this preeminence as Baudrillard does (1981:143–63), I prefer to accept it as the best method for developing a twenty-first-century economic anthropology of Mexico. Wessman's (1981:91–94) discussion of "The Symbol and the Sign" clarifies the origins and uses of semiotics in anthropological discourse.

17. My reading (and rereading) of Bourdieu is focused mainly on two books (1977, 1990), and I will admit to having my doubts about the meaning and analytical fruitfulness of his habitus concept. One of Bourdieu's long definitions of it suffices to provide the basis for a skeptical critique: "The structures constitutive of a particular type of environment (e.g., the material conditions of existence characteristic of a class condition) produce *habitus*, systems of durable, transposable dispositions, structured structures predisposed to function as structuring structures, that is, as principles of the generation and structuring of practices and representations which can be objectively 'regulated' and 'regular' without in any way being the product of obedience to rules, objectively adapted to their goals without presupposing a conscious aiming at ends or an express mastery of the operations necessary to attain them and, being all this, collectively orchestrated without being the product of the orchestrating action of a conductor" (1977:72). This seems to be

Bourdieu's answer to the oppositions between culture and personality or society and individual and seems to posit a semiconscious, unconscious and semi-intended, unintended space in any economy–society–culture formation that mediates between the observable and the unobservable, the subjective and objective dimensions. As such, it is as original, provocative, and useful a concept as anyone else has ever invented and provides a way to express in words the complexities of a process that continues to defy intellectual grasp in any definitive sense.

18. Many of us who instinctively turn to Marx for provocative ideas on economic and social matters also find Weber indispensable. Bourdieu has astutely expressed the rationale for this: "It is evident . . . that Weber saw something that Marx did not, but also that Weber could see what Marx hadn't because Marx had seen what he had" (1990:35).

6

Understanding Peasants, Commodity Economy, and Change in the Mesoamerican Experience

In the half century that has passed since the publication of *Penny Capitalism*, the economic anthropology of Mexico has been influenced by processes of change that have impacted on the nature and role of the countryside as well as on the perspectives, theories, and analytical categories shaping the process of knowledge production. At the time of *Penny Capitalism*'s publication, the category "peasant" was replacing that of "primitive" and "folk" as the unified subject of anthropological inquiry. This process was preceded by a shift in prevailing theoretical orientation from ethnographic particularism to holistic functionalism and was followed by the emergence of several varieties of historical structuralism (cultural ecology, Marxism, and dependency theory), indigenismo (Hewitt de Alcántara 1984:6), and feminism.

The 1980s and 1990s witnessed a continuing theoretical diversification led by several varieties of postmodernism and poststructuralism with deconstructionist and dialogical emphases. This potpourri of theoretical orientations in sociocultural anthropology shared, in varying degrees, a common emphasis on so-called globalization and transnational processes, a critique of the peasant category and of the distinction between rural and urban (Kearney 1996:1), and a rejection of productionist in favor of consumptionist approaches to the economy (usually but not always associated with a rejection of economism).[1]

This dizzying dance of competing approaches to knowledge production in sociocultural anthropology inevitably had some trickle-down effect on the empirical study of the Mexican peasant economy. It is, however, indicative of the singular importance of Eric Wolf's contribution that innovative thought and analysis in this field of study since the 1960s must be evaluated in the context of a paradigm largely of his making.

ERIC WOLF, PENNY CAPITALISM, AND THE PEASANT ECONOMY

The key to understanding Eric Wolf's approach to the economy and economics is that it was developed, for the most part, prior to and outside the framework of the formalist–substantivist controversy. It was forged through his early reading of Karl Wittfogel (esp. 1931, cf. 1968), Julian Steward, and Paul Sweezy and reflects his career-long commitment to "expanding materialist approaches in anthropology" (Wolf 2001:4). The scope of Wolf's work from its inception in Julian Steward's Puerto Rico project (Wolf 1956:171–264; 2001:38–48; see also Roseberry 1978) went well beyond the boundaries of economic anthropology, but his materialist theoretical orientation required him to keep a sharp eye on the economic process. As he became more involved in peasant studies, his approach was influenced by a wide range of sources, including Karl Marx, Max Weber, A. V. Chayanov, Karl Polanyi, cultural ecology/cultural geography, and a variety of historians and ethnographers (Wolf 1966:1–59). His overriding concern was to understand the peasant economy processually—as a "labor process" or the "ways in which people employ tools in carrying out the work of transforming nature" (2001:40) and as "social relations of production" or "the nexus, the link, the articulation . . . between the deployment of social labor . . . and the social allocation of the means of production—the resources of nature and the instruments available for their transformation for human use" (2001:44). His six-step operationalization of how the "relation, the nexus, between these two terms sets up the field of force within which people then carry on material production" completes Wolf's conceptualization of infrastructure (2001:44–45) and set limits on his approach to economics.

But Wolf's knowledge-production agenda could not be contained by infrastructure, much less by the economic field. His driving scholarly interest was in the broader articulation and complex interpenetration of infrastructure with superstructure—especially vis-à-vis the horizontal and vertical flows of political power and cultural symbols that configured social formations synchronically and energized them diachronically, that is, at the level of world-historical or civilizational process. Specific elements of the economic process and, indeed, the entire process itself disappear as a specific object of analysis in a project of this scope. In the final analysis, regarding Mexico, Wolf's primary interest was not the Mexican economic process per se but how that process was encompassed by and evolved within the infrastructure and how the latter, in turn, articulated with superstructure to configure the Mexican social formation as it historically developed through different civilizational forms that in the twentieth century intersected with the emergence of an international market-integrated division of labor (Fröbel et al. 1978).

Wolf's general peasant paradigm, presented in his 1966 book, did not correspond to a specific chronologically limited ethnographic record but to a broader and deeper spatiotemporal historical and ethnographic record that spanned humanity's world-historic experience. Likewise, his more specific paradigm for peasant-Indian Mexico—revolving around the local community but focusing on its interior and exterior relations that locate it processually in a regional, national, and international system—is best understood from the perspective of an intersection of chronological historicoethnographic time and time in the world-historic or "general experience of humanity" sense. Firsthand ethnographic experience was overshadowed by comparative analysis and archival work in shaping Wolf's vision of peasant Mexico (2001:6). His work is a rich source of ideas and hypotheses for a general orientation and point of departure in ethnographic knowledge production about specific time-and-place communities or regions. With some notable exceptions (1967), however, Wolf's theoretically informed generalizations and many of his conceptual constructs dealing with "peasants" are general, comparative, or diachronic and are not correspondent to specific contemporary time-and-place coordinates.

My interpretation of Eric Wolf's work evokes comparison with the work of Oscar Lewis in which the mix between ethnographic and archival experience was reversed—and where the world historic and comparative interest was subordinated to humanistic, developmentalist, and applied anthropological concerns. Lewis's work was more restricted to the level of midrange theory than was Wolf's. Consequently, it was more easily operationalized than Wolf's for purposes of community-based ethnographic studies of rural Mexico. This is readily demonstrable, for example, by comparing Lewis's "levels of organization" (1960:40–53) approach with Wolf's "levels of communal relations" approach (1967:299–316) or Lewis's (1949) approach to group relations with Wolf's (2001:124–38). This comparison could be taken much further to include the two scholars' differing approaches to Indians, the Mexican Revolution, the economy and economic development, and so on.

Lewis, in pioneering the "national citizen" (Cook 1993b:331) approach in the anthropological study of Mexico, set a precedent among anthropologists for seriously examining *Mexicanidad*, or mestizoness, rather than Indianness as a source of social identity among peasant villagers. He rejected "ideological localism whereby each little community is treated as self-sufficient and isolated" (1951:xx–xxi). This put Lewis on a separate trajectory from Mexican *indigenistas* and, to a certain extent, from Wolf, who had a deeper Mesoamericanist orientation than Lewis and enabled him to study the culture of Tepoztlán as "part of the larger culture of Mexico" (1951:xxi) and to document an "increasing identification of Tepoztecans with the Mexican nation and with the state of Morelos" (1951:38).

General differences in Wolf's and Lewis's views are clear from Hewitt de Alcântara's pioneering socioepistemological study of anthropological approaches to Mexican rural otherness (1984:35–40, 73–96) even though she makes no direct comparisons between them. The seven differing schools of thought she identified over six decades of the twentieth century (1920–1980) can be ranged along a continuum "which runs from greatest concern with the ethnographic study of local culture, at one extreme, to greatest concern with the analysis of power at the other" (1984:6). Her own analysis of Wolf's intellectual location in this scholasticized space of Mexican rural studies (that is, as a historical structuralist/cultural ecologist/Marxist) agrees with my distancing of him from the ethnographic pole on the continuum. Lewis, by contrast, would be located much closer to the ethnographic pole and the case study approach, including informant-centered life history.

Although Wolf's understanding of structure insisted on a space for individual maneuver (1959b:142), his work is characterized by the absence of individual voices of human agents and, indeed, of a concern with actual individual decision making. Of primary concern to him was the "ongoing dialectical interpenetration" of "social behavior" and "culturally encoded symbolic forms" (2001:165). The individual in such a process is always hypothetical and always a creature of culturally inscribed social relations—never idiosyncratic or unique but always representative. Individuals as symbolic communicators and actors in Wolf's approach are creatures of social contexts (household, family, community, region, and nation), domains (economics, politics, and religion), and social variables (social origins, gender, age, education, occupation, and class) (Wolf 1999:6–7). There are no Pedro Martinezes (Lewis 1964) or children of Sanchez (Lewis 1961) in Wolf's work, just as the theoretical and comparative world-historical vision of *Europe and the People without History* (Wolf 1982), *Envisioning Power* (Wolf 1999), and *Pathways of Power* (Wolf 2001) is more reduced in Lewis's work.

Despite his early emphasis on "human manoeuver always pressing against the inherent limitations of cultural forms" (1959b:142), Wolf's later work placed more weight on the influence of historically developed structures and social constraints on the exercise of choice than he did on the exercise of choice itself; voluntarism is reduced to a minimum in his approach vis-à-vis, for example, that of Tax. He conceded Tax's point regarding the shrewdness of peasant market habits, but rather than viewing this as a possible basis for the development of peasant economy, he redirected it back into the socially constrained "internal, domestic" realm (1966:14), where it was bound to reproduce, not develop or transform, peasant economy or its elements.

REREADING WOLF ON PEASANT ECONOMY

From the perspective of economic anthropology, a series of Wolf's publications, published between 1955 and 1967, had the greatest impact on establishing the paradigm that would dominate peasant studies. The first of these is his 1955 article titled "Types of Latin American Peasantry: A Preliminary Discussion," in which he elaborated an ideal–typical model of peasant communities, including, most important, what he called the "closed corporate peasant community," which, in Mexico, was most commonly exemplified empirically among indigenous highland populations. Written at the same time and promoting a dualistic view of the corporate peasantry more explicitly (2001:155, 158) was his article "Closed Corporate Peasant Communities in Mesoamerica and Central Java" (2001:147–59).

There are several other foundational contributions by Wolf to the study of the Mesoamerican/Mexican economy. A section of his 1959 book *Sons of the Shaking Earth* is devoted to a discussion of the economy of peasant-Indian communities (1959a:223–32) that is highlighted by his critique of Tax's "penny capitalism" concept. Chapters 1 and 2 from his general introductory book *Peasants* published in 1966 is noteworthy for his conceptualization of the peasant production–consumption unit in a wider field of economic and social relations and conditions, spanning community, region, nation, and world. In addition, his chapter in the *Handbook of Middle American Indians*, "Levels of Communal Relations" (Wolf 1967), emphasized the role of marketing as a mechanism of regional integration. Finally, a posthumously published article, originally written in 1977 (2001:252–59), expanded Wolf's views on the class differentiation of the peasantry. The latter article reiterated his neopopulist/peasantist approach to class associated with the work of Chayanov and Shanin and is especially disappointing for his failure to specifically address the agrarian Marxist approach in Russian studies as developed by Lenin (1964) and further refined in the work of Kritsman and his school (Cox 1984, 1986; Cox and Littlejohn 1984).

Perhaps the conceptual linchpin of Wolf's location of the peasantry (that is, agricultural direct producers) in society is the "rent fund," which he defined as a charge paid out as the result of some superior claim to labor on the land that is paid in labor, produce, or money (1966:9; cf. 2001:260–61). Through rent, according to Wolf, peasant "surpluses . . . are transferred to a dominant group of rulers . . . to underwrite its own standard of living and to distribute the remainder to groups in society that do not farm but must be fed for their specific goods and services" (1966:3–4). This characterization of the place of peasantry in society, as well as the notion of an externalized rent fund, was heavily influenced by Wolf's study of the historic record of feudal European and tributary Asian civilizations. Its applicability in postcolonial

Mexico was limited because of the local control of land and the local class structure that stood between peasant labor and the external state or class structure. The appropriation of peasant surpluses, either from accessed land or agricultural means of production (such as ox teams, plows, and tractors), even during the nineteenth century, was a relational process involving local, relatively well-off households and relatively poor households.[2]

Even in the wake of the early twentieth-century agrarian reforms, which allocated land in free usufruct to significant numbers of peasant households, inequalities in land distribution within Mexican agrarian communities compelled land-poor peasant households to pay rent to other local landowners for access to arable land or for the use of traction animals, tractors, or other agricultural means of production (Cook and Binford 1990:44–45). Rent relations of this type are absent from Wolf's notion of an external rent fund. In short, given the intracommunity differentiation of the Mexican peasantry, Wolf's rent criterion is not necessarily an adequate demarcator of peasant status in postcolonial (and especially postrevolutionary) Mexico, unless it is reconceptualized to also encompass class-based value transfers within the local community. Wolf's model is probably most applicable to colonial Mexico, where the Spanish colonial state and private Spanish and creole landowners effectively extracted rent in Wolf's sense from the peasant-Indian masses.

Wolf's externalization of the "rent fund" set a precedent for his handling of the "profit fund" in economies that are capitalist or are experiencing capitalist development. Since peasants, for Wolf, were producers of social wealth for superordinate others who, by virtue of their superior location in the social hierarchy (status or class), are empowered to appropriate surpluses from the direct producers, the unequal exchange between peasants and capitalists flowed into funds of profit external to the peasantry. This precludes the possibility of the development of capitalist relations of production within the peasantry—a possibility that was foreclosed by Wolf's insistence that the aim and result of peasant production is subsistence, not reinvestment (2001:196), and also to meet replacement, ceremonial, and rent fund requirements (1966:1–17). He recognized the historical tendency toward social differentiation within peasant communities (1966:16) but never was able to link his recognition to peasant participation in commodity economy because he privileged ecological and social factors over market forces and use value over exchange value in constraining everyday peasant economic behavior (2001:257–58). Throughout Wolf's work, despite his rejection of the concept of the peasantry as a single class in an unpublished 1977 paper (2001:252–59), that very concept runs deep.[3]

Wolf asserted, "The peasant . . . does not operate an enterprise in the economic sense; he runs a household, not a business concern" (1966:2), and "the peasant is at once an economic agent and the head of a household. His holding is both an economic unit and a home" (1966:13). Later (2001:257), he admitted that "peasant households may be looked upon as economic firms, but they are firms of a peculiar sort. Because they are . . . kinship units of some kind, what the kinship unit produces and what it consumes will be closely intertwined . . . this introduces particular rigidities . . . [but] the family is especially good at exploiting itself" (2001:257). In this last statement, Wolf appears to be moving toward agreement with Galeski (1972:10–11) that the "basic characteristic of the peasant production unit is *the fusion or (more exactly) the identification of the enterprise (i.e., the commodity-producing establishment) with the domestic economy of the family household.*" Nevertheless, his overall emphasis is on the sociocultural idiosyncrasies of peasants as producers and consumers.

For Wolf, familial self-exploitation could never become "endofamilial accumulation" (Cook 1984a:167), and therefore petty commodity production could never become petty capitalism in the context of peasant economy. This possibility was precluded by virtue of Wolf's structuration of peasant household economics around provisioning of subsistence needs plus ceremonial, replacement and rent fund requirements, and his disengagement of this process from other possible implications of the commodity-producing involvement of the peasant household (for example, profit seeking, capital accumulation, employment of wage labor) (Cook and Binford 1990:113–51).

Indeed, peasant involvement in petty commodity production, like wage labor, was conceptualized by Wolf in Chayanovian terms as "compensatory economic reactions in the field of production" (1955:458; cf. Thorner et al. 1966:108–9). Such reactions by a peasant community were structurally compelled by "any imposition of taxes, any increase in expenditures relative to the productive capacity of the community, or the internal growth of the population on a limited amount of land . . . the lack of resources and the very need to sustain the system of religion and power" (Wolf 1955:458). Wolf referred euphemistically to petty commodity production (including petty trade) as "some specialization which has competitive advantages within the marginal economy of such communities" and views participation in it as entering the "outside market" (1955:458). Nevertheless, in his 1955 article, he equated "production for the market" with "cash-crop production," which he viewed as a creature of the outside capitalist market (2001:207–9). Wolf never really was concerned with the differences between cash-crop and craft production, the complex relationship between them, or with the ways in which they both interact with migratory wage labor in the livelihood strategies of Mexican agrarian households.

THE CCPC, PENNY CAPITALISM, AND THE SIMPLE REPRODUCTION TRAP

In his *Sons of the Shaking Earth*, Wolf berated Tax for losing sight of the communal involvement of peasant Indians and treating them "in terms of capitalist economic theory." According to Wolf, the Mesoamerican Indian subject only superficially resembled the "individual economic agent of classical economics, unrestrictedly exchanging goods in a capitalist market," and "he is not a capitalist, nor free of restrictions" (1959a:224). Two additional statements in this discussion epitomize Wolf's approach to Mexican peasants: "He handles money; but he does not use money to build capital. It is for him merely one way of reckoning equivalences, of appraising the value of goods in exchange" (1959a:224).

More important than the difficulty in locating Wolf's hypothetical peasant-Indian economic agent historically in any specific century is that his discussion downplays the impact of general purpose money on the evolving commodity culture(s) of Mexico's peasant Indians who, at the time the Spanish arrived, were already extensively engaged in marketing and special purpose money use. In short, Wolf seems to arbitrarily close the door on the possible development of indigenous capitalism or even local class differentiation by depriving the peasant-Indian economic agent (a unified subject) of the use of money to accumulate capital.

Wolf's critique of Tax was somewhat blunted in 1966 when he cited Tax positively for drawing anthropological attention to the "proverbial . . . shrewdness of peasants" in negotiating external markets, but then re-sharpened as a means to justify Wolf's own predilection for Chayanov's "special kind of peasant economics" (1966:14): "However, to the extent that a peasant holding serves to provision a group of people, every decision made in terms of the external market also has its internal, domestic aspect" (1966:14). This underlines the critical importance of household demographics, consumer/worker ratios, marginal calculations regarding work/drudgery and needs, and so on that are summarized by Wolf as the "perennial problem of the peasantry . . . in balancing the demands of the external world against the peasants' need to provision their households," which is resolved through the exercise of "two diametrically opposed strategies . . . to increase production . . . [or] to curtail consumption" (1966:14–15).

Paradoxically, the coming into vogue of peasant studies in the 1960s under the stimulus of Wolf's (1955, 1959a, 1966) influential work resulted in the shelving of the Redfield–Tax contribution. I emphasize the paradoxical element in this Wolfian shift because it presumably obliged anthropologists to explore and explain wider system connections with and impacts on the small communities they studied ethnographically—and in Mexico there is no doubt that at least since the nineteenth century, the identity of the wider system has been capitalist. Wolf (1959a:224–28) was partially justified in ridiculing Tax's loose usage of the term "capitalist," but in the process of doing so, Wolf missed an opportunity to emphasize the commodity nature of peasant economy and to support Tax's anti-dualism thesis that Guatemala (and, by inference, Mexico) had a single economy.

Rather, Wolf's critique of Tax and Wolf's elaboration of the closed corporate peasant community (CCPC) model promoted dualism—the thesis that Mexico (and Guatemala) had an asymmetrically bifurcated economic system: a subordinate, ethnoculturally driven peasant-Indian economy (noncapitalist) and a dominant, market-driven mestizo commodity economy (capitalist). This resulted in downplaying the potential for capital accumulation in peasant commodity production and deprived Wolf's approach of the capacity to account for the emergence of indigenous forms of peasant capitalist enterprise and local class differentiation (Cook 1984b:13–14).

Wolf's (1959a:228) thesis that "the Indian's economic involvements are different from those of other participants in the national economy" and that the "individual Indian household is . . . *in* the economy but not *of* it" provided all the theoretical opening that was needed for anthropologists to reject Tax's unitary commodity economy thesis and to resurrect the specter of dual economy, one capitalist and the other noncapitalist, that was in some sort of resistant articulation with external, superordinate capitalism. Kearney succinctly sums up the consequences for anthropological inquiry of the adoption of Wolf's "Indianization" of the closed corporate peasant community: "The combined closed corporateness and Indian cultural identity of these communities resulted in a doubly determined essentialization of them as 'traditional': first as 'indigenous' and second as 'peasant'" (1996:89).

The combined impact of Wolf's rejection of Tax's argument and his elaboration of logically persuasive abstract models of the peasant household (1966) and corporate community (1955) had the unintended consequence of restraining the study of rural class differentiation and complicating understanding that even rural communities with low levels of class differentiation were not, ipso facto, outside the national capitalist class structure. Wolf's approach turned the researcher's gaze beyond the local community to find capitalism—external capitalism penetrated the CCPC to open it; capitalist development at the interior of the CCPC was precluded. By reinforcing the idea that capitalism was external to the peasant-Indian community and downplaying the transformative potential of petty commodity production, Wolf's approach left no room for the study of indigenous capitalist development from within localized peasant economies. Peasant-Indian capitalism or "peasant capitalist industry" were antithetical to his notion of peasant economy. Wolf's embrace of the "nonaccumulation fallacy" found widespread acceptance in Mexican peasant studies (Cook and Binford 1990:15–22).

PRUDENT RATIONALITY AND COMMODITY VALUE

In view of Wolf's objections to viewing Mexican peasants as penny capitalists and his ambivalency regarding structure vs. agency, Daniel Little's

(1989:29–67, 268–71) consideration of the "moral economy" debate in Southeast Asian peasant studies between political scientists James C. Scott (1976) and Samuel Popkin (1979) is instructive. Indeed, it provides hope for those of us who despair over the apparent endless recycling of diametrically opposed approaches to understanding sociocultural phenomena and who are perturbed by the formidable chorus of voices raised against the objectivity claims of empirical reasoning in social science.

Regarding this classic case of contradictory approaches to understanding peasant motivation and social organization, Little's analysis reveals that elements of both views had merit. "Peasants are deliberative—thus bearing out part of Popkin's view—they also are subject to a wide range of other motivations, including moral ideas—thus bearing out part of Scott's view—and their communities embody features that derive from both aspects of their motivational systems" (Little 1989:270–71). Two important conclusions Little draws from his analysis of this and other equally polarized controversies for social science knowledge production are that 1) "any theoretical controversy can likely be resolved or at least narrowed through further empirical research and theoretical analysis" and that 2) "the problems of objectivity and rationality are the humdrum ordinary problems of scientific research anywhere—not special and intractable problems arising from the specifics of social phenomena or social method" (1989:271). As far as I am concerned, both of these conditions are necessary to prevent knowledge production in the social sciences, and economic anthropology in particular, from being exercises in futility.

Regarding the deliberativeness of peasants, Little's analysis of the moral economy controversy yielded a renovated concept of rationality, more broadly applicable than to peasant subjects, which is of critical significance to economic anthropology and is accepted as a fundamental premise in the present study. This renovated concept, "prudent rationality," is summed up by Little in "means–end plus" terms implying that agents categorize and prioritize and are broadly deliberative about the anticipated consequences of their decision making: "[Prudent] rationality incorporates not only means-ends reasoning but deliberation about commitments, moral values, and self-conceptions" (1989:26). Peasants' mixed concerns (subsistence, acquisition, livelihood, influence, status or distinction, and identity) will have an impact on how and when the value (that is, use, exchange, and sign) embodied in or imputed to fabricated artifacts (commodities) is realized through commodity dispositions and movements. These mixed concerns, the deliberative content that serves as a basis for agent choice, are derived from the matrix of commodity culture(s)—norms, ideals, values, beliefs, and value-laden actions by others—the total meaningful environment or context facilitating commodity production and instilling value in commodities, classifying them, and deciding their disposition, which will also determine how and when their value is realized.

Much activity of fundamental interest to economic anthropology, especially that involving human agents and commodities, is unproblematic in the sense that it involves acts and movements whose sole cultural meanings are their "material consequences" and in which actors see "material consequences as the primary factor of deliberation" (Little 1989:57). So-called material consequences are those that meet or satisfy "material" interests or needs having to do with subsistence, livelihood, property, possessions, and other assets or personal and family welfare. In value terms, material consequences typically involve the realization of use value and exchange value or the acquisition or accumulation of the latter.

In cases of social action where material consequences are not the primary factor of agent deliberation but are among several factors of concern, economic anthropology is challenged to find and explain meanings that are not "material" as defined here and inevitably involve the realization of sign or symbolic value (such as distinction, difference, or taste). Notions like gifting and reciprocity invariably appear in discourse about this sphere of social action and its consequences, where they are contrasted with material, utilitarian notions like barter, trade, or equivalence. The study of this sphere is especially challenging either because 1) its functioning depends on the empirically unobservable (such as a posited custom implying indefinitely deferred reciprocity) or 2) it strains strictly defined notions of equivalency and commensurateness.

From the perspective of economic anthropology, the agent deliberations of most concern are those that involve commodities broadly conceived as originating as raw materials in nature but transformed by human labor (combining both thought and energy) and, therefore, made part of culture, society, and history as indicated in the book-opening epigraph by Godelier. It is through a focus on the multiple value content of commodities and its realization that the dialectical interplay between objects and persons, the material and the cultural, can be best exposed and understood.

COMMODITIZATION IN THE EVOLUTION OF THE MESOAMERICAN ECONOMY: THEORY AND THE EMPIRICAL RECORD

Mesoamerica is recognized as one of the independent centers of world civilizational process (Bonfil Batalla 1990:23; Ribeiro 1972). This distinction includes exclusive contributions to that process, such as the domestication of important staple cultigens like maize (*Zea mays*), beans (*Phaseolus*), squash (*Cucurbita*), chile (*Capsicum*), and tomatoes (*Physalis ixocarpa* and *Lycopersicum esculentem*), as well as several cultigens like the stimulants cocoa (*cacao*) and tobacco (*Nicotiana tabacum*) and the industrial crop cotton

(*Gossypium hirsutum*), which would become objects of global capitalist development (Palerm 1967; Wolf 1982:chap. 11). It also includes a plethora of contributions paralleled in other world areas but with unique Mesoamerican features. Among the latter is the development of an intricate division of labor and specialization—with a vast array of technologies, products, markets, traders, and special-purpose monies—as well as the development of a state-integrated, densely populated, class-stratified, urban society based on hydraulic agriculture (Palerm and Wolf 1972; Sanders and Price 1968).

Even more important than these cultural historical facts, however, is that Mesoamerica was one of the independent sites where humanity, already evolved elsewhere as a socially organized and culture-building species that survived through nomadic hunting and gathering, developed unique and more complex approaches to transforming and subordinating external nature to its own life-sustaining purposes. The products of this process became part of Mesoamerican society, culture, and history. Its protagonists were self-conscious human subjects or agents who distinguished themselves and their fellows from the objects they make and who related to both within matrices of value, meaning, and identity. The matrices were (and are) produced and reproduced through cognitions, perceptions, and actions informed and articulated by language, which itself was (and is) a product of social process. The social process, at given spatiotemporal conjunctures, was (and is) organized by relations of production and distribution that structure how labor makes commodities and how the value embodied in them is realized and allocated. Particular groups of Mesoamerican people, their cultural matrices, and their social relations of production can be identified and objectified for study with different criteria and for different purposes. The challenge to economic anthropology is to balance a sensitivity to the specific features of particular sociocultural forms and activities in Mesoamerica/Mexico with a recognition of their general or universal features.

The archaeological, ethnohistorical, and ethnographic records from Mesoamerica are replete with examples of commodity production and exchange that indicate the presence of commodity culture(s) in a variety of societal contexts and with varying degrees of importance in the economic process. There also seems to be ample empirical evidence of the progressive importance, locally and regionally, of commodity culture(s) in the Mesoamerican civilizational process—especially as a concomitant of the development of state-integrated, complex societies in pre-Columbian times, the imposition of European colonialism, and, in the nineteenth century, the development of independent nation-states (Carmack et al. 1996:1–237; Hamnett 1999:24–127; Hodge and Smith 1994; Semo 1973).

As a branch participant in a general evolutionary process of "commoditization" encompassing all of humanity (Hart 1982:39), Mesoamerica and its constituent peoples made a unique and independent contribution to humanity's transformation through a series of "identifiable stages in the progressive abstraction of social labor" (1982:40). The first stage in this process involved the production of things for use (that is, labor's embodiment in a thing external to its producer), and the second stage involved the socialization of useful things (products) through alienation—that is, the products were made social by being produced for the use of others who were foreign to their units of production and reproduction (1982:41). The third stage, inevitably a concomitant of the first and second, involved the development of a division of labor and specialization, first on the basis of gender within a given community but then extended to units of production and reproduction and to the intercommunity level.

Circulation of products of alienated and socially divided labor, by barter or reciprocity, occurred in the fourth stage of the commoditization process. It is important here to emphasize that this process assumes that ancient Mesoamerican subjects made a distinction between persons and things and shared an understanding that fabricated things embodied the work of their fabricators. Given such a cognitive connection among Mesoamerican cultural subjects, the power exercised by alienated products over their producers may be expressed in terms of commodity value.[4]

In the fifth stage, which is acclaimed by scholars as one of the hallmarks of Mesoamerican culture, a market mechanism was developed that operated through barter or exchange of commodities for commodities at negotiated rates. At the time of the early sixteenth-century Spanish Conquest of Mexico, the indigenous market system had local and regional components, including five-day cyclical organization and the use of special-purpose monies (Berdan 1985, 1989:85–91; Marroquín 1978:35–37). According to Michael Smith, "While there was not complete standardization of value among Aztec currencies, the 'medium of exchange' aspect of money was highly developed" (1980:877). This suggests that the Mesoamerican commoditization process was independently on the path to the invention of general-purpose money or that the commodity "crystallized as pure exchange value" (Hart 1982:41), which is the sixth stage in Hart's ten-stage general process of the progressive abstraction of social labor. In short, Mesoamerica was an independent center of the development of commodity production in humanity's civilizational process.[5]

The evolution of commodity culture(s) in Mesoamerica clearly began long before abstract labor became a universal measure of exchange value, that is, before the development of general-purpose money and before labor power itself became a commodity with a market price (that is, was objectified). In other words, luxury and staple commodities were produced and circulated in the Mesoamerican economy long before social reproduction was organized and integrated by commodity production. For example, there is strong evidence that salt was produced seasonally in coastal Belizean workshops specialized beyond the household level (which also produced clay pots for boiling brine) prior to A.D. 900 to supply a growing inland Maya demand (McKillop 2002:175–80). Even prior to the rise of the Belizean salt industry during the Late Classic period, there is substantial evidence of craft production by independent extrahousehold and household-based workshops of utilitarian and ceremonial commodities outside the domain of elite control during the Classic period (A.D.300–600) of Maya civilization (McKillop 2002:24–25).

At the time of the Spanish Conquest, there was an indigenous Mexican social division of labor and specialization that provided the basis for a substantial circulation of commodities through markets (*tianguis*) where haggling was the rule—either involving in-kind or special-purpose money-mediated transactions. There is also evidence that labor power itself was partially commoditized; for example, porters and craftsmen were occasionally employed, but evidence is still lacking for other types of labor (Carrasco 1983:72). The Aztec economy was well on its way to becoming a market-integrated economy by the time of the Conquest where labor-time and special-purpose monies provided some measure of commensurability, but it was still at a stage at which commodity exchanges were incompletely regulated by an objective and universal monetary standard of value (cf. Cook 1976:403).

The Spanish intervention in Mesoamerica, and Mexico in particular, ended this world region's *independent* contribution to humanity's cultural and economic evolution but did not end its peoples' innovative contributions to these processes. From the sixteenth century to the beginning of the twenty-first, thanks to the participation of Mesoamerica/Mexico in international economic relationships, the commoditization process has progressed through Hart's seventh and eighth stages: the use of capital to make profit and the deployment of industrial capital/wage labor. Mexico is presently experiencing the impact, especially through the implementation of the North American Free Trade Agreement (NAFTA), of the ninth stage, when services come to outweigh goods in the sphere of commoditized production, and of the tenth stage, when social labor becomes a computerized, abstract cipher (Hart 1982:41) or, if you wish, a form of cybervalue (see Hart 2001). Thus, Mexico/Mesoamerica remains engaged in both a general and a specific process of commoditization. Although in this stage-ist scheme the process appears to have unfolded teleologically, in reality it has been uneven in the pace and extent of its spatial development and is subject to change or even reversal like any other process involving human agents and their affairs.

In view of the uneven and contradictory course of the commoditization process through time in Mesoamerican/Mexican space, each prior stage has left cultural residue that remains present, if reduced, in successive stages, thus complicating an overall appreciation of its progressive, transformative nature. From the early stages of social evolution in Mesoamerica/Mexico, where the division of labor and specialization was embryonic and human activity was alienated in the form of material products, to the advanced condition under NAFTA of modern service economy in which people are increasingly paid through computerized information systems, a complex cultural fund of knowledge has been elaborated to address the issue of obtaining equivalences for labor and other commodities through exchange.

Regarding labor for labor, labor embodied in goods, labor measured in money, or labor as a computerized cipher, the issue of equivalency and remuneration has been addressed institutionally and through the exercise of prudent rationality by individual subjects. Thus, in Mexico (and Mesoamerica), a process of producing for other use, the repetitive act of alienation of producers from value they have created, has served over the centuries as a foundation of a diversified array of commodity cultures, constituted as funds of knowledge transmitted intergenerationally in units of production and reproduction and subject to continual change in content as a result of ongoing agent experiences.[6]

Furthermore, as socially organized, Mesoamerican/Mexican commodity culture must also be understood in terms of the social relations of production and distribution through which the value of its multiple products is created, allocated, and consumed. Commodity social relations in Mesoamerica and Mexico run the gamut from household and kinship based, tributary and rent based, to merchant and industrial-capitalist based. At the beginning of the twenty-first century, these social relations are still found in complex combinations that, together with regional cultural differences, give Mexican capitalism its uniquely mixed character.

Commodity culture(s) need not be statistically predominant regarding the actual flows of commodities into circuits where equivalences are immediately negotiated or determined through haggling in order to be dominant. Redistributive and reciprocal exchange also involve the creation, disposition, and realization of value. Market-mediated exchange is simply a particular variation of commodity culture(s). In other words, products, objects, goods, artifacts, or anything made with human labor, including that labor itself, is a commodity by virtue of containing use value that is potentially realizable through exchange and consumption. The "social potential" of commodities is, for purposes of the economic anthropology of Mesoamerica, of less consequence than their economic value potential (cf. Appadurai 1986:6).[7]

The twentieth-century ethnographic record, starting with the pioneering contributions of Redfield (1962) and Tax (1963), provides overwhelming evidence for the widespread presence of the market-mediated variety of commodity culture(s)—indeed, so overwhelming that an authoritative recent textbook refers to this focus in contemporary Mesoamerica as "marketing culture" (Goldin 1996:369–70; cf. Aguirre Beltrán and Pozas 1954:226–30). Regionally, for example, Malinowski and de la Fuente, noting the "well-deserved reputation" of the Zapotec Indians for "commercial talent and economic avarice," confirmed this in their own work to the extent that referred to the "'commercial libido' of the Zapotecs" (1957:23, 1982:62). The deep historical tradition of commodity culture(s) among Zapotecs and other indigenous peoples of Mexico and Guatemala, marked by participation in markets of all kinds, including those for land and labor, provides an important intergenerationally transmitted fund of knowledge that Mesoamerican peasants draw on and continue to shape today in circulating through the circuits of North American capitalism to make and earn a living.[8]

The ritualistic, ceremonial, or other so-called community-based culturally reproductive uses of "goods" in Mesoamerica do not in any way diminish commodity status or preclude market circulation. Many *tianguis*-exchanged commodities end up in ritual, ceremonial, or other nonutilitarian (or strictly economic) consumption destinations. Redfield realized this in his 1939 essay where he elaborated extensively on highland Guatemala Indians' being "practical businessmen, as proved both by the great amount of trade and by the extent to which the thinking of the people is commercial and utilitarian," with communities tending "strongly to specialize in certain commodities, although most grow the corn which is the basis of subsistence; and conversely each village and family depend on many others for needed commodities" (1962:204). He also noted that "the market system was well developed and there was some sort of currency" before contact with European culture (1962:209–10). But Redfield stopped short of developing a coherent concept of indigenous Mesoamerican commodity culture(s), rooted in a regional division of labor and specialization with a long history.

In 1954, the economist Sanford Mosk came to the conclusion that "specialization and markets apparently have a long history in the highlands of Guatemala, going back to pre-Columbian times," but he missed an opportunity to link this history to indigenous market culture by opposing "transactions based on market forces" to "custom and tradition" (1954:160–61, 169). Sol Tax, in his rambling and inconsistent contribution to the Viking Fund Seminar's *Heritage of Conquest* (1968), was also presented with an opportunity to identify a common or central underlying feature of Mesoamerican Indian economic culture. This was precluded by his empiricist method that relied on a dichotomic continuum, ranging from extreme self-sufficiency at one pole and local specialization and market dependency on the other, and that emphasized particularistic variation rather than a central or common cultural tendency (1968:44–45). He cited the Lacandon and the Indians of Quintana Roo as reaching the "extremes of self-sufficiency" because they are "tribe-like and isolated," a situation he found "not very interesting" (1968:44–45). Fernando Cámara corrected Tax by pointing out that the Lacandon and the Quintana Roo Indians were market involved (1968:8). It appears that Tax's concern with self-sufficiency was mainly heuristic, given his declaration that "in most places in Middle America the question is the degree to which the local communities enter into a regional market economy" (1968:45; cf. Aguirre Beltrán and Pozas 1954:226).

Tax, despite his dichotomic thinking, did question the notion of self-sufficiency by identifying an "Indian pattern" according to which each family in each community tends to produce the same products, which "causes the Indians of each community to 'look outward' to buy from and to sell to people of other communities" (1968:52). Indeed, he was on the verge of identifying Mesoamerican commodity culture in his declaration that "specialization tends to be by communities and the production individuality of the communities must be considered as part of their general cultural individuality" (1968:46). Tax resisted an unequivocal assertion that the market was "originally an Indian institution" even though he admitted that "it certainly is today . . . the hub of their economic and a good part of their social life" (1968:53).

Manning Nash, in his chapter "Indian Economies" in the *Handbook of Middle American Indians* (1967), refined Tax's typological continuum into three mutually exclusive types of economic organization and avoided viewing the issue of the historical development of Mesoamerican markets and marketing culture. Nevertheless, his concluding paragraph noted that the "overriding presence of money, markets, economic calculations of actors, the concern with price, and the interest in and desire for expanded economic opportunities do not . . . as yet move any of the Indian economies into the category of modern economy" (1967:101). Moreover, Nash acknowledged the possibility that "people who have kept a cultural heritage alive through nearly five centuries of contact with a technologically and politically superordinate society may discover how to blend parts of their cultural heritage with those aspects of economic modernity now absent" (1967:101), thus obliquely implying indigenous Mesoamerican "commodity culture(s)."

This possible route to modernity could be achieved, according to Nash, without the "loss of . . . mechanisms capable of sustaining the social structure in which a distinct Indian heritage is transmitted" (1967:101) but would also presumably require remedying the social organizational lack of "an entity like the firm, an autonomous, corporate group dedicated to and organized for economic activity" (1967:98). Firms, credit mechanisms, and deliberate technical and economic investment needed for economic dynamism, argues Nash, "are part of a social structure not found in the corporate peasantry of Middle America" (1967:99).

These statements show that Manning Nash's thinking at the time was pervaded with modernist developmentalism that inclined him to view external intervention as necessary to developing Indian economies. They also show that he flirted with the notion of an indigenous commodity/market culture. Nash still did not appreciate the possible compatibility of so-called leveling mechanisms with class differentiation at the community level and with indigenous capital accumulation at the level of the household enterprise. He failed to consider the possibility that both class differentiation and capital accumulation were in fact completely compatible with the functioning of the cultural elements that he identified as having "overriding presence" in Indian economic life. In short, Manning Nash's contribution (1966:69–81; 1967) was a modest advance over Tax's regarding the recognition and conceptualization of an indigenous Mesoamerican peasant commodity culture(s). It was no advance whatsoever regarding the notion of "quasi-tribal" household self-sufficiency (Nash 1966:62–64; 1967:88). Finally, it was a step backward regarding the "single economy" thesis that was lost in a concern with "multiple society" (Nash 1966:125–28) and with regard to understanding capitalism (penny or dollar), a discourse that Nash (1966, 1967) strangely ignored.

CONCLUSIONS

The concept of commodity culture(s) suggests new directions for twenty-first-century economic anthropological inquiry in Mesoamerican/Mexican studies and reminds us that capitalist development had an indigenous seedbed that was not implanted by the Spanish or other foreign sources. Rather than representing a complete break with the Wolfian paradigm, the commodity culture(s) approach reprioritizes certain of that paradigm's constituent elements so that more attention is given to endogenous commodity production and to Mesoamerican agency in its development. Wolf's approach never really comes to grips with the parallels between universal commodity development on a global scale and specific commodity development in the Mesoamerican region and, particularly, with the complexities of their sixteenth-century entanglement and subsequent combined and uneven development. The story of how that subsequent combined and uneven development became Mexican capitalism must include the Mesoamerican commodity-cultural experience as well as the European capitalist experience that interrupted and was instrumental in transforming it. There is no question that, as Wolf emphasizes, asymmetries of power were structurally decisive but that indigenous cultural forms, elements, and agency helped shape the Mesoamerican commoditization process.

Precapitalist forms of commodity production developed endogenously in ancient Mexico; indigenous petty commodity and capitalist forms continued to develop after the Spanish Conquest throughout the colonial period and have done so down to the present. Mexican capitalism today is as much a product of *mestizaje* as is the Mexican population. It is a mixed capitalism thoroughly penetrated by commodity logics of market exchange and capital accumulation of indigenous and foreign, precapitalist and capitalist, origins. These realities are often overlooked in discourse about the Mexican economy.

The instrumentality of commodity culture inevitably means that its fit with other aspects of indigenous Mexican culture has not always been and will not always be harmonious. Disharmony, tension, and contradiction are inevitable because culture is devised and practiced by individual human agents who willingly or unwillingly make decisions and act in ways that press against the limits of collective norms or have unintended consequences. Since commodity culture(s) revolves around economic value, however, material interests are always at stake in its practice and, ultimately, physical survival itself. It should not be surprising, then, to find commodity culture(s) entwined in Mesoamerica/Mexico with other dimensions of instrumental and noninstrumental culture—especially those that evoke the relationship between people and nature, people and the "unknowable" supernatural, or people and their identity.

Moreover, since the practice of commodity culture is necessarily social, there is every reason to expect the delimitation of the economic and the social in indigenous Mexican life to be difficult (Bonfil Batalla 1990:55); the whole gamut of social relations—consanguineal and affinal, fictive kinship, age based, gender based, authority or power based, and so on—are mobilized and at play in the practice of commodity culture. Wealth-based or class relations are, of course, uncontested as inseparable from their economic matrix and commodity culture. Regrettably, however, to the degree that class relations are perceived to be absent or are ignored, the economy is melded into society, and commodity culture is replaced with the culture of natural economy. Reproductive, acquisitive, and/or accumulative needs, whether functional prerequisites for social life or not, are historically conditioned and go well beyond physical subsistence to include other economic needs, such as replacement of tools and other material means of production, care of the aged and infirm, rent, and, in the case of petty capitalist enterprises, investment capital. Also inherently part of social reproduction and therefore interactive with the economic field are an array of socioceremonial needs, including kinship and reciprocal duties/obligations, participation in the fiesta cycle, and satisfying communal obligations. Mesoamerican commodity culture, then, is by no means restricted to processes, activities, and relations interior to the economic field proper but necessarily engages a whole range of exterior fields as well.

It seems that Mesoamerican economic anthropological discourse has at the beginning of the twenty-first century come full circle. June Nash, who credited Tax with teaching her and other graduate students at Chicago about the "secular, commercial outlook of the penny-pinching Panajacheleños" who exercised "a rational calculus of . . . greater returns" resulting in "the rational allocation of resources" (1997:13), more recently seems less receptive to the lessons learned from Tax and more inclined to view the Maya, together with other indigenous semisubsistence cultivators, as practitioners of an antimarket logic rooted in a morality of "distinct cultural premises" (2001:14–15).[9]

The Mesoamerican subjects/agents inhabiting this book (some Guatemalans but mostly Mexicans) make, exchange, and use valuable objects—activities that necessarily articulate the processes of making and earning a living with sociocultural fields beyond the economy proper. Mesoamerica and Mexico are located in a world-historical context where their uniqueness is relativized but, nevertheless, remains consequential, especially as a contribution to distinctive commodity culture(s) through their prudent expression of agency.[10]

NOTES

1. According to Clifford Geertz (1984:516), "[Economism] is the view that the moving forces in individual behavior (and thus in society, which is taken to be the aggregate of individual behaviors or some stratificational arrangement of them) are those of a need-driven utility seeker manoevering for advantage within the context of material possibilities and normative constraints." From his substantivist perspective, Geertz "insists that we can only understand a given society within a framework of analysis that gives full attention to the distinctive cultural features of that society—its religious views, its moral and normative context, and the categories of the worldview of its members" (Little 1991:144; cf. Geertz 1984:523). There are other definitions of economism such as "limiting the economic to economics" presumably to the exclusion of the "noneconomic" (Kearney 1996:12) or simply as privileging the economic in any approach to or interpretation of social reality or historical process.

2. Later, in elaborating "a Marxian approach to further clarify and specify the relevance of the concept of rent to an understanding of peasants" (Wolf 2001:260), Wolf still did not address rent in the context of local peasant class differentiation. For him, to the extent that rent is applicable to peasants within capitalism, it must be understood as "a political grant of power to a class of middlemen who are economically empowered to capture monopoly rent in circulation from the peasantry and are permitted to exact a protection rent to secure their economic monopolies" (2001:270).

3. It seems fair to argue that, in one sense, Wolf's ambivalence about the peasantry in class analysis goes back to his experience in the *People of Puerto Rico* project. In his chapter in that project's belatedly published book, Wolf views the peasant coffee/tobacco farmers of Ciales ("San José") as being simultaneously comprised of three classes (lower, middle, and upper) and as representing a segment within a sociocultural whole (1956:255–61, 264). The complicated (and, I would add, confusing) usage in that project (directed by Julian Steward) involving social/class structure, social stratification, and subculture is astutely examined by Lauria-Perricelli (1989:244–54). This does not explain, however, why Wolf's 1977 paper on the class analysis of the peasantry remained unpublished and why his views on that topic,

which were long unshackled from the program of the Puerto Rico project, were underrepresented in his post-1977 writings.

4. This possibility is precluded by the Mauss–Sahlins inalienability thesis, according to which products transferred must eventually be reciprocated only because cognitively and culturally they are understood to be inalienable from their producers. By contrast, the alienability thesis holds that once commodities are transferred from their producers to nonproducers, the process of the realization of their value is an inevitable consequence of alienation. The precise details of how use, exchange, and sign values interact and the preciseness or impreciseness or relative degree of commensurateness in how equivalences are reckoned in any given situation will vary. Nevertheless, the "spirit" of transactions involving the transfer of objects is framed by commodity culture(s), which integrates or articulates specific mixes of exchange/use/abstract value and sign value.

5. Hart's essay is a rigorous exercise in dialectical reasoning so that what appears as teleology is, in fact, dialectics. I have focused on it more as a "historical stages theory" that inevitably downplays the "dialectical reasoning of the cumulative definition of "commoditization"—that each level of the definition pairs what the commodity is with what it is not in a process that includes some quite surprising switches in the content of the idea, especially from objects to subjectivity" (Hart 2004, personal correspondence). Hart's aim "was to reconcile Mauss with Marx, by showing that 'gifts' could be seen as part of commoditization, not abstractly opposed to 'commodities'" (2004). In his essay, Hart explains that "each of the . . . steps . . . represents a further degree of abstraction of human labour from the original condition of organic life, namely from an immediate material symbiosis between the individual and nature. The progress of the social division of labour requires the detachment of human activity from its material context, so that heterogeneous goods and services may find some measure of equivalence in society. In this process, value is quantified and generalized, the formal apparatus of social life is made more elaborate and dominant. . . . This evolution is a process of commoditization, in which a series of commodity forms succeed in enhancing the social potentialities of humanity, while undermining the concrete authenticity of a simpler past" (1982:41–42). My emphasis clearly downplays the negations and emphasizes the interpenetration of opposites throughout the process—but also implies that the steps in Hart's "the commodity is" side of his dialectical pairings is more crucial to understanding social evolution than is "the commodity is not" side (cf. Hart 1982:42). For example, Hart's step/stage 5 pits market exchange of commodities against delayed gift exchange of noncommodities; I prefer to view all transfers of fabricated objects at this stage as involving commodities whose exchange values are realized in different time sequences ranging from immediate to delayed.

There is obviously a relationship between the process of commoditization as outlined by Hart and the process of socioeconomic evolution conceptualized by transformation of modes or production. Dialectical/historical materialism makes no sense in the absence of a notion of general and specific cultural evolution—modes of production clearly are stages in the socioeconomic transformation of humanity that followed different paths at different times and places. Disagreement over the specific stages is legitimate, but to reject unilineal evolution itself is tantamount to rejecting the unity of human history (Gellner 1980:61–62) or, in Semenov's terms, the "unity of the global historic process" (Semenov 1980:40). Humanity has had "torchbearer" societies at every stage in the evolutionary process—not all societies pass through the general stages at the same time or in the same way (Gellner 1980; cf. Semenov 1980). The trick is to understand relationships between abstract dialectical oppositions and interactions as reflective of real historical relationships in the evolution of society.

6. Ollman points out that Marx's view of alienation encompasses four broad relations distributed so as to "cover the whole of human existence . . . man's relations to his productive activity, his product, other men and the species" (1971:137). My use of the concept in the elaboration of the idea of Mesoamerican/Mexican commodity culture focuses on the first three of these relations, which, unlike Marx's original argument, are viewed in the general context of the process of commoditization rather than in the specific context of capitalist relations of production, where they achieve an especially antagonistic degree of estrangement (Marx as quoted in Ollman 1971:148 and expressed in Marx 1964).

I have borrowed the "funds of knowledge" concept from Carlos Vélez-Ibañez, who uses it effectively in *Border Visions* to refer to the intergenerational transmission of "practical means of survival," which are a source of "occupational stability" for many Mexican immigrant families in the southwestern United States (1996:160, 162, 163). There is one important qualification to my use of the concept, namely, to emphasize that each successive generation that taps into a fund of knowledge of commodity culture from a preceding one will certainly change that fund on the basis of its own experience—either by revising, discarding, or adding new elements to it. In short, a fund of knowledge is produced and consumed processually but not necessarily repetitively by individual subjects throughout their entire lives as economic agents.

7. As this statement implies, I do not agree with Baudrillard's insistence that gifting strips an object of its exchange value and use value, that is, of its commodity status, and imbues it exclusively with "symbolic exchange value" (1981:64). I think that "gifts" are better conceived as combining all three types of value—especially given the difficulty of empirically verifying the return of one gift for another in terms of equivalency. In short, I find Baudrillard's positing of four mutually exclusive types of value with their accompanying logics to be important, but I prefer to view the object in all instances as a commodity rather than relegating the commodity to the exclusive domain of the "economic logic of exchange value" (1981:66). In short, I see no reason to accept Baudrillard's declaration that the "logic of ambivalence on the one hand, of difference on the other, are incompatible with the logic . . . of equivalence" (1981:72). Agents can situationally reconcile these logics and, by implication, affect their mutual operational effects (that is, the logic of equivalence, in any given situation, might be relatively suppressed vis-à-vis either of the others).

8. There is an extensive literature that documents the arguments made in this paragraph. Much of it is well summarized in the excellent book by Carmack et al. (1996). A recent collection of relevant articles and a good bibliography is Smith and Masson

(2000:esp. chaps. 9–11). An earlier source that summarizes much important information from the archaeological, ethnohistorical, and ethnographic record on markets and commodity production in Mexico is Caso et al. (1954:23–24, 47–48, 226–29).

9. June Nash has informed me in a recent communication that she hopes I did not get the impression (from reading *Mayan Visions*) that she "turned away from commodity culture" because of her "championing Zapatistas." She continues, "Nor that I think they have. They are as always, very commodity oriented, especially the women artisans, and they see their future in those developments, but on their terms. Whether that is feasible of course will depend on trends in global trade and whether a fair trade ethic will emerge" (June Nash, personal correspondence, December 22, 2003).

10. Arturo Warman's synthesis of the transformation of Mexico's indigenous economy from Spanish contact through the twentieth century, in the substantivist tradition of Polanyi as modified by Wolf, highlights three transactional modes between the indigenous and other components of Mexican society: tributary, ceremonial, and mercantile/market (2003:195–245). His synthesis explicitly focuses on the work-value nexus and implicitly supports my emphasis on labor alienation in a commodity cultural stream, sustained and modified intergenerationally by indigenous subjects, concomitant with the institutionally structured economic transformation. I would emphasize the centrality in understanding this process of commodity value conceptualized as a triangulation of use, exchange, and symbolic components. Commodity cultures, driven by the interaction of these value forms, can then be understood to operate through multiple transactional modes. In other words, I interpret Warman's emphasis on tributary processes like the "reparto de mercancías" (allocation of commodities) (2003:203–6) and redistributive/reciprocal processes (2003:214–16, 222–45) to complement the role of market processes in developing and elaborating commodity cultures.

7

Commodity Culture(s), Livelihood Strategies, and Reproductive Goals: A Critique of Ethnography

For centuries, there has been a wide-ranging participation of indigenous peoples of Mexico in markets through prudently rational combinations of agricultural production for own use and for exchange, craft production, and wage labor in various types of enterprises and branches of production. Many students of indigenous life, however, seem to ignore or deny this empirical record by failing to recognize the existence of a cultural fund specifically attuned to this market experience but also expressed in other activity fields. Instead, they draw rigid boundary lines between market and nonmarket participation and emphasize the peculiar nonmarket morality of indigenous economy, the conservative economic ideology of indigenous communities, and how the indigenous worldview envelops and drives the local economy. By contrast, some authors (Wood 2000a) argue exactly the contrary: that local economy (or one or more of its constituent branches or divisions) is driven by the global market and the rationality of participation in commodity chains. These competing, even contradictory, interpretations challenge the very foundations of our thinking about the "economic other" in Mexico.

Although peasant-Indian participation in commodity production and markets is recognized, commodity culture is never included in the repertory of shared cultural elements with pre-Columbian roots. Indigenous commodity /market culture is either disconnected from or subordinated to external capitalism. This complicates the explanation of change in rural Mexico by assuming that utilitarian forms of accumulation and consumerism violate the "old ways" and represent a "new ideological framework" precipitated by external forces (cf. Goldin 1996:370–71) rather than an updating or modification of "commodity cultural elements" within indigenous funds of knowledge.

Indigenous commodity culture(s) are nourished by participation in external markets for labor, land, and products in ways that are quite compatible with traditional Mesoamerican cultural goals: high priority on land as a valued resource, especially for agriculture; participation in communal fiestas, civic and religious brotherhoods, and the civil–religious hierarchy; generosity; and reciprocity. Sooner or later, all these goals entail or promote acquisition, accumulation, realization, and consumption of commodity-embodied value, represented as monetized abstract labor. In other words, the pursuit of traditional cultural goals in contemporary rural Mexico entails the practice of commodity culture(s) and is not incompatible with external market participation.

What is noteworthy and paradoxical at the beginning of the twenty-first century with advanced internationalization of the economy run by huge capitalist conglomerates is that family and other small-scale enterprises continue to thrive and expand. The creatively destructive pathways of capitalist development have enabled capitalism to achieve international levels of integration without destroying noncapitalist forms of making and earning a living. The tendential laws of motion explaining this process have to do as much with dominant capitalist interests as with popular resistance to those interests and with the pursuit of goals within indigenous commodity culture(s) That is, petty enterprises generate surplus value or serve other interests for hegemonic fractions of capital yet also meet unique needs of urban and rural subalterns that are not served or are poorly served by hegemonic fractions of capital. This is why it is critical to understand the conditions of commodity economy in which petty producers live. These conditions either facilitate or jeopardize their simple reproduction, as they nurture class differentiation and, possibly, expressions of counterhegemonic culture or, paradoxically, of indigenous commodity culture(s).

It is even more important to approach this complexity from a perspective that avoids romanticizing small-scale semisubsistence production and conflating "use value" (in Marx's sense) with gemeinschaft (in Tönnies's sense). Approaches that restrain the "proclivity to marginalize and underplay the calculative, impersonal and self-aggrandizing features" of noncapitalist or small-scale societies (Appadurai 1986:11) should be rejected. Commodity culture(s) encompass "regimes of value" so that every act of commodity exchange does not presuppose "a complete cultural sharing of assumptions" and "the degree of value coherence may be highly variable from situation to situation, and from commodity to commodity" (Appadurai 1986:15). This is consistent with both a very high and a very low sharing of standards by the participants in a particular commodity-economic process and accounts for the capacity of commodity flows to be relatively unaffected by bounded and localized systems of meaning (cf. Appadurai 1986:15) designated as such in specifically ethnocultural terms (such as the Tzeltal of Amatenango).

It must also be emphasized that commodity culture(s) is no more an exclusive element within capitalism than are commodities, markets, marketing, and prudent rationality itself. Capitalist culture, today and historically, embraces much more than commodity culture, but the latter is a critical element of capitalism and an important element in precapitalism. The community and regional cultures of the precapitalist past (or on the periphery of actual capitalism) that inform and are affected by the activities of valuing subjects have done so in ways that often anticipate, parallel, or mimic capitalism but do not replicate it. Once valuing subjects/agents from "peasant" or other small-community origins participate in labor markets, other factor markets, credit markets, or consumer product markets controlled by capital, the commodity funds of knowledge that these subjects/agents bring to such participation are diversified beyond those learned and lived outside the capitalist sphere of relations. The fact remains, nevertheless, that without constituent elements of commodity culture(s) at its core, capitalist culture could not develop and diversify.

In any case, this explicit principle presents the economic anthropology of Mexico with the makings of a more robust economy concept that goes beyond a treatment of economy as destructive of the "genuine" culture and identity of Mexican peasant society and that enables researchers to place greater emphasis on indigenous commodity production and external/internal class differentiation as a historical process. The core of such a concept can be constructed as a paraphrase of Roseberry: economy is at once socioculturally constituted (through present and past productive activity) and socioculturally constitutive (part of the context in which productive activity is given meaning). In operational terms, this requires viewing the economy as a field or sector of sociocultural life, not as separate or disengaged from it. Further, in an economy like Mexico's, where commodity production is the predominant economic form at all levels of the economy, that is, where every product is potentially exchangeable or marketable or convertible to cash or its equivalent, the economic field takes on added weight in its relations/interactions with other sociocultural fields (such as political, religious, kinship, identity, and organizational). The relative weight it has in any given situation must be empirically determined. As an analytical rule of thumb, any given noneconomic field may be economically conditioned, economically relevant, or economically nonconditioned and nonrelevant.

By contrast, the economic field itself, especially in an advanced but mixed-commodity economy like Mexico's, may be conditioned by any other economically relevant fields (for example, politics and religion), and it is always affected by external events that impact on the functioning of society—natural calamities like earthquakes, floods, drought, epidemic disease and human-made catastrophes like war, terrorism, and so on. Like any other sociocultural field, the economy is clearly always a creature of human participation, which itself is conditioned by all fields in the sociocultural system. In practical terms, it makes no sense to conceive of the economic field as any more or less closed or impervious to external conditions or human caprice than any other field. All economies are socioculturally driven but are more directly conditioned by and engaged with the physical environment than other sociocultural fields.

THE OAXACA VALLEY ZAPOTEC

Systematic inquiry on the indigenous, peasant-artisan economy of the Zapotec-speaking region of the central part of the state of Oaxaca began in 1940, when Bronislaw Malinowski (together with Julio de la Fuente) initiated fieldwork there that resulted in a specialized monograph belatedly published in 1957 (Spanish) and 1982 (English). At roughly the same time, fieldwork was also initiated in a team project directed by Lucio Mendieta y Nuñez, director of the Instituto de Investigaciones Sociales at the Universidad Nacional Autónoma de México (UNAM) in Mexico City, that resulted in a comprehensive monograph published in 1949 (Mendieta y Nuñez et al. 1949). The UNAM project included an ethnographic component that specifically addressed agriculture (Alba and Cristerna 1949a:449–69) and rural industry (Alba and Cristerna 1949b:493–595) among the Valley Zapotec and also included a survey of craft industry in Oaxaca City (Alba and Cisterna 1949b:596–600).

Although written descriptively with no explicit theoretical concerns, the UNAM studies contained a great deal of useful analysis and data (including photographs) regarding specific types of a wide range of agricultural and small industrial activity. The analysis focused mainly on labor processes and work organization, costs, market pricing, and earnings. The authors collected data about fourteen different small industries located in twenty-two separate localities in the Oaxaca valley (including Oaxaca City). Their principal findings accentuated the overall importance of agriculture and the low returns from craft production. In their words, "Agriculture constitutes the principal economic activity of the Zapotecs, but not the only one, since some of them also employ their energies, when not required in agriculture, in the practice of small industries . . . only certain industries in the Valley region are sufficiently productive to cover, by themselves, the needs of those that practice them" (Alba and Cristerna 1949b:493, 494). More specifically, they found that, with only some exceptions, income earned from work in small industries was accessory to and merely complemented income from agriculture (1949b:495–96).

The industries Alba and Cristerna classified as "highly productive" (1949b:494) yielded earnings of two pesos daily per worker and included huarache (sandal) making, mescal distillation, construction materials (brick and tiles), and sarape weaving in Teotitlán del Valle. The pattern they discovered of high- and low-capital-accumulating small industries has stood the test of subsequent research that has verified its continuing importance (Cook 1984b, 1993a; Cook and Binford 1990:60–61).

Since the study by Malinowski and de la Fuente of the Oaxaca valley market system represented Malinowski's only sustained fieldwork in the New World and would prove to be his last anywhere, its importance in the history of economic anthropology was ensured. It stimulated and provided a point of departure for subsequent work by several economic anthropologists, most of whom were affiliated with Ralph Beals's Oaxaca market project between 1965 and 1969 (Beals 1975; Cook 1978, 1982; Cook and Diskin 1976; Diskin 1969).

The principal challenge to research in the Oaxaca valley system has been to try to balance the need for quantifying economic performance with the need to explain the meaning of economic activities with regard to prevailing social relations and cultural values. This has been greatly complicated by the organizational complexity of Oaxacan daily life—vertically divided into vectors ranging from household to community (ranging from tiny hamlet to sprawling city) to region to nation to world and horizontally fractioned by class, demographics, ethnicity, age, gender, kinship, and so on. Ralph Beals agreed with me that "our knowledge of such a complicated system will always be conditional and incomplete" (1975:5). I think that he would also agree with me now that the conditional and incomplete state of our knowledge reflects an inevitable lag between lived reality and the attempt to develop concepts to understand it.

The broad field of Oaxaca studies continues to nurture varieties of "ethnocultural survivalism" that are conceptualized as embedding economic process in a shroud of tradition-enforcing and identity-forging sociocultural practice. The most devoted proponents of this cause, among a *carreta* load of fellow travelers, inspired by the idea of the establishment of utopian societies of reenculturated Indians, are Miguel Bartolomé and Alicia Barabas, who have a long history of viewing reciprocity, cooperation, and consumption as expressions of nonmarket, noncommodity, and anticapitalist logic (Cook and Binford 1990:6–7). This is most recently illustrated by their general discussion under the heading "Economic Contradictions and Conditions" (Barabas and Bartolomé 1999:28–32) of an ethnically configured economy that presumably operates (or operated?) across all of Oaxaca's separate ethnolinguistic groupings. In the first place, it is an economy to which wage logic is foreign (lógica salarial que le es ajena; 1999:11) and peasants are "impoverished and submitted to market economy mechanisms over which producers have no control" (1999:28). They also propose that "each primary political segment tends . . . to behave like a production and consumption unit" and that there also exists "a global indigenous logic . . . that is based on different structuring principles of the satisfaction of individual and collective needs" (1999:28).

Predictably, the ethnopopulists' indigenous economy is conceived as a "domestic mode of production" organized through loose kin groupings called "*parentelas*" (kindreds?), articulated and confronted with a global capitalist market economy but integrated locally through relations of redistribution and reciprocity. The "structural substantivist" (Cook 1974b) logic of this kin-based local economy is not to produce profit or to accumulate capital but to produce the "most valuable good imaginable: the community itself" (Barabas and Bartolomé 1999:30).

Together with depriving human economic subjects of agency, the capacity to choose and maneuver, and submitting them to abstract system logics, this approach fails to recognize that underlying market involvement is commodity production. The combination of market involvement and commodity production, at any level of enterprise activity (that is, factory, manufactory, suprahousehold unit, or household), means that the potential for the conversion of exchange value into profit and capital and, hence, class differentiation is likely to be realized sooner or later. This is a fundamental economic connection that is precluded by the ethnopopulist approach.

Until proven otherwise, the empirical record of economic anthropology shows that petty commodity production, endofamilial accumulation, petty industrial capitalism, and class differentiation are present and operative in Oaxaca's commodity economy (Cook 1978, 1982, 1984a, 1984b; Cook and Binford 1990). In some cases (Stephen 1991), local redefinitions or reassertions of ethnic identity are inextricably linked to commodity economy through the internal and external class structure, whereas in others "villagers reinvent and reinterpret cooperation and reciprocity to fit new economic realities, respond to new situations, and support their community in its reproduction . . . and success" (Cohen 1999:xi). This record is completely at odds with an abstract, structurally driven model populated with inert, (re)ethnicized subjects.[1]

British cultural geographer Colin Clarke's (2000) interpretative synthesis of anthropological knowledge of Oaxaca's peasantries provides us with the welcome opportunity to dispassionately take stock of the state of anthropological knowledge about Oaxaca through the sharply focused lens of a knowledgeable representative of a sister discipline. Oaxaca has almost "one-fifth of Mexico's indigenous people, and almost a quarter of its indigenous monolingual population" (Monaghan and Cohen 2000:150) and has justifiably attracted the attention of practitioners of all branches of the sociocultural anthropology of Mexico and other social sciences over the past century. It is unquestionably an ethnographic laboratory for the study of the whole spectrum of problems involving ethnocultural diversity, local/regional/national integration, the criollo/mestizo state project/*política indigenista*, rural/urban relations, migration, petty commodity production, rural class differentiation, and capitalist development. Clarke's exhaustive use of some 600 bibliographic sources (mostly from ethnohistory and sociocultural anthropology) yields a readable, thoughtful, and well-balanced interpretative summary of the state of our knowledge about Oaxaca's economy, society, and culture that addresses all these problems.

Clarke's survey of the ethnohistorical record is, perhaps, the most succinct and uncontroversial part of his interpretative synthesis, but the most important dimension of his contribution may be a perceptive review of the local community from colonial times into the 1990s with a keen eye on political administrative change/persistence, shifting demographics and spatial patterns, and governance. Generalizing about the great transformation in the status of local communities from colonial times through the end of the Porfiriate, he states (2000:29) that the "*pueblos de indios* . . . gave way to *pueblos de ciudadanos*"; the latter, in turn, were further transformed by the Revolution (through article 115 of the 1917 constitution) into *municipios libres*—the "basic unit for the territorial, political, and administrative organization of the federated Mexican states" (2000: 185). Clarke carefully examines the status of the "570 municipios in Oaxaca, about 24 percent of all those in Mexico . . . with an average of 5,200 persons per unit (2000:184). The typical *municipio* is relatively autonomous and encompasses multiple localities (*localidades*), so that the fragmentation of the population is even more striking.

Clarke (2000:255) interprets the ethnographic record of class and ethnic relations in Oaxaca through an eclectic framework fashioned by fitting together elements from three models: 1) class stratification (à la Weber), in which Indians constitute a cultural enclave within the lower, peasant stratum; 2) internal colonialism, which views peasant Indians as dominated culturally as well as exploited economically by mestizos (mostly urban); and 3) pluralism, which focuses on the multiplicity of Oaxaca's ethnic categories while emphasizing their parallel status vis-à-vis one another and their common subordination to mestizos. His contribution here is, in my opinion, too uncritical of the previously mentioned theories and lacks his own explicitly articulated theory of economy, society, and cultural relationships that situates Oaxaca nationally, continentally, and internationally.

Clarke (2000:182–83) proceeds to populate Oaxaca's *localidades* with people representing two cultural sections, the numerically larger mestizo, which is "class ranked," and the smaller, essentially classless Indian. He (2000:163) concedes that putative "classlessness" among Indians is changing under the impact of economic development and observes (2000:184) that whereas the peasant and/or Indian community is "constructed, lived, and expressed" at the local community level, Oaxacan identities are increasingly constructed regionally through language and transnationally through migration to the United States (2000:xii).

When looking at Oaxaca through the lens of peasant economy, Clarke parts company with ethnocultural survivalists to recognize the importance of petty commodity production and even petty capitalism (2000:130–31); and he also does a good job of assessing the impact of modern capitalist activity in the Oaxaca City market and beyond (2000:134). In his words, "Peasants are frequently portrayed as engaged in a distinctive mode of production, but, in the context of Mexico's capitalist economy, it is more logical to regard them as penny-capitalist rather than pre-capitalist" (2000:79). Clarke emphasizes that the "Oaxaca peasantry is not only persistent . . . but highly differentiated" (2000:79; cf. Cook and Binford 1990:27). Although Clarke here is expressing agreement with the results of my project in the Oaxaca valley, our main finding was that the "peasant economy" had been transformed into a commodity economy with complex circuits of value flows and corresponding relations participated in by multiple subjects (and enterprises) none of which could be easily identified as "peasants" (cf. Cook and Binford 1990:12–15).

Economic class is a variable that Clarke handles with considerable ambivalence—alternating between implicit acceptance of the significance of relations of production to explicit rejection of Marxist class analysis in favor of the Weberian "stratification" approach (cf. Clarke 2000: 79, 178, 251–52). Yet he expresses agreement with and selectively accepts the results of Marxist studies like, for example, *Los indios en las clases sociales de Mexico* by Ricardo Pozas and Isabel Horcasitas de Pozas (1971). In addition, his rejection of Marx is belied by his reiteration that the Oaxaca peasantry constitutes a "surplus population" (2000:217), "cheap labor supply" (2000:217), or "reservoir of cheap labor" (2000:249) at the disposal of the capitalist employers at all levels of the system.

Clarke tends to view peasants either as a single class separate and distinct from the national capitalist class structure (a view the Pozases [1971:135] correctly rejected) or, confusingly, as differentiated into peasantries (Clarke 2000:79), "miniature class hierarchies" (2000:80), or "minor class structures within peasantries" (2000:217). I would argue that there is nothing "miniature" or "minor" about the class fractions of the Oaxacan/Mexican peasantry as defined by their specific social relations of production (for example, as piece-waged workers in manufactories, full- or part-time wage laborers in different branches of production, worker–owners of petty enterprises, and so on). In the aggregate, these fractions encompass millions of locations in a North American class structure infinitely more complex than the one sketched out in preliminary fashion by the Pozases (1971:138–55).

Clarke does an imaginative and comprehensively informative job in analyzing the statistical/census record for rural Oaxaca. His statistical analysis employs population and agricultural data from the 1950 and 1970 censuses that are correlated to measure the changing relationship between key variables; he then highlights the key correlations (positive and negative) in a series of linkage diagrams. In combination with his detailed examination of government policies and PRI (Partido Revolucionario Institucional) hegemony, this statistical analysis provides a basis for welcoming the recent electoral success of the opposition and constitutional reform that will continue the trend toward decentralization and increased state and municipal control in the planning and allocation of public expenditures Clarke (2000:186) observes that the "*municipio* as a self-governing entity is increasing."

Perhaps the most significant part of his statistical analysis is on "intergenerational change" between 1950 and 1970. Several findings are worth noting (2000:62): 1) land reform transformed the rural scene, and there were more small units and smaller big ones; 2) polarization took place between urbanization and agricultural development; 3) enduring discrimination occurred against non-Spanish-speaking Indians but with some marginal improvement because of government-confirmed access to communal land; and 4) women's literacy vis-à-vis men's was rising in almost all contexts.

Where does his less-than-glowing appraisal of the record of PRI-Gobierno in Oaxaca since 1950 (2000:38) lead Clarke regarding his assessment of recent political reforms and the resurgence of ethnopolitical movements advocating Indian autonomy? He observes that in mid-1995, the Oaxaca government, under pressure from indigenous groups, revised its electoral legislation to allow 408 (ca. 70 percent) of 570 *municipios* to conduct elections to political *cargos* through community assemblies. The introduction of this practice has been a means of marginalizing the influence of party politics and other forms of factionalism in local communities but, he reasons, "can also be taken as an approximate guide to those communities that consider themselves to be Indian in a cultural sense" (2000:168). "'*Usos y costumbres*,'" Clarke continues (2000:168), "is an expression of an Indian, corporate, cultural, and material existence, which enjoins the sharing of language, land, male assembly, *cargo*, festival, and *tequio*."

He qualifies this interpretation by correlating "*usos y costumbres*" with language group affiliation in my sample of twenty Oaxaca valley communities (Cook and Joo 1995). This leads him to observe, "There is a strong tendency for communities that are Zapotec speaking to use '*usos y costumbres*,' while those that are mestizo or ambiguous may also adopt '*usos y costumbres*' to redefine themselves as indigenous." Clarke's conclusion regarding indigenous identity claims and cultural realities reinforces the validity of an analytical approach that includes considering the situationality of indigenous identity claims (Cook and Joo 1995:54–55): "the absence of traditional culture is by no means a handicap for groups that wish to reinvent themselves as Indian" (2000:170).

There are more concrete issues at play than identity in Oaxaca's recent political reforms. The Ley de Derechos de los Pueblos y Comunidades Indígenas del Estado de Oaxaca, approved on June 16, 1998, recognizes the right of Oaxaca's municipios to elect their officials through mechanisms established by "customary law" (*derecho consuetudinario*)—which is precisely what many indigenous leaders defend as part of what they understand by "autonomy" (Hernández Díaz, personal communication, 2002; also Hernández Díaz 2001b). Unfortunately, Clarke does not give sufficient emphasis to the exclusionary and antidemocratic nature of "customary law" in the 418 Oaxaca *municipios* (73.4 percent) that now practice it. Various population categories—including women, residents of *agencias municipales*, new settlers (*avecindados*), and Protestants—are excluded from voting and/or standing for election in these *municipios*. These exclusions do not occur in those 152 *municipios* (26.6 percent) that vote according to the national party system (Hernández Díaz 2001a:16). Ironically, those who view indigenous identity as a basis for future utopias in states like Oaxaca may find that post-NAFTA national political culture has more democratic potential than the *etnia*-based ones.

Clarke concludes his study by noting that even though the political reform movement continues to be successful in the area of bureaucratic decentralization and increasing municipal autonomy, the real-world situation in Oaxaca is likely to continue to be "substantially 'determined' by the state" as it has been historically (Clarke 2000:247). The safety net provided to the peasantry by postrevolutionary agrarian reform is jeopardized by the "legal change permitting private alienation and sale of land-reform parcels" (2000:258), although the immunity of the communally landed sector from this legal change decreases that jeopardy especially among peasants of the mountain hinterlands. Nevertheless, since opportunities for capital accumulation among Oaxaca's peasants are limited, migration and urbanization continue apace, and education is transferring the children of peasants and petty commodity producers, whether urban or rural, into the semiproletariat and quasi middle class (2000:249, 259). Finally, in a caveat to the utopians, Clarke contends that the persistence of local community difference, and even its association with non-Hispanic ethnic identity, "does not involve an essentialist harking back to the past" but a "means of thwarting outside interference" (2000:257).

Many of the issues raised in general studies of Oaxaca are addressed in Jeffrey Cohen's (1999) study of the village of Santa Ana del Valle, near the better-known community of Teotitlán del Valle, in the Tlacolula arm of the Oaxaca valley. Cohen has taken a sensible approach to the controversial issue of the role of ethnicity in this Zapotec-speaking community: "being ethnically indigenous . . . has little bearing on the structure of local identity and social organization" (1999:21). "Satañeros," he tells us, "do not talk about themselves as Zapotec, nor do they self-identify as Indian; instead, they call themselves Santañero" (1999:21–22). Aside from a good historical survey (1999:23–35), Cohen's best data and most convincing arguments are focused on the thesis that Santañeros "primary means of economic advancement is to place themselves directly in international and transnational markets through commercial textile production and migration" (1999:58). He points out that "many Santañeros are turning to migration, given the uncertainty of farming, the low return on weaving, the lack of wage labor, and the growing demand by villagers for goods and services" (1999:55).

Less convincing and supported by contradictory empirical analysis is Cohen's central argument that "cooperation (often framed as the reciprocal exchange of goods and services or shared support) is the foundation upon which Santañero society is organized and through which it is produced, reproduced, and enacted" (1999:62). Indeed, I can think of no better example of the "glass is half empty versus half full" theme in Oaxaca studies than Cohen's functionalist accentuation of the integrative, harmony-generating effects of cooperation over its disintegrative, disharmony-generating effects, coupled with his decision to recognize but downplay the significance of competitiveness, conflict, and uncooperativeness.

Although I have spent less ethnographic time in Santa Ana than Cohen has, I doubt that life there is characterized more by one set of oppositions than by the other. It shares a balance of oppositions with all other communities in Oaxaca, in Mexico, and in the world. Expressed differently, Santa Ana's continued existence owes to the interplay between these two oppositional sets of behavioral principles. Cohen insists, however, that the foundation of village life is cooperation and reciprocity, which provide a context "for consensus and content, for resistance and hierarchy" (1999:14). Equilibrium is produced by cooperation and reciprocity, whereas atomistic uncooperativeness and avoidance of reciprocity (that is, preference for market-mediated transactions) are disequilibrating.

Cohen's definition of *guelaguetza* as a "formal system of reciprocity and cooperation" (1999:90) is accurate only when the principle is invoked in the context of the fiesta cycle and involves the practice of written accounting. He emphasizes its role in producing and reproducing social solidarity but overlooks the ethnographic record that shows that the principle is often invoked informally in the context of work as a form of mutual assistance according to the motto "you help me now and I'll help you later" (Cook 1968b:113–17, 1982:65–67) and that it is an instrumental principle as much as it is a cooperative one.

In other words, *guelaguetza* is invoked to get access to ceremonial goods when cash is scarce, but it is also widely used to get access to labor and means of production when these are in short supply or not otherwise accessible (Cook 1968b:113–17, 1982:65–67; Martínez Ríos 1964). In all these instances, it has a clear economic function as an equivalent to market exchange when cash is scarce. Moreover, its economic function is always immediate and palpable, whereas its putative social function of building lifelong solidarity between households is contingent on many intervening factors that can impact on interhousehold relations. In any case, as Cohen's data suggest, its function as a solidarity builder is a result more of unintended consequences than of social consciousness (1999:92). In sum, *guelaguetza* may build interfamily alliances and create a "sense of permanence and belonging for both giver and receiver" as Cohen claims (1999:106) but only because it is part and parcel of market culture facilitating and giving meaning to local commodity exchange.

Cohen's analysis of the weaving industry in Santa Ana makes only partial use of the results of a previous survey (Cook and Binford 1990:89–94, 124–25). Regarding the involvement of women as treadle-loom weavers, Cohen observes "that women weave is a change from trends noted as recently as the 1960s" (1999:45) but ignores data from the 1970s that Santa Ana had "proportionately twice as many female weavers as in Teotitlán" (Cook and Binford 1990:91). That study proposed relevant considerations in explanation of this finding, as "many fewer women spin in Santa Ana than in Teotitlán and that product prices are at a lower level in Santa Ana; lower product earnings, therefore, place more pressure on Santa Ana women to earn income through weaving" (Cook and Binford 1990:91). Cohen seems to agree with the conclusion about spinning but is silent on the other argument (1999:46). He is paradoxical in interpreting Santa Ana weavers as directly competing with those in Teotitlán del Valle while at the same time supplying data showing that a majority of them are tied by contract or yarn purchases to Teotitlán buyers through what he calls (apparently following a 1990 federal census category) a "*mano de obra*" arrangement (1999:47–48).

My 1979 project survey disclosed that just over 60 percent of Santa Ana weavers were "self-employed," which meant owning one's own loom and selling one's output for cash or credit; it also disclosed that a common arrangement was for roughly one-third of these weavers to get yarn on credit from five local merchants who also bought up their products (Cook and Binford 1990:93–94). These survey data, when analyzed together with observational, conversational, and survey data from Teotitlán del Valle, provided a more complex picture than the one sketched by Cohen (Cook and Binford 1990:123). Since Cohen did not address these earlier findings in his study of Santa Ana weaving, it is difficult to determine the significance of his findings about how conditions have changed since 1979.

Cohen's discussion fails to make clear the precise nature of the so-called "*mano de obra*" contract and includes an inconclusive analysis of the results of his 1992–1993 survey of forty-eight weavers. According to him, "In 1992 and 1993, fifty households were randomly selected for a survey. Out of this total, only two households were not involved in textile production. Of those that remained, twenty were involved in independent production (selling on the open market). Twelve weavers who identified themselves as independent producers were involved in mano de obra relationships" (1999:47). Depending on how one deals with the issue of "independent production," Cohen's statement leaves many of the weavers in his sample unaccounted for. About all that can be inferred from this and other statements is that in 1992–1993, there were still "independent weavers" in Santa Ana, an indeterminate number who get yarn on credit, in addition to a new group of outworkers for Teotitlán-based workshops and/or merchant putters-out (1999:47–54). I cannot resist speculating about whether the inclusion of the results of my project's 1979 survey would have made any difference in the outcome of Cohen's discussion. In any case, his results appear to confirm our interpretation of Santa Ana weaving as a satellite of the Teotitlán industry but suggest that Santa Ana weavers have now become undisguised proletarians.

In a significant sense, then, Cohen tends to separate his economic from his social analysis—he makes a strong case for market participation and remittances as the key to reproduction of the Santa Ana economy while simultaneously fashioning a sociocultural explanation for the reproduction of Santa Ana society. He never really reconciles these two separate spheres of explanation, demonstrating analytically the dialectical interpenetration of economy and society, of market-mediated principles and those of cooperation/reciprocity. Instead, his analysis seems to render "ideal" what are, in fact, material relations of production and reproduction (cf. Narotsky 1997:222).

Perhaps Michael Chibnik's monograph on Oaxaca valley wood carving is strikingly refreshing because the specific industry he examines has rather shallow ethnohistorical roots in the region and, unlike many others, has experienced remarkable success, until recently, in commodity chains terminating in the homes of consumers throughout the United States (and probably Europe and elsewhere, though Chibnik does not address these markets). Although locating his approach in the now fashionable "multilocal-fieldwork-to-follow-the-commodity" current attuned to the flexible accumulation dynamic in global capitalism (Chibnik 2003:6, 16–18), he does so in a straightforward, low-key way and wisely observes that "flexible" arrangements like piecework and product sharing were around long before the period of so-called late capitalism (Mandel 1978).[2]

The following excerpt summarizes Chibnik's findings and illustrates his approach: "Oaxaca wood carvings are in some ways archetypal examples of a commoditized craft. They were invented recently and have always been sold to tourists, collectors, and merchants. Their sale in large volumes has been made possible by transportation and communication improvements linking Oaxaca, Mexico City, and the United States. Although artisans take pride in their work, they almost always say that they make pieces in order to make money and would abandon the craft if the market for carvings disappeared. Carvers change styles and develop specializations in response to the volume of sales of particular types of pieces. The overall demand for carvings ebbs and flows as the fluctuating exchange rate between the dollar and the peso affects the potential profits of U.S.-based intermediaries" (2003:6).

This is a concise a statement of Oaxaca commodity culture in a NAFTAmerican commodity chain.

In the late twentieth-century period of the commodification of ethnicity and the ethnification of commodities, it is not surprising that these carvings were marketed to tourists and, especially, through intermediaries and dealers in the United States (and websites, brochures, advertisements, and catalogs) as authentic artifacts of ancient Zapotec cultural origin. This sales strategy contrasts markedly with the artisans' (residents of the communities of Arrazola, San Martín Tilcajete, and La Unión in the Oaxaca valley) own representation of their commodities, which they admit are a new art form, and themselves. Chibnik observes that while these artisans "acknowledge indigenous ancestry, they talk about themselves as residents of a particular community, the state of Oaxaca, and the country of Mexico . . . never . . . as 'Indians' or 'Zapotecs.' . . . Very few speak an indigenous language" (Chibnik 2003:242). Chibnik sums this up pointedly: "The wood-carving trade depends in part on intercultural miscommunication" (2003:243).

Although craft studies informed by the social life of a commodities/commodity chain paradigm tend to favor the demand/marketing side of the process, Chibnik does not ignore the production side. Apparently because of fluctuations in demand over the years and even though the wood-carving communities became relatively prosperous, he finds that "many workshops . . . cannot be easily pigeonholed as 'family operations' or 'semicapitalist enterprises' or 'sites of petty commodity production'" (2003:114). He acknowledges a "proliferation of capitalistic forms of labor organization" but hesitates associating this with permanent class differentiation because there has been a "decreased demand for pieces that can be mass produced" (2003:123).

In comparison with other Oaxacan crafts, Chibnik finds that the "returns to labor for carving are similar to those in treadle-loom weaving for wool and better than those for embroidery, treadle-loom weaving for cotton, and backstrap-loom weaving" (2003:119). Even so, he realistically admits that "the amount of money that can be earned from carving is ordinarily less than can be made through immigration to the United States" and that even "in the most prosperous carving villages, the best way for most young people to get ahead is to leave" (2003:240).

In the same comparative vein, he notes that "only the treadle-loom weavers for wool have as much contact as the wood-carvers with intermediaries from the United States and make as many items designed for the high end of the market" (2003:119). One of the outstanding contributions of Chibnik's study is his detailed examination of sales in the United States, where he astutely surveys the marketing landscape through case studies of different-size enterprises located in different market areas. Indeed, his careful analysis provides us with our most complete picture yet of the marketing/demand/consumption side of artistic Mexican craft commodities, including time-series data on inventories and earnings from one large-scale enterprise (Chibnik 2003:210–17). About all that is now lacking with regard to artistic craft consumption is attitudinal survey data from consumers themselves to find out the degree of effectiveness of anthropologically incorrect, dealer-driven advertising. It may turn out that the reasons consumers purchase these special commodities are either more complex or (more likely) simpler than we realize.[3]

THE NAHUA OF GUERRERO

Thanks to the work of Catharine Good (1988), the state of Guerrero is the setting for one of our best views of Mexican penny capitalism as a historically diversifying fund of indigenous market and commodity culture. Her ethnological project has focused on the area known as the upper Balsas River valley, more specifically the village of Ameyaltepec in the district of San Agustín Oapan. Good's project has been informed by a rejection of economistic tendencies in peasant studies that tend to objectify peasant-Indian subjects as reactive subalterns exploited in all dimensions of their economic life through mechanisms of unequal exchange by external capitalism. By contrast, she emphasizes the culturally enabled capacity of Mexico's peasant Indians to achieve remarkable success in creating and accumulating economic value by combining productive skill and marketing prowess in a unique way that not only builds on but also expands and intensifies their ethnocultural heritage concerned mainly with reciprocity and cooperation. Ethnohistorical sources indicate that the region has been settled for five centuries, if not longer, by Nahua-speaking peoples, and it is likely that the intercommunity division of labor and specialization, including barter involving craft and agricultural commodities, was established by the late pre-Hispanic/early colonial period (Good 1988:25–26, 207–20).

Whereas my work in the Oaxaca valley has documented how capitalism can, under certain conditions, develop from within indigenous commodity economy and result in class differentiation, Good's work shows another route for the development of commodity economy that involves a strategy to maximize the capture of exchange value through control of marketing circuits and then to reinvest these earnings in ethnoculturally reproductive circuits of the home economy or, in her words, "to invest surplus money in goods that can circulate within the system, and in that way to get material and moral support from others" (1988:170). It is beside the point to argue that household enterprises, as successful in accumulating money capital through a combination of craft production and trading as those of Ameyaltepec are, assign a value not to money as such but only to what they can acquire with it. Does not the value of general-purpose money lie in its exchangeability?

In all seriousness and with no disrespect intended for Nahua artisan traders, the economic strategy described by Good evokes an analogy to the activities associated with rodents of the Sciuridae family who systematically prowl a habitat for nuts and seeds to store for later use. Unlike the nonmercenary squirrels whose acts reflect an instinct for survival, the behavior of mercenary Nahua artisan traders seeks to capture and store exchange value. The Nahua are "mercenary" because their commercial activity is calculated to aggressively capture exchange value in the form of money rather than objects of congealed use value like nuts and seeds. The analogy is also apt since the Nahua, like rodents, "squirrel away" more than is required to satisfy expected future needs (*Webster's Third New International Dictionary*, p. 2217).

In the specific case of the Ameyaltepec Nahua, the habitat for the calculated capture of monetized exchange value is the market for Mexican crafts that they assiduously ply from the tourist resorts of both coasts and the tourist meccas and upscale market sites of the interior to the urban centers on the U.S. border. Once the money is in hand and expenses involved in its acquisition are paid, the Nahua reconvert it back into less abstract forms of wealth like housing and gift commodities that are introduced into the local reciprocal economy, where they can be later reclaimed with interest (simply by virtue of inflation). This entire cycle is best understood as a peculiar Ameyaltepec Nahua expression of Mesoamerican commodity culture.[4]

The most successful of these very skilled artisan-trader family enterprises combined the sale of pottery and/or paintings (mostly on white or brown bark paper or jute) of their own fabrication with jewelry and carved wooden masks that they buy up from other regional producers or merchants (Good 1988:35–45) and had monthly net earnings of more than six times the minimum wage (1988:56–57). Another characteristic of the most prosperous enterprises is that they sell to three types of buyers: tourists in the streets, regular urban clients cultivated through networking, and other intermediaries (1988:37–39, 59). The best indicator of the relative prosperity of the artisan-trader enterprises of Ameyaltepec is that 83 percent of them enjoyed monthly net earnings of more than twice the minimum wage.[5]

There are several problems with Good's analysis of value circuits and social relations of production/distribution related to them that need to be considered in qualification of her dualistic thesis of a net transfer of value from the extravillage market economy nourishing a classless, reciprocity- and cooperation-organized, nonmarket village economy. The first problem resides in the incompleteness of her analysis of these circuits within the household enterprise itself, which means that the process of endofamilial accumulation (and associated household demographics, composition, and stage in the life cycle) is opaque. A second problem is Good's tendency to exaggerate the success of these units in optimally realizing the exchange value embodied in the commodities of their own fabrication since it is an established fact that in the nested hierarchy of intermediary capital, the highest return on investment occurs at the point of final sale to the ultimate consumer—which in the international craft market means the retail seller in the ultimate consumer's home country. For example, a large, high-quality jute painting that was sold by an Ameyaltepec artisan trader to a Mexico City wholesale/retail merchant in, say, La Ciudadela market for U.S.$50 could be resold to a U.S. wholesale importer for U.S.$100 and resold again to a U.S. retailer for $200 who finally sells it to a private buyer for own use for $400. In this chain of transactions, the Ameyaltepec artisan trader—no matter how adept he or she may be—is a relative bottom-feeder with respect to the process of exchange-value realization.

A third problem lies in Good's underestimation of the net transfers of value from the Ameyaltepec household unit to extravillage merchant and commercial capital through their purchases of commodities for further resale and for direct consumption. A fourth and final problem revolves around her failure to consider the relationship between Ameyaltepec enterprises, in their role as merchant buyers-up of regional craft products (for example, of carved wooden masks from San Francisco Zumatlan and of carved stone from poor mestizos in Taxco and Iguala), as involving unequal exchange (that is, exploitation of the direct producers by buying their commodities cheap and reselling them dear). All these problems make it more difficult for Good to sustain her thesis of the relative autonomy of the Ameyaltepec artisan-trader economy from the process of capitalist development.

Despite these shortcomings, there is a certain plausibility and seductiveness to Good's central thesis. What strikes me most about her ethnographically rich and nuanced analysis of reciprocity as an economic system (1988:159–72) is the extent to which it calls to mind my own ethnographic experience in Zapotec-speaking villages of the Oaxaca valley (1982:91–116, 208–15). Although Good emphasizes the relative paucity of empirical data about reciprocity in the literature on central Mexico (1988:159) and, by implication, the unique importance of her data from Ameyaltepec, she missed an opportunity to consider the latter as a representation of an historical cultural idiom of Mesoamerica—especially well documented, for example, in the Oaxaca literature on *guelaguetza*.

Especially striking is Good's description of the cognitive connection made by her informants between locally grown crops that are ritually gifted or loaned between households and the embodied labor they represent. In her words, "The conceptualization of these goods as a concrete expression of the work that they contain is very explicit. Within the village, there is considerable exchange of the products of the milpa at harvest time. . . . When the first ears of corn (or cantaloupe, or watermelons, or green beans, and so on) are picked, a portion of this crop is distributed among friends, fictive kin (coparents) and relatives. Upon giving it something like the following is always said: 'Have this little ear of corn, here is my work' ['Ten este elotito, aquí está mi trabajo (notequiuh)'], or 'eat something of my work' ['coma de mi trabajo'], and for them to give of their work is a way of expressing affection, respect and friendship" (1988:146). Good's discussion of her own initial misunderstanding of this custom resonates even more with my emphasis on the role of labor alienation in commodity culture(s): "At first I did not understand the custom and I did not want to accept everything that was offered to me that I could not eat. When I explained that I already had a great deal, because I had received 'gifts' from other persons, the inevitable response was: 'Yes, you have, but you have that which is the work of others. It is not my work. Receive what I give you. I want you to have what is mine, I want you to eat my work'" (1988:146).

The similarity between this discourse surrounding the "gifting" of agricultural products in Ameyaltepec and discourse that I heard in the 1960s regarding the sale of metates by producer–sellers in Oaxaca valley marketplaces is extraordinary and, I think, far from coincidental. For example, I documented how the *metateros* employ a sort of homespun labor theory of value that privileges the idea of work expended as representing the value of a product—a theory that often takes the form of specific labor-time calculations that serve the producer–seller as a basis for a minimum acceptable return in the marketplace haggle with buyers (1976:418–20). The producer–seller's withdrawal from an ongoing haggling transaction with a potential buyer will typically be accompanied by a statement like "El trabajo no vale así" (My work is not worth so little) or "El trabajo no resulta" (The work doesn't pay off) (1976:419).

Female petty commodity producers and outworkers in the Oaxaca valley, however, were much less likely than the *metateros* to express the value of their work in labor time. Their earnings are generally so paltry that most of them would agree with one embroiderer who dejectedly admitted, "We don't figure our accounts with a pencil and paper, but we do make an accounting in our heads of the cloth and the thread. It figures out to be a gift. There are no earnings. Our work is given as a gift" (Cook 1990:111). I also found that usufruct rights to communal and ejidal land—whether for agricultural or extractive purposes (such as quarrying)—were essentially transformed into quasi ownership rights by Oaxaca valley peasant artisans owing to a generalized belief that work is determinant of such rights (Cook 1982:44–45, 223–36) as exemplified in the expression "Allí tengo mi trabajo y el que trabaja allí es el dueño" (I have my work there, and he who works there is the owner) (1982:235). In short, I think these views in Oaxaca, like those in Guerrero, are expressions of labor alienation within a historical commodity-market culture generalized throughout Mesoamerica.

Obviously, the sustainability of Good's dual economy thesis hinges on the role of agriculture in the Ameyaltepec quest for subsistence. Once again, her analysis is incomplete and somewhat contradictory and falls short of convincingly supporting her thesis. First, she provides poignant ethnographic support for the importance of agriculture (that is, the milpa) culturally and ideologically but fails to consider the degree to which this discourse reflects a strategy to camouflage from outsiders (especially government tax assessors) the village's actual dependency on craft industry and commerce (1988:140–48). The image of "peasant family subsistence economy" still served as a pretext for government largesse in the pre-Salinas reform days of the 1980s, when Good did her fieldwork. In addition, there appears to be a contradiction between her emphasis on the importance of traditional subsistence agriculture and its renewal through investment of commercial earnings (1988:140) and her description of it as "a highly risky undertaking" (1988:126) that regularly yields corn harvests that cannot meet the annual needs of from 50 to 85 percent of the village's households (1988:139).

To support her claim that the purchase of animals is the most direct way in which capital accumulated in the craft business has subsidized agriculture, she states the following: "The growing number of animals in the village has stimulated subsistence agriculture, since animals facilitate heavy work, and demand ever larger quantities of corn and dried leaves of the corn plant (*zacate*) to maintain them, which are gotten through the cultivation of land and not in the market" (1988:141–42). One wonders how Ameyaltepec agriculture can meet this added demand, given rainfall dependency and otherwise poor quality of available land, and its persistent incapacity to meet the subsistence requirements of even half its households, much less the fodder requirements of a growing animal population.

Good seems to imply that the nonmonetary, nonmarket organization of agriculture in Ameyaltepec reflects a commitment on the part of these successful artisan traders to a subsistence-first strategy coupled with a value system emphasizing reciprocity, cooperation, and the reproduction of Nahua community identity (that is, the avoidance of displacement by secular capitalist relations [1988:144]) and, ultimately, is reinforced by a fundamental worldview in which milpa (plants and crops) is seen as a divine gift and an integral part of individual identity (1988:144–45). It is logical for people who have lived for at least five centuries in a habitat not favored for successful agriculture (1988:144, 211) to attach special importance to whatever crop they manage to produce and to seek divine intervention regarding such a precarious undertaking. It is unrealistic, however, to confuse wishful thinking with actual production possibilities.

Some of Good's own data provide the basis for an interpretation giving more weight to unintentional rather than intentional consequences of individual agency. Given the uniformly marginal quality of Ameyaltepec's land, there is little business incentive to invest in agriculture or, for that matter, to privatize and commoditize land as a factor of production. Clearly, given the relative success of labor-intensive craft production and trading, cash is relatively abundant, and labor is the scarcest and most valuable factor of production. Under such conditions, there is little incentive for households to sell labor and a high incentive on recruiting it by means of family or social duty (1988:143). From where, then, does the threat of capitalist penetration emanate? Surely not from outside developmental interests but, more likely, from the more accommodated artisan-merchant households themselves. Presumably, there should be a high incentive to reinvest earnings in the expansion of the lucrative intermediary side of these household enterprises. Yet Good's emphasis is on "investment" in conspicuous consumption (such as housing, stereos, and cars), the fiesta cycle, ritual commodities, and farm animals and not on investment in enterprise expansion. Given the common economic organization of its household enterprises, this kind of expansion is most likely to find expression in Ameyaltepec's relations with other communities penetrated by its merchant capital, not in relations between artisan-trader households within Ameyaltepec.

Good has recently summarized the results of ethnographic studies in Guerrero, including her own, as suggesting that "internal stratification and the propagation of individualistic behavior are produced by scarcity—not abundance—of wealth. . . . Social disintegration in indigenous communities is not the inevitable outcome of contact with the larger economy or society . . . although disadvantageous articulation with the larger economy is by far the dominant pattern today . . . indigenous peoples can, under favorable circumstances, relate successfully to a global economy in material terms and reproduce their own cultural identity" (2000:139–40).

Several points need to be made about her own work with regard to this summary. First, according to her interpretation, the artisan traders of Ameyaltepec, who operate under conditions of wealth abundance, "manage their merchandise in an individualized way; there is no intent to collectivize craft production, nor the acquisition of merchandise, nor sales" (1988:49). Second, the sphere of development of capitalist relations of production may not be at the level of individual communities so much as at the intercommunity level (Cook and Binford 1990:72–99, 190–98), which means in the upper Balsas River valley the need to examine the relationship between, for example, Ameyaltepec and its merchant buyers-up with communities producing craft commodities like San Francisco Zumatlán (carved wooden masks). Third and last, the degree to which reproduction of cultural identity is an intended or unintended consequence of the process of making and earning a living needs to be carefully considered.

Toward the end of her discussion of Ameyaltepec's internal economic organization, Good posits a method of escape from economic dualism as follows: "At one level of analysis, the reciprocal economic system can be treated simply as an economic strategy in which exchange is reduced to a kind of barter of good for good, or work for work, or even make everything accountable in monetary terms" (1988:172). If she had chosen to adopt this method, she would have eliminated her tendency to conflate monetization with commoditization by recognizing that commodity circulation in a local economy does not require money and that use and exchange value circulate and are realized together in the social reproduction process of the Ameyaltepec economy. In other words, what she views as ceremonial goods, ritual goods, luxury goods, and subsistence goods are, in fact, all commodities moving through particular circuits destined to end in consumption/realization of their embodied use and exchange value (the latter being abstracted through the mediation of money in local or extravillage markets). Although local household enterprises mobilize labor from other local households by family duty or reciprocity, they do resort to wage labor to hire workers from other villages for work in Ameyaltepac. Therefore, there is a local labor market that facilitates accounting for labor in monetary terms.

Good also contends that locally grown agricultural crops (such as maize, beans, squash, fruits) are gifted or bartered rather than sold for a price. Nevertheless, the fact that such crops are marketed regionally and nationally in money-mediated markets has implications for determining their circulatory values in Ameyaltepec. Under conditions of local economy subsumption by capital, as Chevalier (1982) has convincingly argued, the realization of commodity use values through consumption in the subsumed economy can also be understood as involving the realization of exchange value that a given class of commodities has acquired by virtue of its circulation in regional and national markets. Regarding the substantial flow of commodities into the reciprocity system for purposes related to the fiesta cycle or other ceremonial/ritual purposes, a gift commodity (or bundle of commodities) given at time period 1 is consumed by the recipient household, thus realizing its use value but only a portion of its exchange value. The exchange value of that particular commodity (or bundle of commodities), consumed at t^1 is, in fact, only fully realized at t^2, when it is returned by the t^1 recipient to the t^1 donor with an exchange value appreciated by inflation (ΔEV^1). This is why the logic underlying reciprocal transactions in the Ameyaltepec process is a commodity, not a noncommodity, logic. The circuit corresponding to such transactions between two hypothetical households can be represented as follows (HH = household, M = money, C = commodity, t = time, UV = use value, EV = exchange value, Δ =increment to, and → = direction of flow or action):

$$HH1 \rightarrow M^1 \rightarrow C \rightarrow HH2^{t1} \rightarrow UV + EV^1 \rightarrow$$
$$M^2 \rightarrow C \rightarrow HH1^{t2} \rightarrow UV + EV^2 (\Delta EV^1)$$

The important aspect of this process highlighted by this formula is that a social relationship between two separate households HH1 and HH2 is maintained over time at a cost in economic value terms to HH2 equivalent to EV^2.

However, HH2's cost is a savings to HH1 equivalent to the difference between the t^1 and t^2 (inflated) price of the commodity (or commodities) originally donated. For HH1 in monetary terms, this delayed sequence of transactions is tantamount to having put money M^1 in an interest-bearing savings account at t^1 and having collected interest at t^2 (that is, ΔM^1).

Good emphasizes the reproduction of local cultural identity, or the "ability of indigenous peoples to mediate change through existing institutions and social relationships in a manner consistent with collective, historically transmitted values" (2000:139), but is inconsistent about the production, exchange, and distribution of economic value and its corresponding social relations. With regard to the Nahua, she (2000:136) provides many examples of involvement in wage labor: as braceros in the United States, as weavers of palm for hat manufacturers, and as seasonal migrants to harvest sugarcane in Morelos and commercial crops in northern Mexico. She mentions "petty commodity production" explicitly once, but given her lack of attention to enterprise expansion and to the intercommunity relations of merchant capital in her Ameyaltepec study, there is no way to tell if petty capitalist development has occurred. In short, lacking in her otherwise excellent work is, to paraphrase Good herself (2000:126–27), "a more robust economy concept, one that goes beyond a treatment of economy as destructive of the 'genuine' culture and identity of society and that enables researchers to place greater emphasis on indigenous commodity production and class differentiation as an historical process."

THE MAYA OF CHIAPAS

It may surprise some readers to find out that while Chiapas has attracted more anthropological attention that any other state (Köhler 2000:179), Oaxaca (Monaghan and Cohen 2000:150) has a larger and more diversified indigenous population, and Guerrero (Good 2000:127) has an indigenous population that is more isolated, widely dispersed, and out of the national development loop. Köhler (2000:179) estimates that "about half of the ethnographic literature on Mexican Indians published between 1965 and 1995 refers to" Chiapas.

Why has this southernmost Mexican state been the undoubted mecca of so many anthropologists for the past thirty years? Köhler believes that the answer lies in the intrinsic interest in the belief system and lifeways of Maya-speaking Indians "who in comparison to those of other regions *seemed* [emphasis added] to be marginally acculturated" as well as the long-running operation of the Harvard Chiapas Project directed by Evon Z. Vogt, "which accounts for about one-fourth of the published ethnographic record on Chiapas" (2000:179). Another reason why anthropologists have been so attracted to Chiapas probably lies in Köhler's observation that "the Indians of Chiapas are not only growing demographically: their political presence, both nationally and internationally, is also expanding . . . [and] they are much more effective in defending their own interests . . . the 1994 uprising of the EZLN is just one, albeit spectacular, example." This has inevitably produced a literature in sociocultural anthropology on forms of reasserting ethnic identities (Nash 2001).

Köhler's (2000:182) survey of major trends of change since the mid-1960s for the central highlands (Tzotzil and Tzeltal) shows a rather massive and, apparently, mostly successful intervention by the federal government (with the Instituto Nacional Indigenista playing a prominent role) in support of integrated development involving improvements in education, road construction, agriculture, public health, judicial assistance, drinking water, and construction of town halls and Casas de la Cultura. These material signs of progress, however, did not buffer many families from the impact of the post-1982 devaluation/inflation crisis. Köhler identifies and discusses seven strategies pursued by the Tzeltal and Tzotzil in coping with the economic challenges they face: emigration, acquisition of land from Ladinos, cultivation of rented land in the lowlands, work as laborers in construction, transport business, intensifying agriculture, and arts and crafts for tourists.

The lead sentence in Köhler's section on social organization should be a wake-up call to anthropologists: "A clear class structure has emerged in most *municipios* during the last decades." The empirical support for this generalization come from studies of Zinacantan (Cancian 1989, 1992; Collier 1990) and from *municipios* like Chalchihuitlán, Chenhalhó, and Pantelhó of the lower northern regions. The message to anthropologists is clear: if class differentiation is pervasive in the Maya Indian communities of Chiapas—the Mexican national seedbed of persisting, resisting, restructuring indigenous identity—is it not likely to assume a priori that it is occurring in most, if not all, Mexican indigenous communities? At the very least, findings from Chiapas should mean that ignoring (or rejecting) class analysis and capitalist relations in future anthropological knowledge production is unacceptable.

A second generalization by Köhler (2000:199) that caught my attention was made in summary of his own work in which he "interpreted inequality as a survival of Colonial structures, now almost devoid of their former material foundations." This alludes to the fact that one of the critical class bases for the subordination of Indians by Ladinos, landownership in the form of ranches and plantations, has diminished in importance. Indeed, according to him, in the Chiapas highlands almost the entire countryside has been abandoned by Ladinos. The upshot of such changes is that "relations between Indians and Ladinos have changed considerably over the last decades. . . . Indians are much more self-confident now, and Ladinos practice less overt discrimination" (2000:198). Positive change does occur.

Finally, Köhler (2000:205–6) is to be congratulated for ending his essay with a section titled "Perspectives for the Future," where he takes the refreshingly positive step to suggest how labor-intensive industrialization, stimulated by NAFTA and with eventual technical advice and capital investment from East and Southeast Asia, might provide a solution to the economic woes of the land-starved Tzotzil and Tzeltal peoples. After observing that "proficiency in Spanish is no prerequisite for being a skilled worker," he also wryly undercuts the rationale for much of twentieth century's *política indigenista* by proposing that "too much Ladinoization could actually be to the detriment of highland Chiapas as a future industrial location, because it would probably be accompanied by a decline in the work ethic." This is a welcome rejoinder to the retrograde thesis that equates the arrival of NAFTA with the death knell for indigenous identity and culture.[6]

June Nash has a different take on the fate of the indigenous Mayan people of Chiapas in their popular struggle for subsistence and autonomy against international corporate capitalism. She borrows two key concepts, Karl Polanyi's "substantive economy" and Rosa Luxemburg's "natural economy," to help her understand this process, which translates into "framing an alternative path to that of being subsumed in global capitalist circuits as 'people without faces and without voices'" (2001:1). Nash contends that indigenous projects based on "unique worldviews that place them in the center of a collective enterprise to maintain the world in balance" are "predicated . . . on substantive economies responding to the needs of people in a particular society regardless of their power as consumers in a market" and providing a "positive coexisting alternative to a world predicated on universal self-regulating markets" (2001:2). "Mayan rebels are asserting the viability of collectivist noncapitalist alternatives in semisubsistence cultivation coexisting with capitalist exchange," she argues, which "challenges assumptions about lineal evolution and the single dominant mode of production that were central to both Marxist and liberal economic theory" (2001:259 n. 1).

There are elements in this interpretation of the Chiapas situation that can be construed as supporting the view that commodity economy is unnatural, antisocial, and, in its capitalist version, dehumanizing, deculturating, and inimical to subsistence. By implication, these elements also lend support to the thesis that participation in commodity economy is incompatible with the process of materially provisioning communities of indigenous culture practitioners bent on preserving and maintaining an autonomous niche for themselves in a pluricultural nation-state or in the "global ecumene" (Nash 2001:221). There is no silver lining in Nash's vision of the future of international capitalist expansion: her ethnographic work among Bolivian tin miners, Massachusetts factory workers experiencing deindustrialization, and the Mayan peasant artisans of Amatenango gives her "a chilling sense of what will happen worldwide as subsistence enterprises become a diminishing part of world production" (2001:xvii) thanks to transnational capitalist growth.

The anticapitalist, antimarket current in this ethnocultural survivalist interpretative scheme fosters a tendency to misconceive of the "peasant-artisan economy" as embracing a production-for-use logic that is in fundamental opposition to a production-for-exchange logic—the former implying harmony-engendering cooperation, collectiveness, reciprocity, and redistribution and the latter implying conflict-engendering competition, individuality, haggling, and profit seeking. Nash views Chiapas peasant artisans as exemplifying those indigenous peoples who have "demonstrated a remarkable ability . . . throughout the world to carry out commercial transactions with Europeans in their midst while retaining a distinctive logic and practice" (2001:2). As this implies, Nash's concern is restricted not to "economies that are exclusively engaged in self-production for a bounded social group" but rather to "the ends of production, whether it involves commercial transactions in open market or not" (2001:2).

I would emphasize that the "remarkable ability . . . to carry out commercial transactions" Nash rightly attributes to "subsistence enterprises" of indigenous peasant artisans in Chiapas and elsewhere reflects long participation in commodity/market culture(s) rather than retention of a distinctive noncommodity/market logic. Perhaps the most important dimension of the Maya vision for the twenty-first century derives from their creative participation in commodity culture(s) throughout the twentieth century and before in a way reflecting the distinctiveness of their logic and practice. The achievement of the goals of their autonomy movement in the twenty-first century will require them to continue to draw on that experience.

In short, Nash's appropriation of Luxemburg's natural economy concept in combination with Polanyi's substantive economy concept to address her concern with subsistence crisis and domestic/community reproduction suggests that she envisages the future of indigenous Maya economy as involving defensive rather than proactive engagement with the logic of market interdependency. It is as if her focus on the indigenous autonomy movement, Mayan cosmology, and the belief of the people of Amantenango that their town center is the "umbilicus of the World" (2001:xi) has displaced her previous emphasis (1993) on their exercise of prudent rationality through strategic involvement in commodity production and markets. Still, Nash stops short of advocating withdrawal from market economy and rejection of commodity culture(s) as viable options for survival of the Maya or any other Mesoamerican indigenous group in the twenty-first century.

THE GULF NAHUA OF VERACRUZ

A good illustration of my earlier view of the marginalization of the economic anthropological field as such in Mexican studies is the fact that one of the most theoretically and analytically rigorous recent studies of the rural Mexican economy/ecosystem avoids any conscious affiliation with or reference to economic anthropology, preferring instead to identify itself with a purposefully independent approach fashioned from an eclectic theoretical literature including state theory, underdevelopment studies, ecology, gender analysis, and semiotics and united through a sophisticated and totalizing "theory of process" (Chevalier and Buckles 1995:2–3, 337–48). As if to reinforce their effort to "produce a higher-order approach to social phenomena" and to contribute to "a mode of discourse that breaks new ground" and "leads speakers into the unknown and the unspoken" (1995:3), these authors fail to cite George Foster's (1982) pioneering study of the Popoluca economy even though the map of their own study area in southern Veracruz, concentrated on the *municipio* of Pajapan, includes the *municipio* of Soteapan, which was Foster's home base. Presumably, this exclusion is justified on ethnocultural grounds—their study is of the Gulf Nahua, whereas the Popoluca are Mixe-Zoquean language speakers (Chevalier and Buckles 1995:4–5). Thus, in their quest for innovativeness, these authors foreclose any possibility of interrogating a foundational study in the economic anthropology of Mexico based on fieldwork in approximately the same area of southern Veracruz.

The heart of Chevalier and Buckles's contribution to economic anthropology are two chapters (4 and 5) encompassing the midsection of their book; its strength lies in their theoretically informed empirical analysis of social differentiation under changing conditions of state intervention and capitalist "maldevelopment" nuanced by a concern to show the continual functioning of the noncapitalist "patrimonial" domestic economy. Its weaknesses lie in a tendency to conceptualize capital and capitalism in abstract, mechanistic terms as illustrated by their "stupid machine" metaphor (1995:165) and to view capitalism as a system external to the Pajapan economy that is only partially subsumed by it (hence an embrace of dualism that pits capitalism against a kin-based, patrimonial, domestic, and village economy); their failure to distinguish between two different forms of circulating or intermediary capital (merchant and commercial); their flirtation with natural economy through a conflation of commodity production with subsistence production coupled with allusions to an original condition of self-sufficiency; their failure to precisely describe—with regard to organization, function, and value flows—the hierarchically nested structure of markets in which Pajapan household enterprises participate; and, finally, their failure to analyze remittances from absent household members, therefore artificially imposing a closure on the Pajapan economy that surely did not exist in the late 1980s, when their fieldwork was conducted.

The strongest element in Chevalier and Buckles's analysis—namely, of household multioccupationality ("occupational pluralism" [1995::132]), differential access to arable land, and differential involvement in wage labor—provides them with the means for locating households in a "class typology" (1995:132–35). Unfortunately, their heavy reliance on occupational data in generating subclasses and their lack of comparable data on agricultural (such as tractors, traction animals, plows, wagons, and pumps) and other means of production (such as trucks) and rent make it difficult to get a precise picture of the relations of production and distribution between and among the 592 households surveyed.

This is partially offset by their data on cattle ownership, which, as their typology implies and their discussion identifies, is where "capital tends to concentrate" (1995:132). The authors convincingly argue the case for the historically shifting nature of household locations in the class structure (within limits set by differential wealth-generating possibilities of various occupations and other productive activities), but the link between households and enterprises is not always clear with respect to assets and income as tabulated (such as column 5 in table 4.1) or of predominant role in production and distribution of wealth (such as employer vs. employee or lender vs. debtor). Moreover, there are no data presented that enable us to understand how the different class fractions compare by using a standard-of-living index derived from possession (or not), for example, of different types of housing and durable consumer goods (Cook and Binford 1990:118–20); and, although data are presented on land rental by a four-category class grouping (1995:139:table 4.6), these data are not disaggregated by fractional groups of households, and no comparable data on rent incomes (in money or in kind) are provided. The same is true for data on cash savings, ranging from $15 to $3,077 among 11 percent of the households; we are simply told that ranchers and business owners accounted for 48 percent of the households with savings and 60 percent of the total value (1995:152–53).

With regard to cattle raising, especially with a focus on the ranch enterprise, Chevalier and Buckles's analysis is beefier. They have good data on cattle distribution over time that enables them to provide a perceptive analysis of "observable differences in scale, profits and control over capital, variations that have important implications for the accumulation of local capital and the growth of the industry as a whole" (1995:145). One of their major findings is that "cattle ranching contributes little to the creation of local employment or the development of local merchant capital" (1995:145). Paradoxically, they also point out that there are fifteen to twenty cattle brokerages in Pajapan that "make an average net profit of $240 per month and an 18% rate of profit on their initial investment," which means that they "earn more profits than any other small business" (1995:150–51).

In addition, the authors' general hostility toward cattle raising as an economically undesirable and ecologically destructive activity—hence illustrative of capitalism as a "stupid machine" (1995:127–29, 165)—seems to contradict the results of their cost–benefit analysis that shows this to be the most rewarding branch of production in the local economy, yielding a "rate of capital accumulation (sales profits plus the value of the animals retained over the value of the total herd)" of 14.7 percent, "a favorable return on investment compared to other sectors of the rural economy" (1995:146). Together with the savings and liquidity (the relative ease of convertibility into cash) advantages of cattle raising, which they do not mention, it seems to me that these authors' tendency to blame maldevelopment on the expansion of ranching is supported mainly by their ecological data (1995:chap.5) and is certainly contradicted by their economic data.

In the only instance (by my count) when these authors provide a voice in their text for one of their subjects, the content of the admittedly skimpy narrative suggests that more such voices should have been allowed to speak. The concluding sentences of their section titled "Small Businesses and Merchant Capital" read as follows: "The fragmentation of rural merchant capital actually serves the interests of the urban suppliers. In the words of one merchant, small store owners 'don't do business; they work for Acayucan suppliers'"(1995:153). Unfortunately, Chevalier and Buckles do not elaborate on the meaning of this informant's statement to examine the role of Pajapan merchants as "double dealers" (Cook and Binford 1990:195), that is, as both buyers-up of local commodities and local resellers of external, factory-produced commodities. These are, in effect, roles that evoke two forms of intermediary capital often designated by separate terms as "merchant" and "commercial," the former historically linked to petty commodity production and the latter subordinated to industrial capital (Cook and Binford 1990:194–95). In short, this distinction between two forms of intermediary capital could have strengthened Chevalier and Buckles's analysis of the critical sector of circulation capital in the regional economy, which, as it stands, does not adequately explain the nature and implications of the growth in the small-merchant sector to include forty-five stores by 1986 (Chevalier and Buckles 1995:152).

These authors' approach to subsistence and small-scale commodity production (1995:153–62) appears to be tacitly informed by an image of natural economy (or local self-sufficiency) as implied by statements like "reduced in scale and undermined as a self-sustained economy" (1995:126), "peasants *can no longer* [emphasis added] produce all of what they need to subsist" (1995:154), "Pajapeños *no longer* [emphasis added] produce most of what they need as they did a few decades ago" (1995:158), and "these conditions [produce most of what they consume and consume most of what they produce] are *no longer* [emphasis added] characteristic . . . of the area" (1995:261). They attribute the historical movement away from self-sufficiency to external capitalist market penetration (1995:125–27) and view the fluctuating involvement of local households in agricultural production for own use as "not merely a survival strategy" but also a "daily expression of peasant labor's struggle against domination by capital" (1995:131). Finally, they insist that "the persistence of self-employment based on subsistence and simple commodity production points to a domestic and village economy governed by kin-based rules of the patrimonial domain" (1995:125). In short, they embrace a selectively "historical structuralist" (Hewitt de Alcántara 1984:131–77) version of Wolf's looser dual economy thesis, examined earlier in this chapter, that "local economy is *in* but not *of* the capitalist economy," which can be labeled as a variety of "resistant articulationism."

Rather than viewing agricultural production for autoconsumption as an anticapitalist subsistence strategy as these authors (and June Nash) do, I have viewed it (Cook 1988) as one among several defensive strategies that may be employed to situationally strengthen the peasant-artisan household enterprise in periods of inflation or other economic conditions of extralocal origin that impact on the process of labor-power reproduction within these units. A second strategy, in addition to production for own use, that I found to be applied in Oaxaca was combining own agriculture and collection of wild plant foods in a process of substituting wage goods purchased in the capitalist market with goods produced for autoconsumption. A third strategy involved reducing the consumption of wage goods without substituting goods produced for own use. The result of these strategies, which are not mutually exclusive, is identical, namely, to reduce (or avoid the increase of) the cost of reproduction of labor power. I also identified a fourth strategy that consists in selling crops destined for autoconsumption (such as corn), which often has negative consequences later for the household enterprise through the possible need later on of replacing the sold crop at elevated prices (1988:68–69). Several additional strategies were found among self-employed household production units that were designed to reposition them in the process of coping with the impact of inflation on the realization of exchange value (in the case of petty commodity units) or the valorization of capital (petty capitalist units). These included 1) intensifying the production of cash crops, 2) compensatory price increases in commodities produced for sale or for labor power sold, 3) sale of fattened or other animals, 4) downsizing enterprise scale, and 5) migratory labor (1988:68–69).

According to my interpretation, such strategies do not necessarily imply anticapitalist sentiments or initiatives but are perfectly compatible with calculated participation in a changing commodity cultural fund of knowledge constructed around labor alienation. Therefore, household enterprises that turn to the production of maize or other crops for own use is best understood as the exercise of a particular strategy from that fund of knowledge that enables them to strengthen their position vis-à-vis the economic value squeeze they regularly experience in commodity economy. This leaves open the possibility that they may be able to redeploy their labor, directly through wage employment or indirectly through commodity production, to greater advantage later, including in more remunerative external labor markets. The "greater advantage" will accrue through increased income, usually in cash but also in kind, that can be deployed to meet necessary and optional reproductive and/or investment functions (Cook 1978:293–97; Cook and Binford 1990:58–69; 113–23).

Oddly enough, Chevalier and Buckles's analysis of the historically shifting role of production for autoconsumption in the mix of possible allocations of peasant household labor could have been clarified—and definitively disassociated with the image of natural economy—by incorporating the analytical framework from Chevalier's provocative and important study of swidden agriculture farmers in the Pachitea valley in eastern Peru (Chevalier 1982). Presumably, even though only before the 1930s did Gulf Nahua peasants approximate their counterparts in the Pachitea valley regarding the relatively high percentage of produce directly consumed (up to 75 percent in some cases) (cf. Chevalier and Buckles 1995:241), it is reasonable to suppose that their involvement in "subsistence" as opposed to "commodity" production is illusory. In other words, crops grown for own consumption are "subsistence commodities" where the abstract "exchange value" content of the crop commodity is simply not realized through exchange. As Chevalier expressed it, "The peculiarity of 'subsistence commodities' is that they never enter the sphere of circulation not because they are not exchangeable, but rather because their 'abstract' value can best be realized through direct consumption by the producers themselves" (1982:118–19). Thus, production for household consumption is not reflective of a return to "natural economy" but rather of the wider capitalist context of the economy that set in motion a commoditization process in southern Veracruz (as in the Pachitea valley).

Despite rhetorically asserting their objection to "neopopulist . . . theories of an eternal middle peasantry (family labor farms) viewed as undifferentiated *sui generis* economic category, a subaltern mode of production or moral economy struggling to preserve its egalitarian life-world, its subsistence ethic and its Chaynovian drudgery-adverse logic" (Chevalier and Buckles 1995:129–30), Chevalier and Buckles's analysis of household demographics and life cycle data seems to rely mainly on Sahlins's (1972:87–92, 110–21) selective interpretation of Chayanov focused on tribal economics. It does not appear to be based on their own direct reading of Chayanov (1966) and ignores the ample literature generated by the long debate between agrarian Marxists and Chayanovian neopopulists in comparative peasant studies (Cox and Littlejohn 1984; Deere and de Janvry 1981; de Janvry 1981; Harrison 1975; Lenin 1964; Patnaik 1979; Shanin 1972) and Mexican studies (Bartra 1975; Cook and Binford 1986, 1990).

Chevalier and Buckles's analytical findings yield relatively more support for Chaynovian household cyclicity (1995:261–63) and even for the "growth of a 'middle peasantry'" (1995:138–39) than they do for Lenin's thesis that family cooperation is the foundation of capitalist cooperation (Lenin 1963:374) or that the development of household enterprises from conditions of petty commodity production to those of petty capitalism is significantly affected by household demographics through their impact on productive capacity, capital accumulation, and material wealth as measured, for example, by landholdings, means of production, and type of housing (Cook and Binford 1990:115). Indeed, this thesis is not addressed in their analysis. One paradoxical implication of their analysis is a discovery of a reproducing kin-based, patrimonial domestic economy that, for all practical purposes, is a subaltern domestic mode of production subordinated to the capitalist mode (Chevalier and Buckles 1995:253, 263).

The Chevalier–Buckles analysis lacks the variables necessary to shed empirical light on critical processes linking household demographics and life cycle to capital accumulation and enterprise expansion. For example, they assert that "the tendency for middle-aged families to produce and own more than younger and older households seems to confirm the Chayanovian rule which says the smaller the working capacity of the household is, the more its members will work" (1995:261). Yet the crucial variable in a contemporary rural Mexican context is how income per household member is related to the consumer/worker ratio. In Oaxaca, for example, our analysis of this variable showed an inverse relationship and that "growing income per household worker in the context of declining c/w ratios gives rise . . . to a potential for capital accumulation based on the employment of unwaged household labor (i.e., endofamilial accumulation)" (Cook and Binford 1990:118).

In short, Chevalier and Buckles are able to demonstrate empirically the existence of a universe of household enterprises differentiated by predominant source of income, by combinations of subordinate income sources, by income/earnings levels, and by selected assets (such as land, cattle, and cash savings). Nevertheless, they are less successful in providing empirical support for their contention that these household units are integrated through relations of production and distribution—given the lack of crucial data on rent, credit and debt, position in production (that is, employer/employee), and means of production (excluding land, which is a factor of production). They do convincingly establish a basic division between a small minority of household enterprises (6 percent) that own capital invested in cattle and small businesses and a large majority that are either subsistence and wage workers (47 percent) or small-scale commodity producers (47 percent) of whom an undetermined percentage also engage in wage work at least one day a week (1995:134–35). What remains unclear in their analysis is the pattern and volume of value flows between the 6 percent minority and the rest of the households as well as the nature and degree of movement between the two noncapitalist categories and between them and the capital-holding category.

In their elaboration of the nature of the ontological turn back to agricultural production for own use in terms that integrate economy, society, and culture, Chevalier and Buckles get bogged down in contradictory and defensive argumentation. They seem to want to "have their ontological cake (subsistence economy enveloped in Nahua culture) and eat it too" (devoured by capitalist expansion). On the one hand, they emphasize "the impact of a market economy and a class society" on "customary rules" of social hierarchy, exchange, and family relation, whereas, on the other, they insist that "Gulf Nahua kinship continues to play a crucial role in the livelihood of present-day Pajapeños" so that the "domestic economy based on native patterns of organization constitutes a central ingredient of Pajapan society" (1995:253).

To further complicate matters, they view kin-based power and exchange relations as forming "a domain of their own, a bilateral descent system consisting of nuclear households governed by patrimonial rules of residence, marriage and inheritance (polygyny, bride service, male ultimogeniture)." Furthermore, they contend that "from this patrimonial domain emerges a particular view of relations between humans and the universe, a worldview conveyed through narrative discourse" in which the "concept of death as a condition of reproduction is central . . . and touches all aspects of Nahua culture" (1995:6–7). Indeed, the last chapter of the book is a largely unconvincing attempt to demonstrate that "symbolism expressed through discursive practice (narrative, ritual) . . . Gulf Nahua views on relations and problems that govern all life forms dwelling in the universe" (1995:264, cf. chap. 7) are somehow relevant to their economic life today.

Regarding their approach to "native culture" (1995:263), Chevalier and Buckles make repeated references to normative "rules" and "views" and emphasize that "we have been careful to treat the Nahua dimension of life in Pajapan as a critical aspect of all social relations observed in the field, a dimension subject to important changes over time" (1995:263). On the other hand, they make the following disavowals: "Culture has not been confined to a particular set of variables, a fixed sub-system of extant practices (language, religion, kinship) salvaged from the ravages of modern history. We have not equated the cultural with the symbolic or the discursive, as distinct from the practical or the material, the political or the economic . . . we do not believe that ideological practices can be demarcated from other aspects of social life and then combined with political economy to produce a comprehensive view of society" (1995:263). If we take Chevalier and Buckles at their own words, we are hard pressed to arrive at a definitive judgment of their definition of culture, much less its relationship with economy and society.

What is clear is their insistence on distinguishing Nahua or Indian culture from mestizo culture and conceiving "local versus national" economy, society, and culture as structurally separate forms in articulation but with the local still actively resisting full incorporation into the broader domain of capital (1995:1–2). In conclusion, Chevalier and Buckles's findings are much more supportive of the role of labor alienation and an economic value squeeze in Pajapan economic life, which they do not explicitly recognize, than of the role of the Nahua myth of the "corn-god-child" Sintiopiltsin, which they do.

CONCLUSIONS

The contours of the economic anthropological field of study of Mexicans in twenty-first-century North America are best determined by a focus on commodity culture—its diversified development, performance, and outcomes. Spatially, this field is wide open since it encompasses any site where the Mexican agents of commodity culture(s) practice it—for example, within the spatial boundaries of a settlement or its dependent territory or a nonresidential workplace (such as agricultural field, workshop, manufactory, quarry, or mine). Socially, the field is also wide in scope and necessarily encompasses subjects of different ages as well as different gender, class, and ethnic identities. Methodologically and epistemologically, my approach to the study of this field involves attention to symbols and their textual and conversational expression as well as to the actions and activities of subjects and their results, which in most cases can be counted, measured, and otherwise quantified. Theoretically and conceptually, my approach privileges exchange value but also considers its use and symbolic (sign) dimensions. It also assigns priority to expressions of prudent rationality, to the division of labor and specialization and the corresponding branch organization of production, to the enterprise as a unit of analysis, and to economic class identity and corresponding subjective identities. Finally, the approach I mapped out here emphasizes the holistic analysis of the economic process (production, exchange, distribution, and consumption) as well as the selective performance of the exterior operation, that is, to the analysis of interpenetrations and/or relationships between the economic and the noneconomic, especially as the latter is economically conditioned or economically relevant.

There are compelling reasons to argue that within the Mexican branch of North American capitalism today, the logic of commodity culture(s), now heavily fortified by private property and market mediation, is integrative of the entire Mexican social formation to such a degree that nothing that is central to the reproduction of the system or the maintenance of capitalist hegemony (which ethnic divisiveness certainly is) escapes significant, if not prime causal, economic determination. I would argue that this is as equally true of the indigenous rebellion in Chiapas and its anthropological representations emphasizing subsistence crisis and cultural survival as it is of circulatory migration of Mexican workers through the circuits and channels of North American labor markets. These are directly connected to the commodity component of Mexican culture and are, in fact, inconceivable in the absence of that connection—unlike, for example, the umbilical cosmology of the Maya (Nash 2001) or Gulf Nahua myths revolving around the "corn-god-child" known as Sintiopiltsin (Chevalier and Buckles 1995:269), which are not. The cultural domain of highest priority for economic anthropology of Mexico today revolves around commodity value. By contrast, cosmological values occupy a cultural domain that, a priori, can be assumed to have little or no economic meaning or relevance and that probably never had a central, direct relationship to the commodity domain of Mexican culture.

Even though the economic field in the contemporary Mexico sociocultural system is dominated by capitalist forms and dynamics and is market integrated, it includes spaces where household and community reproduction continue to draw on noncapitalist and nonmarket forms (for example, kinship and family relations, reciprocity, redistribution, and communal property and obligations) as well as where commodity production assumes petty forms that are separate from, albeit connected to, the dominant capitalist sector.

For purposes of economic anthropological inquiry in twenty-first-century Mexico, there are still situations in which labor may be performed or services provided outside the money-mediated market, either as social duty, as reciprocal obligation, or for payment in kind. These situations are just as much a part of the economic field and of commodity culture(s) as are those involving money-mediated market transactions. The main difference is that in the nonmarket context, the use-value dimension is subjectively privileged over the exchange-value dimension, although the latter cannot be completely discounted as affecting agency. Indeed, given the pervasive commoditization of labor in the wider economy, it is impossible to eliminate wagelike considerations from situations putatively involving unwaged or reciprocal labor at the local level, as I demonstrated in my study of Oaxaca valley *metateros* (Cook 1976) and as Chevalier (1982) demonstrated in Peru's Pachitea valley.

NOTES

1. See Cook (2003:215–18) for an extended critique of this ethnocultural survivalist current.

2. Ernest Mandel was apologetic for this term, which he deemed "unsatisfactory because it is one of chronology" and emphasized that it did not refer to a new epoch of capitalist development but "merely a further development of the imperialist, monopoly-capitalist epoch" (1978:9). His main analytic concern was to try to understand changes in the "concrete phenomenal forms of 'many capitals'" through the lenses of "the laws of motion of 'capital in general'" (1978:8). Trotsky's notion of combined and uneven development is central to Mandel's analysis (1978:22–23). He accepts the idea of a "capitalist world market" but notes that "it did not everywhere universalize the capitalist mode of production . . . in the so-called Third World it created and consolidated a specific mixture of pre-capitalist and capitalist relations of production

which *prevents* the universalization of the capitalist mode of production, and especially of capitalist large-scale industry, in these countries" (1978:61). Departing from the premise that "capital innately tends to combine international expansion with the formation and consolidation of national markets," he proposed that "depending on the development of productive forces and social conditions . . . world-wide capitalist relations of exchange bind together capitalist, semi-capitalist and pre-capitalist relations of production" (1978:311). I am unaware of any subsequent publication by Mandel in which he has expressed agreement or disagreement with Harvey's hypothesized "shift from Fordism to . . . a 'flexible' regime of accumulation" (that is, more flexible labor processes and markets, geographic mobility, and rapid shifts in consumption practices [Harvey 1989:124]).

3. One critical point I would raise regarding Chibnik's study is that he assumes, incorrectly, that wood carving in the Oaxaca valley is restricted to the three communities he studied and that it is strictly of post-1950 origin (2003:6–7). He ignores the case of Santa Cecilia Jalieza, where the carving of wooden spoons and beverage stirrers (*acahuetes*), which also underwent redesign (by the artisans themselves) as letter openers and bookmarkers, has been practiced at least since the colonial period (Cook and Binford 1990:75–78, 262 n. 8). Granted, this is a less exalted wood-carving industry than the one Chibnik highlights, but it is also more historically and ethnoculturally representative of the Zapotec woodcrafting tradition. Furthermore, my field experience in San Sebastian Teitipac in the 1960s taught me that the crafting of ceremonial masks and figurines from locally available sources of wood is not uncommon among the Valley Zapotec. My compadre Filomeno Gabriel Mateo, a skilled *metatero*, was also a skilled wood carver who occasionally produced masks and figurines for use during the "rite of spring" *carnaval* celebrations in this community that I attended. Some of these carvings form part of my own personal collection. I also saw locally produced masks used in celebrations in the district head town of Tlacolula. Although I never wrote about it, I also knew, and purchased unpainted woodcarvings (figurines) from, an artisan in San Pedro Guegorexe (whose name is buried in my files). The point is that there is evidence of a broader and deeper Zapotec "crafting tradition" in wood carving than Chibnik implies.

Finally, Chibnik participates in the categorization of my work as downplaying "cultural aspects of crafts" to emphasize socioeconomic aspects (2003:61). Such an interpretation admittedly can be inferred from a selective reading of my work, which invariably includes ignoring my book on the *metateros* and various articles in which I address "cultural" dimensions of Oaxaca valley crafts (Cook 1968b, 1981, 1982, 1983, 1995). I trace this tendency in the literature, which Chibnik shares with many others too numerous to cite, to my highlighting over the years of "utilitarian" *crafts* like metate making and brick making and of less artistically exalted industries (such as Xaagá cotton products) in branches like treadle-loom weaving with more artistically exalted industries (such as Teotitlán del Valle). It may also reflect a response to my long-standing critique of ethnocultural/neopopulist discourse (Cook 1978:310–11; 1982:379–82, 2003; Cook and Binford 1990: 6–7) and my promotion of class analysis with a focus on capitalist development from a basis in local petty commodity production.

4. Good notes that the Nahua characterize their commercial activity metaphorically as "haciendo la lucha," implying a "struggle," and describes their aggressive role within the capitalist economic arena as follows: "They created a place within the

dominant economic formation in which they are relatively autonomous, while a vital space exists for their commerce and for them as an ethnic group. They can be conceived of as raiders (Murra, personal communication) who 'assault' urban centers, taking advantage of an international conjuncture that brings waves of tourists to Mexico, disposed to spend their money on the purchase of crafts" (1988:229). Murra's "raider" analogy carries the same implication as my characterization of Nahua traders as mercenary capturers of exchange value.

5. This measure of earnings was adopted by Good to satisfy her informants' concern with possible tax implications of more precise earnings calculations. It has the analytical disadvantage of making it impossible to disaggregate earnings data by family member, by type of product, by labor time, and so on. In fact, since the earnings data are by household enterprise, whereas the wage labor equivalency measure is for an individual worker over a four-week period of forty-eight hours, there is no way for Good to empirically demonstrate her comparative earnings data.

6. The government of the state of Yucatan has aggressively pursued a strategy of inserting its impoverished rural areas, especially in the henequen zone, into the global *maquila* market. "Forty-one of the 111 maquiladora plants in Yucatan are located in the . . . Henequen Zone . . . [and] employ a total of some 25,000 workers, 84 per cent in the garment industry" (Van Dooren and Zárate-Hoyos 2003:184). Since most of these plants are located in the greater Merida area, rural households diversify their incomes through a commuter-type migration (daily or weekly) of young members. This labor market participation now provides most of the total income for these households (2003:182–86). Of course, this type of industrialization—mostly exogenous in orientation—does not necessarily lead to long-term sustainable development. A strategy needs to be found to foster an "endogenous base for . . . sustained competitive advantage" (2003:591).

8

Social Reproduction of Commodity Value: Mapping Interior and Exterior Connections

According to June Nash (2001), the 1980s marked a turning point in sociocultural anthropology and in how subalterns like the indigenous peasantries of Mexico are represented. Just as anthropologists were beginning to undertake class analyses, she argues that it became unfashionable to do so partly because social movement theorists proclaimed that class no longer served as an appropriate analytic category. In addition, a broader range of postmodern/cultural critique/deconstructionist discourse promoted new approaches to the alleged transformations occurring in the postmodern condition (2001:220–21). Nash herself seems to have moved in that direction (only three references to class in her index and a notably non-class-based analysis of conflict and the process of differentiation/wealth distribution [2001:56–66]), yet she seems to do so with some misgivings about postmodernism for ignoring "the conflict of real material interests that are structurally sustained through the institutions of a society that we once thought of as the class struggle" (2001:222). She also notes sardonically that it is "probably not coincident that, just when indigenous people are becoming protagonists in this ongoing drama of class conflict, the pundits within dominant society have denied the existence of the drama" (2001:222).

Susana Narotsky has independently proposed a general approach to social reproduction that seems to be compatible with June Nash's embrace of substantivism without losing sight of the "conflict of real material interests" (Nash 2001:222). Narotsky's approach emphasizes the institutional/structural/cultural matrix which institutes or "embeds" the "economic process" while simultaneously acknowledging but subtly reducing the culturally constitutive role of the economic process. Her approach holds out the promise of being able to maintain a focus on the material process of producing and reproducing life while emphasizing its sociocultural and historical institutionalization or "embeddedness" (Narotsky 1997:3, 49–50, 57, 86–91; Nash 2001:1–6). As I will argue in this chapter, Narotsky's rejection of a specifically economic field of analysis, combined with her reliance on Polanyi's embedment thesis, jeopardizes her approach's promise to maintain a "materialist" focus.

HOLISM, REPRODUCTIONISM, AND CLASS ANALYSIS

If one looks at the sources of resistance to the practice of inquiries focused on commodity and exchange value in economic anthropology, the most common one may be the belief that the real task of anthropological inquiry is to see the whole picture, without emphasizing one element of reality over another, in representing the total situation of the people with whom the anthropologist is collaborating in the knowledge production process. The holistic imperative seems to legitimate anthropological inquiry itself and makes its advocates uneasy with approaches that heuristically privilege economy in the study of culture, or production or commodity value in the study of the economy. Since culture represents the bundle of ties that bind the parts into a whole, with worldview occupying the top rung of the great chain of the integrative cultural process, holism nurtures an essentialist view of otherness revolving around the identification and interpretation of "distinct cultural premises" and idiosyncratic "moral logic" that opposes "rational logic of free market globalization" and whose "morality differs from that of a capitalist Protestant ethic in stressing collective, rather than individual goods" (Nash 2001:24–25).[1]

The question of how one gets from fieldwork experiences primarily in one community to sweeping characterizations of an entire ethnic group and, ultimately, of all indigenous subalterns on the planet is customarily ignored by advocates of the new holistic anthropology. Operational answers to this question are especially important when grand theoretical concepts like "globalization" or collectivistic "moral logic" are at stake in a forum that is no longer strictly academic but part and parcel of antiglobalist politics. The anthropological interpretation of the world seems to be increasingly shaped by human rights and empowerment concerns on the part of anthropologists. Whether or not one agrees with this trend, it should be recognized that in class-organized society, the role of explaining reality in a balanced way is inevitably compromised by taking sides on politically divisive issues as a research credo. It is my conviction that to understand regional and local capitalism in a balanced way, economic anthropologists need to interact professionally with representatives of appropriate fractions from both capitalist and noncapitalist classes. Capitalism is too complex to be understood exclusively from either the subaltern or the hegemonic perspective. Some anthropologists, however, seem to have reinterpreted the activist message from Marx's (1968:30) eleventh thesis on Feuerbach in a way that even Popper (1964:52) did not anticipate: the point is to interpret social development to help in resisting it. The trick is to keep the intention to resist from unduly biasing the interpretation.[2]

A major theme in this book is the divide between those who interpret indigenous Mexican/Mesoamerican economic life by privileging agency and the exercise of prudent rationality and those who emphasize a shared morality of ethnic group survival rather than rationality. As emphasized in preceding chapters, the empirical study of the indigenous peasant-artisan economy of Mesoamerica from Redfield's and Tax's work to the present has shown the importance of labor alienation and all its concomitant elements and processes and how prudent rationality operates through a broad commodity-cultural spectrum of activities of value acquisition, accumulation, and consumption by economic subjects. It has also shown how this operation involves complex mixes and flows of use, exchange, and sign value to underwrite a process of class differentiation and relations that inserts families and communities into regional, national, and transnational nexuses.

This is a sociocultural and socioeconomic process, involving social divisions of labor occupied by active subjects representing particular household enterprises and communities whose value-creating and value-consuming activities, like their corresponding identities, are situationally mobile but ultimately anchored socioculturally and historically. The one thing that these subjects have in common regarding their actual behavior and its consequences is that knowledge of it will be distorted by perspectives that deny commodity economy and that assume natural economy as the context for their action. Distortion will also result from perspectives that reject subjects' exercise of prudent rationality on a false assumption that it is incompatible or lacks correspondence with a higher integrative order of idiosyncratic cultural morality.

There are many pretexts in contemporary social science discourse for avoiding economic class analysis, but they share a common rejection of the notion of a unified class subject and a common emphasis on noneconomic sources of differentiation (such as gender and ethnicity) that provide objective and subjective bases for new social categories and a focus on the "contradictory interaction of an individual's multiple dimensions of social and economic identity" (Gibson-Graham 1997:91). All these tendencies are represented in Mexican studies, including one that views present-day Mexico as a postcapitalist society ruled by a neoliberal bureaucratic/technocratic "new class" where the struggle for social justice is led by indigenous peoples in Chiapas, Oaxaca, and Guerrero and not by an "exploited proletariat" (Hodges and Gandy 2002:186). The apparent lack of economic class-based social protest (hence the failure of "class-in-itself" to become "class-for-itself") or political leadership is certainly not sufficient reason to declassify Mexico as capitalist, just as a focus on gender or ethnicity is a weak pretext for displacing capital-centric discourse that privileges capitalist class relations.

There is, admittedly, a need to overcome the rigidities and categorical imperatives of traditional economic class analysis to account for a wider range of objective and subjective conditions that potentially differentiate subjects, even within fractional categories, and have possible political ramifications. The best way to accomplish this is to subordinate the taxonomical approach to class (that is, relationship to means of production, role in the labor process, and so on) to a value-in-process approach focused on location in the process of production, exchange, distribution, and consumption of commodity value—assigning relatively more weight to exchange value in the process but insisting on attentiveness to the role of the construction of social demand and sign value as a necessary element in value production and to the linkage between the consumption of commodity value, agent identity, and class location (cf. Narotsky 1997:107, 113–14; Kearney 1996:esp. chap. 7).[3]

SOCIAL REPRODUCTION, COMMODITY LOGICS, AND CULTURE

Informed by a theoretical focus on embedment, social reproduction, and a dialectical approach to culture as constituted and constitutive that entered anthropological discourse in the 1980s (Clammer 1985, 1987; Kahn and Llobera 1981; Roseberry 1988), Narotsky has crafted an original and sophisticated framework for economic anthropological knowledge production. She concisely sums up three key elements in her proposed framework: "On the one hand, the rejection of the idea of a separate economic level or bounded region of economic social relations or activities seems to me a first and necessary step. On the other hand, I feel it is useful to narrow the scope of the 'economic' to the social relations involved in the production and reproduction of material life, through the organized interaction of humans and nature. And, last, I would want to put forward the idea that material relations cannot be theoretically separated from their cultural expressions which, in turn, are materially produced and embodied" (1997:7).

If the reader keeps an eye on the "economic" subject in this statement, it appears to sequentially disappear, reappear in a reduced version, and then vanish again with a dialectical flourish. Indeed, there appears to be a contradiction between the first and second elements in her framework—since the "economic" of her second element still implies a separation from the noneconomic. The third element raises the possibility that her proposed framework could lead analysis off the economic mainline to focus primarily on sociocultural structure and institutions. Is this what she means by her reference to "beyond economic anthropology" (1997:1)?

This initial impression is reinforced by Narotsky's programmatic statement that implies a reluctant reliance, for reasons of expository and analytical expediency, on the "'classic' analytic division of the economic process into the distinct moments of production, distribution, exchange and consumption," only to "end in the all-encompassing field of social reproduction" (1997:7), which encompasses a "realm of reproduction" as opposed to the "connected realms of market production and consumption" (1997:39). This is mainly the realm of the domestic group or household where female and other nonwaged labor perform chores or housework related to the reproduction of life and labor power (1997:39, 168–69)—a realm that has been highlighted in studies focused around the "means of livelihood" thesis (Pahl 1984). It is at this intersection of Marx's concept of social reproduction of the economy and the realm of reproduction of life and labor power that Narotsky enters a path leading toward the construction of an approach to social reproduction as a "global concept of social motion" (1997:169)

Before entering this path, however, Narotsky intends to show "how the original self-enclosed categories break down and give way to one another in concrete historical social processes" (1997:169). Her dramatic language gives the impression that her use of the categorical divisions of the economic process is intended to be a onetime epistemological expediency (one that will culminate in its supercession) rather than the demonstration of a method for continuing research. But, as it turns out, despite her failure to provide a prefatory rationale for her "paradoxical route," Narotsky proceeds through an insightful critical reading and refreshing interpretation of Marx in addition to other classic (such as Aristotle, Adam Smith, Thomas Malthus, Alfred Marshall, A. V. Chayanov, and Marcel Mauss) and more recent texts (such as Meillasoux, Miller, Baudrillard, and Bourdieu) to demonstrate that the classic categorization of the economic process is epistemologically indispensable.

In short, it turns out that this classic categorization is the most logical method for not losing sight of the economic process within the enveloping cocoon of sociocultural reproduction (1997:223). Yet Narotsky's journey along the path of "global social motion," which relies heavily on the work of Raymond Williams, seems to seek release from the confines of the economic field to embrace the "'whole material social process' constructed in an endless movement of human practice and experience, and the struggle for change, which is history" (1997:177). This may not lead inevitably to the personalization of society (that is, assuming that the objective of a society is self-reproduction), which Narotsky rejects, but it would seem to encourage the melding of economic anthropology with general Marxist anthropology.[4]

As far as I am concerned, the best counter to such a meld is the maintenance of a central analytic focus on the production, exchange, distribution, and consumption of economic value in the social reproductive circuitry of a given commodity economy. Since the circuitry is socially organized and culturally propelled, it is logical to pursue historical, ideological, and political connections with a focus on particular circuits in order to avoid epistemological excursions seeking more remote or distanced explanations of possible connections between the reproductive circuitry of the economy and other dimensions or realms of sociocultural life that may, in fact, be irrelevant or nonexistent. The circuitry I am referring to has its origins in Marx's *Capital* (1967, 1:105) and is elaborated in a section titled "The General Formula for Capital" (1967, 1:14655) through various combinations in series of the symbols C = commodity and M = money. I have found Geoffrey Kay's (1975:13–55) elaboration of Marx's formula, through the strategic use of subscripts (such as C_n = consumption) and superscripts (such as C^L = labor power), with a focus on the law of social reproduction, production–consumption circuits, and the circuit of capital, to be an indispensable analytical framework for economic anthropological knowledge production in Mexican studies (Cook 1978:302–10). It is especially useful to illustrate the complex linkages within discrete circuits beginning in different types of enterprises (such as peasant-artisan domestic units targeting reproduction through a mixed combination of unwaged and wage labor, merchant capitalist units seeking profit through the resale of peasant-artisan commodities, and industrial capitalist units seeking profit through the resale of commodities produced with C^L [labor power] and C^{MP} [means of production]) as well as linkages between such circuits (Cook 1978:306; 1982:355).[5]

The interdependence of production and consumption underlying social reproduction in all economies of record is represented by Kay (1975:15) in the following circuit: P . . . C_n . . . P . . ., where P represents production and C_n consumption. According to Kay (1975:15), "Material production is the starting point for all social existence since it provides the *means of consumption*—the food, the clothing, the shelter and so on—that enable a population to survive from one year to the next. Production makes possible consumption; but consumption is also necessary for production. For if the producers do not consume their basic essentials, they cannot survive and work." It is not a difficult exercise to move from this very abstract and simple formula to a more concrete and complex one that approximates the main social reproduction circuit for a typical peasant-artisan domestic unit in a specific economy like that of the Oaxaca valley. Moreover, the process of doing so has the great advantage of highlighting the critical role of value creation, flows, destinations, and realization, which in turn compels a consideration of the relations of production and distribution linked to the creation and appropriation of value as well as all the other relevant intersections and connections to economic and noneconomic zones or elements of the sociocultural matrix.

In short, these formulaic maps chart and track value in process and the class relations that organize its production and distribution. As far as I am concerned, those dimensions of social consciousness or of culture that are most accessible to economic anthropological inquiry—and, consequently, most directly connected to making and earning a living—will be expressed around specific lines linking the reproduction circuit of human bearers of labor power to other reproduction circuits (such as those for industrial or merchant capitalist enterprises), to reproduction circuits for other household enterprises in a local or regional division of labor, or to the reproduction circuit of one's own household enterprise. These maps must also be read culturally, however, to ensure that the realization/destruction of commodity value through consumption and the renewal of the process through new production are understood figuratively, not literally, and as part and parcel of a reproductive process (cf. Narotsky 1997:103–4).[6]

This approach gives specific meaning to the thesis that whereas "capitalism embraces a wide range of capital/labor relationships" (Cook and Binford 1990:24), it also embraces even a wider range of cultural differences and agent identities. It forces the specification of abstract commodity logics by specific sets of enterprises in particular social divisions of labor and of production by branch as well as the consideration of ethnic and other local and regional cultural differences.

Theoretically speaking, there are many varieties of consumption and capital accumulation logics, but these need to be substantiated and analyzed empirically at the level of specific enterprises (household based or not) in particular branches of production with specific agents or subjects. There is only limited value in producing discourse about economic logics in general (Narotsky 1997:162–67) simply because such logics are operationally meaningless until reduced to the exercise of prudent rationality by particular subjects in concrete enterprises or economic action units (EAUs). It is only through empirical analysis at the level of EAUs that we can determine the extent to which prudent rationality conforms to ideal–typically posited, form-specific logics.

The following symbolic formula for the circuit of industrial capital has the advantage of serving as the basis for analysis of EAUs ranging in scale from behemoth high-tech machinofactories to petty low-tech workshops and manufactories:

$$M \rightarrow C^{L} + C^{MP} \ldots P \ldots C \rightarrow M^{1}(M + \Delta M) \rightarrow$$
$$C^{L} + C^{MP} \ldots P \ldots C \rightarrow M^{2}\,(M^{1} + \Delta M) \ldots M^{nth}$$

The circuit from M through M^2 represents how an initial investment of money capital M is employed to purchase a given quantity of labor power C^L and means of production C^{MP} to produce a commodity C that is sold at a price that includes an increment to M (symbolized as ΔM) or a profit, hence enabling the circuit of value production to continue in an expanded way (that is, $M^1 \rightarrow M^2 \rightarrow M^{nth}$).

Such formulas can also be used as a framework for analyzing the transition from petty commodity to petty industrial capitalist production as follows:

$$H^L + C^{MP} \ldots P \ldots C \rightarrow M^1(M + \Delta M) \rightarrow H^L + C^L + \Delta C^{MP} \ldots P \ldots \Delta C \rightarrow M^2(M^1 + \Delta M) \ldots M^{nth}$$

Here we see labor power supplied by the household enterprise H^L combined with means of production C^{MP} to produce a given commodity output C for a profit M^1; this accumulated capital, in turn, is invested in wage labor (now supplemented by household labor) and expanded means of production ΔC^{MP} to produce an increased commodity output ΔC and incremental profits $M^2 \ldots M^{nth}$. There are two critical moments in this transition that I have examined in depth for the treadle-loom weaving and brick-making industries in the Oaxaca valley (Cook 1984a, 1984b, 1984c; cf. Cook and Binford 1990:chap. 4): 1) the moment at which M^1 results through a process of endofamilial accumulation resulting when favorable demographics and life cycle conditions provide a relatively abundant unwaged labor supply that, conjoined with labor intensification, results in increased output and earnings and 2) when household labor H^L becomes a supplement to hired labor C^L and, combined with expanded means of production ΔC^{MP}, produces an expanded output ΔC. The only way to infuse these abstract formulas with social and cultural content about human subjects is through empirical case studies of specific enterprises.

One of the great advantages of approaching economic process from the perspective of the social reproduction of commodity value is that it simultaneously exposes the arbitrariness of any attempt to conceptually enclose it within spatial, political, or sociocultural boundaries as well as the heuristic necessity of doing so to approximate an understanding of concrete, everyday behavior of real subjects. It is impossible to successfully achieve such an understanding of any particular universe of subjects in early twenty-first-century Mexico by conceiving of them exclusively as reproducing their lives in an international capitalist economy without also taking into account their participation in processes and relations of narrower range and scope. Far too many of the concrete elements in their actually existing value reproductive circuits would be ignored or left unexplained by an approach at such an abstract level of integrative process.[7]

Such an understanding becomes increasingly distorted as the exclusive focus is reduced in range and scope down to the local community. Whereas access to land for agricultural and other productive purposes continues to provide many rural communities throughout Mexico with the possibility of achieving significant levels of food self-sufficiency, inequality in access to land and agricultural means of production between and among household enterprises, combined with overall demographic growth, relegate such a possibility to the status of a utopian delusion. About all that can be said is that those household enterprises able to access land for productive purposes have a distinct advantage over those that do not in the process of social reproduction of livelihood and lifestyle in a capitalist economy. The thesis that such activity, even when enabling the substitution of home-produced crops for purchased crops, somehow reproduces something other than commodity economy dominated by capitalist relations of production is contradicted by the careful empirical analysis of value flows and transfers as represented in the circuitry mapping approach.

The household is a fundamental unit of analysis of labor reproduction precisely because through membership in it, individuals become value-producing and value-consuming subjects. It becomes a critical hub of economic enculturation and of entry into the internal (domestic) and external (extrahousehold) division of labor. Many of the fundamental elements of commodity culture(s) are learned in this context. Through different mixes of membership composition, demographic, and life cycle variables, the household locates individuals in the organization of production and distribution relations, that is, the class structure. It is in that context that they acquire knowledge about how to produce and consume commodity value consistent with community reproduction.

CULTURE, SOCIAL RELATIONS, AND COMMODITY ECONOMY IN OAXACA

Construction Materials: Adobe versus Brick

Many of these relationships can be illustrated by examining two related commodities, both of which are wholly produced from locally available raw materials—adobe and brick—which, together with thatch, constitute the options for local rural housing construction in the Oaxaca valley. The main difference between the two commodities is that, whereas bricks are kiln fired, adobe blocks are simply sun dried. Firing makes bricks more durable than adobe but also more costly because of the need for kiln construction and the firing process itself, which require more highly specialized labor than does adobe making. This means that historically, throughout Mexico, bricks tend to be produced and consumed predominantly in larger, more urbanized localities and not locally produced in smaller, rural communities. In such communities, when used in local construction, bricks are usually trucked or carted in from external production sites.

The rural demand for these two related commodities is socioculturally constituted in a way that generally reflects the differences in their production. Thatch, by contrast, consisting of a variety of wood and other locally available plant products (for example, palm fronds, dried cornstalks, and reeds), is most prevalent in the housing of the least affluent families in the rural class structure. Adobe has a much wider distribution than thatch or even brick, which tends to be used mostly in the housing of the most affluent families (Cook and Binford 1990:120, 267 n. 10).

In the peasant-artisan context, adobe making is less specialized than brick making and is more likely to be ad hoc and uncommercialized. Both tend to be exclusively dry-season activities involving a varied mix of in-kind and cash-mediated transactions in the production process. Adobe is the more pervasive building material in the Oaxaca countryside because of its relatively less specialized production requirements, lower cost, and higher compatibility with the indigenous cultural matrix.

A composite case from my fieldwork is that of a household of newlyweds in Oaxaca who live with the husband's elderly parents and are building a new adobe house in which to establish an independent household unit. On any given day during this period, we can observe as many as five persons, four men and one woman, at a work site along the banks of a small stream: a small parcel of land has been cleared of brush; one section of it has been smoothed out into a perfectly flat, clean surface, whereas another is being excavated with picks and shovels as a source of clay (cf. Cook 1982:55–56). The clay is piled up and mixed together with burro dung, shredded cornstalks, and buckets of water to a mudlike consistency and then shoveled into square wooden molds, smoothed and formed into the shape of blocks, and laid out on a patio in rows to dry in the sun.

In villages located in the central valleys of Oaxaca, this adobe-making process may be inserted differently into a division of labor and a class structure. The woman on the scene, in this case recently married, could either be there simply to bring food and drink to the men at work and tending grazing animals while the men make adobe (which would reflect a more "traditional" gender division of labor) or be "helping out" with adobe making (as evidence of a "gender crossover" in the division of labor, often reflecting relative poverty). In any case, her labor is a necessary contribution to the reproduction of the household economy and, in the case of her participation in adobe making, is directly productive of commodity value, even though it is unwaged. This example gives some idea of the complexities surrounding the role of female labor in the petty enterprise sector of the Mexican economy (Cook 1984a:167–72; Cook 1990; Cook and Binford 1990:152–89).

The five male workers at the adobe-making site would typically illustrate intersections with wage-mediated and unwaged relations of production/distribution. Let us assume, for example, that in this case the woman's father-in-law, Adalberto, is a full-time agriculturist who also happens to be near the adobe-making site only because he is plowing with an ox team on an adjacent section of the same land parcel, which he owns and where he will plant corn, beans, and squash for own use and for exchange. Adalberto has arranged for his son, Melquiades, to temporarily work for Juan, a home builder (*albañil*) and adobe maker (*adobero*) to whom Adalberto rents the adobe-making site for a share of each batch of adobe produced. Jorge and Marcelino are day laborers employed by Juan for a cash wage. Juan sells the adobe on demand in the village, usually to property owners who contract him to build a house, wall, or other structure. The deal, in this specific instance, is that Melquiades will earn a share of the adobes produced, which will then be added to his father's share until enough are available for him to contract Juan to build a house. Melquiades, in agreement with the others, has asked his brother-in-law, Demetrio, to work with him on a reciprocity basis to add another portion of adobe to his own share.

In this composite example, the relation between Juan and his employees, Jorge and Marcelino, is a straightforward wage-mediated relation, whereas the rent-in-kind relationship between Adalberto and Juan is semicapitalist. The relationship between Adalberto and Melquiades and Melquiades's relationship with Demetrio are kinship mediated; in the latter case, the relationship is also mediated by the Zapotec institution of *guelaguetza*, which will entail a claim on Melquiades's labor on behalf of Demetrio in the future. Thus, in effect, even though Melquiades was able to gain the benefits from Demetrio's work without having to pay for it in cash, he will have to pay for it later with his own labor, which will then have a value equivalent to the locally prevailing day wage rate. Similarly, the adobe blocks resulting from Demetrio's labor can be assigned the same cash value as those produced by Jorge and Marcelino.

The manufacture of handmade kiln-fired brick incorporates elements of adobe making but involves a more complex labor process, reflects a greater degree of specialization of labor and technology, and has more potential for capital accumulation and enterprise expansion. Consequently, compared with adobe making, the brick industry is characterized by more diversified and polarized relations of production/distribution linking wage-dependent households to profit-making enterprises (Cook 1984a). Corresponding to this complex structure of production relations is a complex structure of consumption and demand reflecting this commodity's mass-market potential.

The location of brick production reflects a complex interplay between resource availability, environmental impact, transportation costs, and demand. Therefore, it tends to be concentrated in semirural, periurban zones in as close proximity as environmentally possible to high-density construction markets. I have studied the industry in two contrasting settings: in southern Mexico near Oaxaca City and in northern Mexico along the Texas border (especially the greater Reynosa area of the state of Tamaulipas) (Cook 1984a, 1998, 2001).

Perhaps the most striking change in this branch of production as location shifts from peasant-artisan village to periurban area of Oaxaca City to periurban Reynosa on the Texas–Mexico border is the industry's progressive upsizing and upscaling as measured by geographic space occupied, number of participating personnel and enterprises, and the wide range of variation in enterprise scale and technology (Cook 1998:7–12).

The shift in brick making from village to periurban setting in Oaxaca involves a jump in levels in the division of labor and specialization from an intracommunity to an intercommunity level. The several periurban communities that manufacture handmade clay brick in the Oaxaca valley were historically concentrated in a relatively restricted zone along the Pan-American Highway east of the city limits and not only supplied the city construction market but also construction markets in outlying towns in the Central Valleys region. Except for periods of slowdown during the rainy season, brick production is a year-round activity on privately owned agricultural land, a portion of which has been set aside for establishing a brick plant (*ladrillera*) consisting of clay pits and additional space for molding and stacking bricks as well as for one or more kilns. It is not uncommon for brick plants to have rudimentary rent-free housing for workers and their families, most of whom are immigrants from other regions of the state who are paid a piece-wage per 1,000 unfired bricks molded, sun dried, stacked, and ready for kiln firing. Typically, the male head of household is the principal worker in clay extraction, preparation, and brick molding but is assisted by his wife and children in other tasks. The specific division of tasks depends, nonetheless, on the size, composition, and life cycle stage of the household-enterprise unit.

In any case, the weekly earnings of a brick-producing nuclear household with subteen male dependents are best characterized as a family wage even though the male household head is the sole wage earner. The household's total daily brick output might not have been less in the absence of the labor contribution of other household members, but the principal wage earner's workday was shortened and his drudgery reduced correspondingly. At a later stage in the life cycle, especially in cases where family dependents include teenage males, the daily output of the household unit—and, therefore, its total weekly earnings—will increase markedly. In the case of worker–owner households in the brick industry, it is precisely at this stage where the possibility of capital accumulation and enterprise expansion is greatest. Proletarian households will only enjoy the benefits derived from increased purchasing power.

A definite massification of the brick industry occurs in the movement from peasant-artisan village, to periurban community setting in Oaxaca, and to the periurban context of greater Reynosa on the U.S. border. Total industry output moves from several hundred pieces per week in the village, to many thousand pieces per week in periurban Oaxaca, to many tens of thousands of pieces per week in periurban Reynosa. Plant scale, organizational complexity, and fixed capital investment increases correspondingly in response to the progressive expansion of residential and commercial demand from rural Oaxaca, to urban Oaxaca, to the U.S.–Mexico border.

The greater Reynosa area industry produces brick for the domestic urban residential and commercial construction market as well as for the export market—primarily to Houston, San Antonio, Corpus Christi, and other urban residential and commercial markets in Texas. During its peak in the 1970s, eight of Reynosa's plants were selling an average of two million to three million bricks weekly to Texas buyers. These semimechanized plants occupied several acres and had significant investment in housing for employee families, huge roofed sheds for molding and drying brick, ten or more large-capacity gas-fired kilns, mechanical pug mills for mixing clay, dump trucks for hauling clay, mechanical clay diggers, and forklifts for loading and unloading palleted bricks. Any one of these plants approximated in capacity and fixed capital investment the entire periurban Oaxaca City industry. It is significant that several of these brick plant capitalists in Reynosa also owned agricultural and ranch land that provided them with income in periods of slow or stagnant brick sales; this combination of agriculture and brick making also characterizes the periurban industry in Oaxaca, though on a reduced scale.

In contrast to the periurban Oaxaca City industry—where brick plants tend to produce for inventory, especially in anticipation of the rainy season, when production cycles are often interrupted—the Reynosa export plants have historically tended to avoid large inventory buildups and target production to prepaid orders. This gives Texas-based intermediaries/importers an especially critical role in the circuit of capital as providers of a "wage fund" as follows:

$$M^{WF} + M^{P} \rightarrow C^{LP} + C^{MP} \ldots P \ldots C \rightarrow M^{P} \rightarrow$$
$$C \rightarrow M^{I} \rightarrow C \rightarrow M^{II} \rightarrow M^{WF} + M^{P} \ldots P \ldots \text{nth}$$

In this circuit, the brick production process, P, will not be initiated until the intermediary capitalist (a U.S. importer) provides money capital in the form of a wage fund (that is, a preset amount used for workers' subsistence), M^{WF}, to the Reynosa brick plant owner, who then combines it with his own capital, M^{P}, in order to engage his workers and equipment, $C^{LP} + C^{MP}$, in production, P, to manufacture a targeted output of bricks, C, which will be sold to the intermediary for an agreed-on price, M^{I}, which includes a discount for the wage advance, M^{WF}. The Texas intermediary/importer then resells the bricks in Texas for a profit, $C \rightarrow M^{II}$ ($M^{I} + \Delta M$), and then reinitiates the process, $M^{WP} + M^{P} \ldots P \ldots$ nth (cf. Cook 1998:205–7). It is worth noting that in Mexican brick industry discourse, the Texas intermediary/importer who finances the wage fund is referred to as a *capitalista* (capitalist), whereas the

Mexican manufacturer refers to himself as *industrial* (industrialist) (Cook 1998:229).[8]

Labor reproduction is a challenging and complicated process for both labor and capital in the handmade brick industry in Oaxaca and in Tamaulipas. Historically, the labor supply for the industry in both places has been dependent on migration—from outlying peasant regions in Oaxaca (Costa Chica and Mixteca) and from other northern (Coahuila and San Luis Potosí) and interior states (Guanajuato and Veracruz) in Tamaulipas. The two key jobs in the industry—brick molding and kiln tending and, for that matter, loading and unloading kilns and trucks—require relatively high levels of physical strength, endurance, and muscular coordination; workers are also exposed to higher-than-normal levels of heat, smoke, sweat, and dirtiness during the regular course of a normal workday. In short, it is an industry that many workers avoid or abandon after a trial period. On the other hand, workers in the industry have certain compensations: relatively high wages (for example, vis-à-vis agricultural or construction day labor), relatively little supervision, and a relatively high degree of freedom in determining work schedules and pace of work, work opportunities for other family members in the brickyards or surrounding neighborhoods, free or low-cost housing and utilities, and emergency credit from employer). Therefore, those who find brick culture to their liking have historically stayed with it as a main source of livelihood, with the proviso that they are able to survive the inevitable fluctuations of the business cycle to which the brick (and construction) industry is especially susceptible.

In both Oaxaca and Tamaulipas, there is a history of give-and-take between labor and capital in the brick industry over wages and fringe benefits. Employer paternalism is pressed to the limits by employee demands and their ability to play one employer off against another in a highly competitive industry. On balance, workers have a much harder time making ends meet in periods of economic downturn than do their employers, who, in most cases, have alternative sources of business income (such as agriculture, trucking, and commerce). Many employers will provide wage advances to workers during slumps but also negotiate output reductions so that employees can continue to work, but at a reduced earnings for a reduced output (usually at the going piece rate).

The culturally expressive dimension corresponding to the economic process of brick making ranges from deceptively ideological expressions involving class collaboration to the openly ideological class-antagonistic expressions. In the periurban industry in Oaxaca, for example, outsiders will be presented with a uniformly harmonious view of brick making as an activity engaged in by families to supplement agriculture in the pursuit of livelihood, not as a business involving employers and employees in a quest for wages and profits. I have shown how this ideology is, in effect, a collective defense against government interference in the industry (1984a:chap. 5). On the other hand, inside the industry, discourse reflects an ongoing struggle over the fruits of labor between the *mileros* (piece-wage brick makers) and their *patrones* (employers or owner–operators of the brick plants), moderated somewhat by paternalism (such as pay advances and emergency loans) and the absence of unionization (1984a:139–48).

An equally contradictory situation is found in the Tamaulipas industry, where historically a combination of familism and paternalism operated to camouflage fundamentally commercial activities. Unlike Oaxaca, in Tamaulipas the interface between ideology/cultural discourse and economic process is complicated by a higher degree of class polarization as well as by the question of ethnic (Mexican American vs. Mexican and Anglo vs. Hispanic) and national identity (American citizen vs. Mexican citizen and native born vs. foreign born). Business relationships between Mexican export manufacturers on the one hand and Anglo and Tejano intermediaries–importers on the other are often strained by ethnic prejudice and stereotyping rooted in the ethnically conflictive history of the border region. Although Anglo-Texan intermediaries, for the most part, do not deal directly with brick industry workers, their exposure to them in visits to the Mexican brick plants produces an ambivalent view of the "other" as poverty stricken but artisanally adept. By contrast, Mexican employers and their employees have engaged in their own history of class conflict—including a cycle of unionization, strikes, deunionization, and everyday resistance/negotiation—that has highlighted the critical and indispensable role of labor as the bearer of handmade-brick culture without which capital is left without an industry. My study found that alterity is a factor in interethnic as well as interclass relations of commodity economy on the U.S.–Mexico border (1998:chaps. 9–11).[9]

Metates Revisited

The metate is arguably the quintessential utilitarian commodity in the indigenous market economy, not only of Oaxaca but of Mexico and greater Mesoamerica as well. As such, it also exemplifies the thesis that "there is nothing simple about simple commodity production" (Chevalier 1983) because of its market connections to merchant capital and also its role in sociocultural reproduction. This latter role is crucial to the gender division of labor and to the contradictory status of women as domestic providers through the combined performance of labor reproduction chores in the household and tasks in commodity production/circulation that directly contribute to household income (Cook 1982:51–52, 61–64, 86–87, 291, 348–49 n. 12).

My initial visit to a series of Oaxaca valley villages in 1965 resulted in an immediate attraction to one (San Sebastian Teitipac) that had a resident population engaged in the metate industry. The attraction reflected the receptivity of the *metateros* to the idea of cooperating in a study of their "*oficio*," or craft occupation, and also my realization that the metate industry would present an ideal subject for a comprehensive case study of how peasant artisans in the regional economy made and earned a living.

My 1965 report (Cook 1965), based on ten weeks of fieldwork, produced a research agenda that served as a departure point for two additional years of fieldwork, including every site where metates were produced and marketed in the Oaxaca valley. One of the conclusions of this pilot study was that "the dynamics of market activity in a regional cyclical system can be approached most successfully by going into the market from a satellite village to view the market from the perspective of the villagers . . . who come to the market as producers-seeking-buyers . . . but after selling their products . . . become buyers-for-consumption . . . to focus on the peasant as an economic actor in both village and market-place settings" (1965:37). A surprising result of this "follow-the-metate" approach during subsequent fieldwork was the complexity of the sociospatial patterns and relations involved in its routes of circulation and transfer to its final destination in consumer households (Cook 1976).[10]

This "follow-the-metate" approach was reinforced by reading of Malinowski and de la Fuente's Oaxaca markets study (1957:85), where they argued that "the recognition that it is necessary to observe production in its primary forms—that is, in agriculture, artisan and other regional industries—introduces a principle of order. By studying this aspect of organized activities, not only are data obtained which are indispensable for understanding the economy as a whole but also those which lead directly to many problems that arise in the market." I also noted that Malinowski and de la Fuente's view was compatible with that of the classical economists who believed that "if the phenomena of the market place were to be properly understood, the investigation must begin by penetrating below the surface of those phenomena to the relations between men in their capacity as producers" (Meek 1967:181). I referred to this principle of order as a "production bias" (Cook 1968a:8 n. 3) and clarified its meaning in a discussion of the economic field (Cook 1968a:28–32).

In retrospect, my emphasis on the production and circulation of metates as commodities embodying use and exchange value caused me to give less attention in my earlier work to their symbolic/sign value dimension, which had been suggested, among other features, in a brief commentary by Malinowski and de la Fuente. In their words, "The antiquarian, as well as the sociologist interested in culture change, would not miss the principal pre-Columbian article which appears in the modern market: the grinding-stone or metate. The seasonal variation in sales is connected with the custom that at every marriage a metate painted and decorated in gaudy colours has to be presented ritually to the bride. We were told that in the period between January and May . . . a much larger quantity of decorated metates is to be found.

When buying a metate . . . the woman—for grinding is women's work—would examine the surface, assess the size, and carefully look for any defects. . . . The decoration is indispensable on bridal metates. The godfather of the bride, who is the usual donor, will dance ritually at a certain stage of the marriage ceremony with the metate held on his back. This was actually observed by . . . (B.M.) at a marriage ceremony in the village of Abasolo" (Malinowski and de la Fuente 1982:169–70; cf. Malinowski and de la Fuente 1957:154–55; Cook 1968a:8–9 n. 4; 1982:1, 20, n. 1). During my fieldwork, I took this "bridal gift" role of the metate for granted, simply verifying through observation what Malinowski and de la Fuente described.

It should also be noted that the original English edition of the Malinowski and de la Fuente study, first published in 1982, included many original photos not printed in the 1957 Spanish version which informed my fieldwork. One of these photos shows a large gift metate being tied onto the back of a man, presumably the bride's godfather, for a dance in a wedding ritual. The caption includes the following statements: "Most ingredients used in cooking were ground by women on the metate. It was thus a fitting *symbol of wifely duties*" (Malinowski and de la Fuente1982:photo 27; emphasis added).

In the analysis and write-up of data from fieldwork conducted between 1966 and 1968, I broadened the demand question well beyond Malinowski and de la Fuente's emphasis on "bridal metates" simply because my fieldwork had shown that many of the metates (and especially the manos) sold through the formal marketplace system were ostensibly made and sold for utilitarian rather than bridal gift purposes. Such metates were smaller than gift metates and often were also undecorated (Malinowski and de la Fuente 1982:photo 26; compare with photo of gift metates in Tlacolula in Cook 1982:89). Bridal gift metates, I discovered, were often sold on a special order (or *encargo*) basis and did not necessarily enter the marketplace system (see photo in Cook 1982:426). They were decorated with bas-relief designs on their sides and underside prior to being painted with enamel, were larger in size than utilitarian metates, and consequently were at least double the price of standard metates. Bridal metates were often prominently displayed in households as prestige or status symbols and were given as heirlooms. During the fandango "dance of the metate," which I witnessed in San Sebastian Teitipac, the skillfully decorated underside was displayed by the *padrino* for all to see as he danced with the metate strapped to his back (1968b:314).

In the 1960s and 1970s, the purchase of a metate represented a relatively major expenditure in peasant household budgets. The relatively high price of metates vis-à-vis other traditional commodities was a combined reflection of the hard work and skilled labor involved in their manufacture, the cost of getting them to market, and their versatile status as means of production (some village women regularly sold metate-ground tortillas in Oaxaca City) as well as sources of prestige and distinction. The latter status is underlined by the fact that a bridal gift array may include multiple metates (see Cook 1982:90 for a photo showing six metates). Only one of the metates in such an array is given by the *padrino de bautizo* (or baptismal godfather of the bride) who performs the ritual dance. Other potential donors of bridal gift metates include fictive kinspersons, especially the first-communion godparents or special wedding godparents (*padrinos de la boda*) or relatives. The multiple gifting of metates to one bride reflects the versatile value status of this commodity. Whereas any metate is potentially a gift and is destined to be used rather than simply displayed, there is a definite tendency for gift metates to be larger, more elaborately decorated, and therefore more costly and prestigeful.

The underlying explanation of the January–May upswings in metate supply/demand mentioned in the quote from Malinowski and de la Fuente was the intersection of postharvest phase of the agricultural cycle—when more cash was on hand in peasant households, and effective demand was generally higher for all goods and services across the board—and the *fiesta* cycle (consisting of *mayordomías*, or saints' cult celebrations, and also *fandangos*, or wedding celebrations) that placed special food preparation requirements on sponsoring households, hence the annual surge in demand for metates (to replace or add to the household's inventory). The bottom line is that metates of all sizes and potential uses are factored into my time-series analysis of price and output, so that the proportion of metates sold in the marketplace that were purchased for gift purposes is not really essential to understanding the overall dynamics of price and output fluctuations or the business cycle in the metate market (Cook 1968b:283–94; 1970; 1982:chap. 7).

During the late 1970s and 1980s, I did explore, albeit casually, the role of the metate in reinforcing the gender division of labor as suggested in the Malinowski and de la Fuente photo caption. I summed up the results of this inquiry (that is, casual conversations with several women in two villages conducted in the kitchen areas of their homes, usually while regrinding masa [dough] for tortillas and with their daughters who were observing or were nearby) as follows: "The artifact set, metate and mano, in effect symbolizes the conjugal relationship, the gender division of labor and, more particularly, the role of the peasant housewife as mistress of the hearth and provisioner of the food staple—tortillas. It is this symbolism that is ritually reinforced in Valley Zapotec villages during the *fandango* when the godfather of the bride (or his representative) dances with a metate on his back as it is presented to the bride as a wedding gift. This same symbolism is verbally expressed by Zapotec peasant women of all ages, married or unmarried, in their responses to the question as to why they use metates. According to them, to be a woman is to use a metate and mano to grind maize into dough for making tortillas" (Cook and Binford 1990:74–75).

Even though some crossover has been documented in the gender division of labor, especially with regard to artisanal commodity production, there is little evidence of it in the area of food preparation and child rearing, which remains a nearly exclusive female precinct (Cook and Binford 1990:155–57, 186–89). In sum, the results of this casual inquiry confirmed the symbolic connection recognized by Malinowski and de la Fuente and extended it by suggesting a further connection between metate use and female identity (which surprised me when being affirmed by unmarried, teenage girls, albeit in some cases within hearing distance of their mothers). Nevertheless, this double connection merits more systematic ethnographic inquiry before it is too late.

The previous summary statement quoted in Cook and Binford did not include another finding from these same conversations that consumer taste, both men's and women's, is a factor in the utilitarian rationale justifying the continued use of metates in the preparation of masa for tortillas. Informants repeatedly told me that tortillas made from masa ground on a metate and baked on a *comal* (clay griddle) "taste better" than those that are not so produced (that is, prepared directly from mill-ground masa or factory-made tortillas). Women also noted that tortillas made from reground masa were less prone to crumbling on the comal. Both sets of statements provide a rationale for regrinding masa at home on a metate that has already been ground from *nixtamal* (lime-soaked shelled corn) at the local *molino* (mill).

Metates, through their production and consumption, almost perfectly mirror the gender division that locates women in the spheres of food preparation and child rearing and men beyond the "village settlement area" sphere in quarrying stone and fabricating metates in the quarry area (Cook 1982:chap. 5). I say "almost" because women do "help out" in the home-based finishing of metates and manos (either smoothing out with a handheld chisel a roughed-out mano and/or hand-painted adornment of metates). The only male I ever witnessed grinding corn on a metate was a bachelor who lived alone—but in most cases, bachelors or widowers will either buy tortillas or get them from the household of a close relative where women are the metate users. I never saw a woman doing quarry work or making a metate or mano.

The labor expended by women in the finishing of metates and manos was insignificant compared to that they expended in the use of these utensils in grinding and/or regrinding *nixtamal* and in the grinding of other foodstuffs. The amount of labor saved daily by women, thanks to mechanical grinding mills, amounted to several hours. This elimination of drudgery increased markedly in fiesta-related situations where it has been estimated that "young women work ten to fourteen hours per day making tortillas when they are invited to local fiestas"—labor, incidentally, that is performed on a reciprocity (*guelaguetza*) basis (Stephen 1991:187).

In any case, Mesoamerican metate culture is multidimensional and integrated with economy and society so that the nuances of exchange value and use value intermesh with those of symbolic/sign value to reproduce a gender division of labor. This "intermeshing" is, on the one hand, socioeconomic and utilitarian and, on the other, sociocultural and ideological (Cook 1990). I can think of no other commodity set like the metate and mano whose demise will have a greater impact on weakening the cultural underpinnings of the gender division of labor in indigenous Mesoamerican communities. In short, the metate provides a good example of Miller's insight that "ordinary artefacts have a considerable impact in ordering people" (1997:404); the metate as a cultural artifact is a product of present and past activity and is also part of the context in which activity takes on meaning (cf. Miller 1997:408–13; Roseberry 1989:42). One thing seems certain: if the metate/mano set survives the twenty-first century as a commodity still under production, it will do so on the basis of symbolic, not utilitarian, demand.

CHEVALIER'S "SUBSISTENCE COMMODITY" THESIS, THE LABOR THEORY OF VALUE, AND PETTY PRODUCTION IN CAPITALISM

Before the emergence of widespread concern with the demise of the peasantry and the emergence of a complex transnational subject, Chevalier (1982) theorized simple commodity production and critiqued the thesis that peasant use-value rationale is indicative of natural economy to better understand peasant swidden agriculturists in the Pachitea valley in eastern Peru. His contribution remains unmatched in the Latin American literature for its theoretical sophistication, thought-provoking originality, and elegance of expression—although as we saw earlier he did not extend this approach to his more recent Mexican research (Chevalier and Buckles 1995). In my estimation, Chevalier's approach to the logic and reasoning associated with peasant-artisan involvement in simple commodity and capitalist circuits of value creation, exchange, realization, and reproduction—and the class relations necessarily engaged in the concomitant processes of exploitation and unequal transfers—is pertinent to understanding Mexican/North American/international capitalism at this early juncture of the twenty-first century.

Making imaginative and innovative use of Marx's (capitalist mode of production [CMP]) value-flows circuitry, Chevalier presented a logically powerful and detailed theoretical rationale for his principal thesis that simple commodity production is subsumed by merchant and industrial capital to the extent that production for own use, just like production for exchange, necessarily involves the realization of exchange value that is quantifiable in money terms.[11] Consequently, for him, the proposition that production for own use by rural household enterprises is indicative of a nonmarket economy driven by a subsistence logic within a capitalist market economy is wrongheaded. Rather, production for own household use is driven by a form of calculative pursuit he calls "maximization 'in the concrete'" geared to tangible increases in levels of consumption (1982:115). This contrasts with another form of calculative pursuit Chevalier calls "accumulation in the abstract" geared toward capital accumulation or the appropriation of processional value by capitalist enterprises. To supersede the notion of subsistence goods that embody only use value, he introduces the concept of "subsistence commodities," which embody use and exchange value that are realized through the process of home consumption without ever entering the sphere of circulation.

Chevalier explains the rationale for this dual value realization from the perspective of the Pachitea swidden agriculturists as follows: "It is certainly more economical to retain part of one's own production for domestic use than to sell it entirely and subsequently buy equivalent or identical products at dearer prices from local merchants. By short-cutting market transactions, a farmer is in effect minimizing the cost of his family's food budget, and thus securing his access to other desired commodities that can be obtained with his limited cash earnings. By retaining more than 25, 50, or even 75 per cent of his agricultural output, a farmer is effectively increasing the total utility—the 'abstract' value—derived from both cash earnings and food resources" (1982:118). This leads Chevalier to conclude that production for household consumption "may have nothing to do with the preservation of 'natural economy'" but rather "may result from the need, on the part of simple commodity producers, to obtain the greatest value from their produce, and thus to secure the simple reproduction of their own limited means of livelihood" (1982:119). Maximization in the concrete is, in other words, a situationally appropriate form of economizing.

According to Chevalier, not only the products of labor for own use but also self-employed labor itself and the "free" land that is its object also have exchange value that can be analyzed in quantitative terms. Regarding land, its direct appropriation in a regional context of low population density and ample rain forest represents the "realization of measurable savings in the family budget" just like the home consumption of produce. Self-employed labor power is not merely a use value and a noncommoditized factor of production. It is a "measurable magnitude of exchangeable value" for three reasons: 1) it is occasionally purchased locally at critical moments of the productive cycle and is an essential component of the productive process ("Every farmer is . . . quite aware that the average work he does on his farm in one day is worth [fifty soles—the going wage rate] in the sense that the same work could be, or could have been, performed by a peon in exchange for the sum of fifty soles"); 2) "every farmer is well aware that measurable variations in his labour-time input will have calculable effects upon the overall volume of food commodities he may produce, and upon the total magnitude of use-values he and his family may derive from the consumption or sale of such commodities"; and 3) "the overall level of consumption of an agricultural worker is directly conditioned by the wider market economy, which quantifies (or commodifies) the value of his labour-power and produce in relation to other categories of labour-power and priced goods"—in fact, his labor power and produce are undervalued by the market (1982:121–22).

The strength of Chevalier's approach lies in his recognition that peasant agriculturists in a commodity economy perform "makeshift cost-benefit analyses" using going market rates (Cook and Binford 1990:33), thus strengthening the rationale for assigning market values to factor inputs not directly mediated by market transactions. It should not be forgotten that Marx anticipated this analytical approach in his well-known discussion of the thesis that in the CMP the "independent peasant of handicraftsman is cut up into two persons. . . . As owner of the means of production he is capitalist; as labourer he is his own wage-labourer" (1963:408).[12]

Chevalier neatly schematizes his composite simple commodity production (SCP) circuit to highlight the strategic "subsistence commodity" component by modifying Marx's classic C–M–C formula as follows:

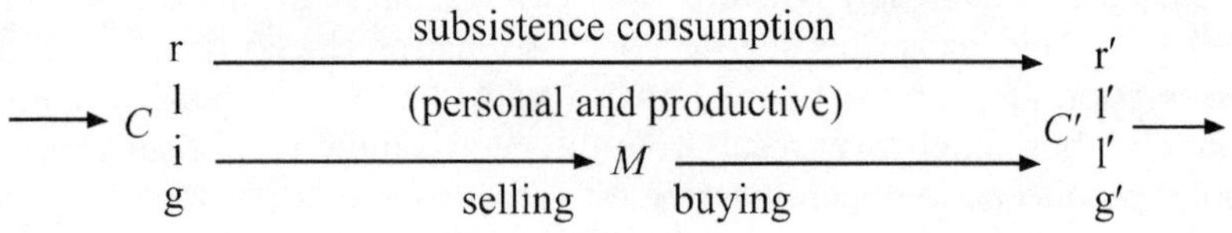

where C = commodity, r = object of labor (natural resources), l = labor power, i = instruments, g = articles of personal consumption, and M = money and credit. The commodities produced or appropriated by a self-employed worker, whether they be articles of personal consumption (g) or factors of production (r, l, and i), are divided into two categories: "subsistence commodities" directly consumed through material acts of household production (the upper circuit) and commodities to be exchanged for money (and credit) and the commodities (C) money can buy (the lower circuit) (Chevalier 1982:122–23). In this model, the subsistence commodity strategy is expressed in the direct transformation of self-employed labor into goods for autoconsumption ($C^l \rightarrow C^g$). It also has the advantage of providing for the "possible necessity for the worker to sell part of his labour-power to other simple commodity producers or agents of capital, or even to supplement his own production with the purchase of other workers' labour-power" and "allows for crucial variations in the relative weight assigned to each component" (1982:123).

On the basis of an earlier cursory reading of Chevalier's 1982 book, I wrongly concluded that he approached SCP as a mode of production (Cook and Binford 1990:9). A more careful reading shows that, in fact, he rejected the articulation of modes of production approach vis-à-vis SCP and viewed it instead as a form subsumed by the CMP. An integral part of Chevalier's exercise in rethinking SCP was a thorough and seductive critique of Wharton's (1971) pioneering and astute operationalization of subsistence rationality, unfortunately flawed by his (Wharton's) positing of a false dilemma between subsistence and profit. Wharton concluded, somewhat ingenuously, that "profit maximization may not be as important in a subsistence or barter economy as the maximization of security and survival" (1971:170).

Chevalier's critique of Wharton, which in retrospect exposes Chevalier's own attachment to "contrast-generalizations" (or conclusions of oppositional thinking) that he criticized others for making (1982:126), hinged on two points: 1) there is no distinction made between subsistence peasants in a commoditized economy and those in a noncommodity context, and 2) the distinction between the subsistence-seeking and profit-seeking peasant is overdrawn and "conceals common elements that may characterize both forms of agricultural production in a commodified economy" (1982:127–28). Chevalier could have also criticized Wharton for implying that individual actors exercise rationality by basing decisions on a "universally operative extremum principle, always seeking to maximize gain and minimize loss optimally" (Cook 1974a:844), except that he shares the same tendency. This runs against the grain of findings from economic anthropology that "an extremum principle operates relatively (situationally) rather than absolutely (uniformly)" (Cook 1974a:844). Little's "prudent rationality" thesis provides a framework for retaining a focus on rational calculation without reliance on an extremum principle.

A paradox in Chevalier's approach is exposed in the juxtaposition of 1) and 2) in the previous paragraph where he first embraces the dichotomy between commodity and noncommodity and then rejects one between subsistence and profit orientation. Can he have it both ways? Probably not. The resolution of Chevalier's paradox lies in accepting the thesis that "commodities," the value tandem that they embody (use plus exchange value) and the cultural/behavioral logics associated with the latter have a long precapitalist history. Historically, commodities, and the economic package that comes with them, did not drop from the sky full blown into capitalism. Their theoretically posited importance in the CMP should not be construed as exhausting their explanatory significance vis-à-vis other historical modes of production or the simple commodity form that preceded the rise of industrial capitalism. Nevertheless, Chevalier's "subsistence commodity" thesis, inspired as much by the kind of market economic logic employed so skillfully by Wharton as it is by Marx's discussion of the CMP's capital circuitry, remains persuasive as an effective counter to those prone to view production for subsistence by subsumed petty commodity producers as evidence of a resurgence of natural economy.

Chevalier's discussion of SCP, apart from his subsistence commodity concept, has several limitations. First and foremost, it does not address the entire range of nonsubsistence funds (rent, replacement, social–ceremonial, and care for the elderly) that must be provisioned to ensure the material reproduction of an SCP household enterprise, nor does it address, except in passing (1982:117, 123), the possibility of capital accumulation and petty capitalist development, which, under certain conditions, can occur in the C–M–C–M' > M circuit where accumulated capital (M' > M) is used to purchase more means of production (C^{MP}) and hire wage workers (C^{LP}) to expand commodity output for sale (>C). Second, he does not address household demographics, life cycle stage, and composition—including child and female labor—as important factors in production planning, performance, and results. Third, he does not incorporate into his discussion cases of SCP in regional economies with long histories of intercommunity division of labor, specialization, and market exchange as, for example, in Mesoamerica.

Fourth, at no point in Chevalier's analysis of value flows and relations in the Peruvian case or in his theoretical discussion of use and exchange value does he tackle head-on the labor theory of value under conditions of SCP or the CMP. In fact, the entire issue of whether Pachitean farmers sell their crops at prices above or below their socially average labor cost or buy commodities from others at prices above or below their socially average labor cost is irrelevant to Chevalier's central argument about their realization of exchange value through autoconsumption. Indeed, his "subsistence commodity" theory essentially ignores what Marx, Engels, and others have said about the law of value under conditions of SCP—probably reflecting his serious reservations about the "materialistic metaphysics that are embedded in the labour-time theory of value and exploitation" (1982:144). The possibility of realizing exchange value in the absence of exchange contradicts Marx's thesis that "to become a commodity a product must be transferred to another, whom it will serve as a use-value, by means of exchange" (1967, 1:41; cf. Engels 1967:897; Marx 1967, 1:180–81). The necessary historical condition that must be present for products to become commodities is, for Marx, that the product "must not be produced as the immediate means of subsistence of the producer himself" (1967, 1:169–70). In other words, a commodity is a product of human labor whose use value can be realized only after it is exchanged to someone other than its producer, that is, after its exchange value has been realized (Cook 1976:396).

Finally, Chevalier's entire theoretical exercise assumes that SCP is a creature of capitalism, which precludes its real history as a precursor of industrial capitalism. He is entitled to define SCP in an ad hoc way but fails to acknowledge the variety of alternative conceptualizations in the literature (Cook 1976:400–404). A more serious problem is that Chevalier's definition of the commodity concept seems to negate a precapitalist history for commodities as such and appears to discard the idea that nonmarket exchange like barter, much less reciprocity and gifting, might involve commodities and the realization of exchange value (perhaps only semicommensurable but abstract nonetheless). He likes Sahlins's idea of exchange without exchange value in precapitalist economies, which restricts exchange value to its capitalist meaning—implying an abstract, commensurable, monetized standard of valuation (1976:114).

Chevalier's concept of "subsistence commodity" is, then, problematic from the perspective of Marx's writings. A concept of "subsistence commodity" more in line with Marx's thinking would emphasize an origin in "other" production, not "own" production—that is, such a commodity would have to be exchanged into a simple commodity producer's household prior to its consumption (use-value realization). In other words, in the circuit C^1–M–C^2, its abstract exchange value would be realized through the transaction C^1–M, where the producer–seller of C^1 exchanges it for money, M, before its concrete use value can be realized by its buyer (assuming the buyer is the consumer and not a reseller); then, through the transaction M–C^2, the producer–seller in the first transaction whose labor embodied in C^1 was transformed into abstract labor represented by M can reconvert the latter back into the embodied concrete labor of another producer–seller represented in the commodity C^2. Only through the consumption of C^2 will its use value be realized and the material needs of the producer–seller of C^1 be met.

Assuming that this sequence of transactions occurred in a regional Mesoamerican marketplace system, it lays bare the situation of a simple commodity-producing household enterprise of the peasant-artisan type: aside from agricultural production for own use, its labor power can meet its own needs only to the extent that it is exchangeable for the labor power of other regional household enterprises. The market system serves as a mechanism for the equalization of different kinds of labor (such as corn producing, metate making, petate making, basket making, pottery making, weaving, and so on). Through money pricing, these are reduced to abstract human labor, and exchange is facilitated because of this implicit abstraction (Cook 1976:415; cf. Rubin 1972:66). Thus, the labor equalization function under conditions of simple commodity economy must be realized through concrete acts of market exchange. Here lies the central meaning of the proposition "value represents labor"; that is, social labor can be realized only through value in its "price form" (Cook 1976:415; cf. Rubin 1972:70, chap.9).

This process is reinforced through marketplace bargaining where artisans like the *metateros* bargain within a cognitive framework, including a minimum expected return (MER), which includes the possibility of earnings above and beyond labor cost of production, a sort of "superior wage" (Meek 1956:23, 26), and a minimum acceptable return (MAR) pegged to the labor cost of production (monetized by reference to the going wage rate) of the metate in question. For example, only under conditions of a household provisioning crisis (for example, no corn from own production) will a *metatero* sell a metate for less than his MAR, illustrating in the process what Galeski referred to as a "'hunger' type of commodity production" (1972:17; cf. Cook 1982:336–39).

Unlike Chevalier's Pachitea valley agriculturists who are apparently less involved in a regional marketing system based on an intercommunity division of labor and specialization of the Mesoamerican variety, peasant-artisan households like those in the Oaxaca valley participate more clearly in a double-tiered system of commodity circulation—one tier operating around commodities produced regionally (in some cases from regions other than the Oaxaca valley) in the intercommunity division of labor by household enterprises (some of which are of the petty capitalist variety) and the other around imported commodities produced in capitalist factories—usually in Mexico but also in other countries. The circulation of tier 1, or regionally produced commodities, is controlled exclusively by local and regional producer–sellers or merchant traders representing enterprises of different types and scales with prices determined mostly through bargaining, whereas tier 2 industrial capitalist commodities are circulated through commercial networks involving distributorships and dependent outlets (such as stores) with fixed, nonnegotiable pricing to the ultimate consumer (Beals 1975; Cook 1982:chap. 8).

One of the interesting features of such a system is that household enterprise production cycles and consumption expenditures are planned to facilitate participation in the regional marketing cycle (a seven-day rotational pattern) so that the C^1–M–C^2 circuit can be realized on market day. The transformation of C^1 (household-produced commodities) into C^2 (target bundle of commodities produced by the full range of other possible production units as outlined previously) is contingent on the C^1–M exchange value realization transaction—with the proviso that cash may be available from many other sources (such as sale of an animal or other commodities in the village, savings, remittance for absent member, loan repayment, and so on) to enable the household to achieve its consumption goals if the latter transaction is not realized on a given market day.

Given the two-tiered structure of commodity circulation for peasant-artisan households in situations like that of the Oaxaca valley, Chevalier's (1982:124) thesis—that for any worker in a capitalist economy "commodities that serve as means of personal or productive consumption are never apprehended as use-values only: the total amount of commodities made available to the worker is always comparable, in a purely quantitative way, to other amounts of 'useful' wealth and, *a fortiori*, to other levels of consumption"—has important implications for twenty-first-century economic anthropological inquiry.

In conclusion, I must reiterate my reservations about Chevalier's banning of commodity circulation from the precapitalist economy, which, in my judgment, is untenable for reasons outlined in this chapter (cf. Cook 1976:398–400). His overall approach, however, has real merit for countering the mistaken interpretation of production for own-household consumption as indicative of a return to natural economy by actors in subsumed mixed agrarian economies in international capitalism.[13]

CONCLUSIONS

The central theme of this chapter has been the importance of a focus on the production, exchange, and distribution of value, derived from Marx's method of analyzing commodity value circuits, to avoid losing sight of the fundamental role of economic process in sociocultural reproduction. This focus is also proposed as a way to avoid the tendency to interpret reciprocal, cooperative, ceremonial–ritual, or conspicuously consumptive flows and deployment of labor or products as indicative of economy within economy. Or, more particularly, it discourages the positing of an ethnoculturally configured nonmarket and noncommodity local economy within a nationally and internationally configured capitalist market-integrated commodity economy—each with its separate, distinctive systemic reproduction logics organizing the economic performances of enterprises and agents. This theme carries the implication that the economic process cannot be properly analyzed, much less understood, from a holistic approach that insists on placing equal weight on linkages from the economy to all other noneconomic fields as on linkages internal to the economic field itself. The relevant exterior connections must be studied, but it is more critical to study primary and secondary internal connections through analytical methods of disaggregation than it is to study irrelevant or tenuous external ones in the context of a unified, aggregate subject.

The focus of economic anthropology in Mexican studies should be the production, exchange, consumption, and distribution of commodity value with an emphasis on the process of social reproduction, which is culturally informed and class and gender differentiated. Formulaic maps, building on the general formula P . . . Cn . . . P . . ., where P represents production and Cn consumption, chart and track value in process and the class relations that organize its production and distribution. Those dimensions of social consciousness or of culture that are most accessible to economic anthropological inquiry (and, consequently, most directly connected to making and earning a living) will be expressed around several specific lines. These include those linking the reproduction circuit of human bearers of labor power 1) to other reproduction circuits (such as those for industrial or merchant capitalist enterprises), 2) to reproduction circuits for other household enterprises in a local or regional division of labor, or 3) to the reproduction circuit of one's own household enterprise. This analysis necessarily entails a consideration of key social and demographic variables (such as sex and age composition, life cycle stage, consumer/worker ratios, and so on) together with class variables as well as expressions of commodity culture(s) and identity.

Undeniably, there has been a production/supply-side bias in the study of commodity culture(s) in economic anthropology: Cn in the previously mentioned formula has typically been underanalyzed vis-à-vis P. There is a long overdue need for studies that give equal attention to the consumption/demand side of the commodity equation. In the specific context of Mexican peasant-artisan studies, the following statement bears reemphasis: "The sociocultural and class origins of the demand for craft commodities correspond closely with the function they serve for consumers (for example, as utensils, status symbols, decorative art, or souvenirs), with the scale and organization of their production, as well as with patterns of marketing and value distribution. One of the notable trends in the global capitalist market for craft commodities is that as their production increases, so does the proportion of their sales to tourists and middle- and upper-income urbanites. This trend represents a new role for small-scale, labor-intensive production within capitalism and provides one important explanation from the demand side for its persistence" (Cook 1993a:60). This statement was made in the context of a comprehensive analysis of social demand, marketing modes, production forms, and patterns of income distribution for seven branches of craft commodity production in the Oaxaca valley. That effort, however, was merely a first step, albeit ex post facto, in a type of inquiry that remains largely a programmatic vision for the future rather than an accomplishment to be emulated.

The challenge to economic anthropology is to identify other elements in "ongoing local and regional logics" (Narotsky 1997:6) and to ascertain how they articulate with dominant commodity logics while simultaneously showing how agents conduct themselves in local, regional, national, and continental spaces. Human maneuver involving the exercise of prudent rationality is, by definition, never irrational and is mostly conscious, and it is "always pressing against the inherent limitations of cultural forms" (Wolf 1959b:142) and their logics. There is still a tendency to view cultural forms and their accompanying logics as overwhelming the "element of human manoeuver which flows through these forms or around them, presses against their limits or plays several sets of forms against the middle" (1959b:142). Logics of systems, forms, or structures are one thing. The exercise of prudent rationality by agents is another and should never be underestimated. The question is to determine how the two domains or levels intersect and what the consequences of that process are.

What is extraordinary about the international commodity economy at the beginning of the twenty-first century is not that there are a relatively few lingering resisters to the strategic or opportunistic insertion of their own household and community economies into local, regional, and international commodity circuits but that there are vast multitudes of petty producers around the world who have found ways to insert their activities for making and earning a living into commodity circuits in ways fully compatible with culturally particularistic household and community reproduction. The international economy, even though dominated by a diverse array of massive, far-reaching, capitalist conglomerates, is replete with a huge pluricultural variety of household-based and other small commodity-producing enterprises.

This vast congeries of enterprises serve the diverse needs of their participants through the mixed pursuit of economic strategies that involve varying degrees and combinations of use value– and exchange value–producing, consuming, and/or accumulating activities to meet ever-increasing and diversifying sets of consumption needs. The problem lies in finding ways to reduce and ameliorate the inequalities and inequities in commodity economy until humanity fashions a better alternative.

NOTES

1. My critique of the holistic approach should not be construed as advocacy of the *ceteris paribus* procedure of economics that predictably leads economists in their cost–benefit analyses to dismiss key variables as bothersome "externalities." For a strong economic anthropological case study that demonstrates the explanatory benefits of integrating so-called externalities into analysis, see Durrenberger and Thu (1998). My argument is against the tendency of holism to fail to distinguish between internal and external variables when examining the economic field.

2. Marx's original thesis was, "The philosophers have only *interpreted* the world, in various ways; the point, however, is to *change* it" (1968:30). Popper uses a later statement by Marx from his preface to the first German edition of *Capital* (1967, 1:10) to propose that the "historicist can only *interpret* social development and aid it in various ways; his point, however, is that *nobody can change* it" (1964:51). The new anthropological tendency toward activism, as a collaborative effort with objectified subaltern subjects, seems to require a revision of Popper's critique of historicism (1964:7–8, 49–54) to account for my change in the wording of his statement.

3. I am sympathetic to Wells's call (which she responded to convincingly in her own study) "to explore the ways in which economic and political systems shape one other [*sic*] and how people acting at the local level reciprocally shape the structures around them" (1996:11). Nevertheless, I would change her emphasis on challenging "the ontological priority of economic events" in the process of pursuing such a call to that of challenging the received ways of conceptualizing ontological priority. In other words, as she implies, the crux of the problem is not epistemological but one of finding a better way to operationalize the priority of economic phenomena in the economic field so as to avoid the substantivist "embedment muddle" critiqued in chapter

3. Otherwise, we end up with a politicalized or a societalized economy with very little autonomy. Politics is on both the inside and the outside of the economy; the point is to show how the two interact, which, of course, is what Wells does a good job of.

4. Although Keith Hart (1983) voiced reservations about the idea of a Marxist economic anthropology, he did propose a ten-item agenda for the possible development of a Marxist economic anthropology, the first item of which was "to write the history of the human economy taken as a whole" (1983:133). The bulk of his essay, however, involved his attempt to answer in a qualified affirmative a question he posed at the beginning: has economic anthropology made any contribution to Marxism (1983:105)?

5. One error I committed in my first use of this circuit approach was to mistakenly describe the peasant-artisan domestic unit circuit as representing a small commodity mode of production rather than simply a "form" of commodity production. Despite my consideration of the theoretical possibility of positing such a "mode of production" (cf. Cook 1977:383–84), I did not do so for long (Cook 1982:355, 389). I am now convinced that given the degree of market penetration of all sectors and spaces in the Mexican economy, it is no longer useful to maintain a distinction between products (use value only) and commodities (use and exchange value). Staple food crops (corn, beans, and squash) that end up being consumed by the direct producing household anywhere in Mexico are, in reality, commodities whose use and exchange values are realized in the act of consumption. This is because these crops, and a whole host of others, are produced by farms of all sizes for sale in the market and circulate as commodities throughout Mexico. Any peasant household that grows these crops can also exchange them for cash and/or for other commodities they need but do not produce. When it does so, the peasant household in question is transforming its private, individual and concrete labor into public, social and abstract labor. If on the other hand it opts to directly consume these crop commodities, it consumes not only their use value but their unrealized exchange value as well. Regarding the peasant household's status within capitalism, all this participation in production for autoconsumption has done is conserve scarce cash for the household and cheapen the cost of labor reproduction, which translates into lower wage bills for employers.

6. This statement does assign substantial importance to subjects' opinions, attitudes, beliefs, interpretations, and other "emic" expressions regarding their economic experience. This does not mean that these expressions are assumed to be error free or are direct, accurate perceptions of reality and will jibe with those of outside experts. It does mean that they should be considered as important data in constructing a composite or representative "emic" view of economic process and that the latter must be combined with the "etic" view in knowledge production (cf. Goodenough 2002:434–35).

7. These concrete elements are implicitly encompassed in Schumpeter's reference to "the inexorable definiteness and . . . the quantitative character that distinguish the economic from other sphere of human action" (1950:123; cf. Cook 1974a:810; Epstein 1967).

8. The presence of a wage fund or wage advance in the border brick industry would seem to vindicate Marx and refute Gudeman and Rivera, who asserted that the "notion of a wage advance is . . . a fiction of economists, for in practice the capitalist holds his money until a work period is completed" (1990:96).

9. Again, the complexities on the production side of the border brick industry are mirrored on the consumption/demand side. I explore this dimension in substantial detail in my 1998 book (Cook 1998:esp. chap. 12).

10. The other sites of metate production at the time were San Juan Teitipac, Magdalena Ocotlán, and Tlacolula de Matamoros (Cook 1982:166–72). I always considered my research in the Oaxaca valley after 1965 to be multilocal or multisited since it culminated in a twenty-village study of many different village-based industries in addition to surveys of artisans in Tlacolula de Matamoros, Ocotlán de Morelos, Mitla, and Oaxaca City (a total of 1,008 household production units in twenty-four localities). In addition, a separate interview schedule, designed to focus on intermediaries as well as sales shops (both with and without direct involvement in production), was administered to a sample of sixty-nine informants in Oaxaca City and to a sample of thirty-one merchant–embroiderers in various localities in the Ocotlán district (Cook 1985; Cook and Binford 1990:243–49).

11. CMP refers to the capitalist mode of production conceived as a theoretical object of analysis, as opposed to a less abstract, more historically specific concept of capitalism. This usage came into fashion with French structural Marxism (Althusser 1970; Balibar 1970) and its offshoots (Hindess and Hirst 1975; cf. Cook 1977).

12. Following this lead of Marx, Roger Bartra (1974) reworked the ICAD group's input/output ratios for farm enterprises in Mexican agriculture (Reyes Osorio et al. 1974) by assigning the value of the prevailing rural wage to peasant household labor, which the ICAD group had excluded. He failed, however, to consider that—given the differentiation of the peasantry—their earnings included not only self-remunerated wages but also self-remunerated surplus value as well as surplus value appropriated from other nonwage family workers and hired hands (Cook and Binford 1990:32–34). Chevalier's analysis acknowledges the class differentiation factor or the capitalist half of Marx's hypothetical "independent peasant" but emphasizes the noncapitalist half.

13. Perhaps the most formidable and persistent critic of the kinds of arguments and interpretations of economic process made by Marxist scholars like Chevalier in the study of the Latin American peasant economy is Stephen Gudeman. Gudeman has made a career out of creatively searching the annals of the history of economic thought to find pathways of knowledge production that avoid or negate Marxist analysis (1978, 1980, 1986), but his 1990 book with Rivera surpasses all his previous performances. This book is essentially a vigorous defense of dualistic thinking about the economy, opposing the "house" to the "corporation" à la Max Weber (1978, 1:339–84), and a concerted attack on the thesis of the household as a hybrid domestic unit plus enterprise (Galeski 1972).

Gudeman and Rivera's travels and conversations in Colombia followed routes that circumvented commodity-producing, exchange value–realizing, and capital-accumulating houses. Hence, the voices and texts that articulate messages contradicting those of the Colombian "house" peoples' antimarket strategies are never confronted. It is asserted that the "house is never fully engaged in or dependent upon the market" (1990:10), and, recognizing vulnerability of their main theses, the authors admit that the "market is one context in which limits on the constructive power of the house model become apparent" and that the "market is . . . one instance in which the limits and incompleteness of the rural folk's model become evident" (1990:15). We are justified in asking why there is no model of the market-dependent house. Surely, it cannot be because rural peasant houses in Colombia are self-sufficient.

One need only read Gudeman and Rivera's labored explanation of the meaning of the term "*fuerza de trabajo*" (that is, not labor power) (1990:30–37) as an example of many points in the text where the conversations ring hollow. Often, their peasant discussants seem to be trying to tell the authors something important about the house-market circuit and its impact on their thinking, but the authors are not listening carefully (for example, labor theory of value, unequal exchange, and role of intermediary capital). The dialogue, in effect, seems to be arbitrarily cut off by the interrogators.

9

The U.S.–Mexico Borderlands: Commodity Culture(s), Labor, and Capital

The uniqueness of the southwestern borderlands of the United States lies in their connection to Mexico, with which they share a 1,952-mile-long international boundary. Beginning with the boundary's delineation in mid-nineteenth-century treaties, the term "border" has been a metaphor for this connection, albeit a paradoxical one. The connectedness of today's border originated in a disconnection by conquest through the 1836–1845 Texas rebellion and annexation, the U.S.–Mexico War of 1846–1848, and a subsequent transferral of the Mexican territories of Texas, Arizona, and California (among others) to U.S. sovereignty through the Treaty of Guadalupe Hidalgo in 1848. The process that configured the borderlands as we know them today was completed when New Mexico became a U.S. territory by means of the Gadsden Purchase in 1854. Thus, the complicated and contradictory meanings evoked by the border metaphor derive from this nineteenth-century disconnection by conquest and expansion, sanctioned by the ideology of Manifest Destiny, that transformed Mexican territory into the southwestern borderlands of the United States.

As we enter the twenty-first century, the first challenge of the U.S.–Mexico border is to understand its complexity both as an international political boundary with distinctive geographical features and as a historical zone of relations, transactions, and movements involving diverse peoples, commodities, and cultures. The second challenge is to understand this complexity by identifying local and regional particularities that necessarily diversify and segment the borderlands. The third challenge is to deal with the impact that the North American Free Trade Agreement (NAFTA) and global capitalism will continue to have in transforming the border/borderlands and our perceptions and understandings of them. Collectively, these three challenges create still another by complicating the conceptualization of the border/borderlands as an object of study and discourse and obliging us to be thoughtful and precise in our use of a variety of applicable concepts.

These challenges must be met by focusing on a set of mirrored interests: the impact of cross-border relations with Mexico on life and culture in the southwestern borderlands of the United States and, conversely, the impact of cross-border relations with the United States on life and culture in the northern borderlands of Mexico. The border is a two-sided interactive space. Owing to its nearly 2,000-mile length, much of which is vacant and unsettled, that space may be operationally segmented into a series of international zones anchored by twin cities strategically located between the boundary's eastern (Brownsville–Matamoros) and western (Tijuana–San Diego) termini. This concept is implied in most of our daily conversational references to the border as a place in statements such as "I am from the border" or "Let's go to the border." The locational referent in such statements is typically a twin city–anchored zone or region.

While making concessions to geography and settlement patterns, however, any comprehensive approach must also consider the cross-border impact of economic transactions and transfers as well as the role of human circulation, sociocultural relations, identity negotiations, and cultural values that shape and are shaped by daily life in the U.S.–Mexico borderlands. This approach highlights deterritorializing processes and evokes the oxymoronic concept of "borderless border" (*frontera sin fronteras*). Accordingly, the geographic discontinuity/duality that gives us a dichotomous "riverine versus landlocked border" is superseded by a focus on transcendent sociocultural processes. These transborder processes involve decisions and actions that operate through or around physical and governmental obstacles.

The borderless border theme is prevalent in Chicano/Mexicano historical and anthropological discourse. The borderlands dating from the eighteenth century are viewed as dependent on the relations between two nation-states in formation, the United States and Mexico. Between the sixteenth and early nineteenth centuries, the area that is today encompassed by the borderlands constituted the frontier of New Spain—the Spanish Empire in North America—a period during which the Hispanic/Indo-Mestizo cultural matrix of the region was forged.[1]

Prior to the arrival of the Europeans, however, this area was impacted by multiple encounters, migrations, inventions, and diffusions involving sedentary and nomadic Amerindian peoples and cultures. The critical prehistoric civilizational axis then was located in what is today central Mexico as the core of Mesoamerica. In this anthropogeographic scheme, the southwestern borderlands is a critical space joining the northern and southern spheres of a North American civilizational process spanning several millennia. Today's migration from south to north across an international boundary is, thus, relativized and absorbed in a process of human circulation that spans millennia, during most of that time span unencumbered by state-imposed boundaries or barriers.[2]

Even when geography provides an empirical basis for conceptualizing "the border," it does not present us with a uniform concept. The notion of the border as a "line in the sand" (that is, a metaphor evoking the western desertic portion of the border from New Mexico to California) contrasts with the notion of the border as a riverine (that is, the 800-mile-long Texas–Mexico portion). Despite the border's geographic bifurcation, it can nevertheless be argued that its riverine expanse has been predominant in shaping discourse about human circulation. For example, undocumented Mexican migrant laborers have been labeled in academic and popular parlance as "wetbacks" (*espaldas mojadas*) or "wets" (*mojados*) even when untold millions of them enter the United States by crossing a fence in the desert, not a river. The border as an international boundary is in some sense a barrier, but one that is necessarily crossed both legally and illegally with regularity.

The borderlands exist only because the borderline is politically maintained and only because of crossings that involve bidirectional flows of people, commodities, and culture. Observation of the cyclical pattern of vehicular and pedestrian traffic flows across bridges linking twin cities like Laredo–Nuevo Laredo, Brownsville–Matamoros, or El Paso–Ciudad Juárez shows that the morning movement is mostly from Mexico to the United States, whereas the late afternoon–early evening movement is reversed. This pattern exposes the large numbers of Mexican commuters who reside in Mexico but work or conduct business in the United States daily and underscores the deep integration of twin-city economic and social life.

The daily commuter worker flow is part and parcel of labor market segmentation in the borderlands that on the U.S. side inclines employers toward hiring Mexican migrant workers (preferably green carders, or "documented" commuters) rather than U.S. citizens of Mexican descent. On the Mexican side, employers seek to employ workers who are perceived to be permanent border residents who, for a variety of reasons, are not prone to seek employment on the U.S. side. The border labor market—thanks, among other things, to the presence of maquiladoras (assembly plants) and the need for seasonal agricultural workers—is, of course, particularly plagued by the "cheap labor" bugaboo.[3]

"CHEAP LABOR" OR FLEXIBLE ACCUMULATION IN THE U.S.-MEXICO BORDER ECONOMY?

The border economy is driven more by the dynamic of flexible accumulation as the modus operandi of capitalist enterprises than by an insatiable demand for cheap labor that pulls Mexican workers into employment in the labor markets of the U.S.–Mexico borderlands or of the U.S. interior. David Harvey defines flexible accumulation as resting on "flexibility with respect to labour processes, labour markets, products and patterns of consumption" and associates it with "the emergence of entirely new sectors of production, new ways of providing financial services, new markets, and, above, all, greatly intensified rates of commercial, technological, and organizational innovation" as well as with "rapid shifts in the patterning of uneven development, both between sectors and between geographical regions, giving rise . . . to a vast surge in so-called 'service-sector' employment as well as to entirely new industrial ensembles in hitherto underdeveloped regions" (1990:147).

Harvey's concept is too abstract to capture the element of diversity of capitalist enterprises within and between branches of the economy that necessarily qualifies the applicability of tendential laws of motion governing capital in the unique space created by NAFTA. A model incorporating the elements of flexible accumulation seems to have been implicit in the drafting and adoption of the agreement and instrumental in producing empirically measurable, albeit contradictory, impacts from its ongoing implementation on the industrialization of the border economy and the concomitant degradation of its ecosystem (Hart 2002:481–83; Wilson 1992:chap. 4). Also impacted is economic life in the U.S. and Mexican interiors, which is paradoxically manifested in the Mexicanization of U.S. production (and to a lesser extent consumption) and the Americanization of Mexican finance, production, and consumption, as symbolized in the emergence of what Hart calls the "Neo-Porifirian Economy" (2002:466–69; see also pp. 459–66, 475–81, 492–98; Heyman 1994).

Although discourse about NAFTA invokes the time-worn theme of "cheap labor," it needs to be pointed out that this theme never adequately captured the complexities of border development or of the interaction between capital and labor in a multinational economy. This is not to deny the truth in Hart's judgment that "American capitalists regard further labor cost reductions as critical to the success of their enterprises despite the fact that in the late 1990s the United States had one of the highest ratios of labor productivity to cost worldwide" and that "American workers received less for the value that they produced than workers did in all but three other industrialized nations" (2002:478). The fact that labor south of the border in some industries apparently provides a higher return per man-hour on capital invested than labor north of the border does attract U.S. capital to Mexico but puts the squeeze on many sectors of Mexican capital that find it increasingly difficult to compete in the domestic labor market. It also appears that in many U.S. labor markets in all sectors of the economy—especially those revolving around various kinds of manual labor—it is not so much the "relative cheapness" but the availability and high performance of Mexican labor that is critical to the hiring of Mexican workers.

The Seductiveness of "Cheap Labor"

The phrase "cheap labor" has been so widely used in academic and popular economic discourse that it has the status of either an axiom or a cliché. This is especially ironic in view of the fact that Manuel Gamio's pioneering study of Mexican labor immigration (1971b:chap. 3) managed to incisively analyze the situation of the Mexican immigrant wage earner without employing this infelicitous and analytically counterproductive term. In any case, it is rare for those who have since employed the phrase ad nauseum to specify its meaning with any precision or analytical rigor. Consequently, the reader of such texts is either obliged to go along with the author in assuming the term's meaning is self-evident or left to infer its possible meaning by identifying euphemisms, metonyms, or synonyms for "cheap labor" in the text. The situation would not be so frustrating if the reader could always dismiss references to "cheap labor" as rhetorical or polemical. Unfortunately, many such references occur in analytical discourse, the value of which is necessarily diminished to the degree that the term's meaning is assumed to be self-evident.

Why is the term so seductive, especially to those friendly to the cause of labor, considering that the modifier "cheap" has pejorative meanings that, when applied to labor, inevitably devalue it in a hegemonic way (that is, vis-à-vis capital)? Why is it that so many critics of capital refer to "cheap labor" ad nauseum but never refer to "cheapskate capital"? According to María Patricia Fernández-Kelly (1983:192), cheap labor is an "abstract category [that] does violence to an accurate description of reality." Her point is well taken but does not explain why the term is so popular with so many scholars who apparently believe that it accurately describes reality. To them, perhaps, the term evokes substantive images of actual human beings at work in the real world of capitalist material production, images that are so powerful as to overwhelm operational concerns for heuristic precision and that reinforce these scholars' macrostructural vision of capitalist economic process. Or is the prolific use of the term simply a matter of expository convenience or style, so that "cheap" is preferred over the less pejorative, more precise, but admittedly more cumbersome phrase "relatively inexpensive"?[4]

Fernández-Kelly's critique of "cheap labor" usage reflects her anthropological involvement in a detailed empirical case study that compelled her, as observer–analyst, to view labor in capitalist maquiladoras as a process of actions and relations involving real human subjects. She found it impossible to adequately explain the complexities of labor and capital relations among different firms and branches in a competitive, market-driven system, much less address substantive issues related to the daily lives of real living subjects such as the "*maquila* women," by employing such imprecise terms as "cheap labor."

A Critical Review of "Cheap Labor" Discourse

The most typical usage of the phrase "cheap labor" is in macrostudies of relations between developed and underdeveloped economies (or regions within one economy). In this literature, it typically refers to the availability in the underdeveloped economy (or region) of an abundant labor force that sells its labor power at a relatively low price in money and/or real terms—that is, in exchange for low money and/or real wages.

Not surprisingly, the literature on the economic development strategy of the Salinas regime in Mexico and on the topic of NAFTA is replete with such references. For example, one widely used reference book succinctly characterizes the Salinas regime's economic growth formula as encouraging "private investment in export-oriented businesses that take advantage of Mexico's comparative advantages in the world economy" and cites "cheap labor" as chief among these (Barry 1992:77–78). Another author, equally beholden to neoclassical discourse, prefers the euphemistic mode of expression: "The sharing of production [in the maquiladora arrangement] exploits [*sic*] the abundant factor of each country, the capital and production processes of the United States and the labor of Mexico, in a least-cost combination" (Weintraub 1990:160–61). My selective sampling of these and other principal sources on U.S.–Mexico economic relations and the border economy discloses a pattern of highlighting the role of "cheap" or low-cost labor in Mexico (or the border region) as the major lure for U.S. capital.[5]

This trend continues into the twenty-first century in important studies such as Hart's detailed history of U.S. capitalist enterprise in Mexico since the Civil War. In a section on "American Maquiladoras" (2002:446–51), he observes that the Border Industrialization Program initiated by the Mexican government in 1965 promoted border locations there for U.S. business by emphasizing the triumvirate of cheap labor, tariff relief, and lower transportation costs. Through the 1990s and into the new century, the growth of the *maquila* industry continued, employing over one million workers in about 4,000 maquiladoras. Again the factor of low wages to mostly female workers (65 percent of the total labor force) is emphasized. Hart, unlike many writers, often avoids knee-jerk use of the term "cheap labor" and provides comparative wage data to support his usage. For example, Hart makes the following statements about comparative labor costs that avoid a reference to "cheap labor" (2002:475):

> American workers complained that their Mexican counterparts earned only one-tenth of their salaries in the United States while performing the same tasks for the same employer. Experts have agreed that the wage differentials between Mexican workers and their American counterparts inspired the motives of American entrepreneurs who built factories in Mexico. Indeed, the earning differentials between American and Mexican workers in electricity-related industries were enor-

> mous. According to one estimate, Mexican electronics workers earned $1.54 per hour in 1996 with very few, if any, fringe benefits, while their American equivalents earned $13.95 per hour plus health care, retirement, and disability support supplied by their employers. The contrast between the benefits received by American workers and those of the Mexican workers was stark. . . . In the automotive industry the differences were even greater. In 1996 workers in Mexican automobile parts factories earned $2.75 per hour, a high wage for Mexican laborers, whereas the average American automobile parts worker made $21.93 per hour plus substantial fringe benefits that were not offered the Mexicans. (2002:448–49)

In other words, Hart specifies what he means when he asserts that NAFTA afforded American entrepreneurs access to inexpensive labor by focusing on wage differentials and avoiding cheap-labor rhetoric.[6]

Why is Mexican labor relatively cheap according to Hart and other authors? Various answers, both implicit and explicit (and nearly always requiring a painstaking search by the reader), are given to this question. There is an excess supply of labor vis-à-vis the demand for it (Hart 2002:475). Labor is prevented by government or union fiat or lack of organization (that is, independent unionization) to negotiate for higher wages or is relegated to low levels in the labor hierarchy by virtue of stigmatized social identity (such as race, ethnicity, gender, and nationality). Another answer is that labor's value (that is, its cost of reproduction) is relatively low either because of its culturally specific standard of living or because of the peculiar conditions/means surrounding the production of its basic reproduction needs (such as production for own use). Or, alternatively, some authors associate labor's low productivity and low cost with lack of skill. Others, taking a more contextual, conjunctural, and applied approach (in the specific sense of the operational needs of U.S. firms in a maquiladora project), hold that Mexican labor is relatively cheap because it is reproduced via wage goods priced and purchased in pesos, which were recently devalued vis-à-vis dollars. Indeed, Hart contends that Mexican leaders supported the 1995 devaluation in part because it would reduce the real cost of labor, which presumably would make Mexican labor more competitive with lower-waged Asian, African, Haitian, and Central American workers (2002:450). The role of the Mexican government, in response to private corporate lobbying and negotiations, clearly plays a critical role in controlling the price and bargaining power of maquiladora labor (Wilson 1992:chap. 3). Any of these factors (as well as others not mentioned), structural together with circumstantial or conjunctural, are identified in the literature as operating singly or in combination to cause Mexican labor to be relatively cheap—cheapness being measured by how much an hour of labor power costs its employer in money terms.[7]

Another characteristic of this literature is that its answer to the questions "Cheap labor for whom?" and "So what?" (or, phrased differently, "From whose perspective is 'cheap labor' good?") is uniformly predictable: Cheap labor is good for cost-conscious ("cheapskate"?) capital. Why? Because, ceteris paribus, in the process of producing commodities with commodities, the lower the prices of commodity inputs, including labor power, the higher the rate of exploitation and, therefore, the higher the rate of profits. In a nutshell, capital is attracted to relatively low cost labor to decrease costs of production so as to increase profits (or, if you prefer, to increase its rate of surplus-value extraction).

In the literature on contemporary U.S.–Mexico economic relations and the border economy, the identity of "cheap labor" is always Mexican, and "cheapskate capital" is always in the maquiladora sector and is non-Mexican. Furthermore, although some attention is paid to the views of Mexican labor, little or no attention is paid to the views of Mexican capital, either within or outside the maquiladora sector, vis-à-vis "Mexican cheap labor." It is almost as if Mexican capital or Mexican entrepreneurs have the status of oxymorons and are insignificant players in the border economy.

Several critiques, theoretical as well as substantive, can be leveled against academic cheap-labor discourse. In the real world, where the services of the Roman pawn ceteris paribus are unavailable, lower labor costs or lower wages do not necessarily translate into higher profits. On the contrary, there is a likelihood that low-paid workers are, in any given case, exploited less than higher-paid ones and thus are less productive of surplus value and, hence, profits. In the words of Geoffrey Kay (1975:53–54), "A lowly paid worker barely able to make ends meet, illiterate, poorly housed, unhealthy, and poorly equipped is much less productive than a highly paid worker who is educated, well-fed and well-equipped. It takes him much longer to produce the equivalent of his wage and therefore the proportion of his working day he is able to give away free is much lower" (that is, the lower the proportion of surplus labor to necessary labor; cf. Bettelheim 1972:302; Dobb 1956:51–54). Moreover, as we find in the case of the border brick industry, one absentee capitalist's perceived cheap-labor pool in a distant or exotic territory may be for the on-site, native capitalist a capricious or even relatively costly labor pool and is apt to be seen as a problematic source of profit.

It is also important to distinguish between two possible meanings of low labor cost in the production of a given output. First, it may mean the "actual amount of work or human energy put into production" (Dobb 1956:50). Second, it may mean the "money that the employer has had to lay out in wages to get the output produced—his wage-outlay" (1956:50). Maurice Dobb spelled out the importance of this distinction by observing that "labour-cost in [the] first sense may be quite independent of the level of wages, and need not be affected by any change of wages" and that "the wage-cost of producing anything will depend both upon the productivity of labour and upon the level of wages, and will be changed by a change in either of these things" (1956:50–51).

Relevant here also is the distinction between real and money wages since not all wage increases automatically translate into higher production costs. This will be the case "where there is a rise, not of money wages, but of real wages due to a fall in the price of things consumed by wage-earners" (Dobb 1956:51). Conversely, not all wage decreases automatically translate into lower production costs. Money wages may remain constant while real wages decline because of an increase in the prices of wage goods. This is especially important in considering the situation of Mexican capitalists after 1982, when the decline in real wages of Mexican labor may be mistakenly assumed to translate into lower production costs for enterprises located in Mexico.

In the case of U.S. capital and Mexican labor, peso devaluations have a double impact: they reduce the real wage of Mexican workers (by raising the cost to them of imported wage goods or of wage goods produced by imported producers' goods) but also reduce the wage cost in dollars that employers pay for Mexican labor power. This is why, in the border brick industry, Mexican brick exporters insist on being paid in dollars by their U.S. customers while always paying their workers in pesos for producing brick. This strategy ensures that peso devaluations function to make Mexican labor power suddenly cheaper for Mexican capital that enjoys sales revenues in dollars and wage bills in pesos. In small-scale Mexican export enterprises like those in the brick industry where rising production costs cannot be absorbed by export price increases (given the competitive nature of the brick market), the combination of dollar sales revenues, peso wage bills, and periodically cheaper pesos (via devaluations) is a key to their capacity to remain viable. Otherwise, inflation and rising money wage costs in pesos would likely squeeze them out of the market. Indeed, many *ladrilleras* were squeezed out of the market during the Salinas years of an overvalued peso.[8]

Another paradox surrounding the notion of "cheap labor" that has arisen in the study of the development of capitalism in the lower Rio Grande corridor hinges on the conflicting interests and views of farming and intermediary capital. Independent Texas retailers were generally opposed to continued Mexican immigration, favored the diversification of the farm economy, and advocated wage increases for the currently employed labor force. The Laredo Chamber of Commerce issued a circular that included the following statements: "We have got about as far as we can with cheap labor. . . . Labor with $1.25 wages can't buy. . . . We don't need more cheap labor. We should not drive out our own labor in the North to provide ourselves with cheap labor here" (Montejano 1987:185). In short, while low wages may be good for the balance sheets of farming enterprises, they keep effective demand low and restrict retail business growth.

The previous discussion simply underlines the extent to which repetitive references to cheap labor often serve as a pretext for a failure to address and analyze wider and deeper implications of differential wage structures, their correspondence to labor market segmentation (Spielberg Benítez 1989), and their relationship to particular branches of the economy and to demographic dynamics (Weeks and Ham-Chande 1992). In the border economy, there are many sources of differentiation in labor remuneration, only one of which is the binational structure of the labor pool. In any case, the cost of wages is by no means the sole or necessarily the most important consideration from the perspective of capital vis-à-vis labor in the border economy.[9]

DISCOURSE IN THE BORDER BRICK INDUSTRY: LABOR VS. CAPITAL

Loosely structured interviews I conducted during 1992–1993, 1995, and 2000 with participants in the artisanal brick industry located in and around Reynosa in the Mexican state of Tamaulipas provided me with a corpus of qualitative data pertaining to labor–capital relations. Two different sets of participants in the industry were interviewed: 1) capitalist owner–operators of *ladrilleras* or brickworks, together with their *ladrillera* foremen (*mayordomo* or *encargado*), and 2) piece-rate brick makers (*hechurero* or *moldeador*).[10]

An apt point of entry into a discussion of some results from an analysis of these interviews focuses on the Spanish word for brick maker, *ladrillero*, or, more specifically, how that word's meaning has been transposed and made ambiguous by the relations between capital and labor. The transposition is implicit in the official name of the artisanal brick industry's association on the Mexican side of the lower Rio Grande corridor, namely, Asociación de Ladrilleros de la Zona Ribereña (Riverine Zone Brick Producers' Association). The members of this association are, in fact, capitalist owners of *ladrilleras* or artisanal brickworks and, therefore, are not themselves *ladrilleros* (in the sense of direct molders or makers of bricks) but are employers of *ladrilleros*. They are, in short, *ladrilleros* (in the sense of indirect makers of bricks) by virtue of their ownership and administration of brickworks and of their appropriative role in the labor market. Their piece-rate employees, the direct producers of bricks, are referred to by various terms, the most common being *hechurero*, but sometimes the term *ladrillero* is also, confusingly, applied to them. Throughout the remainder of this section, I refer to *hechureros* as "brick makers" and as the owner–operators of brickworks as "employers."

It is my contention that this transposition, renaming, and semantic muddling of the term *ladrillero*, associated with the transformation of brick production through the capitalist detail division of labor, ideologically displaces and devalues the real role of labor in the process of material production. This displacement and devaluation is reflected discursively by a typical employer's insistence that anyone can make bricks by hand but not by machine.

As one prominent mechanized brickworks owner expressed it, "I came to the conclusion that anybody could make handmade brick but not everybody can make machine-made brick" or, again, "Handmade brick is easier to manage than machine-made . . . anybody can make handmade brick." The obvious implication is that capital is essential to the process of mechanized brick manufacturing but not necessarily to the process of handmade brick manufacture.[11]

This view is contested head on discursively by the pieceworkers who insist that their capitalist employers are know-nothings in the art of brick making and that special skills and qualities are required by brick-making labor regardless of mechanization. As one retired brick maker, with experience in many unmechanized and semimechanized brickworks, expressed it with reference to several of his past employers, "They [the capitalist brickworks owners] didn't know anything about brick-making. They just didn't have a clue. We were the ones who told them how they could control and make the material. There's more to being a brick-maker than just saying 'I am going to make a brick.' Not every man can make brick." This same informant, who worked as *mayordomo de los patios* (foreman) in a large brickworks, said that he confronted the owner one day in the following blunt terms regarding the owner's lack of knowledge of brick making: "You do not understand the work involved. You just don't understand. You need us to tell you how to do it. You may have the money but the work, we know how to do that." In response to this statement, according to the informant, his employer admitted in no uncertain terms, "No, I am not a brick-maker." The bottom line for this informant is that the employers know accounting but not brick making: "We made the brick, we didn't make the numbers."

What is the background profile of Reynosa-area piece-rate brick makers? In my informal sample of twelve brick makers, a majority were born in rural areas in the interior of border states of Tamaulipas, Nuevo León, or Coahuila and came to the border area as adolescents or young adults with no prior work experience in brick making. A minority were born in rural areas of nonborder states, including Zacatecas, Durango, San Luis Potosí, Guanajuato, and Querétaro. With a few exceptions, most of those who were raised in the Reynosa area were not born there, and their earliest work experience was in ranching or agriculture rather than in brick making. None of the brick makers have more than three years of formal schooling, and most of them have no formal schooling. The average age of the group is fifty, with the range from thirty to seventy-three; the average number of years of work experience in brick making is twenty-eight. Approximately two-thirds of these workers also have some work experience in the United States, mostly in the agricultural fields of the Rio Grande valley. More than half the sample over fifty years of age also spent some time as "wetback" brick makers in artisanal brickworks on the Texas side of the corridor.[12]

The work histories of piece-rate brick makers display a pattern of fluctuation rather than regularity over time with regard to employment. There is interannual turnover with regard to employers in the brick industry as well as a pattern of circulation between three branches: brick making, construction, and agriculture. In addition, in the 1990s—given the overall decline in brick production and the general crisis of labor in Mexico, reflected in unemployment and eroding real wages—it was common for brick makers to moonlight or to supplement income from brick making with income from other part-time, casual jobs. Boredom was also a reason often cited for periodic withdrawals from brick making to work in construction or agriculture. Economic hardship was the main reason cited for seeking supplementary income from odd jobs.

It should also be pointed out that in some cases brick making itself had become a supplementary job, for example, to that of *velador* (watchman). Under conditions of survival in the urban and periurban economy of Reynosa and other border cities, the main household strategy is one of multioccupationality and/or participation in a diverse range of cash-earning activities. There is fluctuation over time in which activities or occupations are practiced and in the degree of participation in them.[13]

Despite the turnover and the possible subordination or displacement of brick making by other jobs or activities, experienced brick makers tend not to permanently abandon this branch not only because jobs are nearly always available in unmechanized brickworks producing for the domestic construction market but also because a higher daily wage can be earned for a shorter, self-directed workday in the brick industry than in construction or agriculture for a longer, supervised workday. For example, during 1993, a brick maker could earn 30 to 45 new pesos ($10–$15) per 1,000 bricks or 120 to 180 new pesos ($40–$60) for a 4,000-brick week of thirty man-hours compared to a day wage of 25 to 35 new pesos ($8–$11) in construction or agriculture, where one must work a five-day, forty-hour week under close supervision. One informant compared the two work situations succinctly: "You earn more here than in construction. In construction they pay $60 a week; here I earn $80. You earn more here. Here, there is no one bossing me around. You work alone. I can cover up my clay and leave without anyone saying anything."

Although the labor supply still fluctuates, there has been significant attrition of brick makers over the years that has permanently reduced the size of the Reynosa area labor pool. Many small brickworks have shut down permanently and have been transformed into garbage dumps by the landowners who may or may not have been brick producers themselves. Most of the garbage haulers, known locally as *carretoneros*, are in fact ex-piece-rate brick makers (*hechureros*). Overall, then, during the past decade there has been a net decline in the local brick industry labor pool (see Cook 1998:esp. chaps. 8–10; see also 2001).

It is a mistake to attempt to analyze brick makers' work patterns strictly according to pecuniary cost–benefit logic for two reasons. First, there is definitely an upper limit on physical productivity per day and per week in brick making that, in turn, limits the capacity of pieceworkers to respond to material incentives to increase output. Second, a significant number of brick makers (from the perspective of their capitalist employers, own testimonies, and my observations) display a propensity to opt for leisure, as opposed to additional work, once a target income is reached. Many brick makers, for example, tend to work a four-day week, reserving Saturday, Sunday, and Monday for rest and relaxation, a period that typically includes high levels of alcoholic consumption. This immediately suggests the possible relevancy of a Chayanovian concern with balancing the marginal utility of an extra batch of bricks with the marginal disutility of the effort to make it. The Chayanovian ceiling on output in this case derives from a combination of achieving the target income (its equivalent in needed goods and services or pressing financial obligations) and the physical cost (that is, drudgery) of producing more bricks (see Cook 1995:84–87).

The following statement by a capitalist brickworks owner, elicited by my question regarding wage incentive schemes, is more expressive than most but otherwise typifies capitalist discourse regarding pieceworker behavior: "[A wage incentive scheme] was always given to them. But they are very special people. Since they are artisans, they work how they want and when they want. Those people and their idiosyncrasies—it's simply that they want to cover their basic needs, and once they have covered them, they have no incentive to work. In general, our people unfortunately have lots of vices and prejudices. That is, independently of the fact that incentives were offered, on a piece rate basis, bonuses were given, these had no great effect, no results. Why? Because those people were saying 'I need X number of pesos to eat and so many pesos to get drunk and since I've already earned them I'm going to work only 3 days this week.' These are people who have never worked a whole week, never. They work 2 or 3 days, 4 days, and then stop working."

Another informant, a longtime brickworks supervisor who had early experience as a brick maker but is now in the capitalist camp, in response to my question regarding how his brick makers responded to wage incentive schemes over the years, said, "They were not interested in earning more. Every raise that was given to them—for example, if they were making 1 peso per brick and were given a raise to 1.20 if they made 1,000 or more bricks, they would produce only 950 because at the rate of 1 peso they earned enough." When a clay-mixing machine was introduced in this brickworks, thus relieving brick makers of the task of preparing clay, the 1,000-brick-per-day quota was then realized by many pieceworkers, but, rather than producing an additional lot of bricks in the time saved by releasing them from clay preparation, these brick makers opted instead, according to this informant, to quit early. In his words, "The people finished sooner, that is all they wanted. The only benefit that came from the mechanical clay mixer was that all the clay was uniform."

From the capitalist perspective, then, productivity increases are best achieved by adding pieceworkers rather than by selectively mechanizing the production process to increase pieceworker efficiency. Moreover, wage increases often fail to significantly boost productivity and may, in fact, decrease it.

Brick-maker discourse both contradicts and reinforces capitalist discourse regarding work patterns but provides a rationale for them. One brick maker who characterizes himself as "ambulante" (ambulatory)—working two, three or four months in the brickyards and then changing to construction—makes 2,500 bricks over a four-day week to earn 75 PN ($25), which he says is "to eat, nothing more" and adds, "If I have food, it's OK" When asked why he didn't make more bricks daily to increase his weekly income, he replied that "it's hard to make a thousand bricks in one day; one struggles a lot to do it and the next day one is tired out; I wake up the next day and can't go to work."

A retired brick maker, a veteran of the export boom days of the 1960s and 1970s, emphasized that although many pieceworkers made relatively good money, they did so "not because the boss paid very well but because you made more than the limit, you forced yourself to make material. That's the reason. Because you forced yourself to get the money you needed, not because the boss rewarded your work." But, he admits, "if you produced more, at the end of the week you got a reward . . . so people would exert themselves more"—an admission that may imply the successful operation of an employer incentive scheme. This same informant also notes that "others produced more because they told themselves, 'I need such and such an amount of money,' to which the patrón responded, 'Well, get to work mixing the clay,'" and went on to admit that he personally "never strove to make a thousand or 1500 bricks a day" and added that those who did so "are no longer with us." He did not do so, he says, because "work is not like food. Work must be sized up. The more you do, the more you need and the more effort you make, well, you end up making life more of a drag."

To sum up, brick makers are a mixed bag: some respond to imposed piece-rate incentive schemes and work harder and longer to produce and earn more, whereas others dance to the beat of their own drum in the form of a targeted income or package of wage goods.

Historically, the brick makers have not only shown roundabout resistance to the low-wage regime but have attempted organized resistance through unionization of the largest brick plants. The height of labor militancy was in the mid-1960s. One of the leaders of the brick-makers' movement put the reason for organizing succinctly: "We joined together to ask for a wage increase that year." According to him, in the initial meeting with the brickworks owner, he justified his petition for higher wages as follows: "We taught you to control brickmaking. We do the work and you put a price on us, on our work." And, he emphasizes, "the bosses have not wanted to pay us very well." Indeed, according to him, a wage of thirty pesos per thousand brick had prevailed for thirteen years during the 1950s and 1960s; the union requested an increase to thirty-five pesos. Regarding this situation, this brickmaker informant commented retrospectively, "Isn't the boss going to notice that the price of potatoes is going up? What consciousness! It's not that you don't want to work, it's that you need the income. You need to take something home. That's the problem." Only two brickworks settled with the union, which had around one hundred members representing all the principal brickworks; the majority of brickworks responded with a lockout that lasted for several months and effectively busted the union. In the words of the union leader, "We scared them." Not surprisingly, it was around this period that many of these same Reynosa brickworks began actively recruiting brick makers from the interior of the states of Nuevo Leon (Monterrey area) and Coahuila (*ejidos* of the Laguna area).

While there is no union activity today in the border brick industry, there is substantial discontent among brick makers, especially those still employed in formal-sector plants, regarding what is perceived to be a persisting low real wage structure. It is clear that real wages have declined at least since the early 1980s; in the years before the 1982 devaluation, real wages are remembered as being relatively good. The following statement by a fifty-seven-year-old brick maker with thirty-three years of work experience at Reynosa's largest artisanal brickworks expresses this well: "In those days [1960s–1970s] I earned 400 pesos weekly. That was big money. Money was worth something. With 100 pesos you bought your groceries and still had money left over. Nowadays with 400 new pesos that you earn you can't buy much because everything is so expensive. Nowadays it doesn't go anywhere, your budget is shot. With my weekly earnings here [$60] I can't buy the groceries we need. The consumer is lost. Things are very uneven. You are forced to eat with the little that you earn."

Despite the overall pattern of irregularity or periodicity in brick-making employment, there are some cases of relatively long-term (one year or longer) ties between pieceworkers and employers. Economics rather than sentiment are operative here—the employer either is willing to extend credit to workers or to keep them producing (and earning), albeit at reduced levels, during market slumps and/or provides them with rent-free housing, water, and electricity (and maintains their social security payments). Employers who do not offer these benefits or who fail to meet payrolls have difficulty in keeping or recruiting brick makers from the local labor pool.

A final paradox in border brick industry discourse regarding labor revolves around the contradictory meanings associated with the modifiers "artisanal" and "cheap." This paradox follows the commodity "handmade bricks" from production sites to sales sites and, finally, to consumption or use sites and is expressed around the contradiction between aesthetic and economic value. In the greater U.S. brick market, "handmade" translates into a pricey, architectural demand. Handmade bricks crafted in the United States are both stylish and expensive, selling for two to three times the price per thousand of common U.S. factory-made bricks. They are used exclusively in custom or architectural construction. By contrast, in the greater Southwest brick market, the highest volume sales of Mexican handmade brick has historically been in the tract-housing market (both private homes and apartments), where the bottom line is low price rather than aesthetic quality.

It is as a consequence of the massive flow of Mexican handmade bricks into the Texas brick construction market that the linkage between poor quality and cheap Mexican labor arose.[14] Not surprisingly, the linkage was spawned and nourished through a sophisticated, multimedia negative advertising campaign sponsored by U.S. brick manufacturers through their industry association, the Brick Institute of Texas—a campaign best known for the widely disseminated image of the president of that association taking a bite out of a Mexican handmade brick, juxtaposed with images of brick-faced homes severely damaged by rain or freeze–thaw cycles (Cook 1998:249–57). The steep decline in Mexican handmade brick exports to the United States since the late 1970s is at least partially attributable to this nexus between cheap labor and poor-quality/low-priced brick, and the surviving brickworks are still struggling to insert their handmade brick into the higher-quality, high-priced architectural/custom building market in Texas. Indeed, it was the inability of the last existing artisanal brickworks on the Texas side of the lower Rio Grande corridor to overcome problems related to this nexus that drove it into bankruptcy in 1980.[15]

CONCLUSIONS

As we enter the twenty-first century, the U.S.–Mexico border is the premier laboratory for observing and evaluating in microcosm global capitalism's transformative impact on the entire gamut of First World/Third World relations. Following the birth of the Border Industrialization Program in 1965 with its maquiladoras (assembly plants), a broad spectrum of discourse—academic, business, government, and the media—proliferated on the "border maquiladoras" theme. This discursive focus remained intense during the 1970s and 1980s.

In the 1990s, this trend has been reinvigorated by the ratification of NAFTA, arguably to the extreme that the "maquiladora" theme has come to define the "border economy" in popular and academic discourse and has made it a global demonstration case either for or against neoliberal capitalist development. This is somewhat ironic since in the 1990s "rapid technological change, the elimination of Tariffs under . . . NAFTA, and changes in Mexican legislation, have combined to create new opportunities for export processing plants located away from the border" (Van Dooren and Zárate-Hoyos 2003:571).

Overshadowed by the celebratory and critical discursive focus on maquiladoras and NAFTA is the sector of small-scale, semi- and unmechanized industries in the U.S.–Mexico border economy that includes artisanal brick making. Ironically, the handmade brick industry in the lower Rio Grande region was a small-scale precursor of multinational corporate industrial arrangements initiated by the Border Industrialization Program. In the 1950s, this industry already had binational arrangements involving the manufacture of unfired handmade brick in Mexico and its export to Texas for firing and, ultimately, resale and utilization in Texas masonry construction. Lower-border brick making is also noteworthy for its development in the nineteenth and early twentieth centuries as a pioneer manufacturing industry in a predominantly ranching, mining, and agricultural economy.

The case of the artisanal brick industry of Reynosa, Tamaulipas, shows why the term "cheap labor" does violence to an accurate description of reality (Fernández-Kelly 1983:192). The term is perniciously pejorative, analytically imprecise, and contested in popular discourse by different fractions of capital as well as by labor. In future academic discourse, a more precise and less pejorative modifier like "lower wage" or "lower cost" should be used in lieu of "cheap" and should be accompanied by specific data regarding wage differentials by branch between the United States and Mexico and within Mexico itself.

NOTES

1. See Bonilla and Morales (1998).

2. This anthropogeographic long view of the border/borderlands, found in pioneering contributions of the geographer Carl Sauer and anthropologist Eric Wolf, is provocatively elaborated in Vélez-Ibañez (1996).

3. These introductory statements were adopted, with slight modifications, from Cook (2001). Maquiladoras, or *maquilas*, are "in-bond companies set up in Mexico generally to perform assembly activity using inputs that are imported tax-free for export back to the country of origin" (Van Dooren and Zárate-Hoyos 2003:571; see also Sklair 1993; Wilson 1992:chap. 3). The relative cost of labor is only one factor that determines the location of production, and its importance varies by branch and type of commodity. For example, in consumer durables such as large appliances, proximity to end market may outweigh labor cost as a determinant in corporate decisions regarding location of production facilities on the Mexican side of the U.S. border (Aeppel 2003).

4. Negative synonyms that imply the devaluation or belittlement of labor, in accord with the hegemonic discourse of capital, include "of little account," "of small value," "mean," "shoddy," "vulgar," "common," "immoral," "inferior," and "base" (*Random House College Dictionary,* rev. ed. 1975:228).

5. The sources consulted are Fernández (1977:113–16, 139–42 1989:121), Fernández-Kelly 1983:27–28, 192), Hansen (1981:12, 87–88, 89, 95, 96, 97, 101, 156), House (1982:79, 91, 163, 166, 223–24, 228), Montejano (1987:chaps. 8–9), Samora (1971:9, 129–30), Weintraub (1990:13, 160–61), and Wilson (1992:9, 40, 53–54). The latest article I read in writing this chapter, dealing with the *maquila*/maquiladora program, also employs this term (Van Dooren and Zárate-Hoyos 2003:592).

6. Recent statistics compiled by the Federal Reserve Bank of Dallas for manufacturing workers' hourly pay (in 2001 U.S. dollars) place Mexico ($2.08) next to last in a rank order of twelve countries, topped by Denmark ($20.23) and bottoming out with China (61 cents). The United States ($16.19) ranks sixth after Denmark, Norway, Switzerland, Germany, and Japan. Total hourly compensation including benefits in 2001 was estimated at $20.60 in the United States compared to $2.33 in Mexico (no estimate given for China). Whereas many enterprises in particular branches of manufacturing (such as electronics and clothing) do relocate specific assembly plants from Mexico to China in response to the wage differential (between 2000 and 2002, for example, an estimated 177 plants were relocated from Ciudad Juárez, Chihuahua, to China), others (such as auto parts) do not, presumably in response to a combination of factors like proximity to the U.S. market or to major assembly unit, transportation costs, or tax-free export status. Although still numbering about 225,000 jobs in Ciudad Juárez alone at the end of 2002, the overall maquiladora employment situation in Mexico is volatile and fluctuates within and between specific industries and branches of the manufacturing sector (Ferriss 2003).

7. Montejano (1987:182–96, 197–99) provides vivid documentation of the linkages between pejorative terms like "cheap" and "dirty" in the pauperization and subjugation of Mexican labor by Anglo capital during the early decades of the twentieth century in the development of the Rio Grande valley. Inexplicably, he often employs the term himself (for example, "The duality of the farm society . . . not only reflected the superiority of the Anglo-American but also served to preserve a cheap Mexican labor force" [195–96]).

8. Incidentally, the impact of peso devaluation and inflation in Mexico on the cost-accounting operations of U.S. firms in the maquiladora sector have been mentioned in the literature by authors like House (1982:223–24; cf. Wilson 1992:39–40), but the impact on dollar-earning Mexican export firms, especially small- to medium-scale firms, has to my knowledge received little attention.

9. In their recent study of the growth of the garment industry via the *maquila* formula to the off-border La Laguna region of the border state of Coahuila, Van Dooren and Zárate-Hoyos find that the "boom of the garment industry in the urban region of La Laguna has resulted in an increasingly tight labour market where competition for workers, especially unskilled or semi-skilled assembly workers, is a concern for industrialists. Competition for workers has driven wages up and improved the range of fringe and other benefits—including transportation, food allowances, sports facilities, etc. offered to workers" (2003:580). The other side of the coin, however, is that "high wages, costly benefits and elevated training cost can be partly avoided by locating in

rural areas, since rural wages are lower and a more limited range of benefits is commonly offered" (2003:580). Here we see both labor market segmentation (rural vs. urban) and labor cost differentials operating within Mexico to show that "cheap labor" is an analytically sterile concept. It remains, nevertheless, a promotional lure used by Mexican state governments like that of Yucatan to attract *maquila* capital (Van Dooren and Zárate-Hoyos 2003:184). It is noteworthy that the spread of the garment industry in Coahuila (and Durango) to small rural settlements involves both cooperatives as well as locally owned subsidiaries of urban-based companies (2003:582).

10. The term "artisanal" refers to both labor-intensive and semimechanized brick production in enterprises ranging from small to medium scale (or micro to small scale, depending on the classificatory scheme or criteria being used). It distinguishes this type of brick production from highly mechanized, capital-intensive factory production. In Mexico, the term *ladrillera* is used to refer to artisanal as well as factory forms of brick production. Although it is possible to identify artisanal *ladrilleras* or brickworks that meet the criteria of informal-sector enterprises, there is at least as high an incidence of artisanal brickworks that bridge or crosscut this sectoral boundary (for example, semimechanized *ladrilleras* that have a core of full-time employees getting fringe benefits but also employ casual pieceworkers in dispersed, off-site campos or brickfields). It is best advised, then, to exercise caution in applying the concept of informality to the artisanal brick branch in the border economy.

11. One of this informant's statements on this matter was even more belittling in an insulting way of artisanal brick-making labor, namely, that "any fool (*pendejo*) can make handmade brick."

12. Handmade fired clay brick manufacture for use in large residential and public building construction was present in the lower Rio Grande corridor from at least the middle of the nineteenth century and was almost surely of Mexican origin. In the earliest period, it was mostly institutionally sponsored (that is, either by the Catholic Church for building churches or the army for building forts), although by the last decades of the nineteenth century brick making was also sponsored by ranches. In the early decades of the twentieth century, with the introduction of irrigated agriculture in the Rio Grande valley and the process of urbanization, on-site brick making was widespread (for example, in places like Edinburg, Harlingen, and Mercedes). Some of these on-site *ladrilleras* were commercialized and were operative until the mid-1950s; one of the most prominent of these was located in Relampago (near Mercedes). Since most if not all of the workers at this *ladrillera* were undocumented Mexicans, the mid-1950s crackdown by U.S. authorities on illegal immigration via "Operation Wetback" (Bustamante 1981:43; Cockcroft 1986:77–78; Samora 1971:52–53) essentially forced the shutdown of the remaining unmechanized *ladrilleras* in the lower Rio Grande valley.

13. It must be emphasized that this profile is of men who either worked or are currently working as brick makers in the Reynosa industry. A few of these men now work as watchmen or do light work in the brickworks other than brick making, an occupation from which they have retired. During the boom days of artisanal brick production for export to Texas during the 1960s, 1970s, and early 1980s, a large volume of handmade bricks was produced through the *campero*, or "brickfield boss," system—a putting-out system in which a master brick maker was employed as a commission agent by a brickworks owner to recruit brick makers and to supervise them

in molding unfired bricks on (usually) rented land outside the main brickworks site. The bricks made in the campos were hauled by truck to the main brickworks and fired there. A significant proportion of the brick makers who worked in the *campero* system were temporary or periodic workers, often recruited and transported either by the *campero* or by labor recruiters (coyotes) from off-border areas of handmade brick production, especially in the Torreón area of Coahuila and the area around Monterrey, Nuevo León. It was typical for members of this campo labor force to use employment in the Reynosa *ladrilleras* as a stepping-stone for a *brinco al otro lado* (jump to the other side), that is, to enter the undocumented labor force in Texas across the river border (see Cook 1998, 2001).

14. The artisanal fired clay brick manufacturers on the Mexican side of the lower Rio Grande corridor from Nuevo Laredo to Matamoros in the state of Tamaulipas have successfully competed against modern, highly capitalized brick factories in major urban construction markets in Texas. Since 1950, hundreds of millions of handmade bricks, worth tens of millions of dollars, from these artisanal brickworks have flowed across the border into the Texas market. Over that period, the flow has been cyclical, reaching a peak in 1977 of 735 million pieces (representing about 50 percent of the total Texas brick market) and a trough in 1991 of 40 million pieces (representing only a 6 percent share of the Texas market). The greater Reynosa area was the principal site for the artisanal brickworks participating in this export market (see Cook 1998).

15. This brickworks was located in Rio Grande City in Starr County; it was owned and operated by Anglo-German Texan capital and employed Mexican American female brick molders. Apart from the actual brick-molding process, this was a capital-intensive, mechanized plant—the last operative plant in what had been a multiplant enterprise, originating in the 1920s, with brickworks in Brownsville, Madero (Mission), and Rio Grande City (Cook 1998:chap. 7).

Although Wells's study of the California strawberry industry is broader in scope and intent than mine on the border brick makers, there are some interesting comparisons. First, in the case of my previous study of brick making in the Mexican interior and of the border study, I found rather more evidence than she did (Wells 1996:3) that point of production or the "local organization of production" was influential on labor–capital relations, including wages, than any other set of influences and less evidence of what she calls the "political construction of the labor market" (1996:13–14). This, of course, may reflect the difference in scale and relative importance in the economy of strawberry production and brick making and certainly reflects the fact that the labor force she studied was predominantly undocumented. Second, Wells seems to define "capitalism" much less inclusively than I do as embracing only the economy and, particularly, the sites where capital is productive (1996:13). Finally, Wells (1996:119–21) talks about "ethnic contrasts in human capital" in reference to the "individual skills, abilities, and experiences which can be brought to bear on farming" by Mexican immigrants, whereas I would emphasize the commodity-cultural funds of knowledge such immigrants bring with them from Mexico to their California job sites. Such funds, as I have emphasized, are developed through enculturation and lived experience and, as such, are diverse and mutable.

10

The New Transborder Space: NAFTAmerica, Migration, and Identity

Although the U.S.–Mexico borderlands are significant sites of distinctive historically shaped human settlements and cultures, they are even more significant as zones of transit for flows of people, commodities, and information moving bidirectionally along north–south axes into the interiors of two nation-states that, together with Canada, share the North American continent. After a fifteen-year period of implementation, the North American Free Trade Agreement (NAFTA), ratified in 1994, has the potential to integrate the economies of the United States, Mexico, and Canada into a duty-free common market. Given the highly legalistic and technical nature of the NAFTA project, it initially became a "symbolic entity invested with hopes, fears, and agency—the power to change lives and nations . . . a vehicle for discussing the particular ways individuals understand, experience, and explain global capitalism" and of issues like "the shifting social contracts between citizens and national governments regarding the right to regulate capital; the decision-making powers of transnational corporations in relation to individual and community livelihoods; or the relationships between stereotypes of migrants and North American nations as they are linked to the fears of job loss" (Kingsolver 2001:2). This controversial discussion included an apocalyptic proclamation by the Zapatistas in Chiapas that equated the initiation of NAFTA with the death knell of indigenous identity and culture in Mexico as well as contributions by anthropologists like June Nash (2001), whose concern with ethnocultural survival in international capitalism has led her to turn away from commodity economy and market logic toward natural economy and indigenous reproduction logic for a way out of the livelihood crisis among Maya peasants.

As NAFTA's implementation proceeds, it has become much more than a symbolic entity as an empirical record of its cost and benefits in the lives of the North American citizenries accumulates (Hart 2002:432–507). The record shows uneven results with an asymmetrical impact on Mexico, especially by U.S. corporate capital, that equals or exceeds in scope and scale the results of collusion between Mexican and U.S. political and business elites during the Porfiriato. Hart's (2002) provocative history exhaustively documents how, after the Civil War, a veritable who's who of American capitalists wheeled and dealed their way across the Mexican economic landscape with the complicity of the Mexican presidency and the U.S. government. By 1910, on the eve of the revolution that ended the thirty-five-year dictatorship of Porfirio Diaz, "15,000 American owners controlled 130,000,000 acres, or almost 27 percent" of Mexico's land, including a substantial portion of its coastlines and border areas (Hart 2002:260). Amazingly, by 1940, thanks to revolution-inspired policies that lasted through the Cárdenas presidency, both resident and absentee U.S. investors had lost most of their material assets in Mexico.

Despite their well-documented shortcomings, official Mexican political economic policy between 1940 and the early 1980s was designed to implement nationalistic and populist agendas embodied in the 1917 Constitution and guided by benevolent statist commitments to import substitution industrialization and a social safety net (Riding 1985:chaps. 7, 11, 12). But by the 1990s, aided by NAFTA and privatization and with the collusion of successive technocratic, neoliberal presidencies and the Mexican business and political elite, U.S. capitalists are again reaping profits across the whole spectrum of Mexico's economy. Hart notes that "the last four years of the twentieth century offered American enterprises their greatest opportunities in Mexico since 1910" (2002:459) and warns that "only a high degree of public awareness and political mobilization in support of wider social benefits can bring about the improvements so desperately needed by the great majority" of Mexicans (2002:507). Hart's warning becomes even more ominous in view of the apparent breakdown of the social pact between the Mexican central government and civil society forged as a result of the 1910 revolution (Hodges and Gandy 2002). The date for the beginning of the breakdown is in dispute (1940? 1968? 1982?), but there is wide consensus that "Mexican elites have killed the programmatic agenda of the Revolution, despite continuing to use the Revolution as a rhetorical reference point" (Gawronski 2002:392). Still, recent national polling data show that the "Mexican Revolution remains deeply embedded in Mexican political culture" (2002:393).

Granting the wisdom of Hart's caveat and acknowledging the poverty that continues to stifle the aspirations of a majority of working-class Mexicans, the NAFTA project may still represent the best available route for twenty-first-century development in Mexico. Ironically, only the events of September 11, 2001, and the consequent reordering of government priorities to combat international terrorism have managed to disrupt the escalated rhythm and flow of cross-border transactions generated by NAFTA's implementation. It remains to be seen how the contradiction between the forces of openness associated with NAFTA and of closure associated with antiterrorism plays out along the U.S.–Mexico border over the next few years.

In addressing NAFTA, several factors must be kept in mind. First, the contours, dynamic, and content of economic relations between the United States and Mexico do not lie in political agreements like NAFTA but in the fundamental asymmetry between the two economies sharing a 2,000-mile-long border—Mexico is a smaller, less diversified, developing economy, whereas the United States is the world's largest, most diversified developed economy. The nature of the border economy and of U.S.–Mexico economic relations from the last quarter of the nineteenth century to the present owes more to this fundamental asymmetry than to anything else.

Second, even though NAFTA may be the "most significant agreement between the United States and Mexico" in the twentieth century (Weintraub 1997:83), principally because it provides the institutional means to achieve common market integration, many trends or processes associated with it, such as industrial relocation, intraindustrial specialization, coproduction arrangements, trade in intermediate products, labor migration, and so on, reflect forces operating at the level of the international division of labor and of the competitive global market and private firms' (including multinational corporations) responses to these, whereas other processes (such as inflation and unemployment) reflect forces operating within either the U.S. or Mexican domestic economies. In either case, they have nothing to do with NAFTA per se and would be operative in the unlikely event that NAFTA were rescinded.

Third, there is nothing irresistible or inevitable about NAFTA. Its implementation is politically contestable by internal and external means, although it is most vulnerable to change by capital rather than by labor or the nonbusiness sector. The retention of antidumping and countervailing duty powers by Mexico and the United States, combined with a grievance process within NAFTA itself, provides a means of dampening, modifying, delaying, or renegotiating specific implementation impacts. Finally, any country can withdraw from the agreement on six months' notice (Orme 1996:296).

Fourth, NAFTA has much greater impact on Mexico than it does on the United States. Weintraub states this well (1997:83–84): "The sheer size of the U.S. economy compared with that of Mexico—U.S. GDP is some 23 times greater than that of Mexico—in combination with the greater diversity of the U.S. export market, means that the potential benefits and losses of NAFTA are more important for Mexico." In 2002, the United States was the destination of 90 percent of Mexican exports and the source of 63 percent of its imports. Given the pre-NAFTA abandonment by Mexico of the import substitution model of development and its joining of the General Agreement on Tariffs and Trade (GATT)—both actions that reflect a neoliberal trade policy—the dependency of Mexico on U.S. trade would have increased without NAFTA.

The upshot of this is that evaluating NAFTA's impact on U.S.–Mexico economic relations is challenging and that its overall impact remains an open question. There seems to be agreement, however, that NAFTA provides an organized forum for addressing trade and related issues (for example, environment, labor relations, and human rights) that did not exist previously (Compa 2001; Orme 1996:297–301) In addition, few would dispute Orme's prediction that "more important than formal trade reforms will be the informal progress towards market unification, with revamped transportation networks, new trade corridors and population centers, and new industrial specializations . . . new subregional economic relationships across national lines" that "will transform a regional free trade zone into something denser, more integrated, and more stimulating" (1996:302).

Stigliz's admonition that the globalization regime has been insensitive to its real and perceived threat to cultural identity and values, as well as to its antidemocratic nature, applies implicitly to regional projects like NAFTA. In his words, "Globalization . . . often seems to replace the old dictatorships of national elites with new dictatorships of international finance" (2002:247). While "dictatorship" may be too strong a word for the NAFTA regime, there is a decidedly antipopular, elitist, and market-fundamentalist character to it that, in combination, are tantamount to disenfranchisement, hence the grassroots resistance to and widespread discontent about NAFTA (cf. Cook 2003:204; Stiglitz 2002:248).

It is ironic that only as a result of NAFTA has Mexican studies undergone a paradigmatic innovation focused on the continentalization of Mexican economy, society, and culture through migration in counterposition to the more traditional focus on internal diversity of the Mexican nation-state. Harbingers of this paradigmatic innovation were present in a line of research connecting scholars like Jorge Bustamante (1978), Carey McWilliams (1968), Julian Samora (1971); in the establishment of El Colegio de la Frontera Norte and its programs; and in the inevitable convergence of the separate fields of Mexican and Mexican American studies through a common focus on the U.S.–Mexico border and its encompassing borderlands or on Mexican workers in the U.S. labor market. Nevertheless, topics like immigration, labor migration, remittances, interethnic (Anglo/Mexican) and intraethnic (Mexican American/Mexican) relations, comparative wage rates, and so on involving the United States and Mexico have been the object of systematic study since the pioneering work of Manuel Gamio.

MANUEL GAMIO, MEXICAN EMIGRATION, AND THE CONTRADICTION OF WAGE EARNERS WITH "FOLKLORISTIC" CULTURE

The work of Manuel Gamio is foundational in two senses. First, he was instrumental in the institutionalization of revolutionary *indigenismo*, which wedded Boasian culturalism to the research goal of "finding adequate forms for combating situations of poverty, ignorance, and unhealthiness in which ethnic identity appears as a problem for which the solution applied is the incorporation of the Indian to Mexican nationality" (Medina 1996:37). Second, by appointment of the Social Science Research Council, he became Mexico's first systematic researcher of Mexican immigration to the United States (Gamio 1971b:ix).[1]

A careful reading of Gamio's pioneering study discloses that many of his findings and interpretations regarding the first major twentieth-century wave of Mexican immigration to the United States either are still valid or have changed only in empirical detail, not in their overall content or thrust. The list is impressive. First and foremost is Gamio's insistence that "Mexican immigration into the United States was, fundamentally, an economic phenomenon" (1971b:30), that it was, at once, attracted by virtue of labor demand but propelled by conditions in Mexico that "obliged Mexicans to leave their country in increasingly large numbers in search of better wages and conditions" (1971b:11). He recognized that this immigration was necessarily incorporated into "the eternal war between capital and labor" by benefiting certain industries in certain regions and being opposed by organized labor in the United States (1971b:33, 50) and also that it had serious repercussions in the arena of ethnic relations, including those between older and current generations of immigrants (and natives) of Mexican origin (1971b:128–32). In addition, he emphasized the significance of remittances to Mexico of U.S. earnings by Mexican immigrants that he submitted to an innovative and rigorous analysis (1971b:30–32).

Finally, Gamio was especially thorough and perceptive in his handling of comparative wage levels (1926–1927) in Mexico and the United States. Employing a concept of the "minimum wage of comfort" focusing on "what is of urgent necessity to life" for a working family of five members, he calculated an average monthly wage for Mexico of 287.88 pesos, or $123.74. Based on average actual monthly wage earnings of 35.65 pesos, or $17.67, in Mexico at the time, Gamio concluded that the "mean wage of a Mexican worker would have to increase approximately eight times in order that he might meet the cost of the normal necessities of life" (1971b:37). His survey of pay conditions for Mexican "common laborers" in the United States found that their earnings were "six times as great as the $17.67 a month which the worker gets in Mexico" (1971b:38). To this day, the irresistible material incentive for the circulation of Mexican labor in U.S. labor markets and the rationale for the establishment of maquiladoras on the Mexican side of the border by U.S. and other foreign capital lie in this disparity in wage levels so carefully documented by Gamio.

The downside of Gamio's analysis derives from his *indigenista* orientation reflecting his zeal for "*forjando patria*" (forging the nation), or, as Medina expresses it, "his [Gamio's] consideration of constructing a homogeneous nation implies in different ways the disappearance of the Indian, with an ingenuous pretension of the scientific possibility of separating positive aspects, in order to retain them, from the negative ones, in order to eliminate them, as a kind of model to be assembled and disassembled" (1996:39). Gamio's characterization of the peasant-Indian cultural background of most of Mexico's migrants (for example, "an environment of personal attitude based on tradition, convention, and supernatural belief" [1971b:73]) emphasized its nonmodern, relatively primitive, folkloristic nature (1971b:74–75), still encapsulated in an inferior stage of civilizational development (1971b:57) and productive of a mentality that was idiosyncratic and anachronistic in a "modern, urbanized environment" (1971b:74). Given this characterization, it was impossible for Gamio to reconcile Mexican immigrants' putative cultural makeup or mind-set with success in negotiating and materially benefiting from their engagement in the U.S. labor market. Nowhere does Gamio credit their cultural background in "folklorism" (1971b:75) with a content that could explain their successful negotiation of the labyrinth of U.S. capitalism. In short, in his selective interpretation of their cultural heritage. Gamio chose to ignore their participation in marketing and commodity culture, that is, their long, collective experience of making and earning a living in Mexico and the funds of knowledge produced, reproduced, and updated through successive generations of that experience.

This selectivity on Gamio's part may have reflected his commitment to the thesis that the experience of Mexican commodity migrants within the United States would result in their reenculturation or, at least, in their learning new information and ways of working that would enable them, on returning to Mexico, to contribute toward making it "a great industrial and agricultural country" (1971b:49). His comparative example of an American and a Mexican woodcutter served to illustrate the ways in which such a transformation from an inefficient to an efficient Mexican economy might occur (1971b:42–43). Hence, Gamio's research findings and the policy recommendations derived from them essentially make him the father and primary champion of what would become the bracero program (1971b:chap. 14). On the basis of this record, it would appear that if Gamio were alive today, he would probably be a strong supporter of NAFTA and transnational migration but less enthusiastic about the extent of the permanent settlement of Mexican immigrants in the United States and the development of a binational Mexican population (Chavez 1992; Torres Sarmiento 2002:28–30).

Likewise, Gamio would probably be troubled by the continuing asymmetry in Mexico–U.S. economic affairs, even if at substantially higher economic index levels than characterized his epoch. He would infer from the steady increases in Mexican immigration to the United States and dollar remittances to Mexico over the last two decades of the twentieth century (Binford 2003:308) that the struggle between labor and capital was marching on to the relative disadvantage of his country vis-à-vis the United States and to that of Mexican labor on both fronts. We can only speculate about how he would interpret the findings over that same period regarding the impact of "migradollars" (Binford 2003:312) in Mexico. Although the findings on this issue are contradictory and inconclusive (2003:309–23), Gamio would no doubt sympathize with Binford's thesis that "the economic consequences of migration cannot be treated in isolation from the social consequences" (2003:326). Finally, Gamio would probably find the extent of Mexico's overall dependency on dollar remittance income today (Binford 2003:308) to be troubling, as he would a consideration of the ways that Mexican labor migration may contribute to "widening the economic gap between Mexico and the United States" (2003:319).

THE ANTHROPOLOGY OF VISIONS AND IDENTITY ON MEXICO'S TWO BORDERS

It may or may not be coincidental that two recent anthropological studies, *Border Visions* (1996) by Carlos Vélez-Ibañez dealing with mestizo Mexico of the northern border and *Mayan Visions* (2001) by June Nash dealing with indigenous Mexico near the southern border, invoke the term "visions" to convey something about their projects that focus on cultural identity. Curiously, neither author specifically explains the rationale for the choice of this term or explicitly defines its intended meaning. The first definition in my dictionary (*Webster's Third New International*), however, seems to be compatible with both projects, namely, "a mode or way of seeing" (p. 2557). The question of exactly whose mode or way of seeing the authors are referring to in their studies also remains implicit.

Prima facie, Nash's usage refers to the worldview of the Maya people; however, her analysis also implies views about the Maya by others, including herself and other anthropologists, non-Maya Mexicans, and other non-Maya. Vélez-Ibañez, on the other hand, given his coupling of "visions" with both a literal and a metaphorical interpretation of "border" (political–geographical and psychological)—as in the U.S.–Mexico border and "border of mind and method" (1996:265–73)—is more explicit regarding the complexity of visions in his project.

Recent contributions to the indigenous cultural survival literature in Mexican studies, represented most prominently by Nash's *Mayan Visions* (2001), forcefully reverberate with issues and arguments in chapter 2 on Traven and have encouraged me to incorporate a reconsideration of these in my elaboration of the commodity-value approach. As exemplified by Nash, ethnocultural survivalists view the aggressive international expansion of capital and market economics as inimical to the autonomous survival of particular idiosyncratic, local–regional, indigenous peasant cultures. Nash's particular concern for the autonomy movement of Chiapas-based Maya has led her to find Polanyi's (1957) approach to the economy as instituted process to be "even more significant in the era of globalization than it was nearly half a century ago" (2001:16). It is ironic that Nash's turn to substantivism and the principle of "natural economy" clashes head on with the Mayan (and other Mesoamerican) peoples' long involvement in and contribution to the development of commodity culture, exhaustively documented by two of her professors at the University of Chicago (Robert Redfield and Sol Tax) and, in fact, in previous work by Nash herself (Nash 1993).

Both Vélez-Ibañez and Nash address the transformative historical impact of capitalist development on the lives and culture of their subjects, and both emphasize the resistance of these subjects as their native land is invaded by superordinate others who relegate the natives to the status of culturally inferior subalterns and their continuing struggle for cultural identity, human rights, and empowerment in which consanguineal and affinal relations and ritual cycles of exchange are instrumental (Nash 2001:chap. 2; Vélez-Ibañez 1996:137–81). Many other comparisons can be made between these two studies, elaborating on the similarities and differences between the historical experiences of Mayans in Chiapas and mestizos in the northern borderlands of Sonora/Arizona and between the approaches of their authors. Of particular interest to me is the contrast between Vélez-Ibañez's use of a "commodity identity" approach to explain the historical experience of Mexican mestizos in Sonora/Arizona and Nash's reliance on a sort of anti–commodity-identity approach rooted in a concept of indigenous "moral logic" (2001:25) to explain the Mayan experience in Chiapas.

For Vélez-Ibañez (1996:7), Mexican migrants and U.S. citizens of Mexican descent were identified as commodities during the capitalist development of the American Southwest and the borderlands because they made up the most abundant source of labor. As such, they were indispensable to whatever productive activity was undertaken. At the same time, however, the relative lack of gainful employment in Mexico and the relatively low standard of living created conditions under which Mexican labor was abundant, inexpensive, and therefore expendable. Under these conditions, the tendency was for Anglos to treat Mexicans impersonally and submit Mexicans to a low-wage regime.

Consequently, "the history of Anglo-Mexican relations," asserts Vélez-Ibañez, "has often been defined by an imposed commodity identity, a determining but not absolute condition that has strongly influenced how Mexicans are perceived by others and how Mexicans perceive themselves" (1996:7; cf. 1996:71). Commodity identity, then, seems to operate to keep Mexicans in the U.S. Southwest, for the most part, occupationally concentrated in lower-income working-class occupations, culturally stigmatized, and suffering from a disproportionate share of poverty, miseducation, physical and mental illness, crime, drugs, and participation in wars (1996:140–42, 182–206).

Vélez-Ibañez's thesis provides a plausible explanation for the origin and reproduction of the general structure of Anglo-Mexican relations in the U.S. Southwest. Still, a great deal of the complexity of everyday relations and discourse in the U.S.–Mexico borderlands cannot be explained through the commodity-identity framework (Cook 1998:chap. 11; Vila 2000). It is limited by the fact that commodity identity is shared by all members of the working class in NAFTAmerica regardless of ethnic, gender, or national affiliation and is an inherent element in the culture of capitalism shared by Mexicans and Anglos alike. Mexicans do not have to migrate to the United States to experience commodity identity and its consequences. Indeed, if one assumes any degree of voluntarism or individual agency in migration, it could be inferred from Mexican migratory behavior over the past century that experiencing commodity identity in the United States is preferable (at least in cost–benefit terms) to experiencing it in Mexico.

Jorge Bustamante (1978:185), in elaborating his important concept of commodity migration, is one of the few writers on the topic who has introduced the cultural element into his analysis of Mexican migrant labor in the United States. In his words, "The process of socialization in which the individual learns to conceive his labor [power] as a commodity is the same in which the workers learn about a labor . . . market and about labor [power] buyers. Migration in this context is nothing else but the self transportation of labor as a commodity to where the capital owner demands it. Social behavior corresponding to these conditions . . . could be called commodity-migration" (1978:185). It is precisely such commodity migration within Mexico and between Mexico and the United States that has underwritten the flow of exchange value in the form of cash remittances to the home-base communities of migrant workers as well as the flow of surplus value into the profit funds of employer enterprises in Mexico and the United States.

Vélez-Ibañez's commodity-identity thesis does not explicitly draw on Bustamante's work. This complicates Vélez-Ibañez's task of demonstrating why the commodity identity of Mexicans in the southwestern United States is any different that that of non-Mexicans who sell their labor power for money in the regular course of surviving in U.S. capitalism. Mexican and non-Mexican wage workers alike, by virtue of their commodity identity, are exploited by capital. In short, the commodity-identity concept alone cannot explain labor market segmentation and cannot explain why Mexicans suffer from racism or ethnic discrimination in the United States.

Bustamante (1978) posits the elements of a proposed explanation of why Mexican commodity migrants are relatively more exploited and also subjected to racism and ethnic discrimination. He notes, first, that "commodity-migrants enter into the relationships of production of a capitalist society occupying the lowest paid positions of that society's occupational structure"; second, that "commodity-migrants are socially defined as deviants and sanctioned through prejudice and discrimination. Thus, the presence of commodity-migrants is used as a factor reinforcing dominant values in accordance with which discriminatory practices are justified and social privileges are maintained"; and, third, that "commodity-migrants are cast into conflict with the lowest paid native workers within whom commodity-migrants compete for the lowest paid jobs" (1978:185–86). Bustamante's first point provides a possible explanation for the relatively greater exploitation of Mexican workers, and his third point provides a possible explanation for what he posits but does not explain in his second point, namely, that Mexicans suffer discrimination because they are competing with the lowest-paid native workers. He subsequently states this more forcefully: "The 'importation' of Mexican workers has had a negative impact on the 'native' labor force" (1978:187).[2]

MEXICAN LABOR, MIGRATION, AND IDENTITY IN NAFTAMERICA: FROM PEASANTS TO POLYBIANS

Part of the complexity confronting students of North American capitalism at the beginning of the twenty-first century lies precisely in the contradictory reproduction of pseudoanachronistic forms involving subjects who are neither unitary nor site confined in making and earning a living. Bustamante (1978), gazing from the Mexican interior toward the U.S. border, perceptively observed that rural Mexicans are pulled into the circuits of American capitalism as "commodity migrants" without realizing the extent to which their participation in the U.S. labor market would mushroom beyond the border into greater NAFTAmerica. It was the Mexican economic crisis—triggered by the 1982 devaluation of the peso—that initiated an upsurge in labor migration from Mexico to the United States in the 1980s. Migratory activity remained at a high level throughout the 1990s, stimulated by another peso devaluation in 1994, together with unprecedented economic growth and labor demand in the United States (Bustamante et al. 1998; Cohen 2001:957–58). Michael Kearney (1996, 2002) has led the way in drawing out the wider implications of this process for anthropological theory.

According to Kearney, generalizing about the Third World, "peasants are mostly gone," and "global conditions do not favor the perpetuation of those who remain" (1996:3). The implication of this ontological condition for Mexican studies, according to Kearney, is that "an adequate ethnography of seemingly rural . . . communities must situate them within transnational and global contexts that effectively dissolve old intellectual oppositions such as rural-urban, modern-traditional, and peasant-nonpeasant" and means that "we must . . . reconceptualize the concepts with which we define identities and communities" (1996:3–4). The "deepening transnationalization and globalization of communities, economies, and identities" (1996:115) necessitates the construction of a new approach to class that views subject positions as reflecting a dialectic between external (relations of production) and internal (processes of consumption) differentiation.

With regard to Mexico, Kearney's transnationalization thesis implies more than deepening involvement in the international economy and more expansive cross-border relations with the United States. During the second half of the twentieth century, foreign capital investment in Mexico has diversified (as in Japan and other Asian countries), but with the implementation of NAFTA, an institutional process of continentalization of the Mexican economy has been set in motion that, even from the perspective of the Porfiriate as documented by Hart (2002) and of early twentieth-century emigration as documented by Gamio (1971a, 1971b), is unprecedented in Mexico's economic history.[3]

The ontological trigger of the epistemological shift advocated by Kearney has unquestionably been human movement or, more specifically, migration—circulatory and otherwise. One common theme in most ethnographic studies of rural Mexico conducted over the last half century is the impact, in greater or lesser degree, of participation by villagers in regional, national, or international migration—a participation that may either temporarily and/or continuously or permanently affect family and community life in multiple ways. Household and village economies have depended on cash remittances from absent members participating in a variety of extravillage labor markets, including regional and national urban centers and agroindustrial areas, as well as a whole spectrum of rural and urban service-sector jobs in the United States. Untold numbers of these absent villagers have become semipermanent residents of the United States, either as officially credentialed or as undocumented, providing support for newly arriving migrants as well as remittances to family in Mexico. Still others, of course, have become permanent U.S. residents and citizens.

This transborder process extends well beyond the border states of California, Arizona, New Mexico, and Texas to include every state in the United States. I have personally witnessed it in Michigan's agricultural fields; in mushroom factories, greenhouses, and nurseries in northeastern Connecticut;

in fruit orchards in western North Carolina; and, most recently, in residential construction and landscaping in central Texas. News reports during the "great burning" summer of 2002 disclosed the high proportion of Mexican migrants in the crews of firefighters dispersed throughout the forests of the western United States. I recently had this driven home to me through an "out of the blue" phone call from member of a family that had hosted me in the village of San Sebastian Teitipac during the 1960s whom I had not had contact with in over two decades. The call originated in Racine, Wisconsin, where the caller informed me that more than 600 ex–San Sebastianos (and their families) live, work, and celebrate in *ausencia*, the annual patron saint's festival of their Oaxaca home village.

Kearney (1996:15–22), from his base in southern California, has been a leading observer of this phenomenon, focusing especially on circular migrants from the village of San Jerónimo in the Mixteca region of Oaxaca whom he first met in 1978 as pickers in the orange groves near Riverside. There is no doubt that the "complex circuits of economic flow and accumulation" that Kearney has documented "within the greater transnational extension of San Jerónimo" (1996:19) do characterize multitudes of other "transnationalized" rural communities throughout Mexico. Perhaps one of the most striking features of this process is that it is by no means restricted to the economic sphere but provides the material means to sustain and enrich the political and ceremonial life of these communities.[4]

Although nothing that Kearney describes was previously unknown (and, indeed, was foreshadowed in Gamio's 1930s vision for Mexican development [Gamio 1971b:170–96]), the implication of his analysis is that the process has developed in recent decades to an extent that represents a difference in kind, not degree, from what had previously been documented. There is, in effect, a new level of transnationalized social reproduction inextricably tying rural Mexican communities to regular and substantial involvement in capitalist circuits that have U.S. loci. Kearney contends that "concentration on productionist aspects of the . . . reproduction would severely slight the importance of local and global social and symbolic influences on the total reproduction of the community" (1996:17), hence his emphasis on developing an approach that expands the definition of economic value and couples that expanded value focus with an attention to power and representational politics. This broad research agenda presses against the outer limits of economic anthropology and is best pursued within a transnationally sensitized version of Marxist anthropology or anthropological political economy (Roseberry 1988), what Kearney conceives as a "robust anthropology" focused on class and identity (2002:9–12). Ultimately, the pursuit of understanding commodities, value, and identity within the framework of cultural production and power leads beyond the boundaries of economic anthropology.

One of the most original proposals in Kearney's project on reconceptualizing peasants revolves around his notion of "internal differentiation," which "recognizes the formative effects on identity of the subjects' position in systems of production" but "enlarges the analytic focus beyond the sphere of production to that of consumption as effecting the constitution of the internally differentiated subject . . . [through] the consumption not only of economic values but also of value-saturated signs that when consumed, nurture the class-based identity of the consuming subject" (1996:168–69; cf. 2002:14–16). Again, the justification offered by Kearney for this radical break with prevailing theoretical approaches and epistemologies based on oppositional thinking (such as subject–object, we–they, developed–underdeveloped, rural–urban, and peasant–nonpeasant) is ontological change—new referents no longer correspond to old concepts. Accordingly, so-called peasant communities in Mexico are inhabited by complex subjects with situationally shifting roles in the division of labor, within and across national borders, and, consequently, of shifting subjective and objective identities. These essentially postpeasant "polybian" subjects occupy multiple economic niches (in contrast to "amphibians," who are restricted to two niches: land and/or water) (1996:141–42; cf. 2002:16).

I fully agree with Kearney's privileging of economic class analysis (that is, social relations of production) in producing knowledge about social differentiation (Kearney's external differentiation). I agree with him, too, that it is necessary to counterbalance a focus on production, exchange, and distribution of economic value with a focus on the consumption of economic, as well as symbolic, noneconomic values, to understand how socioeconomic and cultural differentiation (Kearney's internal differentiation) intersect/interpenetrate (1996:153–54; cf. 2002). Finally, Kearney is also right to emphasize that "the basic principles of political economy are still relevant, although it is necessary to adapt them to the changing historic conditions" (2002:17).[5]

Kearney's highlighting of depeasantization and his call for a corresponding epistemological shift away from the unitary "peasant" subject toward a multi-involved Mexican subject in circulation may be somewhat overdrawn (cf. Watts 2002). He insists that the ontological conditions supporting the transnationalization of Mexican migrants translate into the melding of urban and rural space and the demise of peasant identity in Mexico. I agree that it makes little sense to arbitrarily classify land-poor, marginal agricultural communities heavily involved in specialized craft production and/or a variety of nonagricultural pursuits, as well as in the system of transnational migration and remittance, under the rubric of "indigenous peasant" (Cohen 2001:956).

While I share many of the analytical concerns that underlie Kearney's contention that "the peasant concept . . . no longer accords with contemporary identities and ethnography" (1996:xiii), I think he may have underestimated the degree to which forces and conditions tending to promote the practice of agriculture for family and community reproduction are still operative in Mexican capitalism (not only in heavily indigenous states like Oaxaca, Guerrero, and Chiapas but also in Michoacán, Jalisco, Querétaro, Nayarit, and Colima [Appendini 2002:261–69]). Whether small-scale agriculture is for own use or for sale, it is not necessarily doomed by transnational corporate capitalism and continental/global markets.

Undeniably, peasant agriculture is especially vulnerable to the fads, foibles, and crises in Mexico's political economy, periodically undermining its viability in the process of rural household and community reproduction or as an activity that can meet the needs, expectations, and aspirations of the bulk of the rural population. Nevertheless, there is also solid empirical evidence of peasant agriculture's persistence, increasingly as a supplement to a variety of other cash-earning or commodity-producing strategies but also as a source of corn for self-consumption (Appendini 2002:258, 263). In the last decade of the twentieth century, poverty increased in rural Mexico, as did participation in international migration, but organizational innovations have made agriculture rewarding for many small producers in key areas of the country (2002:257–69). In short, postpeasantism seems to be inappropriate to address the complex ways that "Mexico's rural population has adapted, resisted, and reconstructed its livelihood according to specific circumstances of local and regional contexts, ethnicity, and gender and according to the predominant policy paradigms" during this turn-of-the-century period of NAFTA's implementation (2002:270). Kearney is persuasive, nonetheless, in arguing that agriculture is becoming a less predominant source of livelihood, even among rural Mexican populations where it functioned as such in the recent past.[6]

In short, there remains at least as much empirical support for maintaining a distinction between rural and urban space and for recognizing the socioeconomic importance of agriculture as there is for transnationalism. Kearney himself admits as much in his chapter on San Jeronimo, where the rural agricultural nexus is present at the reproductive core of the village. He observes, for example, that "all households have access to farmland that is communally owned by the town, and most households also have some de facto private land they work" and that "agricultural production is carried out within a complex set of social and economic relationships that include labor exchange, varieties of sharecropping, and hired labor" (1996:15–16). There is no justifiable reason for downplaying the study of these and other localized activities and relations in the study of San Jeronimo's or similar communities' reproduction despite their insertion in transnational processes and the transnational circulation of many of its members. Furthermore, as Appendini convincingly argues, peasant agriculture is not disappearing in Mexico but is immersed in a process of adjustment and reconstitution of people's "livelihoods at the individual, household, and community levels in varying and complex ways" (2002:256).

The performance and outcomes of activities and relations inside and outside the local community must be analyzed to properly understand social reproduction from the perspective of economic anthropology. Ideally, whenever feasible, this analysis should include data from the migrant-receiving communities where remittances are generated. In any case, the migrant-sending communities in Mexico, however much they are impacted by remittances and the culture of migration, are still sites of lived realities and are immersed in Mexican agrarian commodity culture. Thus, on this basis and because of the ongoing popular struggle and negotiations between agrarian sectors and the Mexican state over constitutional issues regarding citizenship, property rights, and local rule, it is premature to proclaim the demise of the corporate agrarian community. In short, it is time to deessentialize the peasantry and emphasize the analytical limitations of the peasant concept but not to discount the persisting role of small-scale agriculture.

MEXICAN IMMIGRANT LABOR, "AGENCY," AND "UNFREEDOM" IN CALIFORNIA AGRICULTURE

One of the more recent and theoretically sophisticated studies of Mexican migrant labor in California agriculture, *Strawberry Fields* by Miriam Wells (1996), wisely avoids references to cheap labor and, in fact, makes a startling admission in the genre of literature dealing with so-called unskilled Mexican labor in California agriculture that "wage workers often intervened to shape the rewards and terms of their labor" (1996:3). She also questions the validity of the flexible specialization/accumulation approach, suggesting the possibility that measures perceived to be adaptive to changing conditions in the global market (such as contingent employment) may, in fact, be motivated by the "control and cost reduction it offers in relation to local class contests" (1996:306). Wells seeks to give agency of Mexican workers its due in the structured game of strawberry production in California fields. Nevertheless, for all her innovativeness in analyzing the role of Mexican origin or descent workers, most of whom are immigrants, monolingual in Spanish, undocumented, and highly mobile (1996:xxi), her analysis of agency could have been strengthened by taking into account the cultural matrix of Mexican agriculture from which these immigrants originated and to which an undisclosed (but presumably high) number return. She emphasizes "how people acting at the local level reciprocally shape the structures around them" (1996:11), but when addressing the anachronism of sharecropping in the California strawberry fields and labor resistance to it, she fails to address the Mexican agricultural experience of Mexican-origin workers. To the extent that they had experienced sharecropping in Mexico, either as employers or as employees, their coping with such relations in California would presumably be less disadvantaged.[7]

As Fred Krissman (2002a, 2002b) mentions in one of his recent expositions of the importance of employer labor recruitment in supplying and shaping the workforce in California agriculture, Mixtec-identity workers find their migratory experience in northern Mexican agriculture to serve as on-the-job training for California: "the relations and technologies of production on both sides of the border are quite similar, right down to packing the product into boxes with the same label" (2002a:21). Although his emphasis here is on California-based agribusiness ownership of Mexican farms, the proposition that Mexican agriculture provides on-the-job training for California or other U.S. agriculture is worth pursuing further. We need to know more about how upbringing and work experience in Mexican agriculture at all levels helps (or not) Mexican immigrant workers in coping with agroindustrial situations in the United States.

The role of enculturated agency needs to be considered both among the majority of Mexican-origin workers who are field hands in California and the minority who have made it into the ranks of the growers (Wells 1996:118–39). The latter group's experiences, for example, with sharecropping in Mexico should be relevant to some extent in their participation in California sharecropping. Unfortunately, rather than exploring this topic, Wells invidiously compares Mexican-origin with Japanese-origin growers as being "least endowed in all regards" concerning "the individual skills, abilities, and experiences which can be brought to bear on farming" (1996:119). She attributes these deficiencies to their Mexican origin and to their Spanish dominance (noting that those who do speak English do so "haltingly") (1996:119). It is surely the case that Mexicans' background and work experience in Mexico cannot alter the organization and modus operandi of California or other U.S. agricultural enterprise but that such background and experience can, perhaps, ameliorate or deflect their impact on Mexican immigrant workers.

It might prove rewarding to view the commodity value–focused enculturation of Mexicans in Mexico, combined with their ongoing lived experience in Mexico, California, and throughout NAFTAmerica, as flowing into a diversifying fund of knowledge that facilitates their deliberative pursuit of labor market opportunities in their own/family's material interest. This knowledge and experience in their memory banks goes some distance in leveling the playing field between Mexican workers and their employers. Mexican workers, whatever their immigration status or ethnic identity, wherever they may be in NAFTAmerica (berry farms in California, beef processors in Iowa, orchards in North Carolina, tree farms or recycling yards in Connecticut, or construction sites in Texas), know that they can get employment somewhere else in the vicinity or in some other space within their experienced labor market (that is, through their networks [Krissman 2002a]).

A case can be made for considering employer-recruited labor as quasi-unfree or quasi-indentured and for considering replacement of mestizo with indigenous labor as favoring employers in value struggles with Mexican employees (Krissman 2000, 2002a; Peck 2000), but the significance of this relative unfreedom to the overall process of Mexican labor immigration is unclear. Presumably, the main impact is that it reduces the values in Gamio's comparative scheme of "minimum wages of comfort" that provide the main material incentive driving the process; but it does so only for the workers on the hook (*enganche*), and it is unlikely to put the squeeze on to the extent that the material incentive disappears (that is, the Mexican worker earns the equivalent or less in the United States of what he would earn in Mexico). The employer strategy of labor segmentation by gender, ethnicity, region, national origin, and so on will reduce the likelihood of organized resistance (for example, protest or unionization) in the long-run but cannot eliminate short-run turnover in a labor force that ultimately reflects action by individual workers.

An increasingly favored paradigm in interpreting the circulation of Mexican immigrant labor through U.S. labor markets emphasizes its relative "unfree" and subaltern condition vis-à-vis U.S. capital. This paradigm raises interesting questions vis-à-vis Marx's thesis that all labor power "freely" contracted in the capitalist market is, in reality, unfree and forced because of the nature of exploitation and the invisible hand of surplus value. Workers are free to get paid for that part of the working day that meets going "standard of living" requirements but is basically unfree with regard to that part of the working day going to the capitalist (surplus labor product/value). The only proviso is that, depending on circumstances, the latter may be subject to reduction by labor resistance/negotiation, implying that the "unfreedom" is qualified. This entire matter is subject to empirical determination in specific cases.[8]

The neoliberal market-fundamentalist approach to free labor assumes that imperfections in factor markets are abnormalities in capitalist market economies so that imperfections that restrict labor movement/choice are viewed as reducing the assumed (via ceteris paribus) freedom. This approach to labor freedom/unfreedom is useful only to the degree that it can systematically show impact on the value-sharing process, that is, rates of exploitation or s/v (surplus value/variable capital), at specific points of production or in specific enterprises. My point regarding Mexican immigrant labor is that since we are not talking about a slavistic regime, hooks (*enganches*) can be unhooked (*desenganchado*) simply by opportunistic disengagement on the part of labor (such as wage advances taken and not repaid or loans given and not repaid). Evidence of such disengagement has accumulated over the years in my research in Oaxaca and on the border, but it is inconclusive.

Worker resistance, agency, and relative freedom/unfreedom are topics very pertinent to understanding piece-rate payment regimes that I have studied in several Oaxaca petty capitalist industries and in the border brick industry. There is an empirical basis for arguing that overly rigid, inflexible regimes can last only in situations where labor supply is open ended with a high degree of interchangeability of workers or where labor is, for whatever reasons, relatively defenseless in bargaining with or resisting capital. This fits the stereotype of the east Los Angeles or other garment industries where a pool of unemployed workers wait outside the shop door to replace recalcitrant, underperforming, or sick/injured employed workers. This has never been the case in industries I have studied but may be the case in California agriculture.

There are, however, certain limits to capital in the absence of de facto/de jure slavery; a piece rate or any other payment regime can go only so far toward complete advantage to capital, or problems will be encountered in the attachment of workers for capital turnover cycles. Worker turnover does create problems in capital turnover or, at minimum, increases the turnover time of capital (Cook and Binford 1990:267–68 n. 11; Harvey 1982:62–64, 71–72, 85–91). This usually translates into profit reductions. The plausibility of this argument appears to be reinforced by Krissman's finding regarding employer-recruited undocumented Mexican labor in a representative sample of twenty-four firms within three labor-intensive crop industries in California and Washington that the "large deductions from their paychecks are a principal source of job dissatisfaction, which is reflected in employee turnover rates averaging 65 percent annually" (2000:284).

The previous discussion suggests that the time may have arrived in California agricultural studies to introduce a working hypothesis that posits labor-intensive sectors (like berry growing) of California agriculture as extensions of Mexican agriculture rather than of U.S. agribusiness. After all, these sectors are completely dependent primarily on undocumented circulatory Mexican migration. Only then will it become obligatory to systematically view Mexicans neither as "commodity migrants" nor as mere pawns of U.S. agribusiness but as commodity enculturated agents/subjects making informed choices in their daily lives to defend their identities and improve their material well-being through circular migration and remittances to their familial home bases in Mexico.[9]

TZINTZUNTEÑOS AND *TLAXCALTECOS* IN FAR-FLUNG REACHES OF NAFTAMERICA

Apropos my earlier critique of George Foster's theorization of the economic culture of Tzintzuntzan, there is a constructive fallout from his long-term interest in that community. This is attributable to Robert Kemper's collaboration with Foster in the study of Tzintzuntzan migration (Foster 1988:389–99; Kemper and Foster 1975), to Kemper's own work on the town as the home base of an extended "community" or "population" (Kemper 1994:124), and to his sharing of data with Torres Sarmiento (2002), who undertook a detailed, long-term study of the formation and dynamics of the "extended community" of Tzintzuntzeños with secondary settlements in California and Washington and worker outposts in Alaska's Aleutian Islands. Although informed primarily by the literature of migration studies and the political economies of gender and of development, Torres Sarmientos's study establishes a precedent for knowledge production in economic anthropology about the contradictory transformative impact on Mexican communities and families of restrictive U.S. border control and immigration policies combined with binational material incentives to integrate the North American economy.

The general story of twentieth-century Mexican immigration to the United States narrated by Manuel Gamio has been concluded by Torres Sarmientos's detailed account of intergenerational experiences of families from Tzintzuntzan, Michoacan in Baja California (Tijuana), California (Santa Ana/Los Angeles), Washington (Tacoma), and Alaska's Aleutian Islands (Dutch Harbor). Her account provides a bridge into the twenty-first-century space of NAFTAmerica as well as a model for future economic anthropology to build on. She has shown how social networks—developed through a process of documented and undocumented immigration to and settlement in the United States, maintenance of identity and ties with relatives in the original base community, and either return or circulatory migration—continue to operate to connect Mexican workers to jobs in the U.S. labor market as an expression of income-generating strategies for distinct sets of consanguineal and affinal relatives that are referred to as "family" without implying coresidence but usually implying income pooling (2002:36). She highlights the critical role of female labor in this process in the sense of both domestic/labor reproducing and cash earning in crafts or other jobs as well as the impact of the job market and nature of employment opportunities (such as fluctuating vs. steady and low wage and no benefits vs. higher wage plus variable benefits). The varied and shifting nature of family organization directly reflects the varied and shifting nature of the labor market, the apparent trend being an increase demand for part-time, nonpermanent, low-wage labor as a consequence of flexible accumulation strategies by employers. This produces multioccupational family income-earning strategies, crosscutting informal and formal sectors, gender and age divisions, national boundaries, and geographic localities.

Interviews with Tzintzuntzeño migrants regarding their premigratory occupational histories document a familiar pattern of multiple involvement in a variety of cash-earning and non-cash-earning activities in the household and extrahousehold division of labor and specialization from a young age. Torres Sarmiento emphasizes agent involvement in "family economic survival strategies" (2002:78) and provides testimonial evidence for the intergenerational transmittal of commodity culture and for the exercise of prudent rationality (2002:75–79) that would serve her informants well in their future economic life across the border. It is clear from these well-documented case studies that commodity culture derived from experience in Mexico prepared family members to negotiate the conditions and obstacles posed by labor markets in the United States and that the exercise of prudent reason by individual subjects—not just impersonal macrostructural forces beyond subject control—must be considered in explaining the positioning and organization of particular families in the cross-border, transnational process at any given point in time.

If Alaska is now part of the labor market negotiated by rural Mexicans, so is Canada. A recent study by Leigh Binford (2002) documents the impact of the participation of Tlaxcalans in an official contract labor program between Mexico and Canada (the Mexico-Canada Program of Temporary Agricultural Workers) on daily life in their northwestern Tlaxcala home communities. This program has grown incrementally in the post-NAFTA period from a modest number of 203 male migrants in 1974 to more than 10,000 migrants (mostly male but now including more than 400 females) in 2001; Tlaxcala regularly sends more temporary agricultural workers to Canada each year than any other participating Mexican state (1,727 in 1999). The study communities (Sanctorum, Atotonilco, and Nanacamilpa) are among those in the state that are heavily dependent on Canada-earned incomes, primarily because of the limitations of their agriculture (dry-land grain farming on eroded hillsides) and the generally small-scale, low-volume, low-return structure of their local economies (2002:9, 12). In Canada, these migrants work in four basic sectors of Canadian agriculture: fruits, field vegetables, tobacco, and greenhouse production of hothouse vegetables and flowers (Binford 2002:6); their earnings, because of deleterious exchange rate trends in recent years between the U.S. and Canadian dollars and the Mexican peso, have translated into a "steady erosion of domestic purchasing power of remittances from Canada" (Binford 2002:11) and make participation in the U.S. labor market more attractive from that standpoint. Binford estimates that "2001 Mexican temporary agricultural workers in Canada earned a before tax equivalent of $42 pesos per hour, considerably lower than the $63.7 peso equivalent paid to agricultural contract workers in the U.S. H2A Program" (2002:11).

Still, contract labor in Canada results in a higher standard of living for the participating families than would have been the case if they had not participated. Binford estimates that "in about five months the 'average' northwest Tlaxcalan migrant remits the yearly equivalent of 2.2 minimum Mexican salaries, and still has 7 months in Tlaxcala to earn more money" (2002:13). The bottom line is that, despite the baseline of poverty that plagues these households, "many substantially improve their standards of living and come to treat as necessities goods and services that a few years earlier were probably thought of as middle class luxury items [such as cars, trucks, satellite dishes, and telephones]" (2002:13).

Paralleling the discourse associated with the employment of Mexican laborers in California and Texas that invariably touts them as highly productive and disciplined, Canadian farmers reportedly praise them for "strong work ethic and obedient attitude" (Binford 2002:10), suggesting the operation of elements of commodity culture brought with them from Mexico. Like the situation in southern Texas, this preferential posture among employers of Mexican labor leads to a tendency to disemploy other workers (in Texas, Tejanos or Mexican Americans; in Canada, Jamaicans and other Caribbeans) and may simply mask more lucrative exploitation (2002:10–11; cf. Spielberg-Benítez 1989; Wells 1996:161).

THE SOCIAL LIFE OF CRAFT COMMODITIES IN TRANSBORDER SPACE

Whereas a line of scholars from Gamio to Bustamante, Vélez-Ibañez, Kearney, Wells, Krissman, and Binford have followed migrant workers from their points of origin in rural Mexico into the U.S. (or Canadian) labor market, W. Warner Wood is among the first to follow craft commodities from their points of fabrication in interior rural Mexico to their points of final sale in the U.S. consumer market. He does so under the heady inspiration of postmodern cultural theory (for example, Bourdieu, Appadurai, and Marcus) combined with an element of "late capitalist" development theory (for example, Harvey). A primary concern derived from the first source is "changes in the value, meaning, and use of commodities as they move from hand to hand and place to place" with an emphasis on the "socioeconomic relations among the various people involved in a trading network and the cultural representations of commodity in different contexts" (Chibnik 2003:16; cf. Appadurai 1986). The second group of sources talk about post-Fordist systems of flexible accumulation that are said to be characteristic of so-called late capitalism (Mandel 1978) and that "allow enterprises to react quickly to new market niches by changing labor processes and creating innovative products" (Chibnik 2003:6; cf. Cook 1998:279–83; Rothstein and Blim 1992).[10]

The cultural meanings of these processes are explained through the method of multisited ethnography elaborated in a series of articles by George Marcus (Wood 2000a, 2000b). Chibnik's caveat about the application of the "social life of commodities" or "commodity chain" (and, by implication, multisited ethnographic) approaches to analyses of the trade in ethnic and tourist arts is apropos here: "A too narrow focus on one commodity may ignore relevant history, culture, and economics in particular localities; a too broad study may result in superficial examination of important topics" (2003:10). Nevertheless, Marcus's method (see Marcus 1995) as applied by Wood is indispensable to the understanding of commodity culture(s).

Wood's eclectic approach raises many questions, not the least of which is that theories of "late capitalism" (Mandel 1978) and concepts like "flexible accumulation" (Harvey 1990) are most relevant to the study of advanced forms of industrial capital accumulation. These theories may not be appropriated unproblematically to explain the role of petty commodity production and petty capitalism in the "global factory" simply because of the diversity and complexity of the petty enterprise sector—even when examined in terms of specific national economies, much less globally (Blim 1992:14–16). From my perspective, the best-case scenario for linking enterprises in this sector to the international division of labor occurs through the "backward or local linkage" effect in contexts like the Asian Tiger industrialization (Wilson 1992:23–26, 121–26) or in special cases like the lower Rio Grande corridor handmade brick industry, where petty enterprises are dependent on larger ones (Cook 1998). In these cases, it is a relatively straightforward exercise to map the production and realization of commodity value through class relations linking petty enterprises to larger-scale enterprises. The linkage logic, however, is driven by the large, not the petty, enterprises.[11]

Petty enterprise in the Mexican ethnic/tourist crafts sector, much of which is a product of long-gestating indigenous development differentially geared to the market (such as local/regional utilitarian vs. national/international tourist), does not participate in the "global factory" (Rothstein and Blim 1992) in the same way that petty enterprises in the noncraft sector do. There may be parallels in organizational, design, and marketing shifts in Mexican craft production to those occurring in the noncraft sector (Wood 2000b), but these are probably coincidental rather than linked to some "global factory" capital accumulation logic.

The fact remains, however, that explanations of enterprise behavior derived from propositions about flexible accumulation, outsourcing, and so on are most convincing when applied to large-scale manufacturing enterprises of wage and capital goods competing in the international market (Wilson 1992:50–60). Such explanations, of course, are usually productionist in orientation and are deficient in addressing consumer demand and the consumption side of commodity circulation. This is where the type of approach Wood favors can make a difference.

Wood's work on Zapotec treadle-loom weaving exposes a tendency in culturalist approaches to subordinate the economic content of production to an all-encompassing notion of cultural production so that the multisited fieldworker follows the use-/symbolic-/sign-value component in craft commodities to the neglect of their exchange-value component. This is puzzling since the goal of capturing and/or accumulating exchange value is really the prime mover of the entire enterprise-organized and enterprise-channeled process of commodity production and circulation. In one of Wood's articles, for example, the reader is told that Zapotec weavers' "participation in the Santa Fe [New

Mexico] economy has dramatically changed the organization of production of Zapotec textiles to the point where they are no longer produced solely in Teotitlán nor solely by the Zapotec" so that "the production of a Zapotec textile begins and ends with a business in the United States" (2000a:135).

This dramatic statement is embellished by a seductive research agenda regarding 1) the distribution of Zapotec textile production across an increasingly dispersed social and geographic space that supposedly fits a pattern typical of post-Fordist or disorganized capitalism, 2) Zapotec households as adaptively dispersed and flexible, and 3) a field of Zapotec textile production encompassing transnational social spaces inhabited by those with vested interests in defining and producing competing versions of Zapotec textiles (2000a:136). This provocative agenda evoked great expectations on my part, not the least of which that Wood had uncovered a type of intermediary capital-driven regime of commodity production resembling the one I mapped in chapter 8 for the lower Rio Grande corridor handmade brick industry (Cook 1998:chap. 10).

Yet my reading of Wood's discussions of flexible production and post-Fordist capitalism, flexible households, and flexible fieldwork produced a relatively low yield of new knowledge about material production. For example, several Teotitecan families have stores, gift shops, or market stalls in Tijuana or important cultural spaces where Zapotec textiles are created, such as the back rooms of galleries in Santa Fe where colors and designs for a new line of textiles are conjured up or Texas where mohair is blended and cleaned before shipment to Oaxaca or a Teotiteca who lives several months a year in southern Colorado weaving in the showroom of a gallery (Wood 2000a:143–44). My expectation was, at the very least, that the reader would be presented with evidence of a significant spatial relocation of Zapotec weavers from Oaxaca to New Mexico at the initiative of Santa Fe–based intermediary capital.

On balance, Wood's dramatic rhetoric about late capitalism, post-Fordism, flexible production, multisited ethnography, and so on may overstate the case for Gringo, rather than Zapotec, agency in his account, and he seems to be only peripherally interested, if at all, in exchange value. His focus is exclusively on use/symbolic/sign value (that is, cultural production). His neglect of exchange value might have been partially justifiable had he provided more information about Zapotec woven goods from the perspective of the consumer. His pursuit of the circulation of these commodities, however, terminated in the shops of the Santa Fe dealers, not in the sites (or minds) of the ultimate consumers. It would be interesting to all of us to learn a great deal more about the penetration of the "southwestern-style" market by Zapotec woven goods—from everyone's perspective (including Navajo weavers) on all sides of the market. My guess is that the tale cannot be told unless exchange value assumes a front-and-center position in analysis.

Cultural production, for Wood, excludes the production and realization of exchange value. Thus, it is of no consequence in his analysis that he paradoxically emphasizes subcontracting and merchant/weaver relations while classifying the weaving enterprises in Teotitlán as representative of petty commodity production (2000a:145). In fact, that industry is organized around weaving enterprises that are either petty industrial capitalist units or dependent units in dispersed merchant capitalist manufactories employing pieceworkers. Unless the situation has changed greatly since the 1980s, when I last worked in Oaxaca, petty commodity enterprises comprise a subordinate element in treadle-loom weaving. A consideration of interbranch (and intrabranch) differences within the craft division of labor in the Oaxaca valley is essential to highlighting the uniqueness of the wool section of treadle-loom weaving (Chibnik 2003:119–22; Cook 1984b, 1993a; Cook and Binford 1990). The lack of such a comparative perspective might explain Wood's repeated references to capitalism as external to the local system, even though both of the industrial complexes within the treadle-loom branch of craft commodity production in the Oaxaca valley (that is, the Teotitlán del Valle–centered wool products industry and the Mitla-centered cotton products industry) has been identified by myself and others as a seedbed of indigenous capitalist and local entrepreneurial development (Cohen 1999:47–51; Cook 1984b, 1986; Cook and Binford 1990:123–27; Stephen 1993:42–43).

Wood's appropriation of the "global factory" approach to petty production (Rothstein and Blim 1992), as already noted, implies that theories intended to explain the dynamics of branches of industry based on machinofacture apply equally to low-tech "craft" manufacture. Translocality and flexible production in treadle-loom weaving (Wood 2000a, 2000b) are one thing, whereas outsourcing, just-in-time inventorying, and computer-controlled machinery in industries like apparel, footwear, furniture, jewelry, toys, and building materials (such as bricks), not to mention home appliances and motor vehicles, are quite another (cf. Cook 1998:279–83; Wilson 1992:chap. 7). In all these branches, subcontracting may, indeed, link relatively small firms to large firms, thus resembling the relationship that exists in craft industries organized by putting-out arrangements. But this resemblance can be misleading since it glosses over many differences in labor process, labor/capital relations, enterprise scale, and associated logics. This same line of reasoning applies a fortiori to Chibnik's study of wood carvers (2003), where fixed capital inputs are much less significant than they are in treadle-loom weaving.

The nature of demand sets limits on "flexibility" in craft industries like treadle-loom weaving and brick making. Whether in the Zapotec weaving industry or in the Reynosa handmade brick industry, capital is restrained in its capacity to enhance labor productivity through mechanization, more so in the former case than in the latter. If the line between machine made and handmade is violated by capital intensification, the market for "handmade" commodities disappears. Moreover, in an ethnified industry like that of Teotitlán del Valle and unlike the Reynosa brick industry, the specific identity of labor is also restricted both by the naturally monopolistic nature of the regional division of labor and specialization and by the ethnic-origin-sensitive market niche for woven goods. Consequently, capital must use organizational or other strategies rather than mechanization to expand the output of craft commodities but in cases like that of Zapotec weaving in Teotitlán del Valle must also employ labor from an ethnically restricted labor pool. Such constraints do not operate in noncraft branches of capitalist industry.[12]

Nevertheless, all is by no means lost in Wood's case simply because his provocative multisited focus on the creation and circulation of use/symbolic/sign value in the Zapotec weaving industry can be improved, integrated with preexisting analyses of exchange value in that branch of production, and then, it is hoped, further combined with his own analysis of exchange value based on new data to provide important new understandings of craft commodity production in NAFTAmerica. There are, after all, many tens (and perhaps hundreds) of thousands of Mexican artisans whose livelihood depends on the circulation of the products of their labor power rather than of their labor power itself in the burgeoning U.S. (and Canadian) "interior-design accouterments" (Wood 2000a:4) market, not only in the "southwestern or Santa Fe style" but in whatever styles the market will bear.[13]

CONCLUSIONS

The NAFTA project builds upon existing processes of continentalization of the border economy and of "*norteñización*" (northernization) (Alarcón 1992) of social infrastructures of communities of "commodity migrants" (Bustamante 1978) in Mexico. As the Mexican and U.S. economies become more integrated, according to Alarcón (1992:305–6), particular Mexican communities specialize in the production of international commodity migrants "through changes in their economic and social structure," thereby establishing close connections between specific areas in Mexico and the United States labor market (Torres Sarmiento 2002:68–69). Once NAFTA is fully implemented, pre-NAFTA discourse surrounding issues like undocumented migrants, "green-carders," or "cheap labor" seems destined to be either superseded or transformed into issues of continental economy, not border economy. Orme is right to assert that "there can never be a true common market in North America if goods and capital can cross borders freely but workers cannot" (1996:316; cf. Cook 2001:14).

The U.S.–Mexico borderlands will remain significant sites of distinctive, historically shaped settlements and cultures but will be more significant as zones of transit for flows of people, commodities, and information moving bidirectionally along north–south axes into the interiors of two nation-states that, together with Canada, share the North American continent. This complicates the process of economic anthropological knowledge production since, inevitably, the boundaries of border-specific phenomena will become more tenuous or porous, just as some of those phenomena are more widely diffused. On the other hand, the process of unique borderlands' development will continue to be stimulated by NAFTA, thus increasing the stakes for twenty-first-century economic anthropology in borderland studies.

This subfield must continue to evolve through studies of the maquiladora sector (Fernández-Kelly 1983; Wilson 1992) but must also expand into the nonmaquiladora sector as well. The handmade brick industry provides one example of many possible contributions to knowledge production that can derive from studies of the nonmaquiladora sector (Cook 1998, 2001). The artistic crafts studies by Chibnik (2003) and Wood (2000a, 2000b) that pursue commodity chains in NAFTAmerica provide others. The borderlands provide an especially fertile ground for the study of themes like identity (Vila 2000), economic otherness, and commodity culture within a broad framework of a posited "regional discursive formation" (Peet 1997:38) premised on the linkage between culture and economy through the mediation of subjectivity (1997:37).

Clearly, the massive expansion of circular migration in geographic and economic space has multiple consequences for life in sending and receiving communities. Thanks to recent studies like those by scholars Socorro Torres Sarmiento (2002), Leigh Binford (2002), and Jeffrey Cohen (2001), we know a great deal about the local-level dynamic and impact of circular migration and remittance in sending communities but much less regarding the impact of circular migration on receiving communities. My familiarity with two such receiving communities—Hendersonville, North Carolina, and Willimantic, Connecticut—suggests that the impact in both is significant economically, socioculturally, and politically. Both towns, for example, have new businesses catering to the needs of Mexican immigrants, and public services (fire, police, education, religion, and health services) inevitably have experienced increased demand for services from that population. In Willimantic, the Mexican population has become part of the wider "Hispanic" sector (mainly Puerto Rican and Dominican), whereas in Hendersonville, it stands alone as the exotic Hispanic minority. But these impressions are no substitute for systematic study of the impact of migration on receiving communities.

The issue of Mexican immigration to the United States—and its many subissues, like remittances, forward and backward linkages, legality versus illegality, identity (ethnic/national/gender), exploitation, human rights, and so on—is more critical today than it was when Manuel Gamio addressed it in his pioneering study in the 1920s. The futures of all three national economies in NAFTAmerica are officially committed to a neoliberal market fundamentalist policy that places transnational corporate capital in a hegemonic position in the globalization process but leaves the immigration question in limbo.

Indeed, the problems of the working classes in these countries are overshadowed by their common subjection to the agenda of transnational capital, which results in outsourcing, downscaling, and segmenting production and exaggerating productivity and profit concerns to the degree that all categories and ranks of labor are increasingly alienated, sweated, and defensive. Agricultural labor and computer engineering labor—indeed, all categories of labor according to classifications by skill, sector, nationality, ethnicity, gender, and so on—are directly experiencing the impact of globalization in ways that place more of a burden on workers to defend or advance their material interests while limiting their capacity to effect change for the better.

NOTES

1. In his introduction to the 1971 Dover edition of Gamio's book, John Burma phrases this differently: "Dr. Gamio was one of the few persons perceptive enough to recognize the importance of this immigration, and to study it in accordance with what then were the best methodological techniques" (1971a:v).

2. Wells makes a convincing argument that undocumented workers, because of the "political construction" of their labor market status, in their strategy to avoid the *migra* (Border Patrol) "aim not for the highest-paying, largest ranches, but for the medium and smaller ranches in more secluded locations, where they are more likely to develop a personal relationship with the grower or foreman and to have access to a barn, a shed, over even a protected gully, for shelter" (1996:161). Refreshingly, she also gives a more balanced picture of how wage and working conditions are negotiated in shifting ways conjuncturally and locally (1996:chap. 5).

3. Trouillot (2001:128–29) argues convincingly that it is important to recognize that such developments represent not so much deepened globalization as they do "fragmented globality."

4. My rereading of Gamio's (1971a) pioneering study of Mexican immigration to the United States for this book reminded me that his exhaustive research, including official census data, demonstrated the presence of Mexican immigrants, mostly working class, in every state of the United States since 1900. His own innovative method of tracking U.S. postal money-order remittances to Mexico for 1926 showed that "with the exception of Maine, Vermont, and North and South Carolina, Mexican immigrants sent money to Mexico . . . from all the states in the American union" (1971a:29).

5. In economic anthropology, Josiah Heyman (1994) made a pioneering contribution to the study of consumption and its impact on local culture and identity in a Sonoran section of the border. From a different perspective, I have also attempted to address the impact of consumption and demand on output in the border brick industry

(1998:esp. chap. 12). Both contributions strike me as being compatible with Appadurai's thesis that the demand for commodities is part of a wider process of cultural production (1986:29–41). In contrast to Appadurai (1986:3), I am not prepared to abandon the linkage between the labor process of commodity production and commodity value and to conceptualize the latter exclusively as a creature of exchange. I do agree with his effort to broaden the meaning of the commodity category beyond capitalism and with his emphasis that commodities may be regarded as "existing in a very wide range of societies (though with a special intensity and salience in modern, capitalist societies)" (1986:6–7).

6. The record on agriculture in contemporary Mexico is admittedly inconsistent and varies greatly by region. For example, the situation in the La Laguna region of the border state of Coahuila is relatively bleak for agriculture because of a combination of factors, ranging from drought, decline in cotton prices, and policy reforms, so that "agriculture is now surpassed by industry as a source of income" (Van Dooren and Zárate-Hoyos 2003:575). In Yucatan, on the other hand, although the "very divide between urban and rural is blurred by the increasing importance of non-agricultural income derived from the younger generation's participation in the urban labour markets," there is a notable "return to some form of indigenous agricultural activity especially by the older members" (2003:586).

7. It is not my intention to imply that Mexican immigrant workers can set in place the relations of production in California or other U.S. agricultural settings. Rather, I wish to emphasize that their enculturated agency helps them maneuver/negotiate within those structures, perhaps in a way that impacts on work conditions or value share. My assumption is that any experience Mexican workers have in Mexican agricultural labor markets will be potentially helpful to them in U.S. labor markets. Obviously, the closer the relations experienced in Mexico to those experienced in the United States, the better. But any experience vis-à-vis, for example, strawberry production in Mexico—even in small capitalist horticultural enterprises—is better than none. The reason for my emphasis is simply to counter the notion that Mexican labor is naive, helpless, and mercilessly exploitable in its encounter with Gringo capital. I do not refer to agency with a necessary implication that its exercise is collective or involves coordinated or organized activity like unionization. It is exercised by individual subjects (or agents) to achieve their perceived material interests; it may or may not be socially coordinated or organized and typically involves coping with existing structural conditions rather than changing them for new ones (changing employers as a means to get higher wages or better working conditions rather than engaging in a social protest to get all employers to provide higher wages or better working conditions).

Regarding sharecropping in California agriculture, the resurgence of which surprised Wells (1996:2–3), our understanding would be strengthened by a comparative approach—first in specifying exactly what its constituent elements are and second in explaining its resurgence. No matter how unique the California situation may be, something significant can be learned about it by drawing on case studies in other capitalisms, including the Mexican variety.

8. The concept of so-called free labor in a capitalist economy is problematic, even in the absence of ethnic, gender, or other kinds of market segmentation or other imperfections. For Marx, laborers' freedom to sell labor power is illusory not simply because of subsistence need but because there is no wage equivalent for a critical part

of the working day sold to the capitalist (that is, that part that yields surplus labor or surplus value). According to Marx (1967, 3:819), "Capital obtains . . . surplus-labour without an equivalent, and in essence it always remains forced labour—no matter how much it may seem to result from free contractual agreement" (cf. 1977, 1:415). In other words, so-called free labor is, in fact, forced by the invisible hand of surplus value. To argue that undocumented Mexican labor in the United States is unfree because "workers' formally illegal status impedes free movement about the labor market and thus prevents the sale of labor power on the best available terms" (Binford 2003:332 n. 24) makes sense only from the perspective of neoliberal market fundamentalism that assumes an absence of imperfections in factor markets. In those niches of the labor market accessed largely through social networks, it is reasonable to assume that most undocumented workers are aware of more than one employment option and do have some degree of choice regarding terms and conditions of employment. They also have the "advantage" of binational mobility between home and foreign sources of employment, even if qualified by the risk factor.

9. I am aware that there is considerable asymmetry in agriculture, as in other branches of the NAFTA economy, favoring U.S. capital (including farm operation in Mexico), which supports the predominant thesis of Mexican dependency. Nevertheless, the labor supply side of the Mexico–California connection provides overwhelming ontological support for the antithesis. The work of scholars like Kearney (1995), Mines (1981), and Zabin et al. (1993) shows some of the explanatory potential of such a focus.

10. Chibnik (2003:esp. chap. 12) does a comprehensive job, from a refreshingly straightforward, non-Marcusized perspective, of analyzing the sales of Oaxaca carvings in the United States and provides a good model for future research—although it did not explore extensively the end consumer's perspective on these fascinating craft commodities. All those with tendencies to wax romantic or celebrate indigenous ethnicity with regard to Mexican crafts must read Chibnik's conclusion (2003:242–43).

11. My rereading of Harvey's chapter "Flexible Accumulation—Solid Transformation or Temporary Fix?" reinforces this contention. His discussion, to the degree that it gets specific, is focused primarily on machinofacture sectors of the world economy like auto production in the United States, Japan, or South Korea. His reference to "more traditional production systems (such as those of Singapore, Taiwan, or Hong Kong) resting on 'artisanal,' paternalistic, or patriarchal (familial) labour relations . . . [that] have undoubtedly grown (even within the advanced capitalist countries) since 1970, often at the expense of the Fordist factory assembly line," fails to identify specific industries. I doubt, however, that he is referring to artistic handicraft industries like treadle-loom weaving or wood carving. If so, in my opinion, he has overextended his thesis. Moreover, in a later publication, Harvey argues that if in fact new types of accumulation like a post-Fordist flexibility principle are operating in global capitalism, they will have concrete spatial expressions. "New territorial divisions of labor and concentrations of people and labor power, new resource extraction activities and markets" (Harvey 1996:295). Such concrete spatial expressions have not occurred in artistic craft industries like treadle-loom weaving or wood carving, with the possible exception of market expansions that, in any case, follow the capriciousness of consumer vogues rather than accumulation crises related to the labor process of commodity production.

12. This proviso apparently is put into question by market forces making caveat emptor ever more the rule in the ethnic arts and craft market. According to Wood (2000a:135), the southwestern/Santa Fe–style designs (many of which are of Navajo origin) are being produced for Santa Fe–based enterprises by outworkers in the Oaxaca valley. To the degree that "design" or "style" is more important than ethnic origin in the market, this trend will undoubtedly grow in importance.

13. There are no reliable census data on artisans in Mexico. The figure of ten million indigenous artisans has been cited recently. In 1995, Fonart estimated that there were about 100,000 potters (*alfareros*) in Mexico. However, a 1998 survey by the Instituto Nacional de Estadística, Geografía e Informática (INEGI), reported 8,436 pottery manufacturing units in Mexico with nearly twelve thousand workers (Amador Tello 2002:64).

Afterword

Commodity Culture(s), Economic Value, and the Future

There is a subtle yet fundamental relationship between the objectivity of economically derived logics and the subjectivity of agency/identity. Richard Peet convincingly argues that the logic of economic action, understood as the "reasons people have for behaving in certain ways as economic agents . . . is formed, and displayed discursively, in the rationalized structures of explanations agents offer for their economic behaviour and the reasons they give for their overall success or failure" (1997:37–38). This rationality implies both motives for behavior as well as ethics that justify it. As logic and motive, Peet continues, "rationalities derive from the broader experiences of socialized and encultured persons; they are signs of identities, rather than being divined from the inherent structural logics of economic systems" (1997:37–38). The systemic logics of economic forms are created through the repetition of rationalized actions. In sum, according to Peet, "economic forms are culturally created, economically maintained, interact with subjective processes of agents' identity formation, and to a degree are self-generating or at least self-maintaining" (1997:37–38). Peet's thoughtful statement provides a fertile point of departure for identifying and discussing some general implications of my analysis of commodity culture(s).

Prudent rationality at the core of commodity culture(s) in Mexico/Mesoamerica has a continuity, consistency, and relatively autonomous dynamic for at least two reasons: 1) agents derive power from their positions within existing economic forms, and 2) elites culturally represent economic logics as naturally efficacious (cf. Peet 1997). This means that, historically, the construction of hegemony by elite fractions is facilitated by the subjective dimension of commodity economy present among subaltern fractions.

Even revolution and crisis in Mexico during the twentieth century were unable to alter this connection, which conflates "penny capitalism" with "dollar capitalism" as it reproduces the dominance of capital.

The carriers and producers of Mexican commodity culture(s), the economic agents whose repetitive acts of value production and alienation, are real people with sociocultural and class identities (which, incidentally, have both objective and subjective dimensions). Their repetitive acts of value production and alienation imply culturally informed participation in a social division of labor and specialization as well as in different commodity exchange modes (such as barter, gifting, reciprocity, and market sale) and destinations (such as utilitarian consumption, festive or ceremonial consumption, and conspicuous or prestige consumption) that modulate how the logic is played out, or how exchange value is realized by agents of alienated labor (that is, what kind of equivalency—monetary or in-kind, immediate or deferred, and so on).

This process implies objective economic action of value production followed by exchange as a prelude to consumption. The objective structure itself is a product of sociocultural processes involving "socialized and encultured" person–agents exercising prudent rationality. Each and every branch of the commodity-producing division of labor and specialization and every specific social relation of production and distribution is culturally informed and is a source of cultural reproduction and/or innovation.

In addition, agents' identity is objectively and subjectively at stake through their activity as carriers and makers of commodity culture(s). The quest for equivalency or accumulation of exchange value and/or for the consumption of use value by economic agents as alienated laborers will feed back into their self-images and/or consciousness of their social locations as well as impact on their objective social locations (that is, upward, downward, or horizontal mobility is contingent).

There is a complementarity between agents' involvement in value circuits. The realization or accumulation of exchange value directly facilitates consumption of use value and, therefore, may reinforce either consensual judgments on intrinsic aesthetic values or their instrumentalization as an aid to "strategies of distinction" (Bourdieu 1984; Sayer 1997:23). For example, peasant-artisan petty capitalists clearly pursue exchange value as well as use value in the sense of sign value (Baudrillard 1981:65–66). That is, they may choose to rechannel exchange value (as purchasing power for additional means of production or labor power) into status-enhancing ceremonial expenditures (such as purchase of a new saint's image for the home altar or church, possibly in conjunction with sponsorship of a *mayordomía*). Obviously, a similar connection between exchange-value realization and the consumption of use value as sign value exists in the commodity cultures of all class locations within Mexican capitalism.

Although the sign value of commodities (that is, "their symbolic significance as means by which lifestyles and identities can be constructed" [Sayer 1997:18]) must be taken into account, I agree with Sayer that it "has certainly not replaced exchange value as the regulator of economic activity in capitalism" (1997:18). To assert that such a displacement has occurred would be tantamount to "agreeing that the consumer demand for lean pork drives the re-organization of the swine industry from production of pigs to slaughter" (Paul Durrenberger, personal communication). The other side of the coin, however, is illustrated by the fact that pork is essentially decommoditized by sign value among Middle Easterners (Islamic/Jewish); it is removed from the realm of preferred consumables by religious fiat. Among Islamics, the meat preference is slanted toward lamb, hence an organized industry dedicated to the production and slaughter of that tasty animal and hence the need to add sign value to exchange and use value in conceptualizing commodity value.

The logics of commodity cultures are accessible dialogically. They are present in agents' consciousness and, therefore, are subjects of agents' explanations, attitudes, and opinions. In Peet's terms, Mexican commodity cultures comprise a "discursive formation" (1997:38). This does not mean that such a formation is without an unconscious or subconscious dimension, but it does mean that speculation about these is not essential to production of knowledge regarding its intended and unintended consequences. It also implies that discursive spheres do not exist in the absence of particular social relations of production and distribution of commodity value.

Finally, as an economic form, commodity cultures are premised on labor alienation. Consequently, their production and reproduction occurs because of repetitive labor alienation and because alienated laborers as economic agents are socialized and encultured people. Clearly, there can be no commodity cultures without commodity value—exchange value, use value, and sign value do not drop from the sky but are historically and socioculturally constituted through specific relations of production and distribution.

Commodity culture(s) is akin to a Weberian "ideal type" in the sense that it is a "construction based on the deliberate and one-sided accentuation of certain 'real' conditions in accordance with the idiosyncratic values and interests of the investigator" (Hindess and Hirst 1975:2). But I have also attempted to conceptualize this cultural construct according to my interpretation of Marx's method of political economy—perhaps combining his own way of conceptualizing the capitalist mode of production with Lenin's study of the "conditions of a determinate concrete social formation" (1975:4). In any case, I agree with Hindess and Hirst that "it is the general concepts that make possible the analysis of the concrete" 1975:4). It is just as important to emphasize that the concretization of general concepts occurs only through the identification and study of specific time-and-place social relations of production and related distribution of economic value.

For centuries, commodity cultures have developed in counterpoint to pervasive labor alienation in the economic life of Mexico's indigenous peasants. These cultural developments are at once specific to particular classes or class fractions and other (for example, geographic, ethnic, and gender) population segments and more generalized. As transmitted and innovated funds of knowledge, commodity cultures encompass a vast and diverse repertory of beliefs, attitudes, stories, and other symbolic forms of conscious expression that stimulate, reflect, and give meaning to economic interaction and define economic identities. The innovative nature of commodity culture(s) reflects the productive and reproductive role of particular social relations of production and distribution. Economic anthropology in Mexican studies has implicitly recognized and exhaustively documented general and specific expressions of commodity culture(s) and their social relations but has not given them the theoretical attention they deserve. For example, the identification of several generations of ethnographers working in the Oaxaca valley of the "Zapotecs" propensity to monetize and to perceive and evaluate things, events, and behavior from the perspective of a trader (Cook 1982:94; cf. Beals 1975:186–87; Leslie 1960:6771; Malinowski and de la Fuente 1957:23; Parsons 1936:12–13, 445) has not been exhaustively studied locally, regionally, or comparatively or in terms of its social relational distribution.

Such a study could begin by focusing on recurring clichés in popular economic discourse as indicative of the moral or normative structure of the economy, as, for example, with those describing economic personality types as the "*persona legal*" (honest or custom abiding) and the "*persona tramposa*" (deceiver or cheat) (Cook 1982:95). There are also idiomatic expressions or terms that are employed by specific class fractions of rural or transnational migrant Mexican working people, as, for example, the reference to "Juan Garabato," a mythical petty commodity producer who is perpetually in a situation of having to "*vender barato y comprar caro*" (sell cheap and buy dear), the expression "*la necesidad obliga*" (need obliges) (Cook 1982:282–83; Cook and Binford 1990:58–59), "*haciendo la lucha*" (making ends meet) (Good 1988:15), or "*el gasto*" (the amount of money required to obtain what is necessary to sustain the family (Torres Sarmiento 2002:165). Recording and interpreting these elements of expressive, conversational culture would help put flesh and blood into the meat-and-bones profiles of economic performance and its quantified results, but it would have to also be accompanied by a systematic analysis of consciousness and identity corresponding to specific locations in local/regional economic class structure or division of labor and specialization.

In any case, commodity culture interactively permeates objective economic structure; it is the other side of the coin of structure without which the latter is socially meaningless. It is pointless in economic anthropology to describe a specific social division of labor and specialization or class structure without showing how real subjects interact with their total environment through their use of cultural information and symbols to produce, exchange, and consume commodities. I have tried to follow this approach in my studies of metate culture (1982) in the Oaxaca valley and of brick culture (1984a) there and on the Texas–Mexico border (1998). The same intent, admittedly less visible, was present in my more comprehensive study of rural petty industry in the Oaxaca valley (Cook and Binford 1990) that focused on social differentiation.[1]

There is no question that, from the perspective of the evolution of commodity economy, Marx was right to emphasize the transformative nature of the commoditization of labor. Through this reproduction process, which can be represented symbolically as C^{LP}–M^{W}–Cn (wage goods), workers exchange the use value of the only commodity they possess, their labor power, in return for a money wage that they must convert into "commodities sufficient to reproduce their own existence" (Harvey 1982:46). It is also axiomatic that under such conditions, which predominate in capitalist economies, direct producers have only a modicum of influence over the price of their labor power (wages) and none whatsoever over its value (its reproductive equivalent in wage goods) (cf. Harvey 1982:47–52). The fundamental alienation of wage workers who produce value they do not consume and consume value they do not directly produce, while more attenuated in its effect on value deliberations compared, for example, to petty commodity producers, is not completely disengaged from such deliberations, as exemplified in such diverse cases as California strawberry production and Texas–Mexico border brick production.

Much of the behavior of Mexico's peasant artisans recorded by ethnographers regarding price inquisitiveness, propensities to monetize or to perceive and evaluate things like a trader, marketplace haggling over price in money or in kind, wage disputes, disputes between spouses over control of household budgets or the disposition of earnings, and narratives or other representations of relations of production or exchange or distribution are part and parcel of commodity economy (Cook 1976:416; cf. Rubin 1972). These and many other behaviors are not, as Foster (1988:122) would have us believe, products of subconscious cognition of absolute scarcity, an abstract image of limited good, but rather reflect conscious responses to labor alienation and to the economic consequences of the social organization of Mexico's commodity economy.[2]

Cultural expressions of labor alienation essentially mirror the economic consequences of its social organization; that is, they are increasingly compartmentalized and asymmetrical as they reflect greater involvement in and dependency on capitalist markets or as the social organization becomes more complex in its differentiation. For example, whereas peasant-artisan producer–sellers are more apt to express frustration regarding buyers-up or merchant capitalists and regarding commercial capitalists or sellers of machinofactured commodities, piece-wage workers are more apt to combine complaints about wage-good prices with complaints about employers low or irregularly paid wages. But, as I noted earlier, in a capitalist economy the agency of workers as subalterns is very much constrained by their dependency on capital for employment and subsistence.

Commodity culture impacted by general-purpose money always tends to focus consciousness directly on the value question and, more specifically, on the ratio between own labor and other labor as mediated in the market. Logically, this is not simply a quantitative ratio reckoned in utilitarian terms with varying degrees of precision but is a qualitative ratio representing social relations not only between different sets of laborers who create value but also between them and those who intervene in its realization (that is, as merchant or commercial capitalists) or those who (in capitalist production) organize it. Depending on prevailing objective conditions at particular times and places, commodity culture may be expressed as economic class (for example, independent direct producer, piece-rate outworker or other wage worker, worker–owner, or employer) or status (for example, as a consumer, a woman, or an Indian) consciousness. Its expressions can range from inchoate to varying degrees of relative coherency.

There is no certainty that such expressions will occur, much less that they will have political ramifications. There are a multiplicity of possible political ramifications, ranging from none to low-intensity resistance at the point of production or realization of value to high-intensity class warfare within a given social landscape. Since commodity cultures are only one source of class and status consciousness, albeit ones with a historical record as a social force, among many other competing sources, it is never easy to predict under what specific circumstances such forms will become significant movers of subject behavior.

Moreover, there is a slippery maze of possible connections and disconnections between competing cultural fields that imperil the direct link from economic value to social organization to social consciousness. This slippery maze tends to become more disconnective in state-organized societies and especially so under corporate capitalism where a combination of massed private and public sector power is focused precisely on disconnective operations at every level of the social formation. This process is relatively successful in the United States, as evidenced in 2001–2002 with the exposure of massive corporate fraud that ramified asymmetrically throughout the economy with life-shattering consequences for class fractions dependent on corporate employment and/or investment in a stock market reliable in the long run only for rewarding insider trading. This led to palliative legislative reforms, punishment for a few egregious corporate offenders, and a diffuse, inchoate response from the shattered class fractions that may or may not, at some point, be measurable at the ballot box.

In Mexico, on the other hand, peasant subjects' collective actions appear to be reflective of conscious awareness of current or anticipated economic value squeezes linked to their particular social locations in the national class structure. This is illustrated by the recent example of the uprising of Texcoco *ejidal* communities (most prominently San Salvador Atenco) over imminent expropriations by the federal government of 13,000-plus hectares of agricultural land for airport construction that caused the Fox administration to cancel the airport project. It is also illustrated by the ongoing neo-Zapatista rebellion in Chiapas that continues to defy a federal government solution and where land poverty and subsistence crisis appear to be significant causal factors.

Admittedly, most expressions of commodity culture are much less dramatic and much more part and parcel of the normal routines of everyday existence. Rather than threatening the disruption of family and community reproduction cycles, they reinforce these cycles and cushion their contraction or facilitate their expansion. They involve drawing on and, when appropriate, modifying intergenerationally transmitted funds of knowledge necessary to inform and facilitate work, the acquisition of consumption, and similar economic activities that ensure subsistence and define and substantiate identity. As already mentioned, this facilitates the maintenance of hegemony by elites who simply have to identify themes that tap into the commodity cultural matrix in conjuncturally appropriate ways.

If the Mexican economy has been historically configured through its participation in a Mesoamerican cultural process, it has been continentalized in an unprecedented way through the late twentieth- and early twenty-first-century implementation of NAFTA. As a result of the latter process, the Mexican economy has institutionally become part of a North American economy—a transborder, transnational space through which people, commodities, and information circulate across national boundaries under a regime of progressive, if selective, government deregulation. The twenty-first-century development of the Mexican economy will be marked by a dialectic between its dual identification with NAFTAmerica and Mesoamerica as well as by its changing pattern of participation in the extracontinental global economy.

The neoliberal capitalist impulse behind NAFTA looks toward the future and holds out the possibility of parlaying common-market integration into the formation of a wider North American community comparable to the European Community. Among the many obstacles NAFTA faces, the most formidable is how to democratize its implementation and administration so that the transnational corporate power behind it is counterbalanced by the public interest of its trinational citizenries and labor constituencies. To the extent that this democratization fails and public input is either ignored or co-opted, resulting disputes within and between its member nation-states could jeopardize the entire NAFTA project. Like every capitalist project for economic reform since World War II, the success of this one will depend on its "pacing and sequencing" to ensure that job creation exceeds job destruction and that institutions are put in place to cope with risk, "including effective safety nets" (Stiglitz 2002:87).

One of the principal loci of resistance to the NAFTA project has come from the Chiapas-based neo-Zapatista movement (Ejército Zapatista de Liberación Nacional) headed by subcommandant Marcos, who in 1994 led an uprising that coincided with the inauguration of the NAFTA/TLC (Tratado de Libre Comercio) (Berger 2001:149). This movement has selectively appropriated elements from Mexico's Mesoamerican past and seeks to revert the unicultural national vision of the 1917 Constitution to a pluricultural one that would decentralize and fragment the Mexican state into a pluriethnic entity consisting of a congeries of "distinct ethno-linguistic communities each striving to safeguard its identity" (Hamnett 1999:21). This would also entail a redefinition of the meanings of citizenship and patriotism while nurturing primordial ethnolinguistic loyalties lost or attenuated as a result of the acculturative process of colonialism among many segments of the peasantry (cf. Cook and Joo 1995:33–34; Hernández Díaz 2001b:7–10, 325–44; Stavenhagen 1992). The economic vision of the leadership of this anti-NAFTA movement, together with its intellectual sympathizers, not only is anticapitalist but also is in denial about the commodity cultural heritage of Mesoamerica, preferring instead to advocate utopian notions of communal natural economy sustained through principles of reciprocity and redistribution where subsistence is the rule and accumulation the exception.

Despite NAFTA and global market strategizing by multinational corporations and international financial and trade organizations and organized resistance to it, it is at the level of specific work sites, industries, and communities that most struggles between capital and labor related to value distribution, working conditions, standard of living, and quality of life will be waged. There is no more convincing demonstration of this than Miriam Wells's study of the role of Mexican immigrant labor in California agriculture where she ethnographically documents her thesis that "economic reconfigurations—too often portrayed as the inevitable and value-neutral outcomes of changing global economic structure—may instead be primarily the result of local sociopolitical conflicts" (1996:xv). Ideological expressions of globalism or antiglobalism ring hollow in the early twenty-first-century struggle in Mexico between continental integrationism, Mesoamerican commodity culture(s), and ethnopopulist utopianism. Whatever direction the future economic development of Mexico may take, including a difficult-to-imagine but possible reversion to a nationalist model that would reduce participation in the international economy and reconfigure national, regional, and local economies, the individual and cooperative exercise of prudent rationality by Mexican subjects in defense of and to advance their perceived material interests will be decisive.

There is an important message here that should be comforting to those in the United States who are threatened by or uneasy about the growing presence of Mexican migrants in our midst. It should also give pause to others who are quick to emphasize, even exoticize or romanticize, the cultural or ethnic differences between Mexicans and Americans. With regard to fundamental aspirations and considerations related to making and earning a living, including sociopolitical understandings, there is really very little difference between us. Too much has been made in the past of the concrete economic differences between our two countries represented in abstract, statistical terms (or in systemic terms regarding politics/political culture) as an asymmetrical First World–Third World divide. This notion of economic (and political) difference or "otherness" has been reinforced by a conflictive and controversial history that has shaped the international border between the United States and Mexico and reverberated in our respective national identities since the middle of the nineteenth century. It has also been accentuated by the impersonal, instrumental discourse of international capitalist development that has made "maquiladora," "*indocumentado*," and "cheap labor" household words in both countries. Against this litany of economic (and political) difference, the lesson to be gleaned from the record of study of Mexican/Mesoamerican commodity culture, from the highlands of Guatemala to the valleys of Oaxaca or Guerrero to the coasts of Veracruz and along the Rio Bravo side of the border, is that its bearers and fashioners, the peoples of this vast region south of the Rio Grande and Rio Bravo, think and act about making and earning their livelihood just as we would in their space. It is this fundamental recognition of our common humanity that should be uppermost in all our minds as we negotiate and struggle our respective ways together through NAFTAmerica in the twenty-first century.

NOTES

1. My reference to objective economic structure is derived from the concept of capitalist class structure but is broader in the sense that it emphasizes the social location of producers, exchangers, and consumers of commodity value without necessarily specifying the relation of surplus-value appropriation, which is central to the class structure of capitalism.

2. I am not disagreeing here with Raymond Williams's argument that "the characteristic world-view or general perspective of a class or other social group . . . will include formal and conscious beliefs but also less conscious, less formulated attitudes, habits and feelings, or even unconscious assumptions, bearings and commitments" (1981:26). I am asserting, however, that much of what I call "commodity culture" is within the realm of the "conscious" and "less conscious" and, therefore, can be assumed to inform subject behavior. This means that the ethnographer, through standard fieldwork procedures, can elicit expressions of commodity culture from informants related to past,

present, or anticipated behavior and that the results of behavior informed by commodity culture can be observed and, if appropriate, quantified for further analysis and interpretation. As far as I am concerned, economic anthropology should be focused mainly on this zone of commodity culture; the realm of the unconscious, as it relates to commodity culture, can be only a matter of speculation or, at most, of informed guesswork.

To the extent that the subjects in economic anthropological inquiry are objectively determined to be located in a specific class or class fraction, it is also necessary to heed Williams's warning that a "social class is by no means always culturally monolithic" (1981:74). However, I assume from his discussion of this point that as the observer–analyst moves from the larger social aggregate down to fractional social aggregates (that is, through the process of statistical disaggregation of a universe), in recognition of a process of internal differentiation, the probability for cultural variability lessens. At any rate, this was a tacit assumption in my study of Oaxaca valley peasant artisans (Cook and Binford 1990)

Bibliography

Aeppel, Timothy. 2003. "Three Countries, One Dishwasher." *Wall Street Journal*, October 6, B1, B8.

Aguirre Beltrán, Gonzalo. 1967. *Regiones de refugio*. Ediciones Especiales 46. Mexico: Instituto Indigenista Interamericano.

———. 1970. "Los símbolos étnicos de la identidad nacional." *Anuario Indigenista* 30 (December): 101–40.

Aguirre Beltrán, Gonzalo, and Ricardo Pozas. 1954. "Instituciones indígenas en el México actual." In *Métodos y resultados de la política indigenista en Mexico*. Edited by Alfonso Caso et al. Memorias del Instituto Nacional Indigenista VI. Mexico: Ediciones del Instituto Nacional Indigenista, 171–268.

Alarcón, Rafael. 1992. "Norteñization: Self-Perpetuating Migration from a Mexican Town." In *U.S.–Mexico Relations: Labor Market Interdependence*. Edited by Jorge Bustamante, Clark Reynolds, and Raul Hinojosa. Stanford, Calif.: Stanford University Press, 302–18.

Alba, Carlos H., and Jesus Cristerna. 1949a. "La agricultura entre los zapotecos." In *Los zapotecos: Monografía historica, etnografica y economica*. Edited by Lucio Mendieta y Nuñez et al. Mexico City: Imprenta Universitaria, 449–92.

———. 1949b. "Las industrias zapotecas." In *Los zapotecos: Monografía historica, etnografica y economica*. Edited by Lucio Mendieta y Nuñez et al. Mexico City: Imprenta Universitaria, 493–600.

Althusser, Louis. 1970. *For Marx*. New York: Vintage Books.

Althusser, L. L., and E. Balibar. 1970. *Reading Capital*. New York: Pantheon.

Amador Tello, Judith. 2002. "Fonart da un giro." *Proceso*, no. 1350 (September 15): 62–65.

Andrews, Anthony P. 1983. *Maya Salt Production and Trade*. Tucson: University of Arizona Press.

Appadurai, Arjun, ed. 1986. *The Social Life of Things: Commodities in Cultural Perspective*. Cambridge: Cambridge University Press.

Appendini, Kirsten. 2002. "The Challenges to Rural Mexico in an Open Economy." In *Mexico's Politics and Society in Transition*. Edited by Joseph S. Tulchin and Andrew D. Selee. Boulder, Colo.: Lynne Rienner, 255–75.

Arensberg, Conrad M. 1957. "Anthropology as History." In *Trade and Market in the Early Empires*. Edited by Karl Polanyi, Conrad M. Arensberg, and Harry W. Pearson. Glencoe, Ill.: Free Press, 97–113.

Báez-Jorge, Félix. 1978. "Prologo." In *La ciudad Mercado (Tlaxiaco)* by Alejandro Marroquín. Número 4 Colección INI (Clásicos de la Antropología Mexicana). Mexico, D.F.: Instituto Nacional Indigenista, 9–12.

Balibar, E. 1970. "The Basic Concepts of Historical Materialism." In *Reading Capital*. Edited by L. L. Althusser and E. Balibar. New York: Pantheon, 199–308.

Barabas, Alicia M., and Miguel A. Bartolomé, eds. 1999. *Configuraciones etnicas en Oaxaca: Perspectivas etnográficas para las autonomías. Vol. I: Introducción, macroetnias*. Mexico, D.F.: INAH-INI.

Barry, Tom, ed. 1992. *Mexico: A Country Guide*. Albuquerque, N.M.: Inter-Hemispheric Education Resource Center.

Bartra, Roger. 1974. *Estructura agraria y clases sociales en México*. Mexico City: Ediciones Era.

———. 1975. "La teoria del valor y la economía campesina: invitación a la lectura de Chayanov." *Comercio Exterior* 25, no. 5: 517–24.

Baudrillard, Jean. 1975. *The Mirror of Production*. St. Louis, Mo.: Telos Press.

———. 1981. *For a Critique of the Political Economy of the Sign*. St. Louis, Mo.: Telos Press; originally published as *Pour une critique de l'economie politique du signe* (Paris: Gallimard, 1972).

Bauer, Peter T., and Basil S. Yamey. 1957. *The Economics of Underdeveloped Countries*. Chicago: University of Chicago Press.

Baumann, Friederike. 1987. "B. Traven's Land des Frühlings and the Caoba Cycle as a Source for the Study of Agrarian Society." *In B. Traven: Life and Work*. Edited by Ernst Schürer and Philip Jenkins. University Park: Pennsylvania State University Press, 245–59.

Beals, Ralph L. 1946. *Cherán: A Sierra Tarascan Village*. Institute of Social Anthropology Publication no. 3. Washington, D.C.: Smithsonian Institution Press.

———. 1970. "Gifting, Reciprocity, Savings and Credit in Peasant Oaxaca." *Southwestern Journal of Anthropology* 26: 231–41.

———. 1975. *The Peasant Marketing System of Oaxaca, Mexico*. Berkeley: University of California Press.

———. 1976. "The Oaxaca Market Study Project: Origins, Scope, and Preliminary Findings." In *Markets in Oaxaca*. Edited by Scott Cook and Martin Diskin. Austin: University of Texas Press, 27–44.

Becerril Straffon, Rodolfo, and Adalberto Rios Szalay, eds. 1981. *Los artesanos nos dijeron. . .* Mexico City: Fondo Nacional para Actividades/Fondon Nacional para el Fomento de las Artesanías.

Belshaw, Cyril. 1965. *Traditional Exchange and Modern Markets*. Englewood Cliffs, N.J.: Prentice Hall.

———. 1969. *The Conditions of Social Performance*. London: Routledge & Kegan Paul.

———. 1979. "The Data Base in Economic Anthropology." In *Currents in Anthropology: Essays in Honor of Sol Tax*. Edited by Robert Hinshaw. The Hague: Mouton, 69–84.

Belshaw, Michael. 1967. *A Village Economy: Land and People of Huecorio*. New York: Columbia University Press.

Benson, John. 1983, *The Penny Capitalists: A Study of Nineteenth-Century Working Class Entrepreneurs*. New Brunswick, N.J.: Rutgers University Press.

Berdan, Frances F. 1985. "Markets in the Economy of Aztec Mexico." In *Economic Anthropology*. Edited by Stuart Plattner. Stanford, Calif.: Stanford University Press, 339–67.

———. 1989. "Trade and Markets in Precapitalist States." In *Economic Anthropology*. Edited by Stuart Plattner. Stanford, Calif.: Stanford University Press, 78–107.

Berger, Mark. 2001. "Romancing the Zapatistas: International Intellectuals and the Chiapas Rebellion." *Latin American Perspectives* 28, no. 2: 149–70.

Bernstein, Henry. 1979. "African Peasantries: A Theoretical Framework." *Journal of Peasant Studies* 6: 421–43.

Bettelheim, Charles. 1972. "Theoretical Comments." In *Unequal Exchange: A Study of the Imperialism of Trade*, by Arghiri Emmanuel. New York: Monthly Review Press, 271–322.

Bhaskar, Roy. 1991a. "Dialectics." In *A Dictionary of Marxist Thought*. 2nd ed. Edited by Tom Bottomore, Lawarence Harris, V. G. Kiernan, and Ralph Miliband. Oxford: Basil Blackwell, 143–50.

———. 1991b. "Determinism." In *A Dictionary of Marxist Thought*. 2nd ed. Edited by Tom Bottomore, Lawarence Harris, V. G. Kiernan, and Ralph Miliband. Oxford: Basil Blackwell, 139–41.

Binford, Leigh. 2002. "Social and Economic Contradictions of Rural Migrant Contract Labor between Tlaxcala, Mexico and Canada." *Culture & Agriculture* 24, no. 2: 1–19.

———. 2003. "Migrant Remittances and (Under) Development in Mexico." *Critique of Anthropology* 23, no. 3: 307–38.

Blim, Michael L. 1992. "Introduction: the Emerging Global Factory and Anthropology." In *Anthropology and the Global Factory: Studies of the New Industrialization in the Late Twentieth Century*. Edited by Frances A. Rothstein and Michael L. Blim. New York: Bergin and Garvey, 1–30.

Boeke, J. H. 1942. *The Structure of the Netherland Indies Economy*. New York: International Secretariat, Institute of Pacific Relations.

Bohannan, Paul, and George Dalton, eds. 1962. *Markets in Africa*. Evanston, Ill.: Northwestern University Press.

Bonfil Batalla, Guillermo. 1990. *México profundo: Una civilización negada*. 2nd ed. México, D.F.: Editorial Grijalbo.

———. 1996. *México Profoundo: Reclaiming a Civilization*. Austin: University of Texas Press. (first published in 1987 as *México profundo*: *Una civilización negada*. México, D.F.: Secretaría de Educación Pública)

Bonilla, F., and R. Morales, eds. 1998. *Borderless Borders: U.S. Latinos, Latin Americans, and the Paradox of Interdependence*. Philadelphia: Temple University Press.

Bottomore, Tom. 1985. *Theories of Modern Capitalism*. London: George Allen and Unwin.

———. 1991. "Economism." In *A Dictionary of Marxist Thought.* 2nd ed. Edited by Tom Bottomore, Lawrence Harris, V. G. Kiernan, and Ralph Miliband. Oxford: Basil Blackwell, 168–69.

Bottomore, Tom, Lawrence Harris, V. G. Kiernan, and Ralph Miliband, eds. 1991. *A Dictionary of Marxist Thought.* 2nd ed. Oxford: Basil Blackwell.

Bourdieu, Pierre. 1977. *Outline of a Theory of Practice.* Cambridge: Cambridge University Press.

———. 1984. *Distinction: A Social Critique of the Judgement of Taste.* Cambridge, Mass.: Harvard University Press.

———. 1990. *In Other Words: Essays towards a Reflexive Sociology.* Stanford, Calif.: Stanford University Press.

———. 1998. *Practical Reason.* Stanford, Calif.: Stanford University Press.

Braverman, Harry. 1974. *Labor and Monopoly Capital: The Degradation of Work in the Twentieth Century.* New York: Monthly Review Press.

Bretón, Yvan, and Marie France Labrecque, eds. 1981. *L'Agriculture, la pêche et l'artisanat au Yucatan.* Quebec: Université Laval.

Burling, Robbins. 1962. "Maximization Theories and the Study of Economic Anthropology." *American Anthropologist* 64: 802–21.

Bustamante, Jorge A. 1978. "Commodity Migrants: Structural Analysis of Mexican Immigration to the United States." In *Views across the Border: The United States and Mexico.* Edited by Stanley Ross. Albuquerque: University of New Mexico Press, 183–203.

———. 1981. "The Immigrant Worker: A Social Problem or a Human Resource." In *Mexican Immigrant Workers in the United States.* Edited by A. Ríos-Bustamante. Los Angeles: UCLA Chicano Studies Research Center, 97–102.

Bustamante, Jorge A., Guillermina Jasso, J. Edward Taylor, and Paz Trigueros Legarreta. 1998. "Characteristics of Migrants: Mexicans in the United States." In *Migration between Mexico and the United States.* Vol. 1. Austin, Tex.: Ministry of Foreign Affairs and the United States Commission on Immigration Reform, 91–162

Bustamante, Jorge, Clark Reynolds, and Raul Hinojosa, eds. 1992. *U.S.–Mexico Relations: Labor Market Interdependence.* Stanford, Calif.: Stanford University Press.

Camara, Fernando. 1968. "Discussion." In *Heritage of Conquest.* By Sol Tax et al. New York. Cooper Square Publishers.

Cancian, Frank. 1965. *Economics and Prestige in a Maya Community.* Stanford, Calif.: Stanford University Press.

———. 1966. "Maximization as Norm, Strategy, and Theory: A Comment on Programmatic Statements in Economic Anthropology." *American Anthropologist* 68: 465–70.

———. 1967. "Political and Religious Organizations." In *Handbook of Middle American Indians.* Vol. 6, *Social Anthropology.* Edited by R. Wauchope. Austin: University of Texas Press, 283–98.

———. 1972. *Change and Uncertainty in a Peasant Economy: The Maya Corn Farmers of Zinacantan.* Stanford, Calif.: Stanford University Press.

———. 1989. "Economic Behavior in Peasant Communities." In *Economic Anthropology.* Edited by Stuart Plattner. Stanford, Calif.: Stanford University Press, 127–70.

———. 1992. *The Decline of Community in Zinancantan.* Stanford, Calif.: Stanford University Press.

Carlsen, Robert S. 1993. "Discontinuous Warps: Textile Production and Ethnicity in Contemporary Highland Guatemala." In *Crafts in the World Market: The Impact of*

Global Exchange on Middle American Indians. Edited by June Nash. Albany: State University of New York Press, 199–224.

Carmack, Robert M., ed. 1992. *Harvest of Violence: The Maya Indians and the Guatemalan Crisis*. Norman: University of Oklahoma Press.

Carmack, Robert M., Janine Gasco, and Gary H. Gossen, eds. 1996. *The Legacy of Mesoamerica: History and Culture of a Native American Civilization*. Upper Saddle River, N.J.: Prentice Hall.

Carrasco, Pedro. 1983. "Some Theoretical Considerations about the Role of the Market in Ancient Mexico." In *Economic Anthropology: Topics and Theories*. Edited by Sutti Ortiz. Society for Economic Anthropology Monographs in Economic Anthropology, no. 1. Lanham, Md.: University Press of America, 67–82.

Carrier, James G., ed. 1997. *Meanings of the Market: The Free Market in Western Culture*. Oxford: Berg.

Carver, Terrell, ed. 1975. *Karl Marx: Texts on Method*. New York: Barnes and Noble.

Caso, Alfonso, et al. 1954. *Métodos y resultados de la política indigenista en Mexico*. Memorias del Instituto Nacional Indigenista VI. Mexico City: Ediciones del Instituto Nacional Indigenista.

Cassady, Ralph, Jr. 1968. "Negotiated Price-Making in Mexican Traditional Markets: A Conceptual Analysis." *América Indígena* 28, no. 1: 51–79.

Chavez, Leo. 1992. *Shadowed Lives: Undocumented Immigrants in American Society. Case Studies in Cultural Anthropology*. Fort Worth, Tex.: Harcourt Brace.

Chayanov, A. V. 1966. *The Theory of Peasant Economy*. Edited by D. Thorner, B. Kerblay, and R. E. F. Smith. Homewood, Ill.: Irwin.

Chevalier, Jacques M. 1982. *Civilization and the Stolen Gift: Capital, Kin, and Cult in Eastern Peru*. Toronto: University of Toronto Press.

———. 1983. "There Is Nothing Simple about Simple Commodity Production." *Journal of Peasant Studies* 10, no. 4: 153–86.

Chevalier, Jacques M., and Daniel Buckles. 1995. *A Land without Gods: Process Theory, Maldevelopment and the Mexican Nahuas*. London: Zed Books.

Chibnik, Michael. 2003. *Crafting Tradition: The Making and Marketing of Oaxacan Wood Carvings*. Austin: University of Texas Press.

Clammer, John. 1985. *Anthropology and Political Economy: Theoretical and Asian Perspectives*. London: Macmillan.

———, ed. 1987. *Beyond the New Economic Anthropology*. London: Macmillan.

Clark, Margaret, R. V. Kemper, and C. Nelson, eds. 1979. *From Tzintzuntzan to the "Image of the Limited Good": Essays in Honor of George M. Foster*. Berkeley, Calif.: Kroeber Anthropological Society Papers.

Clarke, Colin. 2000. *Class, Ethnicity, and Community in Southern Mexico: Oaxaca's Peasantries*. Oxford and New York: Oxford University Press.

Cockcroft, James. 1986. *Outlaws in the Promised Land: Mexican Immigrant Workers and America's Future*. New York: Grove Press.

Cohen, Jeffrey H. 1999. *Cooperation and Community: Economy and Society in Oaxaca*. Austin: University of Texas Press.

———. 2001. "Transnational Migration in Rural Oaxaca, Mexico: Dependency, Development, and the Household." *American Anthropologist* 103, no. 44: 954–67.

Collier, George. 1990. "Seeking Food and Seeking Money: Changing Productive Relations in a Highland Mexican Community." Discussion Paper II. Geneva: United Nations Research Institute for Social Development.

Collins, Jane L., and Martha Gimenez, eds. 1990. *Work without Wages: Domestic Labor and Self-Employment within Capitalism*. Albany: State University of New York Press.

Compa, Lance. 2001. "NAFTA's Labor Side Agreement and International Labor Solidarity." *Antipode* 33, no. 3: 451–67.

Cook, Scott. 1965. *The Metateros of Teitipac: An Ethnography of a Zapotec Peasant Artisan Group*. Oaxaca Archives, Stanford University. Summer Field Training Program in Anthropology. Mimeograph.

———. 1966a. "Maximization, Economic Theory, and Anthropology: A Reply to Cancian." *American Anthropologist* 68: 1494–98.

———. 1966b. "The Obsolete 'Anti-Market' Mentality: A Critique of the Substantive Approach to Economic Anthropology." *American Anthropologist* 68, no. 2, pt. 1: 323–45.

———. 1968a. "Review of *Primitive, Archaic and Modern Economies: Essays of Karl Polanyi*." *American Anthropologist* 70: 966–69.

———. 1968b. "Teitipac and Its Metateros: An Economic Anthropological Study of Production and Exchange in a Peasant-Artisan Economy in the Valley of Oaxaca, Mexico." PhD diss., University of Pittsburgh.

———. 1969. "The 'Anti-Market' Mentality Re-Examined: A Further Critique of the Substantive Approach to Economic Anthropology." *Southwestern Journal of Anthropology* 25, no. 4: 378–406.

———. 1970. "Price and Output Variability in a Peasant-Artisan Stoneworking Industry in Oaxaca, Mexico: An Analytical Essay in Economic Anthropology." *American Anthropologist* 72, no. 4: 776–801.

———. 1973. "Production, Ecology and Economic Anthropology: Notes toward an Integrated Frame of Reference." *Social Science Information* 12, no. 1: 25–52.

———. 1974a. "Economic Anthropology: Problems in Theory, Method, and Analysis." In *Handbook of Social and Cultural Anthropology*. Edited by John. J. Honigman. Chicago: Rand McNally College Publishing, 795–860.

———. 1974b. "'Structural Substantivism': A Critical Review of Marshall Sahlins' *Stone Age Economics*." *Comparative Studies in Society and History* 16, no. 3: 355–79.

———. 1975. "Comment." *Current Anthropology* 16, no. 3 : 380–81.

———. 1976. "Value, Price and Simple Commodity Production: The Case of the Zapotec Stoneworkers." *Journal of Peasant Studies* 3, no. 4: 395–427.

———. 1977. "Beyond the *Formen*: Towards a Revised Marxist Theory of Precapitalist Formations and the Transition to Capitalism." *Journal of Peasant Studies* 4, no. 4: 360–89.

———. 1978. "Petty Commodity Production and Capitalist Development in the Central Valleys Region of Oaxaca, Mexico. *Nova Americana* 1: 285–318.

———. 1981. "Crafts, Capitalist Development, and Cultural Property in Oaxaca, Mexico." *Inter-American Economic Affairs* 35, no. 3: 53–68.

———. 1982. *Zapotec Stoneworkers: The Dynamics of Rural Simple Commodity Production in Modern Mexican Capitalism*. Lanham, Md.: University Press of America.

———. 1983. "Mestizo Palm Weavers among the Zapotec: A Critical Re-Examination of the 'Albarradas Enigma.'" *Notas Mesoamericanas* 9: 39–46.

———. 1984a. *Peasant Capitalist Industry: Piecework and Enterprise in Southern Mexican Brickyards*. Lanham, Md.: University Press of America.

———. 1984b. "Peasant Economy, Rural Industry and Capitalist Development in the Oaxaca Valley, Mexico." *Journal of Peasant Studies* 12, no. 1: 3–40.

———. 1984c. "Rural Industry, Social Differentiation, and the Contradictions of Provincial Mexican Capitalism." *Latin American Perspectives* 11, no. 4: 60–85.

———. 1985. "Craft Businesses, Piece Work, and Value Distribution in the Oaxaca Valley, Mexico." In *Economic Anthropology*. Edited by Stuart Plattner. Stanford, Calif.: Stanford University Press, 235–58.

———. 1986. "The 'Managerial' vs. the 'Labor' Function, Capital Accumulation, and the Dynamics of Simple Commodity Production in Rural Mexico." In *Entrepreneurship and Social Change*. Edited by Stanley Greenfield and Arnold Strickon. Monographs in Economic Anthropology, no. 2. Lanham, Md.: University Press of America, 54–95.

———. 1988. "Inflation and Rural Livelihood in a Mexican Province: An Exploratory Analysis." *Mexican Studies/Estudios Mexicanos* 4, no. 1: 55–78.

———. 1990. "Female Labor, Commodity Production and Ideology in Mexican Peasant-Artisan Households." In *Work without Wages: Domestic Labor and Self-Employment within Capitalism*. Edited by Jane L. Collins and Martha Gimenez. Albany: State University of New York Press, 89–115.

———. 1993a. "Craft Commodity Production, Market Diversity, and Differential Rewards in Mexican Capitalism Today." In *Crafts in the World Market: The Impact of Global Exchange on Middle American Indians*. Edited by June Nash. Albany: State University of New York Press, 59–83.

———. 1993b. "Toward a New Paradigm for Anthropology in Mexican Studies." *Mexican Studies/Estudios Mexicanos* 9, no. 2: 303–36.

———. 1995. "B. Traven and the Paradox of Artisanal Production in Capitalism: Traven's Oaxaca Tale in Economic Anthropological Perspective." *Mexican Studies/Estudios Mexicanos* 11, no. 1: 75–111.

———. 1998. *Mexican Brick Culture in the Building of Texas, 1800s–1980s*. College Station: Texas A & M University Press.

———. 2001a. "The Mexican Connection in the Southwestern Borderlands: An Introduction." *Journal of the West* 40, no. 2: 5–14.

———. 2001b. "In the Maquiladoras' Shadows: The Handmade Brick Industry in Transborder Development." *Journal of the West* 40, no. 2: 32–41.

———. 2003. "Struggling to Understand Complexity: The Sociocultural Anthropology of Mexico at the Beginning of the Twenty-First Century." *Mexican Studies/Estudios Mexicanos* 19, no. 1: 203–41.

———, ed. 2001. "The Mexican Connection in the Southwestern Borderlands—Trends and Prospects." *Journal of the West* 40, no. 2.

Cook, Scott, and Leigh Binford. 1986. "Petty Commodity Production, Capital Accumulation, and Peasant Differentiation: Lenin vs. Chayanov in Rural Mexico."*Review of Radical Political Economics* 18, no. 4: 1–31.

———. 1990. *Obliging Need: Rural Petty Industry in Mexican Capitalism*. Austin: University of Texas Press.

Cook, Scott, and Martin Diskin, eds. 1976. *Markets in Oaxaca*. Austin: University of Texas Press.

Cook, Scott, and Jong-Taick Joo. 1995. "Ethnicity and Economy in Rural Mexico: A Critique of the Indigenista Approach." *Latin American Research Review* 30, no. 2: 33–60.

Cox, T. 1979. "Awkward Class or Awkward Classes? Class Relations in the Russian Peasantry before Collectivization." *Journal of Peasant Studies* 7, no. 1: 70–85.

———. 1984. "Class Analysis of the Russian Peasantry: The Research of Kritsman and His School." *Journal of Peasant Studies* 11, no. 2: 11–60.

———. 1986. *Peasants, Class, and Capitalism*. Oxford: Clarendon Press.

Cox, T., and G. Littlejohn, eds., 1984. "Kritsman and the Agrarian Marxists." *Journal of Peasant Studies* 11, no. 2.

Dalton, George. 1961. "Economic Theory and Primitive Society." *American Anthropologist* 65: 1–25.

———. 1965. "Review" of *Capital, Saving and Credit in Peasant Societies*." *American Anthropologist* 67: 121–22.

———. 1969. "Theoretical Issues in Economic Anthropology." *Current Anthropology* 10, no. 1: 63–102.

———, ed. 1968. *Primitive, Archaic and Modern Economies: Essays of Karl Polanyi*. Garden City, N.Y.: Doubleday Anchor.

———. 1971. *Studies in Economic Anthropology*. Anthropological Studies, no. 7. Edited by Paul J. Bohannan. Washington, D.C.: American Anthropological Association.

Deere, Carmen D., and Alain de Janvry. 1981. "Demographic and Social Differentiation among Northern Peruvian Peasants." *Journal of Peasant Studies* 8, no. 3: 335–66.

de Janvry, Alain. 1981. *The Agrarian Question and Reformism in Latin America*. Baltimore: Johns Hopkins University Press.

de la Peña, Sergio. 1981. *Capitalismo en cuatro comunidades rurales*. Mexico City: Siglo Veintiuno.

Delpar, Helen. 1992. *The Enormous Vogue of Things Mexican: Cultural Relations between the United States and Mexico, 1920–1935*. Tuscaloosa: University of Alabama Press.

Dinerman, Ina R. 1974. *Los tarascos, campesinos y artesanos de Michoacán*. Mexico City: SepSetentas.

Diskin, Martin. 1969. "Estudio estructural del sistema de plazas en el valle de Oaxaca." *América Indígena* 29: 1077–99.

Dobb, Maurice. 1956. *Wages*. Cambridge: Nisbet and Cambridge University Press.

———. 1963. *Studies in the Development of Capitalism*. New York: International Publishers.

Donham, Donald. 1990. *History, Power, Ideology: Central Issues in Marxism and Anthropology*. Cambridge: Cambridge University Press.

Drucker-Brown, Susan, ed. 1982. *Malinowski in Mexico: The Economics of a Mexican Market System*. London: Routledge and Kegan Paul.

Durkheim, Emile. 1964. *The Division of Labor in Society*. Glencoe, Ill. Free Press.

Durrenberger, E. Paul, ed. 1984. *Chayanov, Peasants, and Economic Anthropology*. Orlando: Academic Press.

Durrenberger, E. Paul, and Nicola Tannenbaum. 2002. "Chayanov and Theory in Economic Anthropology." In *Theory in Economic Anthropology*. Edited by J. Ensminger. Walnut Creek, Calif.: AltaMira Press, 137–53.

Durrenberger, E. Paul, with Kendall Thu. 1998. *Pigs, Profits, and Rural Communities*. Albany: State University of New York Press.

Durston, John W. 1976. *Organización social de los mercados campesinos en el centro de Michoacán*. Mexico City: Instituto Nacional Indigenista.

Earle, Timothy. 2002. "Commodity Flows and the Evolution of Complex Societies." In *Theory in Economic Anthropology*. Edited by J. Ensminger. Walnut Creek, Calif.: AltaMira Press, 81–104.

Eaton, John. 1966. *Political Economy: A Marxist Textbook*. New York: International Publishers.

Eber, Christine, and Brenda Rosenbaum. 1993. "'That We May Serve beneath Your Hands and Feet': Women Weavers in Highland Chiapas, Mexico." In *Crafts in the World Market: The Impact of Global Exchange on Middle American Indians*. Edited by June Nash. Albany: State University of New York Press, 155–80.

Edgley, Roy, 1985, "Dialectical Materialism." In *A Dictionary of Marxist Thought*. 2nd ed. Edited by Tom Bottomore, Lawrence Harris, V. G. Kiernan, and Ralph Miliband. Oxford: Basil Blackwell, 142–43.

Emmanuel, Arghiri. 1972. *Unequal Exchange: A Study of the Imperialism of Trade*. New York: Monthly Review Press.

Engels, Friedrich. 1967. "Supplement to Capital, Volume Three." In *Capital*, vol. 3, by Karl Marx. New York: International Publishers, 889–910.

———. 1972. "The Part Played by Labor in the Transition from Ape to Man." In *The Origin of the Family, Private Property and the State*. New York: International Publishers, 251–264.

Ensminger, Jean, ed. 2002. *Theory in Economic Anthropology*. Walnut Creek, Calif.: AltaMira Press.

Epstein, A. L., ed. 1967. *The Craft of Social Anthropology*. London: Tavistock.

Epstein, T. S. 1967. "The Data of Economics in Anthropological Analysis." In *The Craft of Social Anthropology*. Edited by A. L. Epstein. London: Tavistock, 153–80.

Fernández, Raul A. 1977. *The United States–Mexico Border: A Politico-Economic Profile*. Notre Dame, Ind.: University of Notre Dame Press.

———. 1989. *The Mexican–American Border Region: Issues and Trends*. Notre Dame, Ind.: University of Notre Dame Press.

Fernández-Kelly, María Patricia. 1983. *For We Are Sold, I and My People: Women and Industry in Mexico's Frontier*. Albany: State University of New York Press.

Ferriss, Susan. 2003. "Mexican Factory Workers Undercut by China, Economy." *Austin American-Statesman*, Sunday, November 2, J1, J6.

Findeis, J. L., A. M. Vandeman, J. M. Larson, and J. L. Runyan, eds. 2002. *The Dynamics of Hired Farm Labor*. London: CAB International.

Fine, Ben. 1991. "Production." In *A Dictionary of Marxist Thought*. 2nd ed. Edited by Tom Bottomore, Lawrence Harris, V. G. Kiernan, and Ralph Miliband. Oxford: Basil Blackwell, 447–48.

Firth, Raymond. 1939. *Primitive Polynesian Economy*. London: Routledge.

———. 1946. *Malay Fishermen: Their Peasant Economy*. London: Routledge.

———. 1951. *Elements of Social Organization*. London: Watts & Co.

———. 1965. *Primitive Polynesian Economy*. 2nd ed. London: Routledge and Kegan Paul.

———. 1966. *Malay Fishermen: Their Peasant Economy*. 2nd ed. London: Routledge and Kegan Paul.

———, ed. 1967. *Themes in Economic Anthropology*. A.S.A. Monographs, no. 6. London: Tavistock.

Foladori, Guillermo. 1981. *Polémica en torno a las teorías del campesinado*. Mexico City: Escuela Nacional de Antropología e Historia, Instituto Nacional de Antropología e Historia.

Foner, N., R. G. Rumbaut, and S. J. Gold, eds. 2000. *Immigration Research for a New Century: Multidisciplinary Perspectives*. New York: Russell Sage Foundation.

Foster, George M. 1948a. *Empire's Children: The People of Tzintzuntzan*. Institute of Social Anthropology Publication no. 6. Washington, D.C.: Smithsonian Institution Press.

———. 1948b. "The Folk Economy of Rural Mexico with Special Reference to Marketing." *Journal of Marketing* 13: 153–62.

———. 1965. "Peasant Society and the Image of Limited Good." *American Anthropologist* 67, no. 2: 293–315.

———. 1972. "The Anatomy of Envy: A Study of Symbolic Behavior." *Current Anthropology* 13: 165–202.

———. 1982 [1942]. *A Primitive Mexican Economy*. Reprint of American Ethnological Society Monograph no. 5. Westport, Conn.: Greenwood.

———. 1988 [1967]. *Tzintzuntzan: Mexican Peasants in a Changing World*. Prospect Heights, Ill.: Waveland Press.

Frank, Andre Gunder. 1969. *Latin America: Underdevelopment or Revolution*. New York: Monthly Review Press.

Fraser, L. M. 1947. *Economic Thought and Language*. London: Adam and Charles Black.

Fried, Morton H. 1967. *The Evolution of Political Society*. New York: Random House.

———. 1968. "Introduction to Karl Polanyi's 'Anthropology and Economic Theory.'" In *Readings in Anthropology*. 2nd ed. Vol. 2, *Cultural Anthropology*. Edited by Morton H. Fried. New York: Thomas Y. Crowell, 215–16.

———, ed. 1968. *Readings in Anthropology*. 2nd ed. Vol. 2, *Cultural Anthropology*. New York: Thomas Y. Crowell.

Fröbel, F., E. Heinrichs, and O. Kreye. 1978. "The New International Division of Labor." *Social Science Information* 17, no. 1: 123–42.

Fusfeld, Daniel B. 1957. "Economic Theory Misplaced: Livelihood in Primitive Society." In *Trade and Market in the Early Empires*. Edited by Karl Polanyi, Conrad M. Arensberg, and Harry W. Pearson. Glencoe, Ill.: Free Press, 342–56.

Galeski, Boguslaw. 1972. *Basic Concepts of Rural Sociology*. Manchester: Manchester University Press.

Gamio, Manuel. 1971a. *The Life Story of the Mexican Immigrant: Autobiographical Documents*. New York: Dover Publications; originally published as *The Mexican Immigrant: His Life Story* (Chicago: University of Chicago Press, 1931).

———. 1971b [1930]. *Mexican Immigration to the United States: A Study of Human Migration and Adjustment*. New York: Dover Publications.

García Canclini, Nestor. 1982. *Las culturas populares en el capitalismo*. Mexico, D.F.: Editorial Nueva Imagen.

Gawronski, Vincent T. 2002. "The Revolution Is Dead. ¡Viva la revolución!: The Place of the Mexican Revolution in the Era of Globalization." *Mexican Studies/Estudios Mexicanos* 18, no. 2: 363–97.

Geertz, Clifford. 1984. "Culture and Social Change: The Indonesian Case." *Man* 19: 513–32.

Gellner, Ernest, ed. 1980. *Soviet and Western Anthropology*. London: Duckworth.

Gibson-Graham, J. K. 1997. "Re-Placing Class in Economic Geographies: Possibilities for a New Class Politics." In *Geographies of Economies*. Edited by Roger Lee and Jane Wills. London: Arnold, 87–97.

Gillin, John. 1955. "Review of *Penny Capitalism* by Sol Tax." *American Anthropologist* 57, no. 3: 631–32.

Glantz, Susana, ed. 1987. *La heterodoxia recuperada: En torno a Angel Palerm*. México: Fondo de Cultura Económica.

Godelier, Maurice. 1971. "'Salt Currency' and the Circulation of Commodities among the Baruya of New Guinea." In *Studies in Economic Anthropology*. Anthropological Studies, no. 7. Edited by Paul J. Bohannan. Washington, D.C.: American Anthropological Association, 52–73.

———. 1972. *Rationality and Irrationality in Economics*. New York: Monthly Review Press.

———. 1986. *The Mental and the Material*. London: Verso.

Goldin, Liliana R. 1996. "The Political and Cultural Economy of Mesoamerica." In *The Legacy of Mesoamerica: History and Culture of a Native American Civilization*. Edited by Robert M. Carmack, Janine Gasco, and Gary H. Gossen. Upper Saddle River, N.J.: Prentice Hall, 353–78.

Good, Catharine. 1988. *Haciendo la lucha: Arte y comercio nahuas de Guerrero*. Mexico: Fondo de Cultura Económica.

———. 2000. "Indigenous Peoples in Central and Western Mexico." In *Ethnology*. Vol. 6, *Supplement to the Handbook of Middle American Indians*. Edited by John D. Monaghan. Austin: University of Texas Press, 120–49.

Goodenough, Ward H. 2002. "Anthropology in the 20th Century and Beyond." *American Anthropologist* 104, no. 2: 423–40.

Goodfellow, D. M. 1939. *Principles of Economic Sociology*. Philadelphia: Blakiston.

Goody, Esther N., ed. 1982. *From Craft to Industry: The Ethnography of Proto-Industrial Cloth Production*. Cambridge: Cambridge University Press.

Graburn, Nelson H. H., ed. 1976. *Ethnic and Tourist Arts: Cultural Expressions from the Fourth World*. Berkeley: University of California Press.

Graham, Richard, ed. 1990. *The Idea of Race in Latin America 1870–1940*. Austin: University of Texas Press.

Gramsci, Antonio. 1957. *The Modern Prince and Other Writings*. New York: International Publishers.

Granovetter, Mark. 1992. "The Nature of Economic Relations." In *Understanding Economic Process*. Edited by Sutti Ortiz and Susan Lees. Monographs in Economic Anthropology, no. 10. Lanham, Md.: University Press of America, 21–40.

Greenberg, James B. 1981. *Santiago's Sword: Chatino Peasant Religion and Economics*. Berkeley: University of California Press.

Greenfield, Sidney M., and Arnold Strickon, eds. 1986. *Entrepreneurship and Social Change*. Monographs in Economic Anthropology, no. 2. Lanham, Md.: University Press of America.

Gregory, C. A. 1997. "Exchange and Reciprocity." In *Companion Encyclopedia of Anthropology: Humanity, Culture and Social Life*. Edited by Tim Ingold. London: Routledge, 911–39.

Gudeman, Stephen. 1978. *The Demise of Rural Economy: From Subsistence to Capitalism in a Latin American Village*. London: Routledge and Kegan Paul.

———. 1980. "Physiocracy: A Natural Economics." *American Ethnologist* 7: 240–58.

———. 1986. *Economics as Culture: Models and Metaphors of Livelihood*. London: Routledge and Kegan Paul.

Gudeman, Stephen, and Alberto Rivera. 1990. *Conversations in Colombia: The Domestic Economy in Life and Text*. Cambridge: Cambridge University Press.

Guthke, Karl S. 1991. *B. Traven: The Life behind the Legends*. Brooklyn, N.Y.: Lawrence Hill Books.

Habermas, Jürgen. 1971. *Knowledge and Human Interests*. Boston: Beacon Press.

Halperin, Rhoda H. 1977. "Production in Peasant Societies." In *Peasant Livelihood: Studies in Economic Anthropology and Cultural Ecology*. Edited by Rhoda Halperin and James Dow. New York: St. Martin's Press, 17–21.

———. 1984. "Polanyi, Marx, and the Institutional Paradigm in Economic Anthropology." *Research in Economic Anthropology* 6: 245–72.

———. 1985. "The Concept of the Formal in Economic Anthropology." *Research in Economic Anthropology* 7: 339–68.

Halperin, Rhoda, and James Dow, eds. 1977. *Peasant Livelihood: Studies in Economic Anthropology and Cultural Ecology*. New York: St. Martin's Press.

Hammel, Eugene, and Laura Nader. 1979. "Will the Real George Foster Please Stand Up? A Brief Intellectual History." In *From Tzintzuntzan to the "Image of the Limited Good": Essays in Honor of George M. Foster*. Edited by Margaret Clark, R. V. Kemper, and C. Nelson. Berkeley, Calif.: Kroeber Anthropological Society Papers, 159–64.

Hamnett, Brian. 1999. *A Concise History of Mexico*. Cambridge: Cambridge University Press.

Hansen, Niles. 1981. *The Border Economy: Regional Development in the Southwest*. Austin: University of Texas Press.

Harris, Marvin. 1980. *Cultural Materialism: The Struggle for a Science of Culture*. New York: Vintage Books.

Harrison, Mark. 1975. "Chayanov and the Economics of the Russian Peasantry." *Journal of Peasant Studies* 2, no. 4: 389–417.

Hart, John Mason. 2002. *Empire and Revolution: The Americans in Mexico since the Civil War*. Berkeley: University of California Press.

Hart, Keith. 1982. "On Commoditization." In *From Craft to Industry: The Ethnography of Proto-Industrial Cloth Production*. Edited by Esther N. Goody. Cambridge: Cambridge University Press, 38–49.

———. 1983. "The Contribution of Marxism to Economic Anthropology." In *Economic Anthropology: Topics and Theories*. Edited by Sutti Ortiz. Society for Economic Anthropology Monographs in Economic Anthropology, no. 1. Lanham, Md.: University Press of America, 105–44.

———. 2001. *Money in an Unequal World: Keith Hart and His Memory Bank*. New York: Texere.

Harvey, David. 1982. *The Limits to Capital*. Chicago: University of Chicago Press.

———. 1989. *The Condition of Postmodernity: An Enquiry into the Origins of Cultural Change*. Cambridge, Mass.: Blackwell.

———. 1990. *The Condition of Postmodernity*. Cambridge, Mass.: Blackwell Publishers.

———. 1996. *Justice, Nature and the Geography of Difference*. Malden, Mass.: Blackwell Publishers.

Heath, Dwight B., ed. 1974. *Contemporary Cultures and Societies of Latin America*. 2nd ed. New York: Random House.

Helm, June, ed. 1965. *Essays in Economic Anthropology*. Proceedings of the 1965 Annual Spring Meeting of the American Ethnological Society. Seattle: American Ethnological Society/University of Washington Press.

Herman, Theodore. 1956. "The Role of Cottage and Small-Scale Industries in Asian Economic Development." *Economic Development and Cultural Change* 4 (July): 356–70.

Hernández-Díaz, Jorge. 2001a. "Elecciones municipales y conflictos postelectorales: Una preocupación permanente." *En Marcha*, no. 31: 16–17.

———. 2001b. *Reclamos de la identidad: La formación de las organizaciones indígenas en Oaxaca*. México, D.F.: Universidad Autónoma Benito Juárez de Oaxaca.

Herskovits, Melville J. 1940. *The Economic Life of Primitive Peoples*. New York: Alfred A. Knopf.

———. 1960 [1952]. *Economic Anthropology: A Study in Comparative Economics*. New York: Alfred A. Knopf.

Hewitt de Alcántara, Cynthia. 1984. *Anthropological Perspectives on Rural Mexico*. London: Routledge and Kegan Paul.

Heyman, Josiah McC. 1994. "The Organizational Logic of Capitalist Consumption on the Mexico–United States Border." *Research in Economic Anthropology* 15: 175–238.

———. 2001. "On U.S.–Mexico Border Culture." In *Journal of the West* 40, no. 2. Edited by Scott Cook, 50–59.

Higgins, Benjamin. 1956. "The 'Dualistic Theory' of Underdeveloped Areas." *Economic Development and Cultural Change* 4, no. 2: 99–117.

———. 1959. *Economic Development: Problems, Principles, and Policies*. New York: W. W. Norton.

Hindess, Barry, ed. 1977. *Sociological Theories of the Economy*. London: Macmillan.

Hindess, Barry, and Paul Q. Hirst. 1975. *Pre-Capitalist Modes of Production*. London: Routledge and Kegan Paul.

Hinshaw, Robert, ed. 1979. *Currents in Anthropology: Essays in Honor of Sol Tax*. The Hague: Mouton Publishers.

Hoare, Quintin, and G. N. Smith, eds. 1971. *Selections from the Prison Notebooks of Antonio Gramsci*. New York: International Publishers.

Hodge, Mary G., and Michael E. Smith, eds. 1994. *The Economies and Polities of the Aztec Realm*. Albany: State University of New York, Institute for Mesoamerican Studies.

Hodges, Donald C., and Ross Gandy. 2002. *Mexico: The End of the Revolution*. Westport, Conn.: Praeger.

Hopkins, Terence K. 1957. "Sociology and the Substantive View of the Economy." In *Trade and Market in the Early Empires*. Edited by Karl Polanyi, Conrad M. Arensberg, and Harry W. Pearson. Glencoe, Ill.: Free Press, 271–306.

Hornborg, Alf. 2001. *The Power of the Machine: Global Inequalities of Economy, Technology, and Environment*. Walnut Creek, Calif.: AltaMira Press.

Hoselitz, Bert. 1956. "Economic Development in Central America." *Weltwirtschaftliches Archiv* 76: 267–308.

———. 1964. "Introducción a la versión Española." In *El capitalismo del centavo: Una economía indígena de Guatemala*, vol. 1, by Sol Tax. Guatemala, C.A.: Centro Editorial "Jose de Pineda Ibarra, Ministerio de Educación Pública, 13–19.

House, John W. 1982. *Frontier on the Rio Grande: A Political Geography of Development and Social Deprivation*. Oxford: Clarendon Press.

Humphrey, Caroline, and Stephen Hugh-Jones, eds. 1992. *Barter, Exchange and Value: An Anthropological Approach*. Cambridge: Cambridge University Press.

Ingold, Tim, ed. 1997. *Companion Encyclopedia of Anthropology: Humanity, Culture and Social Life*. London: Routledge.

Isaac, Barry L. 1965. "'Rational' and 'Irrational' Factors in Southern Mexican Indian Capitalism." *America Indígena* 25: 427–36.

———. 1993. "Retrospective on the Formalist-Substantivist Debate." *Research in Economic Anthropology* 14: 213–33.

Jenkins, Alan. 1977. "'Substantivism' as a Comparative Theory of Economic Forms." In *Sociological Theories of the Economy*. Edited by Barry Hindess. London: Macmillan, 66–91.

Jones, Bryn. 1977. "Economic Action and Rational Organization in the Sociology of Weber." In *Sociological Theories of the Economy*. Edited by Barry Hindess. London: Macmillan, 28–65.

Kahn, Joel. 1997. "Demons, Commodities and the History of Anthropology." In *Meanings of the Market: The Free Market in Western Culture*. Edited by James G. Carrier. Oxford: Berg, 69–98.

Kahn, Joel, and J. R. Llobera, eds. 1981. *The Anthropology of Pre-Capitalist Societies*. London: Macmillan.

Kaplan, David. 1965. "The Mexican Marketplace Then and Now." In *Essays in Economic Anthropology*. Edited by June Helm. Proceedings of the 1965 Annual Spring Meeting of the American Ethnological Society. Seattle: American Ethnological Society/University of Washington Press, 80–94.

Kaplan, Flora S. 1993. "Mexican Museums in the Creation of a National Image in World Tourism." In *Crafts in the World Market: The Impact of Global Exchange on Middle American Indians*. Edited by June Nash. Albany: State University of New York Press, 103–26.

Kay, Geoffrey. 1975. *Development & Underdevelopment: A Marxist Analysis*. New York: St. Martin's Press.

Kearney, Michael. 1995. "The Effects of Transnational Culture, Economy, and Migration on Mixtec Identity in Oaxacalifornia." In *The Bubbling Cauldron: Race, Ethnicity, and the Urban Crisis*. Edited by Michael Peter Smith and Joe R. Feagin. Minneapolis: University of Minnesota Press, 226–43.

———. 1996. *Reconceptualizing the Peasantry: Anthropology in Global Perspective*. Boulder, Colo.: Westview Press.

———. 2002. "Transnational Migration from Oaxaca, the Agrarian Question and the Politics of Indigenous Peoples." *Osterreichische Zeitschrift für Geschichtswissenschaften* 13, no. 4: 7–21.

Kellner, Douglas. 1989. *Jean Baudrillard: From Marxism to Postmodernism and Beyond*. Stanford, Calif.: Stanford University Press.

Kemper, Robert V. 1977. *Migration and Adaptation: Tzintzuntzan Peasants in Mexico City*. Beverly Hills, Calif.: Sage Publications.

———. 1994. "Extendiendo las fronteras de la comunidad en teoría y práctica: Tzintzuntzan, México, 1970–1990." In *Estudios Michoacanos. V.* Edited by Victor Gabriel Muro. Zamora, Michoacan: El Colegio de Michoacán, 119–29.

Kemper, Robert V., and George M. Foster. 1975. "Urbanization in Mexico: The View from Tzintzuntzan." In *Latin American Urban Research*. Vol. 5. Edited by A. Cornelius and Felicity M. Trueblood. Beverly Hills, Calif.: Sage Publications, 53–75.

Kingsolver, Ann E. 2001. *NAFTA Stories: Fears and Hopes in Mexico and the United States*. Boulder, Colo.: Lynne Rienner.

Kirchhoff, Paul. 1968 [1952]. "Mesoamerica: Its Geographic Limits, Ethnic Composition and General Characteristics." In *Heritage of Conquest: The Ethnology of Middle America*, by Sol Tax et al. New York: Cooper Square Publishers, 17–30.

Knight, Alan. 1990. "Racism, Revolution, and Indigenimso: Mexico 1910–1940." In *The Idea of Race in Latin America 1870–1940*. Edited by Richard Graham. Austin: University of Texas Press, 71–113.

Knight, F. H. 1941. "Anthropology and Economics." *Journal of Political Economy* 49: 247–68.

Köhler, Ulrich. 2000. "The Maya of Chiapas since 1965." In *Ethnology*. Vol. 6, *Supplement to the Handbook of Middle American Indians*. Edited by John D. Monaghan. Austin: University of Texas Press, 179–206.

Kowalewski, Zbigniew. 1969. "Comment." *Current Anthropology* 10, no. 1: 85–86.

Krissman, Fred. 2000. "Immigrant Labor Recruitment: U.S. Agribusiness and Undocumented Migration from Mexico." In *Immigration Research for a New Century: Multidisciplinary Perspectives*. Edited by N. Foner, R. G. Rumbaut, and S. J. Gold. New York: Russell Sage Foundation, 277–300.

———. 2002a. "Apples and Oranges? Recruiting Indigenous Mexicans to Divide Farm Labor Markets in the Western U.S." Paper delivered at the October 11 conference on "Indigenous Mexican Migrants in California," University of California, Santa Cruz.

———. 2002b. "Cycles of Deepening Poverty in Rural California: The San Joaquin Valley Towns of McFarland and Farmersville." In *The Dynamics of Hired Farm Labor*. Edited by J. L. Findeis et al. London: CAB International, 183–96.

Kroeber, Alfred L. 1948. *Anthropology*. New York: Harcourt, Brace & World.

Kuhn, Annette, and AnnMarie Wolpe, eds. 1978. *Feminism and Materialism*. London: Routledge and Kegan Paul.

Kuznets, Simon. 1953. *Economic Change*. New York: W. W. Norton.

Lange, Oscar, 1945–1946. "The Scope and Method of Economics." *Review of Economic Studies* 13(1), no. 33: 19–32.

Lauria-Perricelli, Antonio. 1989. "A Study in Historical and Critical Anthropology: The Making of the 'People of Puerto Rico.'" Doctoral diss., New School for Social Research, New York.

LeClair, Edward E., Jr. 1962. "Economic Theory and Economic Anthropology." *American Anthropologist* 64: 1179–1203.

LeClair, Edward E., Jr., and Harold K. Schneider, eds. 1968. *Economic Anthropology: Readings in Theory and Analysis*. New York: Holt, Rinehart and Winston.

Lee, Roger, and Jane Wills, eds. 1997. *Geographies of Economies*. London: Arnold.

Lenin, Vladimir I. 1963. *Collected Works of V. I. Lenin*. Vol. 2, *1895–1897*. London: Lawrence and Wishart.

———. 1964 [1899]. *The Development of Capitalism in Russia*. Moscow: Progress Publishers.

Leontyev, L. 1975. *Political Economy: A Condensed Course*. New York: International Publishers.

Leslie, Charles. 1960. *Now We Are Civilized*. Detroit: Wayne State University Press.

Lewis, Oscar. 1949. "Aspects of Land Tenure and Economics in a Mexican Village." *Middle American Research Records* 1, no. 13: 195–209.

———. 1951. *Life in a Mexican Village: Tepoztlán Restudied*. Urbana: University of Illinois Press.

———. 1960. *Tepoztlán, Village in Mexico*. New York: Holt, Rinehart and Winston.

———. 1961. *The Children of Sanchez: Autobiography of a Mexican Family*. New York: Random House.

———. 1964. *Pedro Martínez: A Mexican Peasant and His Family*. New York: Random House.

Little, Daniel. 1986. *The Scientific Marx*. Minneapolis: University of Minnesota Press.

———. 1989. *Understanding Peasant China: Case Studies in the Philosophy of Social Science*. New Haven, Conn.: Yale University Press.

———. 1991. *Varieties of Social Explanation: An Introduction to the Philosophy of Social Science*. Boulder, Colo.: Westview Press.

Littlefield, Alice. 1976. *La industria de las hamacas en Yucatan, Mexico*. Mexico, D.F.: SEP-INI.

———. 1979. "The Expansion of Capitalist Relations of Production in Mexican Crafts." *Journal of Peasant Studies* 6, no. 4: 471–88.

Löffler, Lorenz G. 1969. "Comment." *Current Anthropology* 10, no. 1: 86–87.

Luxemburg, Rosa. 1968. *The Accumulation of Capital*. New York: Monthly Review Press.

Malinowski, Bronislaw. 1921. "The Primitive Economics of the Trobriand Islanders." *Economic Journal* 31: 1–16.

———. 1960. *A Scientific Theory of Culture and Other Essays*. New York: Oxford University Press.

———. 1961 [1922]. *Argonauts of the Western Pacific*. New York: Dutton.

Malinowski, Bronislaw, and Julio de la Fuente. 1957. *La economía de un sistema de mercados en México. Acta Anthropologica Epoca* 2, vol. 1, no. 2. México, D.F.: Escuela Nacional de Antropología, Sociedad de Alumnos.

———. 1982. *The Economics of a Mexican Market System*. London: Routledge and Kegan Paul.

Mandel, Ernest. 1969. *An Introduction to Marxist Economic Theory*. New York: Merit Publishers.

———. 1970. *Marxist Economic Theory*. Vol. 1. New York: Monthly Review Press.

———. 1971. *The Formation of the Economic Thought of Karl Marx*. New York: Monthly Review Press.

———. 1978. *Late Capitalism*. London: Verso.

Marcus, G. E. 1995. "Ethnography in/of the World System: The Emergence of Multi-Sited Ethnography." *Annual Review of Anthropology* 24: 95–117.

Marín de Paalen, Isabel. 1974. *Historia general del arte mexicano: Etno-artesanías y arte popular*. Mexico City: Editorial Hermes, S.A.

Marroquín, Alejandro. 1957a. "Introducción al mercado indígena mexicano." *Ciencias Políticas y Sociales* 3, no. 8.

———. 1957b. *La ciudad mercado (Tlaxiaco)*. Mexico City: Imprenta Universitaria.

———. 1978. *La ciudad mercado (Tlaxiaco)*. Mexico City: Instituto Nacional Indigenista.

Marshall, Alfred. 1890. *Principles of Economics*. London: Macmillan.

Marshall, Gordon, ed. 1998. *Oxford Dictionary of Sociology*. Oxford: Oxford University Press.

Martin, Ron, and Peter Sunley. 2001. "Rethinking the 'Economic' in Economic Geography: Broadening Our Vision or Losing Our Focus?" *Antipode* 33, no. 2: 148–61.

Martínez Peñaloza, Porfirio. 1978. *Arte popular y artesanías artísticas en México: Un acercamiento*. Mexico City: Jus.

Martínez Ríos, Jorge. 1964. "Análisis funcional de la 'guelaguetza agrícola.'" *Revista Mexicana de Sociología* 26, no. 1: 79–125.

Marx, Karl. 1904. *A Contribution to the Critique of Political Economy*. Chicago: Charles H. Kerr.

———. 1963. *Theories of Surplus-Value*. Part 1. Moscow: Progress Publishers.

———. 1964. *The Economic and Philosophic Manuscripts of 1844*. New York: International Publishers.

———. 1965. *Pre-Capitalist Economic Formations*. New York: International Publishers.

———. 1967. *Capital*. 3 vols. New York: International Publishers.

———. 1968. "Theses on Feuerbach." In *Selected Works in One Volume*, by Karl Marx and Friedrich Engels. New York: International Publishers, 28–30.

———. 1970. *A Contribution to the Critique of Political Economy*. Edited with an introduction by Maurice Dobb. New York: International Publishers.

———. 1971. *The Grundrisse*. Edited and translated by David McLellan. New York: Harper and Row.

———. 1973. *Grundrisse (Foundations of the Critique of Political Economy)*. Translated with a foreword by Martin Nicolaus. Middlesex: Penguin Books.

———. 1975. "Notes (1879–80) on Adolph Wagner." In *Karl Marx: Texts on Method*. Edited by Terrell Carver. New York: Barnes and Noble, 179–219.

———. 1977. *Capital*. Vol. 1. New York: Random House.

Marx, Karl, and Friedrich Engels. 1947. *The German Ideology*. New York: International Publishers.

———. 1968. *Selected Works in One Volume*. New York: International Publishers.

Mauss, Marcel. 1954 [1925]. *The Gift: Forms and Functions of Exchange in Archaic Society*. London: Cohen and West.

McBryde, F. W. 1945. *Cultural and Historical Geography of Southwestern Guatemala*. Institute of Social Anthropology, no. 4. Washington, D.C.: Smithsonian Institution Press.

McKillop, Heather. 2002. *Salt: White Gold of the Ancient Maya*. Gainesville: University Press of Florida.

McWilliams, Carey. 1968 [1948]. *North from Mexico: The Spanish-Speaking People of the United States*. New York: Greenwood Press.

Medina, Andrés. 1996. *Recuentos y figuraciones: Ensayos de antropología mexicano*. Mexico, D.F.: UNAM/Insto. De Investigaciones Antropológicas.

Medina, Andrés, and Noemí Quesada. 1975. *Panorama de las artesanías del valle del mezquital*. Mexico, D.F.: UNAM, Instituto de Investigaciones Antropológicas.

Meek, Ronald L. 1956. *Studies in the Labour Theory of Value*. London: Lawrence and Wishart.

———. 1967. *Economics and Ideology and Other Essays*. London: Chapman and Hall.

Mendieta y Nuñez, Lucio, et al. 1949. *Los zapotecos: Monografía historica, etnografica y economica*. Mexico City: Imprenta Universitaria.

Miller, Daniel. 1991. *Material Culture and Mass Consumption*. Cambridge, Mass.: Blackwell.

———. 1997. "Artefacts and the Meaning of Things." In *Companion Encyclopedia of Anthropology: Humanity, Culture and Social Life*. Edited by Tim Ingold. London: Routledge, 396–419.

Mines, Richard. 1981. *Developing a Community Tradition of Migration to the United States: A Field Study in Rural Zacatecas, Mexico, and California Settlement Areas*. San Diego: Program in United States–Mexican Studies, University of California, San Diego.

Mohun, Simon. 1991. "Division of Labor." In *A Dictionary of Marxist Thought*. 2nd ed. Edited by Tom Bottomore, Lawrence Harris, V. G. Kiernan, and Ralph Miliband. Oxford: Basil Blackwell, 153–56.

Monaghan, John D., ed. 2000. *Ethnology*. Vol. 6, *Supplement to the Handbook of Middle American Indians* (Victoria R. Bricker, ed.). Austin: University of Texas Press.

Monaghan, John D., and Jeffrey Cohen. 2000. "Thirty Years of Oaxacan Ethnography." In *Ethnology*. Vol. 6, *Supplement to the Handbook of Middle American Indians*. Edited by John D. Monaghan. Austin: University of Texas Press, 150–78.

Montejano, David. 1987. *Anglos and Mexicans in the Making of Texas, 1836–1986*. Austin: University of Texas Press.

Mosk, Sanford A. 1954. "Indigenous Economy in Latin America." *Interamerican Economic Affairs* 8, no. 3: 3–26.

Mulhare, Eileen M. 2000. "Mesoamerican Social Organization and Community after 1960." In *Ethnology*. Vol. 6, *Supplement to the Handbook of Middle American Indians*. Edited by John D. Monaghan. Austin: University of Texas Press, 9–23.

Murillo, Gerardo (Dr. Atl). 1980 [1922]. *Las artes populares en México*. Mexico City: Instituto Nacional Indigenista.

Narotsky, Susana. 1997. *New Directions in Economic Anthropology*. London: Pluto Press.

Nash, June. 1994. "Global Integration and Subsistence Insecurity." *American Anthropologist* 96, no. 2: 1–31.

———. 1997. "When Isms Became Wasms: Structural Functionalism, Feminism and Postmodernism." *Critique of Anthropology* 17, no. 1: 11–32.

———. 2001. *Mayan Visions: The Quest for Autonomy in an Age of Globalization*. New York: Routledge.

———, ed. 1993. *Crafts in the World Market: The Impact of Global Exchange on Middle American Indians*. Albany: State University of New York Press.

Nash, Manning. 1958. *Machine Age Maya*. Glencoe, Ill.: Free Press.

———. 1961. "The Social Context of Economic Choice in a Small Society." *Man* 219: 186–91.

———. 1966. *Primitive and Peasant Economic Systems*. San Francisco: Chandler.

———, ed. 1967. *Social Anthropology*. Vol. 6, *Handbook of Middle American Indians* (R. Wauchope, ed.). Austin: University of Texas Press.

Neale, Walter C. 1964. "On Defining 'Labor' and 'Services' for Comparative Studies." *American Anthropologist* 64: 1300–1307.

———. 1976. *Monies in Societies*. San Francisco: Chandler and Sharp.

Nicolaus, Martin. 1973. "Foreword." In *Grundrisse (Foundations of the Critique of Political Economy)*, by Karl Marx. Translated with a foreword by Martin Nicolaus. Middlesex: Penguin Books, 7–64.

Novelo, Victoria. 1976. *Artesanías y capitalismo en México*. Mexico, D.F.: SEP-INAH.

Ollman, Bertell. 1971. *Alienation: Marx's Conception of Man in Capitalist Society*. London: Cambridge University Press.

Orlove, Benjamin. 1977. "Inequality among Peasants: The Forms and Uses of Reciprocal Exchange in Andean Peru." In *Peasant Livelihood: Studies in Economic Anthropology and Cultural Ecology*. Edited by Rhoda Halperin and James Dow. New York: St. Martin's Press, 201–14.

Orme, William A., Jr. 1996. *Understanding NAFTA: Mexico, Free Trade, and the New North America*. Austin: University of Texas Press.

Ortiz, Sutti, ed. 1983. *Economic Anthropology: Topics and Theories*. Society for Economic Anthropology Monographs in Economic Anthropology, no. 1. Lanham, Md.: University Press of America.

Ortiz, Sutti, and Susan Lees, eds. 1992. *Understanding Economic Process*. Monographs in Economic Anthropology, no. 10. Lanham, Md.: University Press of America.

Othón de Mendizábal, Miguel. 1946. *Obras completas*. 6 vols. México, D.F.: Talleres Gráficos de la Nación.

Pahl, R. E. 1984. *Divisions of Labour*. Oxford: Basil Blackwell.

Palerm, Angel. 1954. [Review of *Penny Capitalism* by Sol Tax]. In *Boletín Bibliográfico de Antropología Americana*. Vols. 15 and 16, 1952–1953, part 2. Mexico: Instituto Panamericano de Geografía e Historia, 205–7.

———. 1967. "Agricultural Systems and Food Patterns." In *Social Anthropology*. Vol. 6, *Handbook of Middle American Indians*. Edited by Manning Nash. Austin: University of Texas Press, 26–52.

Palerm, Angel, and Eric Wolf. 1972. *Agricultura y civilización en Mesoamerica*. Mexico City: SepSetentas.

Paré, Luisa. 1975. "Tianguis: Y economía capitalista." *Nueva Antropología* 1: 85–93.

Paredes, Américo. 1993. *Folklore and Culture on the Texas–Mexican Border*. Austin: CMAS Books, Center for Mexican-American Studies, University of Texas Press.

Parsons, Elsie Clews. 1936. *Mitla, Town of the Souls*. Chicago: University of Chicago Press.

Parsons, Talcott, and Neil J. Smelser. 1956. *Economy and Society*. Glencoe, Ill.: Free Press.

Patnaik, Utsa. 1979. "Neo-Populism and Marxism: The Chayanovian View of the Agrarian Question and Its Fundamental Fallacy." *Journal of Peasant Studies* 6, no. 4: 375–420.

Peattie, Lisa. 1979. "Economic Anthropology and Anthropological Economics." In *Currents in Anthropology: Essays in Honor of Sol Tax*. Edited by Robert Hinshaw. The Hague: Mouton Publishers, 85–94.

Peck, Gunther. 2000. *Reinventing Free Labor*. Cambridge: Cambridge University Press.

Peet, Richard. 1997. "The Cultural Production of Economic Forms." In *Geographies of Economies*. Edited by Roger Lee and Jane Wills. London: Arnold, 37–46.

Plattner, Stuart, ed. 1985. *Markets and Marketing*. Society for Economic Anthropology, vol. 4. Lanham, Md.: University Press of America.

———, ed. 1989. *Economic Anthropology*. Stanford, Calif.: Stanford University Press.

Polanyi, Karl. 1957 [1944]. *The Great Transformation: The Political and Economic Origins of Our Time*. Boston: Beacon Press.

———. 1947. "Our Obsolete Market Mentality." *Commentary* 3: 109–17.

———. 1966. *Dahomey and the Slave Trade*. Seattle: University of Washington Press.

———. 1968a. "Anthropology and Economic Theory." In *Readings in Anthropology*. 2nd ed. Vol. 2, *Cultural Anthropology*. Edited by Morton H. Fried. New York: Thomas Y. Crowell, 215–38.

———. 1968b. "Appendix." In *Primitive, Archaic and Modern Economies: Essays of Karl Polanyi*. Edited by George Dalton. Garden City, N.Y.: Doubleday Anchor, 120–38.

Polanyi, Karl, Conrad M. Arensberg, and Harry W. Pearson, eds. 1957. *Trade and Market in the Early Empires*. Glencoe, Ill.: Free Press.

Popkin, Samuel L. 1979. *The Rational Peasant*. Berkeley: University of California Press.

Popper, Karl R. 1964. *The Poverty of Historicism*. New York and Evanston: Harper Torchbooks.

Poster, Mark, ed. 1988. *Jean Baudrillard: Selected Writings*. Stanford, Calif.: Stanford University Press.

Pozas, Ricardo, and Isabel H. de Pozas. 1971. *Los indios en las clases sociales de México*. Mexico City: Siglo Veintiuno Editores, S.A.

Raskin, Jonah. 1980. *My Search for B. Traven*. New York: Methuen.

Redfield, Margaret Park. 1962. *Human Nature and the Study of Society: The Papers of Robert Redfield*. Vol. 1. Chicago: University of Chicago Press.

Redfield, Robert. 1962 [1939]. "Primitive Merchants of Guatemala." In *Human Nature and the Study of Society: The Papers of Robert Redfield*. Vol. 1. Edited by Margaret Park Redfield. Chicago: University of Chicago Press, 200–209.

———. 1971 [1931]. "Introduction." In *The Life Story of the Mexican Immigrant: Autobiographical Documents*, by Manuel Gamio. New York: Dover Publications, xi–xv.

Reyes Osorio, S., R. Stavenhagen, S. Eckstein, and J. Ballesteros. 1974. *Estructura Agraria y desarrollo agrícola en México*. Mexico City: Fondo de Cultura Económica.

Ribeiro, Darcy. 1970. "Reply." *Current Anthropology* 11: 426–34.

———. 1972. *The Americas and Civilization*. New York: E. P. Dutton.

Ricardo, D. 1911. *The Principles of Political Economy and Taxation*. London: J. M. Dent and Sons Ltd.

Richards, Audrey I. 1932. *Hunger and Work in a Savage Tribe*. London: Routledge and Kegan Paul.

Riding, Alan. 1985. *Distant Neighbors: A Portrait of the Mexicans*. New York: Alfred A. Knopf.

Ríos-Bustamante, A., ed. 1981. *Mexican Immigrant Workers in the United States*. Los Angeles: UCLA Chicano Studies Research Center.

Robinson, Joan. 1958. "Some Reflections on the Philosophy of Prices." *The Manchester School of Economic and Social Studies* 26:116–35.

———. 1962. *Economic Philosophy: An Essay on the Progress of Economic Thought*. Garden City, N.Y.: Doubleday Anchor.

Roseberry, William. 1978. "Historical Materialism and *The People of Puerto Rico*." *Revista/Review Interamericana* 8: 26–36.

———. 1988. "Political Economy." *Annual Review of Anthropology* 17: 161–85.

———. 1989. *Anthropologies and Histories: Essays in Culture, History, and Political Economy*. New Brunswick, N.J.: Rutgers University Press.

Ross, Stanley R., ed. 1978. *Views across the Border: The United States and Mexico*. Albuquerque: University of New Mexico Press.

Rothstein, Frances A., and Michael L. Blim, eds. 1992. *Anthropology and the Global Factory: Studies of the New Industrialization in the Late Twentieth Century*. New York: Bergin and Garvey.

Rottenberg, Simon. 1958. "Review of *Trade and Market in the Early Empires*." *American Economic Review* 48: 675–78.

Rubin, Isaak I. 1972 [1928]. *Essays on Marx's Theory of Value*. Detroit: Black and Red.

Rubinstein, Robert A., ed. 1991. *Fieldwork: The Correspondence of Robert Redfield and Sol Tax*. Boulder, Colo.: Westview Press.

Sahlins, Marshall D. 1969. "Economic Anthropology and Anthropological Economics." *Social Science Information* 8: 13–33.

———. 1972. *Stone Age Economics*. Chicago: Aldine-Atherton.

———. 1976. *Culture and Practical Reason*. Chicago: University of Chicago Press.

Salisbury, Richard F. 1962. *From Stone to Steel*. Melbourne: University of Australia Press.

———. 1968. "Anthropology and Economics." In *Economic Anthropology: Readings in Theory and Analysis*. Edited by E. E. LeClair Jr. and Harold K. Schneider. New York: Holt, Rinehart and Winston, 477–85.

———. 1969. "Comment." *Current Anthropology* 10, no. 1: 89.

Samora, Julian. 1971. *Los Mojados: The Wetback Story*. Notre Dame, Ind.: University of Notre Dame Press.

Sanciprián, Nancy. 1991. *B. Traven en México*. Mexico City: Consejo Nacional para la Cultura y las Artes.

Sanders, William T., and Barbara J. Price. 1968. *Mesoamerica: The Evolution of a Civilization*. New York: Random House.

Saussure, Ferdinand de. 1986. *Course in General Linguistics*. Chicago: Open Court.

Sayer, Andrew. 1997. "The Dialectic of Culture and Economy." In *Geographies of Economies*. Edited by Roger Lee and Jane Wills. London: Arnold, 16–26.

Schaff, Adam. 1963. *A Philosophy of Man*. New York: Monthly Review Press.

Schneider, Harold K. 1974. *Economic Man: The Anthropology of Economics*. New York: Free Press.

Schneider, Jane, and Annette Weiner, eds. 1989. *Cloth and Human Experience*. Washington, D.C.: Smithsonian Institution Press.

Schumpeter, Joseph A. 1950. *Capitalism, Socialism, and Democracy*. New York: Harper and Brothers.

Schürer, Ernst, and Philip Jenkins, eds. 1987. *B. Traven: Life and Work*. University Park: Pennsylvania State University Press.

Scott, James C. 1976. *The Moral Economy of the Peasant*. New Haven, Conn.: Yale University Press.

Seldon, Arthur, and F. G. Pennance. 1965. *Everyman's Dictionary of Economics*. London: J. M. Dent & Sons.

Semenov, Yu. I. 1980. "The Theory of Socio-Economic Formations and World History." In *Soviet and Western Anthropology*. Edited by Ernest Gellner. London: Duckworth, 29–58.

Semo, Enrigue. 1973. *Historia del capitalismo en México: Los orígenes, 1521–1763*. Mexico City: Ediciones Era.

Shanin, Teodor. 1972. *The Awkward Class*. Oxford: Oxford University Press.

Sklair, Leslie. 1993. *Assembling for Development: The Maquila Industry in Mexico and the United States*. San Diego: Center for U.S.–Mexico Studies, University of California, San Diego.

Smelser, Neil J. 1959. "A Comparative View of Exchange Systems." *Economic Development and Cultural Change* 7: 173–82.

Smith, Adam. 1937. *The Wealth of Nations*. New York: The Modern Library.

Smith, Carol. 1976. "Markets in Oaxaca, Are They Really Unique?" *Reviews in Anthropology*, July–August, 387–99.

———. 1984. "Does a Commodity Economy Enrich the Few while Ruining the Masses? Differentiation among Petty Commodity Producers in Guatemala." *Journal of Peasant Studies* 11, no. 3: 60–95.

Smith, Michael E. 1980. "The Role of the Marketing System in Aztec Society and Economy: Reply to Evans." *American Antiquity* 45, no. 4: 876–83.

Smith, Michael E., and Marilyn A. Masson, eds. 2000. *The Ancient Civilizations of Mesoamerica*. Oxford: Blackwell Publishers.

Smith, Waldemar. 1977. *The Fiesta System and Economic Change*. New York: Columbia University Press.

Sombart, Werner. 1967 [1915]. *The Quintessence of Capitalism*. New York: Howard Fertig.

Spielberg Benítez, Joseph. 1989. "Some Potential Impacts of the Mexican Crisis on Mexican Commuter Workers in the Segmented Labor Market of the Lower Rio Grande Valley of South Texas." *Occasional Papers in Latin American Studies*, no. 10. Storrs, Conn.: Center for Latin American and Caribbean Studies, University of Connecticut and Brown University.

Starr, F., 1900–1902. "Notes upon the Ethnography of Southern Mexico." *Proceedings of the Davenport Academy of Sciences* 8 (1899–1900): 102–98; 9 (1901–1903): 63–172.

———. 1908. *In Indian Mexico: A Narrative of Travel and Labor*. Chicago.

Stavenhagen, Rodolfo. 1969. *Las clases sociales en las sociedades agrarias*. Mexico: Siglo Veintiuno Editores SA.

———. 1975. *Social Classes in Agrarian Societies*. Garden City, N.Y.: Anchor Books.

———. 1978. "Capitalism and the Peasantry in Mexico." *Latin American Perspectives* 3, no. 18: 27–37.

———. 1992. "Los derechos de los indígenas: Algunos problemas conceptuales." *Nueva Antropología* 13, no. 43: 83–99.

Stephen, Lynn. 1991. *Zapotec Women*. Austin: University of Texas Press.

———. 1993. "Weaving in the Fast Lane: Class, Ethnicity, and Gender in Zapotec Craft Commercialization." In *Crafts in the World Market: The Impact of Global Exchange on Middle American Indians*. Edited by June Nash. Albany: State University of New York Press, 25–58.

Steward, Julian, et al. 1956. *The People of Puerto Rico*. Urbana: University of Illinois Press.

Stiglitz, Joseph E. 2002. *Globalization and Its Discontents*. New York: W. W. Norton.

Stone, Judy. 1977. *The Mystery of B. Traven*. Los Altos, Calif.: William Kaufmann.

Stromberg, Gobi. 1976. "The Amate Bark-Paper Painting of Xalitla." In *Ethnic and Tourist Arts: Cultural Expressions from the Fourth World*. Edited by Nelson H. H. Graburn. Berkeley: University of California Press, 149–62.

———. 1985. *El juego del coyote: Platería y arte en Taxco*. México, D.F.: Fondo de Cultura Económica.

Taussig, Michael. 1980. *The Devil and Commodity Fetishism in South America*. Chapel Hill: University of North Carolina Press.

Tax, Sol. 1963 [1953]. *Penny Capitalism: A Guatemalan Indian Economy*. Chicago: University of Chicago Press; originally published as Smithsonian Institution Institute of Social Anthropology Publication no. 16. Washington, D.C.: U.S. Government Printing Office.

———. 1957a. "Changing Consumption in Indian Guatemala." *Economic Development and Cultural Change* 5, no. 2: 147–58.

———. 1957b. "The Indians in the Economy of Guatemala." *Social and Economic Studies* 6: 413–24.

———. 1964. *El capitalismo del centavo: Una economía indígena de Guatemala*. Book 1. Guatemala, C.A.: Centro Editorial "Jose de Pineda Ibarra, Ministerio de Educación Pública.

Tax, Sol, et al. 1968 [1952]. *Heritage of Conquest: The Ethnology of Middle America*. New York: Cooper Square Publishers.

Thorner, Daniel, Basile Kerblay, and R. E. F. Smith, eds. 1966. *A. V. Chayanov: The Theory of Peasant Economy*. Homewood, Ill.: Irwin.

Thu, Kendall, and E. Paul Durrenberger, eds. 1998. *Pigs, Profits, and Rural Communities*. Albany: State University of New York Press.

Thurnwald, Richard. 1932. *Economics in Primitive Communities*. London: Oxford University Press.

Torres Sarmiento, Socorro. 2002. *Making Ends Meet: Income-Generating Strategies among Mexican Immigrants*. New York: LFB Scholarly Publishing.

Traven, B. 1928. *Land des Frühlings*. Berlin: Büchergilde Gutenberg.

———. 1956. *Canasta de cuentos mexicanos*. Translated from the English by R. E. Lujan. Mexico City: Cia. General de Ediciones, S.A.

———. 1966. *The Night Visitor and Other Stories*. Introduction by Charles Miller. New York: Hill and Wang.

———. 1969a. *The Cotton-Pickers*. New York: Hill and Wang.

———. 1969b. *Gobierno*. 4th ed. Mexico City: Cia. General de Ediciones, S.A.

———. 1969c. *La carreta*. 6th ed. Mexico City: Cia. General de Ediciones S.A.

———. 1969d. *La rebelíon de los colgados*. 7th ed. Mexico City: Cia. General de Ediciones, S.A.

———. 1969e. *La rosa blanca*. 6th ed. Mexico City: Cia General de Ediciones, S.A.

———. 1969f. *The Treasure of the Sierra Madre*. New York: The Modern Library.

———. 1970. *The Carreta*. New York: Hill and Wang.

———. 1979. *The White Rose*. Translator's note by Donald J. Davidson. Westport, Conn.: Lawrence Hill.

———. 1993. *The Night Visitor and Other Stories*. Chicago: Elephant Paperbacks, Ivan R. Dee, Publisher.

———. 1994a. *March to the Montería*. Chicago: Elephant Paperbacks, Ivan R. Dee, Publisher.

———. 1994b. *Trozas*. Chicago: Ivan R. Dee.

Trouillot, Michel-Rolph. 2001. "The Anthropology of the State in the Age of Globalization." *Current Anthropology* 42, no. 1: 125–38.

Tulchin, Joseph S., and Andrew D. Selee, eds. 2002. *Mexico's Politics and Society in Transition*. Boulder, Colo.: Lynne Rienner.

Van Dooren, Robine, and Germán A. Zárate-Hoyos. 2003. "The Insertion of Rural Areas into Global Markets: A Comparison of Garment Production in Yucatan and La Laguna, Mexico." *Journal of Latin American Studies* 35: 571–92.

Vélez-Ibañez, Carlos G. 1996. *Border Visions: Mexican Cultures of the Southwest United States*. Tucson: University of Arizona Press.

Vila, Pablo. 2000. *Crossing Borders, Reinforcing Borders: Social Categories, Metaphors, and Narrative Identities on the U.S.–Mexico Frontier*. Austin: University of Texas Press.

Vogt, Evon Z. 1974. "Penny Capitalist or Tribal Ritualists?—The Relationship of Market Behavior to Ceremonial Life in a Modern Maya Community." In *Contemporary Cultures and Societies of Latin America*. 2nd ed. Edited by Dwight B. Heath. New York: Random House, 158–63.

Warman, Arturo. 1976. *Y venimos a contradecir: Los campesinos de Morelos y el estado nacional*. Mexico, D.F.: Ediciones de la Casa Chata.

———. 1980. *"We Come to Object," the Peasants of Morelos and the National State*. Baltimore: Johns Hopkins University Press.

———. 2003. *Los Indios Mexicanos en el Umbral del Milenio*. Mexico: Fondo de Cultura Economica.

Waterbury, Ronald. 1989. "Embroidery for Tourists." In *Cloth and Human Experience*. Edited by Jane Schneider and Annette Weiner. Washington, D.C.: Smithsonian Institution Press, 243–71.

Watts, Michael J. 2002. "Chronicle of a Death Foretold: Some Thoughts on Peasants and the Agrarian Question." *Osterreichische Zeitschrift für Geschichtswissenschaften* 13, no. 4: 22–50.

Wauchope, Robert, ed. 1967. *Handbook of Middle American Indians*. Vol. 6, *Social Anthropology*. Austin: University of Texas Press.

Weber, Max. 1947. *The Theory of Social and Economic Organization*. Glencoe, Ill.: Free Press.

———. 1949. *The Methodology of the Social Sciences*. Glencoe, Ill.: Free Press.

———. 1958. *The Protestant Ethic and the Spirit of Capitalism*. New York: Charles Scribner's Sons.

———. 1961. *General Economic History*. New York: Collier Books.

———. 1978. *Economy and Society: An Outline of Interpretive Sociology*. 2 vols. Edited by Guenther Roth and Claus Wittich. Berkeley: University of California Press.

Weeks, John R., and Roberto Ham-Chande, eds. 1992. *Demographic Dynamics of the U.S.–Mexico Border*. El Paso: Texas Western Press.

Weintraub, Sidney. 1990. *A Marriage of Convenience: Relations between Mexico and the United States*. New York: Oxford University Press.

———. 1997. *NAFTA at Three: A Progress Report*. Washington, D.C.: Center for Strategic and International Studies.

Wells, Miriam J. 1996. *Strawberry Fields: Politics, Class, and Work in California Agriculture*. Ithaca, N.Y.: Cornell University Press.

Wessman, James W. 1981. *Anthropology and Marxism*. Cambridge, Mass.: Schenkman Publishing.

Wharton, Clifton R. 1971. "Risk, Uncertainty, and the Subsistence Farmer: Technological Innovation and Resistance to Change in the Context of Survival." In *Primitive, Archaic and Modern Economies: Essays of Karl Polanyi*. Edited by George Dalton. Garden City, N.Y.: Doubleday Anchor, 151–78.

White, Leslie A. 1959. *The Evolution of Culture*. New York: McGraw-Hill.

Wilk, Richard R. 1996. *Economies and Cultures: Foundations of Economic Anthropology*. Boulder, Colo.: Westview Press.

Williams, Raymond. 1981. *Culture*. Glasgow: Fontana Paperbacks.

Wilson, Godfrey, and Monica Wilson. 1945. *The Analysis of Social Change Based on Observations in Central Africa*. Cambridge: Cambridge University Press.

Wilson, Patricia A. 1992. *Exports and Local Development: Mexico's New Maquiladoras*. Austin: University of Texas Press.

Wittfogel, Karl A. 1931. *Wirtschaft und Gesellschaft Chinas. Part I, Produktivkräfte, Produkts-und Zirkulations-Prozess*. Schriften des Instituts für Sozialforschung an der Universität Frankfurt am Main, 3. Leipzig: C. L. Hirschfield.

———. 1968. "The Theory of Oriental Society." In *Readings in Anthropology*. 2nd ed. Vol. 2, *Cultural Anthropology*. Edited by Morton H. Fried. New York: Thomas Y. Crowell, 179–98.

Wolf, Eric R. 1955. "Types of Latin American Peasantry: A Preliminary Discussion." *American Anthropologist* 57: 452–71.

———. 1956. "San Jose: Subcultures of a 'Traditional' Coffee Municipality." In *The People of Puerto Rico*, by Julian Steward et al. Urbana: University of Illinois Press, 171–264.

———. 1959a. *Sons of the Shaking Earth*. Chicago: University of Chicago Press.

———. 1959b. "Specific Aspects of Plantation Systems in the New World: Community Sub-Cultures and Social Class." In *Plantation Systems of the New World*, Social Science Monographs, 7. Washington, D.C.: Pan American Union, 136–46.

———. 1966. *Peasants*. Englewood Cliffs, N.J.: Prentice Hall.

———. 1967. "Levels of Communal Relations." In *Social Anthropology*. Vol. 6, *Handbook of Middle American Indians*. Edited by Manning Nash. Austin: University of Texas Press, 299–316.

———. 1982. *Europe and the People without History*. Berkeley: University of California Press.

———. 1999. *Envisioning Power: Ideologies of Dominance and Crisis*. Berkeley: University of California Press.

———. 2001. *Pathways of Power: Building an Anthropology of the Modern World*. Berkeley: University of California Press.

Wood, W. Warner. 2000a. "Flexible Production, Households, and Fieldwork: Multisited Zapotec Weavers in the Era of Late Capitalism." *Ethnology* 39, no. 2: 133–48.

———. 2000b. Stories from the Field, Handicraft Production, and Mexican National Patrimony: A Lesson in Translocality from B. Traven." *Ethnology* 39, no. 3: 183–203.

Woolfson, Charles. 1982. *The Labour Theory of Culture: A Re-Examination of Engels' Theory of Human Origins*. London: Routledge and Kegan Paul.

Wyatt, Will. 1980. *The Secret of the Sierra Madre: The Man Who Was B. Traven*. New York: Doubleday.

Young, Kate. 1978. "Modes of Appropriation and the Sexual Division of Labour: A Case Study from Oaxaca, Mexico." In *Feminism and Materialism*. Edited by Annette Kuhn and AnnMarie Wolpe. London: Routledge and Kegan Paul, 124–54.

Zabin, C., M. Kearney, A. Garcia, D. Runsten, and C. Nagengast. 1993. *Mixtec Migrants in California Agriculture*. Davis: California Institute of Rural Studies.

Zogbaum, Heidi. 1992. *B. Traven: A Vision of Mexico*. Wilmington, Del.: SR Books.

Index

About the Author

After completing undergraduate studies at the University of Texas and American University (BA, economics, 1959), **Scott Cook** did graduate work at the University of Wisconsin (economics), the University of Puerto Rico (graduate diploma in the social sciences, 1962), and the University of Pittsburgh (PhD, anthropology, 1968). He taught anthropology at Michigan State University from 1968 to 1971 and at the University of Connecticut from 1971 until 1997. From 1987 to 1992, he directed the Center for Latin American and Caribbean Studies and from 1996 to 2000 served as interim director of the Puerto Rican and Latino Studies Institute at the University of Connecticut. His most recent book is *Mexican Brick Culture in the Building of Texas, 1800s–1980s* (1998, Texas A&M University Press) based on research conducted along the Texas–Mexico border. Four earlier books and many journal articles dating back to the 1960s address various themes in economic anthropology and peasant-artisan studies and draw heavily on extensive fieldwork in Oaxaca, Mexico. Scott Cook resides in San Marcos, Texas, and can be reached via e-mail at hscook@grandecom.net.